PRAISE FOR *IKE AND DICK*

"Perhaps the most intriguing—and dysfunctional—political marriage in history was the one between the subjects of Jeffrey Frank's meticulously researched *Ike and Dick*. . . . A highly engrossing political narrative that skillfully takes the reader through the twisted development of a strange relationship that would help shape America's foreign and domestic agenda for much of the 20th century."

—Front page, *The New York Times Book Review*

"*Ike and Dick* is an elegant example of how pleasurable political history can be when written by a skilled teller of fictional tales who has a careful reporter's respect for facts. It is top-drawer as political history, unusually well written, and stuffed with forty pages of notes providing sources for an extraordinary variety of information. It is also an entertaining human tale of generational conflict, filled with the elements that enliven popular novels and soap operas."

—Russell Baker, *The New York Review of Books*

"One of the best books ever written about Richard Nixon. . . . *Ike and Dick* shows how much life remains in artfully straightforward narrative history."

—Thomas Mallon, *The New Yorker*

"Engrossing . . . worthwhile. . . . At the heart of *Ike and Dick* are marvelously cringe-inducing anecdotes that capture an awkward relationship that improved over time without ever truly blooming."

—*The Wall Street Journal*

"[A] rare and understatedly important book that suggests a subtle rethink, offering both the casual reader and the student of history a surprisingly candid and humane look at the national villain-in-chief, Richard Nixon. And just as significant, Frank helps to round out our portrait of Nixon's venerable political mentor, the equally wily and fickle President Dwight D. Eisenhower. . . . [A] carefully argued and nuanced book."

—*The Post and Courier* (Charleston, SC)

"Jeffrey Frank knows a good story when he sees one, or sees two. . . . Ambition and hesitation, intrigue and indifference, scheming and serenity, infuse 31 chapters. His saga evokes the seamy underside of the sunny 1950s. . . . [A] detailed and charming history."

—Martin F. Nolan, *San Francisco Chronicle*

"Jeffrey Frank is a nimble writer with a clear-eyed understanding of power . . . [His book] reveals the nuances of the complex relationship between Nixon and the man under whom he served as vice president, Dwight Eisenhower, nuances that should resonate with Republicans who are waging an internecine struggle over the future of their party."

—*The Miami Herald*

"Frank constructs a marvelous account of political history as well as astute portraits of the two men. . . . The rich, inside-politics mix of rumor and maneuver in which connoisseurs of political history love to marinate."

—*Booklist*

"Fascinating."

—*Minneapolis Star-Tribune*

"Frank sorts through these layers of angst and irony with a skillful hand and a sense of empathy for the troubled man at his book's center.

—*Pittsburgh Post-Gazette*

"Absorbing and worthwhile."

—*The Plain Dealer* (Cleveland)

"The elegant writing in this book reflects Frank's skills as a political novelist and is several cuts above most historians' prose. Both Eisenhower and Nixon appear here as three-dimensional characters."

—*The New Republic*

"A gracefully written, sober, and judicious book that manages to humanize both of its subjects while capturing the strange amorality of politics."

—*National Review*

"A story arc that's studded with insider perspectives and with intimate and sometimes excruciating anecdotes."

—*The Buffalo News*

"Evocative, clear-eyed."

—*Newsday*

"This deeply researched account, which includes more than 60 author-conducted interviews, is the only complete book treatment of the enduring yet shaky political connection that guided the United States through some of the most critical decades of the Cold War."

—*Library Journal*

"Revelatory."

—*Richmond Times-Dispatch*

"Eminently readable, with clever characterizations . . . and an eye for telling detail. Frank has delved into presidential libraries, university archives, and oral history, and conducted numerous new interviews . . . an increasingly distant era come[s] vibrantly alive."

—*Washington Monthly*

"This is superlative, compelling, can't-put-it-down history. Jeffrey Frank is an elegant writer with a novelist's eye; the relationship between Eisenhower and Nixon, in all its complexity and weirdness, is a treasure chest that he unpacks brilliantly. This is the perfect time for us to reconsider the trajectory of the Republican Party in the late twentieth century, and this book is a perfect way to do it."

—Joe Klein, *Time* columnist

"To read this book is to be reminded of Richard Nixon's singularly tortured character in all its cussedness and genius—and to learn anew of Dwight Eisenhower's capacity for shrewd political cunning and often insouciant human coldness. *Ike and Dick* deeply textures our understanding of two outsized American personalities and the complex layers of their long and consequential relationship—and it's full of delicious gossip, too."

—David M. Kennedy, Pulitzer Prize–winning author of *Freedom from Fear*

"The mating of Dwight Eisenhower and Richard Nixon was one of the strangest and most fateful in all of American political history. With psychological acuity and perfect pitch for the not-so-distant past, Jeffrey Frank has captured the story beautifully. *Ike and Dick* will surprise and greatly entertain as well as enlighten you."

—Sean Wilentz, author of *The Rise of American Democracy*

"*Ike and Dick* is enthralling, innovative, and judicious. It rivets the reader. Jeffrey Frank knows Washington and national politics inside and out. He employs numerous interviews and recently declassified information superbly. In critical respects, and by using their own words with meticulous care, he peels away layers of disingenuousness from both men. The cast of characters, including indiscreet aides, ranges from bright red to shady gray."

—Michael Kammen, Pulitzer Prize–winning author and past president of the Organization of American Historians

ALSO BY JEFFREY FRANK

The Columnist
Bad Publicity
Trudy Hopedale
The Stories of Hans Christian Andersen
(translator, with Diana Crone Frank)

IKE

— AND —

DICK

Portrait of a Strange
Political Marriage

Jeffrey Frank

SIMON & SCHUSTER PAPERBACKS
NEW YORK   LONDON   TORONTO   SYDNEY   NEW DELHI

Simon & Schuster Paperbacks
1230 Avenue of the Americas
New York, NY 10020

First Simon & Schuster trade paperback edition November 2013

SIMON & SCHUSTER PAPERBACKS and colophon are registered trademarks
of Simon & Schuster, Inc.

For information about special discounts for bulk purchases,
please contact Simon & Schuster Special Sales at
1-866-506-1949 or business@simonandschuster.com.

The Simon & Schuster Speakers Bureau can bring authors
to your live event. For more information or to book an event,
contact the Simon & Schuster Speakers Bureau at
1-866-248-3049 or visit our website at www.simonspeakers.com.

Designed by Akasha Archer

Manufactured in the United States of America

10 9 8 7 6 5 4 3 2

The Library of Congress has cataloged the hardcover edition as follows:
Frank, Jeffrey
   Ike and dick : portrait of a strange political marriage / Jeffrey Frank:
      p.   cm.
   Includes bibliographical references and index.
1. Eisenhower, Dwight D. (Dwight David), 1890–1969. 2. Nixon, Richard M. (Richard
Milhous), 1913–1994. 3. United States—Politics and government—1945–1989.
4. Presidents—United States—Biography. I. Title.
   E836.F73 2013
   973.921092—dc23
   [B]   2012015138
ISBN 978-1-4165-8701-9
ISBN 978-1-4165-8721-7 (pbk)
ISBN 978-1-4165-8820-7 (ebook)

For Vibeke Elise Frank,
her parents, and, as always, Diana

CONTENTS

1

The war in Europe ended on May 7, 1945, when the chief of staff of the German army came to a small red schoolhouse in Reims, France, headquarters of the Supreme Allied Commander, General Dwight David Eisenhower, and signed Germany's unconditional surrender. Six weeks later, Eisenhower was in Washington for a parade in his honor. Stores and offices were closed and signs said "Welcome Home, Ike!"—the nickname he'd been given by childhood friends, soldiers, and total strangers. A million citizens watched the olive drab motorcade make its way from National Airport to Capitol Hill, where the general spoke to a cheering joint session of Congress.

In Manhattan on the following day, some four million people turned out to see Ike as his open car traveled through the city. They filled the sidewalks and peered from windows, fire escapes, and almost any perch that let one claim a fleeting glimpse. The motorcade—twenty-one cars, including the newsreel brigade—went from the airport across the Triborough Bridge and entered Central Park at East 96th Street. There it made its way through the park where Eisenhower was applauded by thirty thousand schoolchildren lined up along the side of the road; now and then, a supervising teacher, or a nun in a black habit would tell the kids to step back, to get out of the way.

With music provided by the Army band, the parade reached 60th Street and headed down Fifth Avenue, where the crowds grew thicker, pushing against barricades to see the general, a smiling fifty-five-year-old just under six feet tall, who stood and waved, occasionally returning a salute when he spotted men in uniform, some of whom were on crutches or had empty sleeves. At 44th Street, the police department's band took over from the Army's, and then, at 23rd Street, the fire department band replaced the NYPD's. At Union Square, as the caravan turned east and then motored south along the East River Drive, Eisenhower was able briefly to relax. It was a hot day—temperatures were already in the 90s—and when the cars approached the Fulton Fish Market, the sour air started to fill with a mist of ticker tape and torn paper—seventy-seven tons of it, by one account. Eisenhower again rose to his feet and raised his arms to make them look like stiff cornstalks.

One of the spectators was a Navy man, Lieutenant Commander Richard Milhous Nixon, who in his last months in uniform had been assigned to negotiate contract terminations with defense suppliers and, since the first of the year, had been moving around—from Baltimore to Philadelphia to New York, where he happened to be on this June day, on Church Street. He watched the parade from the vantage point of a high window, which gave him an excellent view as the procession moved along lower Broadway. "Maybe I just think it was that way—I was about thirty stories up—but I have the picture that there he came, with his arms outstretched and his face up to the sky, and that even from where I was I could feel the impact of his personality," Nixon recalled on several occasions. "I could just make him out through the snowstorm of confetti, sitting in the back of his open car, waving and looking up at the cheering thousands like me who filled every window of the towering buildings. His arms were raised high over his head in the gesture that soon became his trademark." A variation of this—two arms aloft with two fingers held up in victory symbols—would become a Nixon trademark, too.

• • •

Years later, even after all that happened between them, even though Eisenhower frequently made his life miserable, Nixon still saw him as a large historical figure, distant and even unapproachable despite his startlingly friendly smile. When Nixon talked about him to crowds and reporters, his language could veer toward reverence; in moments of ecstatic campaigning, he might refer to him as a man singled out by destiny, the heroic figure of that victory parade. But as Nixon got to know Eisenhower, he came to see a different man: someone who could radiate kindness and bonhomie while acting with cold indifference and even casual cruelty; and someone comfortable with issues of war and peace but far less so when it came to the problems of his own country and the politics of Washington.

On a personal level, Nixon's early relationship with Eisenhower, who was old enough to be his father, had a filial aspect, though one without much filial affection. He saw the president as someone who rarely appreciated his contributions and as someone used to rapid, absolute obedience. During his eight years as vice president, he often felt "like a junior officer coming in to see the commanding General," and sometimes a junior officer who had to endure rebukes and snubs, some of them more imagined than real. The journalist and Nixon confidant Ralph de Toledano told a friend, "There were times when I would find Nixon literally close to tears after a session at the White House during which Eisenhower humiliated Nixon."

Nixon, though, was an attentive pupil. He observed Eisenhower's responses to international crises and domestic emergencies and saw the value of an orderly, hierarchical White House, the importance of gestures, and the virtues of patience. Some of these lessons would fade, but Nixon absorbed them with the steady focus of an A student, eager to play a larger role in the eyes of a superior who regarded him as a bright synthesizer rather than as a proponent of imaginative views. Eisenhower did not have a high regard for professional politicians, but he valued Nixon's logical mind and his expressions of loyalty; and after a time, he listened to his opinions on questions ranging from civilian control of space to civil rights. It was understood that Nixon, as a veteran Red hunter, helped to protect Eisenhower from the resentful Republican right; Eisenhower returned the favor by giving Nixon an increasingly useful veil of moderation. Neither man regarded this as a partnership; vice presidents since the time of John Adams traditionally filled a distinctly peripheral role. But by accident as well as design, their association, in and out of office, grew and that helped to shape the ideology, foreign policy, and domestic goals of the twentieth century.

When Eisenhower ran for president in 1952, he was an elderly sixty-two; the war had worn him down—years of heavy smoking, too much coffee, and nonstop stress. When he selected the thirty-nine-year-old Nixon as his running mate, he relied on his advisers, most of whom he didn't know well and who hadn't come up with many choices; in any case, he wasn't personally acquainted with the potential field. Apart from an occasional stateside visit, he'd been away from America (in Panama as a young officer; in the Philippines as an aide to General Douglas MacArthur; in North Africa and Europe during the war) a lot more than he'd been home. He had met Nixon only twice, and briefly—at a Bohemian Grove summer retreat in the summer of 1950 and in Paris in the spring of 1951, when he was at SHAPE, the Supreme Headquarters Allied Powers Europe. He was aware of all the anti-Communist excitement in the States in which Nixon had played a significant part, but he never recorded an impression of Nixon himself.

On the surface, the two men could not have been less alike. Nixon was a talented speaker, but he often seemed miserable in his political appearances; the journalist Russell Baker saw him as "a painfully lonesome man undergoing an ordeal," and sympathized with "his discomfort with the obligatory routines of his chosen profession." As a public man, he knew that he was unloved and sometimes spoke of the pain that cartoonists inflicted ("I'm not exactly amused to see myself pictured as a lowbrow moron," he said of the Herblock drawings that appeared with some regularity in the *Washington Post*). The aspect that so delighted caricaturists—the close-set eyes, dark, heavy brows, what Garry Wills called his "spatulate nose"—were all the more striking in contrast to those of Eisenhower, who had an expressive, mobile face (his skin turned dark red when he was angry) and that dazzling grin—a spectacular display of surface warmth. Ike's appearance sometimes seemed to change as new thoughts occurred to him, which made him seem, as the military historian B. H. Liddell Hart observed, spontaneous and transparently honest.

Despite that surface candor, though, Eisenhower was as private a man as Nixon, and sometimes an intimidating man. Many were struck by his eyes—"those cold blue laserlike eyes," an early campaign volunteer recalled. When he got angry, his longtime aide Bryce Harlow said, it was like "looking into a Bessemer furnace." Those moments passed quickly; what was far more difficult was being subjected to his chilliness when, as Harlow put it, "those blue eyes of his turned crystal cold." Nixon sometimes felt that unsettling chill, even when nothing was said. He came to realize that the president might refer to him in embracing terms—"We are very close. . . . I am very happy that Dick Nixon is my friend"—just as he was aiming to be rid of him. And while Nixon acquired and kept a reputation for duplicity, Eisenhower was equally accomplished in the arts of deception and misdirection. He had no trouble ordering Nixon to undertake some of his nastiest chores, such as firing his top White House aide, and he tried to disassociate himself from Nixon's meanest campaign rhetoric, as if his vice president was speaking for someone else. As Nixon later put it in a much cited phrase—language over which he carefully deliberated—Eisenhower was "a far more complex and devious man than most people realized." Nixon's vice presidential years were sometimes a struggle for survival. He was nearly forced off the ticket—and into political oblivion—in 1952, and Eisenhower wanted to jettison him four years later; both times, Nixon outwaited and outmaneuvered the general. When Nixon lost the presidency to John F. Kennedy in 1960, the most damaging—and memorable—words of the campaign were uttered by Eisenhower. Nixon thought that he knew who his enemies were—Eisenhower's favorite brother, Milton, had little use for him; the president's press secretary, James Hagerty, could be distinctly unhelpful when Nixon most needed him, Eisenhower's close friend General Lucius Clay didn't trust him—and sometimes he didn't know whether to number Eisenhower among them.

Nixon was always alert to the trap that he'd gotten himself into: doing what the party and the president expected of him could undermine his future, and it could be worse for him if he rebelled. It was a costly bargain.

He was always on call to express the angry id of the party, but when he did so his opponents would resurrect a label he acquired in his 1950 Senate race: "Tricky Dick." Because of this dilemma, Nixon often acted in a certain carefully controlled way; in his perfect, modulated responses, there was an aura of artifice—not exactly calculating but as if he were measuring and judging each word, the "tight-lipped, over-tense, and slightly perspiring manner of a desperately earnest man determined to make no slightest mistake, but not quite at home and not likely to be," in the words of William S. White. "I was constantly aware of an inner man, one who was very private, very elusive," the Eisenhower adviser Gabriel Hauge wrote in an unpublished autobiography, and at the same time, the outward man was much like any striving employee—exceptionally well prepared, taking careful notes, in a constant quest for commendation from a boss whose approval could always lift his uncertain spirits.

Even in their worst moments, there was never a real breach; there was, rather, a fluctuating, unspoken level of discomfort. So it was a curious thing that their relationship, which was both political and personal, lasted and evolved as it did for nearly twenty years. Its duration alone was highly unusual. Presidents and vice presidents, whether Herbert Hoover and Charles Curtis (America's first and only Native American vice president) or Franklin Roosevelt and his three running mates, tended to have little or nothing to do with each other in or out of office. Eisenhower and Nixon had much to do with each other although Nixon was never in Ike's inner circle (his offices were across town, in the Capitol, where he could fulfill his only constitutional duty, as president of the Senate). During his presidency, though, Eisenhower tried to include Nixon in the decision-making machinery of the administration (Nixon kept count of the number of cabinet and National Security Council meetings over which he presided); he used him as a goodwill emissary, sending him to more than fifty countries over eight years while steadily increasing his responsibilities; and there was a barely perceptible shift in power as Eisenhower, limited by the Constitution to two terms and weakened by illness, saw Nixon's presidential goals become clearer and increasingly plausible.

The two men were also drawn together at the end of Ike's life for personal reasons: in November 1967, over the general's objections, his grandson and namesake, Dwight David Eisenhower II, and Nixon's younger daughter, Julie, both of whom were born in 1948, announced their engagement; a year later, the Eisenhower and Nixon families were united by marriage. Yet even teenagers in love could become entangled in politics when the teenagers belonged to these two families. The relationship between David and Julie played a real part in Nixon's 1968 comeback campaign and it affected his relationship with Eisenhower, who, though he said that Nixon was ready for the presidency, seemed doubtful about his ability to win, and not entirely pleased by the prospect of actually having him in the White House.

2

In June of 1945, Dick Nixon was in many ways the model of the bright young postwar American professional out to improve his lot, a type recognizable to readers of novels by James Gould Cozzens or Sloan Wilson. He had been a lawyer in his hometown, Whittier, California (named after the Quaker poet John Greenleaf Whittier), and worked briefly in Washington, in the tire-rationing section of the Office of Price Administration. He got a Navy commission in August 1942, and served fourteen months in the South Pacific, in Bougainville; his last Navy assignment brought him to Middle River, Maryland. At thirty-two, he was older than most returning veterans, and he had no clear idea what was next for him, although he would likely return to the Whittier law practice that he'd joined after graduating from Duke in 1937. He had responsibilities now. In June 1940, after an intense and single-minded courtship, he had married Thelma Catherine Ryan, known as Pat, an attractive young woman with dark red hair. Jessamyn West, a Nixon cousin and the author of the novel *Friendly Persuasion,* thought that Pat looked a little like Marlene Dietrich—"The same slanted, almost Slavic eyes. . . . The same strong nose and clear jawline. The same long torso and fine legs."

Although Nixon had finished near the top of his law school class (a classmate described him as "a very studious individual—almost fearfully so"), his career options were surprisingly few. He had tried without success to find a position with several New York firms and had even applied to be an FBI agent. He'd given some thought to politics, too. Before the war, Herman Perry, a banker and a Nixon family friend (he'd gone to college with Nixon's mother), had asked half seriously if he was interested in running for an open seat in the State Assembly.

Perry played a large role in what happened next, a story that sometimes got exaggerated as it did in a note that the excitable broadcaster Paul Harvey sent years later to Nixon's personal secretary, Rose Mary Woods: "Somebody related a secondhand story about Dick Nixon answering a want ad for a Congressional candidate," Harvey wrote and asked for details for his broadcast, adding, "Young people need every possible reminder that the American dream is still good." Woods did fill in the details, although by then they were familiar to anyone who had followed Nixon's career. The "want ad" was actually a handout mailed in the late summer of 1945 to newspapers in California's 12th Congressional District; it invited prospective candidates to apply to a Republican fact-finding committee, whose goal was to defeat the five-term Democratic incumbent. Perry knew that Nixon met the qualifications: he was young, educated, and a veteran. In a letter to Nixon—airmailed, which gave it a special urgency—Perry asked how he'd feel about getting into the race, and as one would expect of an ambitious young man presented with a path to change his life in so alluring a fashion, Nixon was elated. This was an altogether exciting opportunity, something that could combine many of his talents: his cleverness, a gift for public speaking, the lawyerly logic and boundless energy that he brought to a courtroom. He got so wound up that he placed a long-distance call to Perry, who advised him to calm down: he explained that Nixon still had to go through a selection process, and even then might face a primary. On the other hand, Perry was ready to work in Nixon's behalf, and told his colleagues that "Lt. Nixon comes from good Quaker stock and is about thirty-five years of age [sic]. . . . He is a very aggressive individual."

Nixon was chosen after his second appearance before a local selection committee (the *Los Angeles Times* ran a smudgy photograph of "Lt. Cmdr. R. M. Nixon" in his Navy uniform, and said that his supporters characterized him as "a natural-born leader and . . . a well-known debater and orator in collegiate circles"), and although the election was still a year off, he was consumed by it. He wasn't polished and never would be: "He has terrifically large feet"—actually, 11-D—"and we had trouble getting a pair of shoes that was big enough for him," Roy Day, the Republican Central Committee chairman, said. Day also worried "that he wouldn't look women in the eyes, in the face. He'd turn his head; he was shy." Nixon, though, was determined. He campaigned all over the district and lured the incumbent, Horace Jeremiah (Jerry) Voorhis, into a series of debates for which Nixon, the strategic litigator, had prepared himself, as if for a chess match. People who had known him as a polite and deferential young man, a lawyer embarrassed by the intimacies of marital lawsuits, were surprised by his ferocity, in particular the Red scare rhetoric that he added to the mix: a claim that Voorhis had been endorsed by a political action committee that was infiltrated by Communists. Communism was not yet the issue that it would become four years later, in the prime of Senator Joseph McCarthy, but it was very much in the air; and Nixon was tutored by Murray Chotiner, a chubby, cigar-smoking, quick-witted criminal defense lawyer (his firm often defended bookmakers and drunk drivers), Jewish, and a veteran of California politics. Chotiner had helped to elect Earl Warren as governor in 1942 and would one day get credit for the idea that a successful politician needed to run a "permanent campaign" and for some nasty modern campaign practices, including the dictum that to be successful you need to "deflate the opposition candidate before your own campaign gets started." Nixon won with 56 percent of the vote, and almost as soon as he arrived in Washington with his wife and an infant daughter, Patricia—"Tricia"—he began to make a name for himself.

3

If Nixon's entry into politics was a triumph of will and hard work, Eisenhower's was the result of circumstance and, in the end, acclamation. His appointment in 1943 to command the Anglo-American Overlord operation—a relatively sudden ascent from lieutenant colonel to four-star general—had a lot to do with luck and timing; the post would otherwise have gone to his mentor and benefactor, the Army chief of staff, General George C. Marshall. The assignment acknowledged Eisenhower's intelligence as well as a gift for dealing with difficult personalities—Churchill and de Gaulle, General George Patton and Field Marshal Bernard Law Montgomery among them—and his disinclination (in contrast to General Douglas MacArthur, under whom he had served in the Philippines) to preen.

On the day that Washington put on its victory parade, a column by the influential Walter Lippmann began, "The cheering in the streets will die down, but his renown will endure," and went on:

> Although he bore the majestic title of Supreme Commander, in fact he commanded by leading and he led by consent. It is an art which is not described in any book of rules because it is reserved for those who are gifted with a happy nature and are faithful to a good philosophy. Everyone likes Eisenhower.

Lippmann did not employ the word "president" in this column, but that would have seemed almost anticlimactic after asserting that Ike's "genius is to have in an uncommon balance, common sense and common humanity." These qualities seemed to be on display during the last leg of his journey as he went by train from Kansas City to his hometown, Abilene (pop. 5,760), and watched the most extravagant parade in the town's history; 35,000 people from the surrounding area came to applaud. When he was asked about politics, he said, "All I want is to be a citizen of the United States, and when the War Department turns me out to pasture that's all I want to be." And yet he also sounded like someone with more on his mind. "We are not isolationists," he said. "We are a part of the great civilization of this world at this moment, and every part of the world where a similar civilization prevails is a part of us."

If Eisenhower in 1945 wasn't yet talking about a political future for himself, other people, including Harry Truman, were. In Eisenhower's war memoir, *Crusade in Europe*, published early in 1948, he revealed an astonishing conversation with the president in Potsdam, in July 1945, during which Truman "suddenly turned toward me and said, 'General, there is nothing that you may want that I won't try to help you get. That definitely and specifically includes the presidency in 1948.'" Ike's response was to laugh and say that it would never happen. There was, though, a practical difficulty in pushing Eisenhower toward presidential politics: there was no place for him in 1948 despite the urging of disaffected Democrats, including James Roosevelt, one of FDR's sons, to enlist him as a substitute for the increasingly unpopular Truman; and besides, no one seemed to be sure of his party affiliation, which he waited until 1952 to declare. The smart political columnists regarded the idea of an Eisenhower candidacy as a "complete chimera," and just before the 1948 election it all seemed moot: Eisenhower was appointed president of Columbia University and Governor Thomas E. Dewey of New York was expected to defeat Truman.

After the 1948 election, though, many influential Americans began to look again at the general. In fact, on the morning after Truman defeated Dewey, a man named Edward Bermingham, a Chicagoan who had made his fortune as an investment banker, asked Eisenhower to come to dinner in Chicago—Ike would be the guest of honor. Bermingham had put together a list of well-to-do Americans, people like Fred Gurley, the president of the Atchison, Topeka & Santa Fe Railway System; and newspaper publishers like Colonel Robert McCormick of the *Chicago Tribune*, and Marshall Field of the *Chicago Sun-Times;* the chairmen of the board of Sears Roebuck and Montgomery Ward, along with the presidents of the Swift and Armour meatpacking companies; several bankers; and even Robert Hutchins, president of the University of Chicago. These were the sort of men whose company the general enjoyed and the sort who began to encourage him to seek the presidency.

4

Dick Nixon, as a freshman congressman on the House Un-American Activities Committee, stood out from a disreputable crew—among them the racist and outspokenly anti-Semitic John Rankin of Mississippi and the committee's chairman, J. Parnell Thomas, who led the investigation of alleged Communist influence in Hollywood and later went to jail on tax fraud charges. Nixon also stood out by managing actually to expose someone—namely Alger Hiss, who was accused of passing classified documents to the Russians. The case was revelatory as well as puzzling because Hiss, then the president of the Carnegie Endowment for International Peace, was a model of New Deal achievement and aplomb—a Harvard Law School graduate, the secretary-general of the United Nations Charter Conference, in 1945, and the well-connected friend of people like Dean Acheson, the secretary of state, and John Foster Dulles, who was then the president of the Carnegie Endowment's board of trustees. In the end it was Nixon who let Hiss trap himself with his increasingly convoluted testimony and lawyerly avoidances. Alice Roosevelt Longworth, Theodore Roosevelt's daughter, was so drawn to the twists and mysteries of the Hiss affair that she sent copies of *Seeds of Treason,* a celebratory book about the case, to friends.

In his first term Nixon also served on the Select Committee on Foreign Aid, led by Christian Herter of Massachusetts. From August to October 1947, the Herter Committee, as it came to be known, toured Europe, and the misery that they saw deeply impressed them. "Hamburg, Berlin and the other German cities looked up at us just like great gaunt skeletons," one of Nixon's typical diary entries said. "We could not understand how it was possible that three million people could be living . . . there like a bunch of starved rats in the ruins." The committee's report helped the European Recovery Program—the Marshall Plan—win the support of Congress in March 1948 and was the sort of stand that brought Nixon closer to the internationalist Republicanism of people like Governor Dewey and General Eisenhower. Congressman Nixon in 1947 also came out in favor of a U.N. peacekeeping force, which led to accusations that he was an agent of world government.

Nixon was restlessly ambitious, and by the fall of 1949 he was in pursuit of a Senate seat. His eventual opponent, following a ferocious Democratic primary, was Helen Gahagan Douglas, a former Broadway star who since 1944 had served in the House. Nixon was once more coached by Murray Chotiner and ran an unusually harsh campaign, insinuating while never quite saying that Mrs. Douglas was not a loyal American. The *Nation* magazine characterized him as a "dapper little man with an astonishing capacity for petty malice," and even his loyal congressional staff considered the race a "nasty, sordid" effort. Although such excesses more or less ended after the midterm elections of 1954, Nixon's reliance on casual smears and the sneering dismissal was most pronounced when he ran against Mrs. Douglas, and until the Watergate affair, critical biographers tended to focus on that Senate race. His opponents never forgot it or forgave him.

They were reared in different countries. Eisenhower was born in 1890, and his first memories of "the war" were of the Civil War veterans he'd seen when he was growing up in Abilene. For Nixon, born in 1913 in Yorba Linda, fifteen miles from Whittier, it was the Great War. If Nixon, as Arthur Schlesinger Jr. suggested, was a product of "the mobility of the new technical society," appealing to other Americans who were "rootless, sectionless, classless," then Eisenhower was a product of a rural, more homogeneous America that was steadily vanishing, a nation now so distant that despite the film and recordings of some of its people and locales, its true images are difficult to summon. They moved in different circles. Eisenhower maintained a few old friendships from his Army days, but he was more drawn to his new ones from America's business elite, with whom he spent hours playing golf and bridge, competing furiously at clubs like Augusta National, where Nixon was never a guest. Nixon was not a popular figure in Washington; he lacked the chumminess of many politicians, and his early, intemperate campaigns had made many journalists wary of him. He did have Republican allies on Capitol Hill, where he enjoyed the company of the Chowder and Marching Society, a loose, congenial band of small-town congressmen, and as vice president he formed a sympathetic bond with, among others, John Foster Dulles, the secretary of state, whose view of the Cold War he shared and whose social stiffness resembled Nixon's. Nixon also liked just being alone, often jotting notes on one of the yellow legal pads that were his constant accessory; he could be silently absorbed for hours. Eisenhower, by contrast, always liked to have people around.

One might think that they belonged to different classes, but in fact their backgrounds were curiously similar. Both came from modest circumstances, and were reared by devout mothers—Ida Stover and Hannah Milhous—and short-tempered fathers: David Eisenhower, who worked as a mechanic in a local creamery, and Frank Nixon, who ran a general store in East Whittier, where Dick helped out. "His temper could blaze with frightening suddenness but when things were going along at a casual tempo, he was a good companion," Ike said of his father, "My father had an Irish quickness both to anger and to mirth," Nixon wrote. "It was his temper that impressed me most as a small child."

Both were deeply affected by early deaths in the family. Dick was the second oldest of five Nixon brothers, only three of whom lived into their mid-twenties. Arthur was seven when he died in 1925; Dick was twelve. "We never really knew for sure what killed Arthur," Nixon told the biographer Jonathan Aitken, but he believed that it was a tubercular fever caused by the milk of an infected cow—and Frank Nixon had pushed his family to drink unpasteurized milk. "My father was very firm in that idea," Nixon told Aitken, who recalled that he had tears in his eyes. "He just kept going and stuck to his guns on raw milk." Harold, who was four years older than Dick, suffered from tuberculosis. Hannah Nixon took him to the dry climate of Prescott, Arizona, a fourteen-hour drive from East Whittier; mother and son stayed there for almost three years. Edward Nixon (born in 1930) believes that Harold's death, in 1933 at the age of twenty-four, affected his older brother's life "forever." Everyone adored Harold—"he was blond and blue-eyed—more like my father," Ed Nixon said. Jessamyn West remembered Harold as a "brighter, more handsome fellow" than Dick, adding, "I'm sure in his family they felt the best had been taken."

Eisenhower was the third of seven brothers, one of whom died in infancy. His parents were members of the River Brethren, a sect closely related to the Mennonites who had emigrated from the south of Germany; Ida was a regular participant in the Abilene Ecclesia of the International Bible Students Association, which became Jehovah's Witnesses. The pacifistic impulses in Eisenhower's speeches and writings were very likely influenced by this upbringing, in much the way that the Nixon brothers were influenced by the beliefs of Hannah Milhous, a Quaker.

When Eisenhower was twenty-five and an Army lieutenant stationed in San Antonio, Texas, he met and soon married nineteen-year-old Mamie Doud. A year later, they had a son—Doud Dwight, nicknamed Icky, who died of scarlet fever when he was three. A half century later, writing about Icky's death, Eisenhower said, "I have never known such a blow. This was the greatest disappointment and disaster in my life, the one I have never been able to forget completely." Not even the birth of a second son, John Sheldon Doud, born in 1922, could get Dwight and Mamie over the loss of their firstborn.

5

Both Eisenhower and Nixon—the citizen-soldier from Kansas and the lawyer-politician from Southern California—were engaged by the problems and conflicts of the world and by the personalities of American politics; in the 1960s, when both were out of office, they could shake their heads in appalled unison over the early mistakes of the Kennedy administration, such as the bungled invasion of Cuba at the Bay of Pigs, and over Lyndon Johnson's handling of the Vietnam War; and they could create a fiction of party unity to get them past the embarrassment of the 1964 presidential campaign of Barry Goldwater. In 1963, when Nixon joined a Wall Street law firm and started to accumulate wealth for the first time, it was as if he'd metamorphosed into one of the contented businessmen to whom Eisenhower had always been attracted. By the time he was fifty, Nixon had become a prosperous Republican elder while Eisenhower was receding into history.

Over years of casual familiarity, Eisenhower's view of Nixon kept changing—from the disdain that he felt for most professional politicians to doubts about Nixon's "maturity" to a kind of hesitant respect. Nixon's feelings about the general could change, too—from neediness and even awe to rare bursts of hateful rage, as when he called him a "goddamned old fool" or by one account "a senile old bastard." Yet at the very end, when the general was dying and Nixon had become the nation's thirty-seventh president, Eisenhower still had a powerful hold on him; just as he had affected the intense young man Nixon had been—insecure, smart, and curious, capable of nasty practices and benevolent acts—he affected the man he had become. "After Nixon got elected, he invited a few of us to go upstairs and see what the living quarters were like," the political strategist John Sears said. "And all he talked about was how it looked when Eisenhower was president—where he had his medals and what he had over there and where he had his desk and all that stuff. All the time we were running, he was always anxious that Eisenhower be filled in on what we were doing, and how well we were doing. He felt better if he thought Eisenhower thought he was doing well." Nixon could never be sure what Eisenhower really thought of him, but it never ceased to matter, and his restive pursuit of Ike's good opinion remained one of the few constants in an extraordinary life.

CHAPTER 1

The Men's Club

1

Herbert Hoover, the last living Republican president in mid-century America (his predecessor, Calvin Coolidge, died in 1933), treasured his membership in the Bohemian Club, which was founded in San Francisco in 1872 as a center of western influence and wealth. Hoover had joined in 1913 and for most of his life kept an eye out for recruits who might enliven the Bohemian Grove, the club's summer encampment, 2,700 acres covered by redwoods and situated seventy miles north of San Francisco. The motto of the Bohemian members is the Shakespeare line "Weaving spiders come not here"—a warning to visitors to avoid self-promotion and networking—but for many guests and members the whole point of the Club was precisely that, and for them the Grove each summer was a natural habitat for web-weaving spiders. Hoover regarded his annual weeks at the Grove as "the greatest men's party on earth."

There are innumerable private clubs in America—city clubs and country clubs and Rotary Clubs and university clubs; General Eisenhower was familiar with many of them as part of his growing circle of wealthy, clubbable Americans. But the Bohemian Club is set apart by its rituals, its efforts at secrecy, and the exclusion of women as guests, although women eventually were permitted to work on the Grove's grounds. In the 1950s, the club's membership included bankers, politicians, influential journalists, and show business personalities like Edgar Bergen and Bing Crosby, and while the names changed, the traditions continued. Each year, as many as two thousand Bohemians and members and their guests still get together in the woods where they carry out the rites of the Grove: the serious and also somewhat vulgar entertainments (called High Jinks and Low Jinks), lectures (particularly the Lakeside Talks, during which prominent men give off-the-record speeches), and, most unforgettably, if only for its quasi-Masonic tendencies, the Cremation of Care ceremony, during which men in red hoods and red robes—some playing dirgelike music and others carrying torches—bear a mock coffin to a nearby lake, where a mock corpse that represents Dull Care is "cremated." These private ceremonies have become less secret, and therefore perhaps less interesting, in the age of YouTube.

Richard Nixon stayed at the Grove in late July 1950, because Herbert Hoover, whom his associates and friends called the Chief (and who liked being called Chief), had taken a liking to him even before they'd met; he particularly admired Nixon's work with the House Un-American Activities Committee. In January 1950, after Alger Hiss was found guilty of perjury (for lying about committing espionage, for which the statute of limitations had expired), Hoover wrote—"My dear Mr. Congressman"—to say that Hiss's conviction "was due to your patience and persistence alone. At last the stream of treason that existed in our Government has been exposed in a fashion that all may believe."

The Chief always gave a lot of thought to Cave Man Camp—Hoover's camp, one of several dozen separate camps at the Grove, where he was known as the No. 1 Cave Man. He was particularly interested that year in bringing in Nixon as well as Conrad Hilton, the hotel man, and soon enough it was shaping up to be a first-rate Grove summer, all the more so because General Eisenhower, also paying his first visit, had accepted an invitation to give the Lakeside Talk. Eisenhower had turned down a number of earlier invitations, but Fred Gurley, the railroad man whom Ike had met two years before in Chicago, not only invited him to the Grove, but, as the president of the Atchison, Topeka & Santa Fe, was able to offer a superior means of transport.

• • •

By tradition, the speakers who "gave a Lakeside" did so at Cave Man Camp. These talks were sometimes regarded as a way to take the measure of a politician, and interest in Eisenhower in 1950 had a lot more to do with his political future than with his job as president of Columbia University or his career as a soldier, although the nation was at war again. This time it was in Korea, where the United States had become the major actor in a United Nations "police action." At the camp lunch, Hoover, as he usually did, sat at the head of the table; Eisenhower was next to him on his right and Nixon was on his left, three seats down. As Nixon recalled the summer day when Eisenhower spoke, the general "was deferential to Hoover but not obsequious," and "He responded to Hoover's toast with a very gracious one of his own." Nixon was sure that Ike knew he was in "enemy territory among this generally conservative group"; Hoover had become increasingly encrusted with conservative views since his defeat by FDR in 1932. When it came to the Republican Party's nominee for president, most of Hoover's friends—and the Chief himself—favored the candidate of the old guard, Robert Alphonso Taft, the Ohio senator, who had gone after the nomination before and would go after it again in 1952.

Although Nixon had seen Eisenhower again in 1948, walking in the funeral cortege for General John J. Pershing, he had never seen him close up, and he paid sharp attention. "It was not a polished speech, but he delivered it without notes and he had the good sense not to speak too long," he recalled. "The only line that drew significant applause was his comment that he did not see why anyone who refused to sign a loyalty oath should have the right to teach at a state university." After the talk, the attendees sat around a campfire and discussed what the general had said. "The feeling," Nixon thought, "was that he had a long way to go before he would have the experience, the depth, and the understanding to be President."

Nixon and Eisenhower talked briefly that day, a conversation that did not leave enough of an impression for Eisenhower ever to refer to it. Afterward, Eisenhower went by rail to Denver, where his mother-in-law lived and where he spent the next six weeks, while Nixon returned to his increasingly shrill senatorial campaign, which ended with him defeating Helen

Douglas by a margin of more than 600,000 votes. Nixon was thirty-seven years old, and on election night Pat and Dick and some of their friends celebrated; they went from party to party, and when they came to a room with a piano, the senator-elect, an autodidactic pianist who played by ear and always in the key of G, would pound out "Happy Days Are Here Again," not caring that Democrats liked that song, too. The victory, and the insistent focus on Communism during the campaign, gave Nixon a kind of national credential; it brought him into contact with movie stars like Dick Powell and Dennis Morgan and the politically engaged gossip columnist Hedda Hopper. ("Watch that boy! He's presidential timber!" Hopper wrote when Nixon was a senator.) He got another note from the Chief, this one saying, "My dear Mr. Congressman: Your victory was the greatest good that can come to our country," followed by an invitation: "My dear Senator Nixon: This is just by way of suggesting that if you ever come to New York, I will gladly produce food." Those who had never liked Nixon very much began to look at him with something close to hatred.

2

Once in a while that fall, someone would mention General Eisenhower, who was back in Morningside Heights. Governor Dewey did so when he appeared on *Meet the Press* in mid-October and declared that he, person-ally, was through running for president. When a questioner asked, "Gov-ernor, if you are not going to run, do you have any candidates in mind?" Dewey replied, "Well, it's a little early, but we have in New York a very great world figure, the president of Columbia University, one of the great-est soldiers of our history, a fine educator, a man who really understands the problems of the world, and if I should be re-elected governor and have influence with the New York delegation, I would recommend to them that they support General Eisenhower for president if he would accept the draft." Dewey's statement was not only an endorsement but a warning to the old guard that the eastern branch of the Republican Party was still around, that its internationalist principles remained unshaken, and that people like Dewey were prepared to fight for them.

At the end of 1950, Eisenhower, at President Truman's request, took a leave of absence from Columbia to return to active duty, becoming the first Supreme Allied Commander Europe (SACEUR). In April 1951, he set up SHAPE, and in keeping with his reputation for modest living, turned down a chance to locate his office at the Palace of Fontainebleau, which the French had offered. He chose instead a prefabricated building fifteen miles from Paris. Europeans were impressed by Eisenhower. "He fascinates them as a heroic fictional character of a type they have never read about before—a non-Napoleonic, unmilitary-minded, professional general of high class," Gênet (Janet Flanner) wrote in *The New Yorker.* "They think him humane, a tactician, a great soldier, an honest democrat."

Eisenhower had mixed feelings about this move. He and Mamie had been enjoying life in Morningside Heights, though he once said that he never went out for a walk at night without carrying his service revolver. But he could not turn down a president—and this was an appealing request, not least because it kept him removed from the contagions of American politics, a subject that kept being broached not only by restless journalists but by visitors, especially a group of relatively new friends, well-to-do businessmen to whom he sometimes referred as "the gang." This set included William Robinson, executive vice president of the *New York Herald Tribune*; Clifford Roberts, a partner in the investment banking firm Reynolds & Company and, perhaps more importantly, a cofounder (with the celebrated golfer Bobby Jones) of the Augusta National Golf Club; Ellis (Slats) Slater, the chairman of Frankfort Distilleries; and George E. Allen, an insurance executive and, for a few years, a commissioner of the District of Columbia, who was sort of an odd man out—he was not very wealthy and had been a friend of Harry Truman's. But like the others, he enjoyed golf and bridge, and his wife, Mary, had been close to Mamie Eisenhower during the war. Not all the gang members were fond of each other; Cliff Roberts even tended to be jealous of his time with Eisenhower, almost as if he was in competition for the hand of a woman. Ike was probably most comfortable around Allen and a later arrival, Freeman Gosden, who belonged to the Augusta National and was known for his roles as the Kingfish and Amos on the radio version of *Amos 'n' Andy*.

Like background noise, the chatter about Eisenhower as a presidential candidate got louder, so much so that there developed a hallucinatory view of Eisenhower's place in the political scene—one that ascribed to him a spiritual affinity with both major political parties. At one point in the spring of 1951, Senator Paul Douglas of Illinois, a Democrat, suggested that if Truman didn't run again and the Republicans chose Eisenhower, Democrats should go ahead and nominate him, too. Douglas pointed out that the two parties could still distinguish themselves by selecting different vice presidential candidates. Eisenhower was not immune to that sort of improbable idea. "You don't suppose a man could ever be nominated by both parties, do you?" he once asked Walter Lippmann. Richard Nixon, who was as aware as anyone of all the interest in Ike, saw the general for a second time when he visited SHAPE headquarters in May. The stopover was a detour on what had started as a trip by an American delegation to the new World Health Organization in Geneva. For Nixon, it was an opportunity to have a conversation with the general nearly a year after their inconsequential chat at the Bohemian Grove. For Eisenhower, it was a chance to get briefed on a domestic concern—the purported peril from homegrown subversives. After all, who was better equipped to fill him in on the Red threat than the man who had bagged Alger Hiss? Their meeting came about through the intervention of Alfred Kohlberg, a rich textile importer (one journalist described him as a "round, bald little man with snapping brown eyes"), who was one of America's most active anti-Communists, a believer in the "someone-lost-China" theory of history—and someone with a seemingly unlimited supply of unfounded suspicions.

On May 1, 1951, Kohlberg, who also had an overactive busybody side, wrote to Nixon, saying, a little mysteriously, that "General Eisenhower feels a need for more information about the communist conspiracy. There are two men with whom he would like to talk on this. You are one of them." For some reason, Kohlberg did not reveal the identity of the second man and felt it necessary to add that "The friend of the General's who spoke to me is not acquainted with either you or the other man." In any case, on May 9, 1951, a message from DEPTAR (the Department of the Army) arrived at SACEUR reporting that Senator Nixon was on his way, and SACEUR then told DEPTAR that they were holding open May 18, at ten-thirty in the morning. Nixon later told Kohlberg that he'd spent an hour with the general and "incidentally, was very impressed with his understanding of the nature of the problems we face both abroad and at home in respect to the Communist conspiracy." All in all, Nixon after seeing Eisenhower came away in much the same frame of mind as when he'd left the Bohemian Grove, and he later recalled the meeting in some detail: Eisenhower "was erect and vital and impeccably tailored, wearing his famous waist-length uniform jacket, popularly known as the 'Eisenhower jacket.' . . . He spoke optimistically about the prospects for European recovery and development," a subject in which Nixon remained interested. "What we need over here and what we need in the States is more optimism in order to combat the defeatist attitude that too many people seem to have," Eisenhower said. They didn't discuss American politics—as Nixon saw it, they stepped cautiously around that topic—but Nixon noted that "it was clear he had done his homework," which included knowing something about Senator Nixon.

Rather than staying behind a desk, the general invited Nixon to sit on a couch beside him, and went on to tell him that he'd read about the Hiss case in *Seeds of Treason* and that "The thing that most impressed me was that you not only got Hiss, but you got him fairly." Nixon was proud of that compliment and found the visit memorable enough to enter some thoughts in the *Congressional Record,* which was the first public juxtaposition of their names: "I was impressed, let me say parenthetically, with the excellent job he is doing against monumental odds, in the position he holds," Nixon said, adding that Eisenhower had told him that "one of the greatest tasks" he had was to convince America's allies "of the necessity for deferring . . . expenditures for nonmilitary purposes and for all those countries to place the primary emphasis in their budgets upon the necessity of rebuilding their armed forces to meet the threat of Communist aggression." Years later, Nixon had a distinctly different recollection, recalling an Eisenhower observation that "being strong militarily just isn't enough in the kind of battle we are fighting now"—struck by that because "then as now it was unusual to hear a military man emphasize the importance of non-military strength." Very likely, Ike said both things; and very likely Nixon adapted each message to the times—the peak of the Cold War and the arrival of détente—in which he lived.

For Nixon, paying this call was a way to make an impression on someone who might one day be a national leader as well as a chance to let the general know that they were two men of one mind on the issues of the day. "I felt that I was in the presence of a genuine statesman," Nixon recalled, "and I came away convinced that he should be the next President. I also decided that if he ran for the nomination I would do everything I could to help him get it."

By the fall of 1951, columnists and poll takers had decided that there were two major Republican candidates: the declared Senator Taft and the undeclared General Eisenhower. The general already had a wide following in the press, starting with the *Herald Tribune,* the magnetic pole of eastern Republicanism, as well as the Luce publications: *Time, Life,* and *Fortune.* Henry Robinson Luce, *Time's* founder, was dazzled by the general. "Harry fell in love with Eisenhower as people fall in love with beautiful girls," Allen Grover, a former *Time* vice president and Luce's personal aide, told one biographer. "Here was this marvelous man who came from the heartland of America, the fair-haired boy, the leader of the great armada of World War II, a crusader, honest and straight!" (Luce's wife, Clare Boothe Luce, the charming and slightly mad former Connecticut congresswoman—Cecil Beaton supposedly described her as "drenchingly beautiful"—saw Eisenhower in the fall of 1949 to discuss, as he put it, "the future of the country and the opportunities of the Republican party to affect that future favorably.") The *Herald Tribune* publisher Bill Robinson, a gang member, knew everyone in the business—or he knew people who knew people. The *Trib's* most important political writers were Walter Lippmann and the Alsop brothers, Stewart and Joseph; Robinson was also acquainted with other influential columnists of the day, such as Roscoe Drummond of the *Christian Science Monitor* (later with the *Trib*) and Arthur Krock of the *New York Times.* The *Times's* Paris-based correspondent C. L. Sulzberger had been on friendly, bridge-playing terms with Eisenhower since the war.

One reason for this interest was a belief that any Republican was bound to defeat Harry Truman, who had been embarrassed by an unusual number of scandals—among them the claim that someone could land government contracts for a fee plus 5 percent and an official who got a $9,000 mink coat for his wife, a White House stenographer. Terms like "five percenters" and "mink coats" had become part of the political discourse; so had reports of a perfume manufacturer who sent gratis freezers to several people, among them Truman's wife, Bess, and Truman's long-time friend and military aide, Major General Harry Hawkins Vaughan. Truman's popularity declined further in April, when he dismissed General MacArthur from his Far Eastern command. MacArthur had not only been insubordinate, but Truman believed, as most historians have also come to believe, that he was close to turning the Korean conflict into a wider war. The initial reaction was a burst of support for MacArthur—the archconservative *Chicago Tribune* called his firing "the culmination of a series of acts which have shown that [Truman] is unfit, morally and mentally, for high office," and called for impeachment—but that level of enthusiasm quickly dissipated.

The *Herald Tribune* in late October almost impulsively endorsed Eisenhower for the presidency—its comment, headlined "The Time and the Man," ran at the top of page one—with the newspaper's editorialist writing, "At rare intervals in the life of a free people the man and the occasion meet." As to what political party Eisenhower belonged, the paper finessed that delicate question, saying, "By deed and word General Eisenhower has shown himself a keeper of the great liberties to which Republicanism is dedicated. . . . He is a Republican by temper and disposition." This idea did not appeal to newspapers like the *Chicago Tribune*, which let it be known that it would not be jumping on any Eisenhower bandwagon, but the endorsement was considered meaningful enough for the *New York Times* to treat it like news.

A Citizens for Eisenhower group, started by a couple of war veterans, the aviators Stanley Rumbough and Charles Willis, had been growing since the spring of 1951, and soon after the *Trib*'s endorsement his candidacy was being planned and promoted by a group of political professionals that included Senator Henry Cabot Lodge Jr. of Massachusetts, who had talked to Dewey about running Ike's campaign; Herbert Brownell, a New York lawyer who had run Dewey's campaign in 1948; and Ike's friend General Lucius Clay. In early January 1952, Sherman Adams, the governor of New Hampshire, wrote to Lodge to say that they were ready to go ahead and work for Eisenhower in his state, but "There is one question which we would like to have answered by Jan. 10, if possible. The question is, to which political party does General Eisenhower belong?"

That little mystery was finally solved when the general hurriedly came out as a Republican. The declaration was enough for Truman, the amateur history buff and unembarrassed partisan, to compare Eisenhower's prospects to those of General Winfield Scott, who ran on the Whig ticket in 1852 and was defeated by Franklin Pierce, a Democrat. Truman had every reason to feel aggrieved; just ten days earlier, the general had written to him to say, "I do not feel that I have any duty to seek a political nomination, in spite of the fact that many have urged to the contrary," adding that to do so would be a violation of Army regulations and that "the possibility that I will ever be drawn into political activity is so remote as to be negligible."

Ike's declared affiliation made him all the more attractive to Senator Nixon, who in mid-January wrote an ingratiating letter, reminding the general of their brief acquaintanceship and drawing his attention to a far-right organization that called itself the Partisan Republicans of California, "which has been issuing some very defamatory literature directed against you." (One mailing included a cartoon of Stalin pinning a medal on Eisenhower.) Nixon continued, "As a Californian, I am ashamed of the fact that we seem to attract so many crackpots to our state," and he wanted to disassociate "the great majority of good Republicans and Democrats" from outfits like the Partisan Republicans. If the point of Nixon's letter was to remind the general that he was still around and still an admirer, he accomplished that in his concluding paragraph, where he wrote, "I remember with great pleasure our visit to Paris in May and I am looking forward to meeting you again sometime in the future. I want you to know that I am among those who believe you are rendering a great service to the country under very difficult circumstances." Eisenhower replied—it appears to have been his first letter to Nixon—saying, "I suppose that defamatory attacks are the 'occupational hazards' for people such as you and I, but they are nonetheless vexatious." In February, Nixon wrote to a family friend to say, "The political pot is really boiling and I only hope that Eisenhower can see his way clear to come back to the states about a month before the convention. I, frankly, believe this will be necessary if he is to get the nomination."

A Citizens for Eisenhower office opened in New York in February 1952, followed by a late-night Eisenhower-for-President event at Madison Square Garden, where at least fifteen thousand people and several movie stars (among them Henry Fonda, Lauren Bacall, Humphrey Bogart, and Clark Gable) showed up and cheered. Mary Martin sang "I'm in Love with a Wonderful Guy" over a shortwave hookup from London, accompanied by the song's composer Richard Rodgers. After the show, the aviatrix Jacqueline Cochran flew to Paris, carrying an unedited film of the evening. The film went on too long, but Eisenhower was, as Cochran later put it, "flabbergasted." Following the personal screening, she raised a glass and said, "To the President." Ike's reaction, she said, was to "burst into tears."

Perhaps the cumulative weight of these Hollywood stars and the images of thousands of cheering spectators really did make him weep—and Eisenhower in his diary confessed that it was "a real emotional experience for Mamie and me"—but Jackie Cochran, a self-made cosmetics entrepreneur as well as a flier, was something of a fabulist. The Garden event, though, was bound to increase the pressure on Ike, and even if he had wanted a way out of the political trap that had gripped him, the calendar was closing in—with one date in particular: the New Hampshire presidential preference primary, set for March 11. General Eisenhower had never run for office, and yet his postwar mystique was strong enough for him to easily defeat Senator Taft without ever showing up to campaign. At the same time, President Truman was challenged by Estes Kefauver, a Tennessee senator, and was outpolled five to one—a result that helped persuade him to announce that he wasn't going to seek another term.

CHAPTER 2

The Ticket

1

Even Dick Nixon was probably never sure when he began seriously to think about the vice presidency, but the idea certainly occurred to him—at least in a ruminative, what-might-be-next-for-me sort of way—after Governor Dewey suggested it a couple of months before the 1952 Republican National Convention. The occasion was a May 8 dinner for the New York Republican State Committee at the Waldorf-Astoria, where Nixon had been invited to talk. He was already a party celebrity—Republicans around the country sought him out as a guest speaker—and he was terrific in that role: he was young, partisan, smart, though perhaps a little too lawyerly in the way he liked to present an argument in linear steps, stating one all-too-obvious side and then dismissing it. But in those days he could summon a fiery, even evangelical rhythm, and he usually managed to impress his audiences, even if they didn't always take to him personally. Dewey saw something of himself in him, both good and bad. "Dick Nixon's got the same trouble I have," he once said. "Too many people don't like us both," and it was also true that Dewey, like Nixon, was catnip for caricaturists: his face, in *The New Yorker* writer Wolcott Gibbs's words, "on the whole, has a compressed appearance, as though someone had squeezed his head in a vise."

Nixon at the Waldorf held forth on some of the subjects that he'd mastered since coming to Washington. During the Truman era, he said, the Communists had gained—and the West lost—600 million people, most of them Chinese. Nixon liked that sort of formulation—everyone could understand the geopolitical map when it was transformed into a scorecard. But Nixon also knew when to add flourishes of moderation, of bipartisanship, the language that the Dewey wing of the party liked to hear, and so he said that Republicans "should offer . . . a program based not on a return to isolationism but on the necessity for more effective American international leadership." When he'd finished, Dewey, who was standing to the side and smoking, stamped out his cigarette and went over to Nixon and shook his hand. "That was a terrific speech," Dewey said. "Make me a promise. Don't lose your zeal, don't get fat, and you can be President someday!" Later that night, the governor invited the senator to his suite and told him straight out that he might well be on a presidential ticket with General Eisenhower. "He had a very fine voting record in both the House and the Senate, good, intelligent, middle-of-the-road, and at this time it was important to get a senator who knew the world was round," Dewey said years later. "His age was a useful factor. He had a fine record in the war. Most of all, however, he was an extraordinarily intelligent man, fine balance and character." Nixon later told Dewey that he thought the suggestion was "only a polite gesture" but Nixon was being disingenuous. The encouragement he got from Dewey—the governor of the most populous state, a man eleven years his senior who was twice the party's presidential nominee—made it hard to resist considering such possibilities, however distant, and to do so in a focused, realistic way.

Dewey had long since declared his preference for Eisenhower—starting the year before on *Meet the Press*—but there was not much of a personal connection between Eisenhower and Dewey and never would be; Eisenhower didn't warm up to professional politicians the way he did to his military friends and his circle of businessmen cronies. But Dewey was sure that Eisenhower shared many of his beliefs and, above all, believed that he could win a national election—a belief that Nixon already held.

2

Yet even in the late spring of 1952, a month before the Republican National Convention, Eisenhower did not quite seem like a real candidate. Primary voters in New Hampshire and Minnesota (where he almost won a write-in victory) liked him, but something wasn't right, and one could see that in June, when he gave a nationwide television and radio address from what was already called Eisenhower Park, in Abilene. It had rained that afternoon, and the grandstands had emptied out, but what struck viewers peering at small TV screens was that he no longer looked like General Ike, the Supreme Commander. Rather, he resembled an elderly man reading a mediocre speech and not reading it particularly well. This was not someone who had the qualities of a winning candidate, and so a month later there was not a lot of joy to be found inside the International Amphitheatre on Chicago's Southwest Side, the site of the convention. For all the "I Like Ike" buttons around the hall, many delegates, as Richard Rovere observed in *The New Yorker*, considered the general "a parvenu, an amateur, and a heretic of sorts." Despite the polls and primaries that showed Eisenhower's strength, these delegates were more inclined toward Senator Taft than to someone who was being cheered on by the same band of easterners who'd been running things, and losing elections, since Alf Landon's defeat in 1936; and by many estimates, Taft had enough delegates to win the nomination on the first ballot. Taft, though, was burdened by the adjective "unelectable" that often accompanied his name; and in an era when more Americans owned television sets, he wasn't helped by his rimless glasses, comb-over, and a mouth that seemed to contain too many teeth.

Television had never been so present at a political convention, and the three networks that summer tried to cover the event with all the technology available. Seven large cameras watched the convention floor; at least seventy cameras were elsewhere in the hall, and correspondents showed off innovations like the "walkie-lookie" or "peepie-creepie," which let them mingle with delegates and give viewers the chance to witness squabbles in real time. They could watch the Taft and Eisenhower forces as they engaged in major floor fights over credentials in three states—particularly Texas, which was crucial to Ike's strategy and where Taft was outplayed and outfought. The TV critic for the *New York Times* was annoyed when the networks switched away from the thrilling Texas battle to watch Senator McCarthy speaking from the podium.

Nixon's support of Eisenhower was as real as Dewey's ("Nixon is a dyed-in-the-wool Ikeman," the Los Angeles newspaperman James Bassett wrote to his wife from Chicago), but it was not an open commitment and Nixon did not behave honestly in the weeks leading up to the convention. He wanted to accommodate various alliances and agendas, but that goal proved to be just beyond his reach. As a member of the California delegation, he was committed to supporting the state's favorite son and the delegation's leader, Governor Earl Warren, who had his own agenda—he saw the possibility of being nominated in the event of an Eisenhower-Taft stalemate. Before Nixon even got to Chicago, though, he had begun to make mischief by sending out a questionnaire to his state's chairmen and precinct workers in which he asked for an appraisal of other candidates in the event that Warren released the delegation. When Warren and his supporters learned about Nixon's private canvass, they concluded that its only purpose was to undercut the governor. Warren never said anything publicly, but he never forgot it; ten years later, his son Earl Warren Jr. told a reporter, "Mr. Nixon through backdoor tactics pulled the rug out—for political gain for himself"—in order to get the vice presidential nomination.

Warren had about as much chance of winning the nomination as did the former Minnesota governor Harold Stassen, who had competed with Dewey in 1948 and likewise hoped for a stalemate; or the seventy-two-year-old General MacArthur, who was greeted like an arriving royal and who gave the keynote in which he warned of a "deep sense of fear that our leaders in their insatiate demand for ever more personal power might destroy the Republic." (Herbert Hoover, looking old and weary when he spoke—"We were in fear that he'd drop in his traces before the speech was over," Jim Bassett told his wife—had the fanciful idea that Eisenhower could be stopped if Taft, whose support was fading, would ask his delegates to support MacArthur.) Senator Nixon at the convention was in constant motion. He could be spotted in the hall and in hotel lobbies, milling about with delegates and hangers-on; at the Knickerbocker Hotel he ran into Jackie Robinson, the Brooklyn Dodger and a Republican, who on Tuesday night in Philadelphia had hit a first-inning home run that helped the National League win the All-Star Game. Nixon, a true sports fan, had been aware of Robinson since he'd played football at UCLA and he told him that he'd seen him in a game against Oregon, a moment of total recall that impressed Robinson.

Nixon was being careful, and ever more so as the week wore on and more people began mentioning him in connection with the national ticket. When he talked with journalists, he kept insisting that the chance of that happening was too remote for him even to consider it, but he naturally knew better, and so did his staff in Washington, who knew something was going on. The *New York Times* on the convention's third day noted that he was one of seven people in contention for the job; furthermore, before the end of the week he had already met at least once with Herbert Brownell and other Eisenhower advisers. When the presidential contenders stopped to chat with the California delegation, Eisenhower was greeted at curbside by Nixon, who never left the general's side.

On Thursday, July 10, the day before the balloting, John S. Knight, the editor and publisher of the *Chicago Daily News*, wrote a front-page column predicting that Eisenhower would be the nominee and that Nixon would be his running mate; James Reston reported in the *New York Times* that Ike's advisers were leaning strongly to Nixon for vice president. Nixon kept dodging any encounters with veracity, and when a *Los Angeles Times* reporter asked about an Eisenhower-Nixon ticket, he said, "It's the first time I ever heard of it and I expect it will be the last."

Eisenhower occupied adjoining suites at the Blackstone Hotel, and during the week he went from one to the other to meet delegates or party leaders or journalists or friends. By the time the roll call of states began in late morning on Friday, July 11, the general was curiously detached. "As you know," he wrote to an acquaintance, "that vote did not take very long— and so I had no real opportunity to get stirred up." It was over at 1:30 P.M., when Eisenhower won on the first ballot.

The general was not used to being a political leader. He was not even aware that the choice of a running mate was up to him rather than to a horde of exhausted delegates, most of whom probably would not have been able to find their way around Chicago, much less make such an important decision on their own.

The vice presidential selection was made on Friday afternoon by a group of men in a classically smoky room at the Conrad Hilton. Among them were Dewey and Cabot Lodge (who was facing a Senate race in Massachusetts against Representative John F. Kennedy); some Republican governors, including New Hampshire's Sherman Adams, a slight, intense man of fifty-three, who had been Ike's floor manager and was about to become his chief aide and campaign manager; several senators; Congressman Christian Herter (who was running for governor of Massachusetts); Arthur Summerfield, a onetime Chevy dealer from Flint, Michigan, and now chairman of the Republican National Committee; several RNC officials, observers, and Ike's old friend General Lucius Clay. Considering how important this moment was, it is surprising that no one seems to have a clear memory of what happened. The key person in the room was probably the former Dewey adviser Herbert Brownell. He had gone to dinner with Eisenhower the night before the balloting, and apparently it was then that he informed the general that he could fill out the ticket just by letting the delegates know his preference. The selection process, Sherman Adams later wrote, "reminded me of a ward committee in Philadelphia discussing the selection of a candidate for alderman."

The *New York Times* correspondent C. L. Sulzberger, who had come to Chicago from Paris, noted in his diary that Eisenhower liked Nixon "primarily because he is young (only thirty-nine) and the general wants to capture the imagination of American youth," and Eisenhower told a supporter soon afterward that he wanted Nixon because "he is dynamic, direct and square." It was also obvious that Nixon offered geographical balance and, as a busy anti-communist, some ideological comfort to the party's right. He was by then known not only for the Hiss case but for a bill mostly written by Nixon and introduced in 1948 with Senator Karl Mundt of South Dakota—an attempt of dubious constitutionality to restrict the domestic activities of the Communist Party. Three years later, at a press conference, James Reston asked the president, "Could you recall for us, sir, what your role was in the selection of Mr. Nixon for Vice President," and Eisenhower, with surprising candor, conceded that he basically had no role—that, as many suspected, he had been a political novice. "The first thing I knew about the President or any presidential nominee having any great influence in the Vice-Presidential selection was, I think, about the moment that I was nominated. I said I would not do it, I didn't know enough about the things that had been going on in the United States. I had been gone two years. And so I wrote down the names of five, or maybe it was six, men, younger men, that I admired, that seemed to me to have made a name for themselves. And I said, 'Any one of these will be acceptable to me.' And he was on the list."

Nixon, meanwhile, was feeling ever more edgy, and no matter how often he had shrugged off the vice presidential question, he knew that it was time to level with himself and with his wife. For much of Thursday, he had been on the floor of the convention hall, and he didn't get back to his room at the Stock Yard Inn, which was next door, until midnight. Pat was waiting up, and was not in a particularly good mood. Campaigning was "the worst part of politics," as Nixon described her thinking, and she knew that if he were offered the job, it wouldn't mean just traveling around California, which was hard enough, but going through most of the forty-eight states. It would be especially grueling for a mother with two young daughters (Tricia was six, and her younger sister, Julie, had just turned four). They kept discussing it, and at about four in the morning, Dick suggested that they talk to Murray Chotiner, who had come to Chicago as a Warren alternate.

Pat had little affection for Chotiner—with his cigars, his frenetic, distractible energy, and mordant wit, he was not her type. But she knew that he was deeply, honestly loyal to her husband, and very quickly the momentum in this argument, insofar as it was an argument, shifted. When Chotiner came to the Nixons' hotel room late that Thursday, he said, "There comes a point when you have to go up or go out," and then elaborated on that argument. Sometime after that, the Nixons talked some more—the night was gone by now—and Pat Nixon, certainly aware that she had no choice, said, "I guess I can make it through another campaign."

When the convention briefly adjourned after nominating Eisenhower, Nixon returned to the Stock Yard Inn, hoping to take a nap. "The room was not air-conditioned," he recalled, "and the temperature must have been 100 degrees when I opened the door. I stripped down to my shorts and lay on top of the covers, trying to think cool thoughts." There was not much air-conditioning to be found anywhere in the summer of 1952, and when the day was as warm as it was in Chicago on July 11—the temperature outside was recorded at about 98 degrees—one had to make the best of it. In the modern International Amphitheatre, at least, the Carrier Corporation had installed a cooling system that got the temperature down to about 78.

While Nixon was trying to rest, Pat had gone to the hotel's Saddle and Sirloin Coffee Shop to have lunch with a good friend, Helene Drown— they'd known each other since they'd both taught at Whittier High School—and Phyllis Chotiner, Murray's wife. Nixon did not have much time to rest, because Chotiner in an excitable mood showed up a few minutes after he'd lain down. He told Nixon what he'd just learned: that he was on a list of candidates acceptable to Eisenhower and that the list was now in the hands of Ike's inner circle. Also, Brownell had asked him how to reach Nixon, just in case.

Pat Hillings, a Nixon protégé who had won Nixon's former congressional seat in 1950, joined Chotiner in the hotel room, and when the telephone rang, Hillings picked it up. "This is Herb Brownell," the caller said. "We want to speak to Dick Nixon." While Hillings called Nixon to the phone, he could hear people talking, and he heard Brownell say, "It's Nixon." That was enough for Hillings to yell, "It's you!" When Nixon pressed the receiver against his ear, he realized that Brownell at that moment was talking to Eisenhower and informing the general whom the advisers had recommended. Then Brownell said, "We picked you" and also that Ike had asked "if you could come see him right away. . . . That is, assuming you want it."

Nixon wanted it, and yet he was curiously out of sorts. He was not, for instance, dressed for a job interview; he was still in his underwear, trying to deal with the heat. (Jim Bassett later told his wife that "with the damndest wet tropical wind I ever felt oozing through the Venetian blinds, I'd swear I was back on Guadalcanal.") "I felt hot, sleepy, and grubby," Nixon recalled. By the time he got to the Blackstone, he was wearing a wrinkled light gray suit, but he hadn't had time for a fresh shave. He was greeted at the door of the Eisenhower suite by Sherman Adams, who took Nixon to see the general. They had seen each other just the other day, when Eisenhower had visited the California delegation, but the dynamics had changed considerably. The general who had led the Allies to victory and had just claimed his party's nomination was greeting a sleep-deprived, thirty-nine-year-old junior senator who needed a shave. As Nixon recalled it, he greeted Eisenhower with the words, "Hi, Chief," and immediately sensed "a little coolness developing"—the general didn't like being addressed that way. Mrs. Eisenhower didn't come out to say hello; she had a toothache and was resting in another room.

Pat Nixon, who hadn't seen her husband since breakfast, was still in the coffee shop of the Stock Yard Inn. She had been holding a BLT and was taking a bite when a restaurant television interrupted an old movie to broadcast the news—news that, despite what she'd talked over with her husband and Murray Chotiner, was startling enough to make her drop the sandwich. "That bite of sandwich popped right out of my mouth," she recalled. She left Phyllis Chotiner and Helene Drown and hurried up to the now empty hotel room to change clothes; then, wearing high heels, she ran next door to the convention hall.

Stephen Hess, a University of Chicago student who later worked in the White House for both Eisenhower and Nixon, had gotten a summer job at the convention and was in the hall when Senator Nixon arrived. "Because I had a job," Hess said, "I could hear the stuff coming in on the radio back and forth. And I heard, 'Nixon's just been announced as vice president.' And then, 'Nixon's coming in from door three.' And so I ran to door three—and there's Nixon! The door opens, he grabs my hand, he shakes my hand, I don't know him, he doesn't know me, he's in a trance—he doesn't even know that he's shaking." Nixon was nominated by acclamation, after which he spoke very briefly, almost impromptu. "Haven't we got a wonderful candidate for the Presidency of the United States?" he asked as Eisenhower, seated behind him, absently scratched his head; and soon enough, the traditional tableau—candidates, wives, and assorted party luminaries—filled the stage.

Pat Nixon, wearing a black-and-white print dress and a white hat, arrived on the podium as the band played "California, Here I Come." When she reached Dick's side, he hugged her, pulling her to him hard; she leaned in and kissed him on the cheek. He had a giddy expression, his eyes wide and his mouth open as if he were about to say something, and then he gripped Eisenhower's left wrist and shook his arm, almost violently. Eisenhower, who hated being touched by people he didn't know, managed to grin anyway. "I sensed when I held the general's arm up that he resisted it just a little," Nixon said years later. "Oh, he didn't indicate displeasure, but that—he didn't quite like it." Afterward, while the candidates shook hands with delegates, Pat Nixon sat on the platform next to Mrs. Eisenhower. "You're the prettiest thing!" Mamie said to Pat, and then went on to complain about her aching tooth.

CHAPTER 3

The Silent Treatment

1

General Eisenhower and Senator Nixon had become a team, and yet they barely knew each other. After Nixon's groggy meeting with the general at the Blackstone and the cheering acceptance of the ticket, the two men went their separate ways—Nixon to California, accompanied by his family and his new campaign manager, Murray Chotiner, and Eisenhower to Denver, where he set up operations at the grand old Brown Palace Hotel. "I'm sure that Sherman Adams and the others occasionally talked to Nixon," Stephen Benedict, a young Eisenhower speechwriter, said. "But there wasn't any of the sort of coordination of who was going to say what on what day and so forth. I don't think Ike took it terribly seriously." Eisenhower and Nixon got together briefly in Fraser, Colorado, seventy miles from Denver, at the ranch of Ike's good friend the mortgage broker Aksel Nielsen. The general was an expert, even obsessive fly fisherman; he tied his own flies and liked to create combination lures. He tried to teach the art to Nixon, but the tutoring was not a success—after several tries, Nixon's hook caught Ike's jacket; a newsreel from the time shows Nixon trying out the general's fishing rod and looking baffled by the apparatus.

Nixon understood that Eisenhower wanted to take an "above-the-battle position" and that any "hard partisan campaigning" would pretty much fall to Nixon, but both candidates focused on those delectable Truman scandals—the mink coats and five percenters—and Eisenhower promised to clean up "the mess" in Washington. "When we are through, the experts in shady and shoddy government operations will be on their way back to the shadowy haunts in the sub-cellars of American politics from which they came," the general said at campaign stops, which seemed to guarantee that his once friendly relationship with Truman was not recoverable. Nixon said that the Truman administration was filled with "crooks and incompetents" and accused Truman of "gutter politics." He also began to show a fondness for rodent imagery, referring to the Democratic nominee, Adlai Stevenson, as a "waltzing mouse" with a "mouse-like dependence on Harry Truman." But then he went too far: he came up with the phrase "Dean Acheson's College of Cowardly Containment," and late in the campaign, at a rally in Texarkana, Texas, with excited references to "Communist coddling," he said that Truman, Acheson, and Stevenson were "traitors to the high principles in which a majority of the nation's Democrats believe," a statement that Truman, believing he had been accused of treason, never got over.

All that emphasis on Democratic misdeeds created the perfect environment for the episode that changed Nixon's life: a report that a fund, amounting to about $18,000 and supported by the contributions of some wealthy backers, had been set up to offset his day-to-day office expenses. The story first appeared on Thursday, September 18, on the front page of the *New York Post* with the headline "Secret Nixon Fund!" (its typeface was smaller than the two-line banner under the mast that advertised "SIX SEX ARRESTS"); and it claimed to reveal "a 'millionaires' club' devoted exclusively to the financial comfort of Sen. Nixon." There had been talk about such a fund; Nixon had been asked about it after a *Meet the Press* appearance by a Washington newspaperman named Peter Edson, who had been chasing the rumors since late July. ("[T]here was considerable doubt as to just who was behind Sen. Nixon," Edson wrote to a prospective source. "There were repeated stories that Sen. Nixon first got into California politics with the backing of a group of one hundred business men.") Nixon told Edson that the money supplemented his office allowance of $50,000 (as a United States senator, he earned $12,500 and got a personal expense stipend of $2,500); he gave Edson the name of a Pasadena lawyer,

Dana C. Smith, who had been finance chairman in his senatorial campaign and had set up the fund. In ordinary circumstances, the *Post* story might quickly have disappeared, even with the languid news cycles of 1952. Instead, in the midst of a campaign that focused on the purported sleaze of the Truman administration, this news about a "millionaires' club" and anonymous wealthy Southern Californians not only attached itself to Nixon but then, in a lasting way, to his relationship with Eisenhower.

When the *New York Post* published its story, Eisenhower was on his train, the Look Ahead, Neighbor Special, about to deliver a speech in Omaha, where he pledged "to give America what everybody wants—an honest deal." His staff didn't even learn about the fund until the next morning, Friday, and Eisenhower waited until that afternoon, at a stop on his way to Kansas City, to issue his first, less-than-supportive statement: "I believe Dick Nixon to be an honest man. I am confident that he will place all the facts before the American people fairly and squarely. I intend to talk with him at the earliest time we can reach each other by telephone." It was possible to read that in any number of ways, and just about everyone did. Those who knew Eisenhower saw this as the typical response of a man who never liked to hurry into a decision. This judiciousness (or, depending on one's view, hesitance) was no comfort to Nixon, who saw it as something else—a sign of weakness, of disloyalty even. Why wasn't General Ike rushing to defend his troops when they were under fire? For that matter, why hadn't Eisenhower made an effort to hear his side? What sort of leadership was that? "If Ike can't make up his mind on this," a Nixon worker said, "what's he going to do when he's dealing with Stalin?"

On that Friday, Nixon was in California; he was finishing a speech at the Marysville Depot when someone shouted, "Tell us about the sixteen thousand [*sic*] dollars!" Nixon, appearing for the first time a little trapped, held the train, the Nixon Special, and informed his audience that "the purpose of those smears is to make me, if possible, relent and let up on my attacks on the Communists and the crooks in the present Administration." It was all prompted by the Hiss case, he said, and continued, "As far as I am concerned, they've got another guess coming: because what I intend to do is to go up and down this land, and the more they smear me the more

I'm going to expose the Communists and the crooks and those that defend them until they throw them all out of Washington."

Most likely it was not a Communist—not even a left-leaning Democrat—who had tipped off reporters, but rather a disgruntled supporter of Earl Warren, someone still bitter over Nixon's alleged duplicity at the Chicago convention. The source was never identified as more than a resident of Pasadena, but he was said to be angry enough to have urged a number of journalists to investigate Nixon's "secret" backers.

For Nixon, embarrassment rapidly evolved into mortification. He was also becoming uneasy at the silent treatment he was getting from Eisenhower—and at what Ike was said to be telling others. He would have been even more uneasy if, right after the story appeared, he could have overheard Eisenhower telling Sherman Adams, "I do not see how we can win unless Nixon is persuaded to withdraw," or been there when Eisenhower told reporters on Saturday, September 20, that Nixon had to come "clean as a hound's tooth." And what did the general mean when, at a speech to the National Federation of Republican Women's Clubs in St. Louis, he began to cite approvingly some conventional maxims, among them "Honesty is the best policy" and "He that goes a-borrowing, goes a-sorrowing." And as for extirpating the corruptions of Washington, Ike quoted the Bible—"The axe laid at the roots of the tree." A campaign that had been ebullient had lost its fizz.

Journalists could not get enough of the fund story. Eisenhower told some reporters that the idea of a private fund made him uncomfortable, and his brother Milton had what he'd thought was an off-the-record chat with James Reston, during which Milton, thinking out loud, mentioned that the Senate Ethics Committee might look into the matter. Their chat leaked out at once. "God—I tell you, in five minutes, all over the train," Milton said years later, still furious at Reston even though the press liaison, Jim Hagerty, had warned him that nothing is off the record in a presidential campaign. Even more alarming than Ike's silence and those biblical quotations was an editorial in the *Herald Tribune* saying that Nixon's "financial arrangements . . . were ill advised," and that while Eisenhower had "correctly withheld judgment" until he could talk with his running mate, "The proper course for Senator Nixon in the circumstances is to make a formal offer of withdrawal from the ticket." Nixon knew how connected the *Trib* was to Eisenhower's inner circle—William Robinson, a gang member, was its publisher—and he later wrote with almost comical understatement that "it occurred to me that this might well be the view of Eisenhower himself." And yet Eisenhower tried to keep his distance. "I have a feeling that in matters of this kind no one can afford to act on a hair-trigger," he wrote to Bill Robinson the day after the *Trib* published its editorial.

2

A young woman named Marjorie Peterson (later Marjorie Acker) had joined Senator Nixon's staff in 1951 as an assistant to Nixon's personal secretary, Rose Mary Woods. Because Nixon knew that her hometown was Portland, Oregon, she was aboard the Nixon Special as it headed north, and she remembers how odd it was to be so isolated. There was no communication with the outside world until the train stopped, at which point telephones would get plugged in—for the staff and the press—and that was when it became clear that the fund story had the potential to destroy Nixon. "The thing just kind of snowballed," Acker said. Nixon was now calling the story the "big lie," and when the train reached Eugene, Oregon, he was not only attacking Truman and his crowd but starting to use phrases that would serve him well in the days ahead—observing that the Alabama senator John Sparkman, his Democratic counterpart, kept his wife on the Senate payroll and adding "No mink coats for Pat Nixon . . . I'm proud she wears a good Republican cloth coat, and she is going to continue to do so."

Speculation that Nixon was about to be dropped from the ticket was increasing, although it was not clear how he would be replaced—this sort of thing had never happened. If Eisenhower had made a substitution, he might have chosen California's senior senator, William Knowland, another man he barely knew; Sherman Adams had already invited Knowland to travel on the Eisenhower train, but after the fund story appeared, he asked him to hurry it up. Knowland, an overweight and graceless man with, in one description, "a great fold of muscle and flesh at the back of his neck," was the privileged son of J. R. Knowland, the editor and publisher of the *Oakland Tribune;* he quickly got the idea that he was not only there to campaign but to play the role of a relief pitcher. When the Nixon entourage arrived in Portland, "There was all kinds of stuff going on," Acker said. As they walked from their car to the entrance of the Benson Hotel, they saw hecklers: "You heard people, and they had those little cups that said 'Pennies for Nixon.' "

Inside the Eisenhower campaign, the candidate was being pulled in different directions by his advisers. More people were asking why Eisenhower still hadn't called Nixon—not that one could simply pick up a telephone on the Look Ahead, Neighbor Special and chat with someone on the Nixon Special. At least the two campaigns had made contact; an Eisenhower representative in Nebraska spoke to Nixon, after which Eisenhower issued a statement saying, "Knowing Dick Nixon as I do, I believe that when the facts are known to all of us, they will show that Dick Nixon would not compromise with what is right." That, though, was far from the full defense that Nixon had hoped to get.

Another thing that Eisenhower had not yet done was to offer Nixon any sort of advice or reassurance. He did, though, ask for a full audit of Nixon's finances, and soon enough Gibson, Dunn and Crutcher, a Los Angeles law firm, and Price, Waterhouse & Co.—in all about fifty lawyers and accountants—plunged into the particulars of the fund, which also meant an extra burden for Nixon's office. "I remember in one small town we stayed at a tiny old-fashioned hotel, and I stood on a stool, using a wall phone and calling all over the country for figures," Nixon's secretary, Rose Mary Woods, recalled. The general's silence, apart from tormenting Nixon, was sending its own message. When the Eisenhower train arrived in St. Louis on Sunday, September 21, reporters asked Jim Hagerty, a veteran of the two Dewey campaigns, why Ike would pass up the chance to talk directly with Nixon. "That's a question I'm not going to answer," Hagerty said, unhelpfully.

• • •

The Nixons on Sunday morning in Portland attended services at the First Friends church, and later that day the candidate was handed a telegram from Harold Stassen, the former Minnesota governor, who a year before had contemplated his own presidential run and had asked Nixon to consider joining this notional ticket. Stassen had exchanged friendly notes with Nixon as far back as 1946, when Nixon was competing in his first congressional race, but this time he was not the least bit solicitous. Rather, the telegram, which went on at some length and which urged Nixon to volunteer to quit the ticket, probably set the tone for what became a slightly creepy lifelong relationship between them. "I am certain that for the success of the Eisenhower campaign he must have the opportunity to make a clear-cut decision," Stassen wrote. "In the long run it will also strengthen you and aid your career, whatever may be the immediate decision or results." Stassen suggested that Ike could ask Governor Warren to step in, but only because Stassen could not admit that he wanted the job for himself.

Nixon was scheduled to speak that evening at Portland's Temple Beth Israel Men's Club. "For all we knew, it was going to be the last speech of the campaign for him," Murray Chotiner told reporters, and Nixon was starting to give hints that, as one campaign worker put it, he "was ready to chuck the whole thing." Rumors that Nixon was about to be dropped had circulated all day and reporters stood outside the Broadway entrance to the Benson Hotel, waiting to hear the latest. Nixon meanwhile saw that in a survey of a hundred newspapers, the nation's editorial pages (among them Portland's *Oregonian*) were running two to one against him. When he was handed a telegram from his mother—GIRLS ARE OKAY... WE ARE THINKING OF YOU AND KNOW EVERYTHING WILL BE FINE—he broke down, crying.

At Temple Beth Israel, Nixon spoke about the threat of international Communism and his support for civil rights, and he addressed recurring charges that he was anti-Semitic, which he called a "libel." Murray Chotiner, he pointed out, "is a member of your faith." At the Benson Hotel, he got a neck massage and talked more with his entourage, a group that also included Pat; Rose Mary Woods; his friend Jack Drown, a magazine distributor (he was married to Pat's close friend Helene), who was arranging travel; the Los Angeles newspaperman James Bassett, now helping with the campaign; and William Rogers, a young lawyer with whom

Nixon had been friendly ever since Rogers, as counsel to a Senate committee in the 1940s, had encouraged him to pursue the Hiss investigation. Nixon knew that Eisenhower could remove him from the ticket simply by uttering those words, but would he? He wanted to believe that they were partners and that the general had enough respect for him to trust his word. Eisenhower, though, had an altogether different view; he did not feel the least bit close to Nixon and, as Herbert Brownell later wrote, "was not sympathetic to Nixon's predicament and felt that it was up to Nixon to justify his actions and that if he could not do so convincingly he had to leave the ticket." Nixon and his group talked repetitively—Rogers said that it was all up to Eisenhower; Chotiner was scornful of the general's amateurism—and during one lull, Nixon said, as though to himself, "I will not crawl."

One of Nixon's most valuable allies was Robert Cunningham Humphreys, a publicist for the Republican Party. Humphreys's résumé included stints as a radio sports commentator, a newspaper reporter, and a few years as the national affairs editor of *Newsweek*. He was forty-seven and like Chotiner was a political operative ahead of his time—a master of campaign strategies and of staging events that were meant to appear spontaneous. Among his talents was an ability to find a way to the roots of a political dilemma and on that Sunday, with the Eisenhower campaign in St. Louis, Humphreys saw that Ike and Dick needed to speak to each other and that Sherman Adams was the person best equipped to make that happen.

Adams, thin and white-haired and always in motion was already acquiring a reputation for cold impatience, and Humphreys began his conversation by asking, "What do you plan to do? Change every piece of literature, every billboard, every campaign poster, every sticker in the land with Nixon's name or picture—and how the hell do you think we are going to do that?" He reminded Adams that Eisenhower on Friday had said "I intend to talk with him at the earliest time we can reach each other by telephone" and asked, "Do you mean to tell me we can convince the American people that for the last sixty hours Dick and Ike have not been able to get together on the telephone . . . ? No wonder everybody thinks there is a plot to throw Nixon off the ticket." Humphreys expected Adams to get angry, but Adams said that he was willing to give it a try and told an operator to set up a call. That was all; arrangements finally were made for Eisenhower and Nixon to speak from separate stationary locations, and just before midnight on the East Coast they connected.

According to the notes that Nixon took as they spoke, Eisenhower started by saying, "You've been taking a lot of heat the last couple of days," and asked, "Has it been pretty rough?" When Nixon said that it had been, the general said, "You know this is an awful hard thing for me to decide." He told Nixon that during dinner the other night, his friends had agreed on one thing: that Nixon ought to have the chance to tell his story (Humphreys takes credit for suggesting television). That was only partly true. Some of Ike's dinner companions, among them Bill Robinson, Milton Eisenhower, and General Clay, simply wanted Nixon gone—to put this episode behind them as quickly as possible. But a consensus had emerged that Nixon should be allowed publicly to explain himself, and Eisenhower said to him, "I think you ought to go on a nationwide television program and tell them everything there is to tell, everything you can remember since the day you entered public life. Tell them about any money you have ever received."

"Well, General, do you think after the television program then an announcement should be made one way or the other?" Nixon asked.

"Well, I am hoping that no announcement would be necessary at all—that maybe we could tell after the program what ought to be done," Eisenhower replied.

"Well, General, I just want you to know that I don't want you to give any consideration to my personal feelings," Nixon said, although his personal feelings were all that he could think about. "I will get off the ticket if you think my staying on it would be harmful. You let me know and I will get off and I will take the heat. On the other hand, this thing has got to be decided at the earliest possible time."

"Yes, I think you ought to go on television on Tuesday, if possible," Eisenhower said, avoiding the question.

"After the television, General, if you think I should stay on, I think you should say so," Nixon said, persisting. "The great trouble here is the indecision."

To that, Eisenhower replied, "We ought to wait three or four days after the television show to see what the effect of the program was." It was about then that Nixon said something shockingly rude for a man in his position to say to his party's presidential nominee—and for a former Navy lieutenant to say to a five star general. But after his insincere offer to immolate himself, he could no longer contain his anger. "There comes a time in matters like this," Nixon informed Eisenhower, "when you've either got to shit or get off the pot." (In his memoir *Six Crises,* the phrase was genteelly rendered as "fish or cut bait.")

Despite the evident fury of his running mate, Eisenhower was still not about to be rushed, just as he hadn't been rushed during the war when his friend George Patton had overstepped and Ike had been forced to react. He said, "Well, Dick, go on the television show, and good luck," and also, "Keep your chin up." It was at about this time that Pat Nixon said to her husband, "Why should we keep taking this?"

Later that Sunday, Nixon was told that three Republican Party organizations had pledged $75,000 to pay for his radio and television time. The spot after CBS's *I Love Lucy* on Monday night was available, but that was less than twenty-four hours away and Nixon said that he needed more time; instead, they booked the half hour immediately following the popular *Milton Berle Show,* which aired on Tuesday nights on NBC from eight to nine. Batton, Barton, Durstine & Osborne—BBD&O, the Republican Party's advertising agency—contracted for a national hookup of 64 NBC television stations, 194 CBS radio stations, and practically the entire 560-station Mutual Broadcasting System radio network.

The Nixons and their entourage flew to Los Angeles on Monday, September 22, and checked in at the Ambassador Hotel. That night, Nixon walked the nearby streets with Bill Rogers and swam in the hotel pool. He felt pressure from every side: A *Wall Street Journal* reporter took note of Senator Knowland's presence in the Eisenhower entourage and wrote that he might be Nixon's replacement. The *Herald Tribune* continued to express doubts, saying, "A high ethical level in government requires not only that men be individually honest but that they avoid any circumstances which might cause the disinterestedness or good faith of their public acts to be doubted." A United Press dispatch based on something overheard in a hotel bar said that Nixon had decided to withdraw "within the next seven days" and that he "has been thrown to the wolves." Nixon spoke by telephone to Helene Drown, who said that she'd ask the Carmelite nuns to pray for him.

"Just before the broadcast I had my worst moment," Nixon said later. "I turned to Pat and said: 'You know, I don't think I can go through with it—I don't think I can make the speech.'" Nixon had been waiting at the El Capitan Theatre in Hollywood, from where such NBC programs as *This Is Your Life* were broadcast, and that worst moment probably came a half hour or so before airtime. As he waited, he was told that a "Mr. Chapman" was on the phone and wanted to speak to him. Nixon knew what that meant—"Mr. Chapman" was going to be Governor Dewey, who had assumed the role of intermediary between the Eisenhower and Nixon camps. When Nixon got on the line, Dewey began by saying "I hate to tell you this, Dick," and went on to inform him that "There has just been a meeting of all of Eisenhower's top advisers, and they have asked me to tell you that it is their opinion that at the conclusion of the broadcast tonight you should submit your resignation to Eisenhower. As you know, I have not shared this point of view, but it is my responsibility to pass on this recommendation to you."

"What does Eisenhower want me to do?" Nixon asked, as if he hadn't quite understood what had just been said.

Dewey said that he couldn't give a definite answer, but to Nixon it couldn't be clearer that the general wanted him to dematerialize. Nixon had it right—and at that moment Dewey knew that Ike wanted Nixon to resign. It was Nixon's first experience with that side of Eisenhower—the invisible commander who liked to issue an order and have it carried out as if the order had arisen spontaneously. "It's kind of late for them to pass on this kind of recommendation to me now," Nixon said. "I've already prepared my remarks," he added, and in fact he had sketched them out—in detailed notes—on five pages of yellow legal paper.

Dewey, though, had what he thought was a creative proposal: "We've got another suggestion as to how you can follow this up and come out of all of it the hero rather than the goat. What you might do is announce not only that you are resigning from the ticket, but that you're resigning from the Senate as well. Then, in the special election which will have to be called for the Senate, you can run again and vindicate yourself by winning the largest plurality in history."

At this point, there was silence—it lasted perhaps as long as two minutes, and was broken only when Dewey said, "Well, what shall I tell them you are going to do?"

Nixon managed to contain his rage and nervousness as he said that he hadn't the slightest idea what he was going to do—that they'd better watch the broadcast to find out. But after that burst of defiance, as Pat Hillings remembered it, "Dick looked like someone had smashed him," and he went to sit alone for the next half hour, thinking things through. He knew that he wasn't going to voluntarily wreck his political career, or make it easy for someone else to ruin it. He was a quick learner who had already run two hard campaigns, and he was beginning to understand that when it came to his own future, the only one he could rely upon was himself, and his own devices. He was also beginning to realize that when it came to raw political combat, the legendary soldier Dwight D. Eisenhower might not be in his league.

CHAPTER 4

"The Greatest Moment of My Life"

1

Nixon's speech—delivered just five days after the *New York Post* story appeared—was seen by some 58 million people, or about a third of the population of the United States. It lasted thirty minutes and was to be forever identified by its reference to a cocker spaniel named Checkers. It was like nothing ever seen in American politics, set apart by its intimacy, its pathos, the apparent revelation of a private life from a public man, and its use of television. Its structure was a trial lawyer's closing (or, perhaps, opening) argument, which ranged from the explanatory to the exculpatory to the defiant; buried within it was not only Nixon's defense of himself, but occasional jabs at his opponents and probably at General Eisenhower. It is still a remarkable document.

The set was simple: Nixon sat behind a desk, his hands loosely clasped over his notes, and Pat Nixon was several feet away in a chair that seemed too large for her. Looking earnestly into the camera, Nixon said:

> My fellow Americans, I come before you tonight as a candidate for the Vice Presidency and as a man whose honesty and integrity have been questioned. Now, the usual political thing to do when charges are made against you is either to ignore them or deny them without giving details.

I believe we've had enough of that in the United States, particularly with the present Administration. . . .

I have a theory, too, that the best and only answer to a smear or to an honest misunderstanding of the facts is to tell the truth. And that's why I'm here tonight. I want to tell you my side of the case.

Nixon went on to do just that, often conducting a dialogue with himself in a style and rhythm that he would continue to employ and to improve upon throughout his public life:

I'm sure that you have read the charge and you've heard it said that I, Senator Nixon, took eighteen thousand dollars from a group of my supporters.

Now, was that wrong? And let me say that . . . it isn't a question of whether it was legal or illegal; that isn't enough. The question is: Was it *morally* wrong? I say it was morally wrong if any of that eighteen thousand dollars went to Senator Nixon, for my personal use. I say that it was morally wrong if it was secretly given and secretly handled. And I say it was morally wrong if any of the contributors got special favors for the contributions they made.

But that never happened, Nixon insisted. And then he posed another question to himself: "Well, then, some of you will say, and rightly, 'Well, what did you use the fund *for*, Senator?' 'Why did you have to have it?' " That permitted him to explain the economics of a Senate office—his salary, his travel expenses, and the rest. But there were, he added, other expenses that needed to be covered and for which there was no federal reimbursement. How, Nixon asked, does one pay for that—and do it legally? "The first way," he said, "is to be a rich man. I don't happen to be a rich man; so I couldn't use that one." Then, using the language of quiet insinuation that infuriated his detractors, he took the night's first slap at the Democrats—starting with Senator Sparkman—while bringing Pat Nixon into an increasingly personal narrative:

Another way that is used is to put your wife on the payroll. Let me say, incidentally, that my opponent, my opposite number for the Vice Presidency on the Democratic ticket, does have his wife on the payroll, and has had her on his payroll for ten years—for the past ten years.

Now just let me say this: That's his business and I'm not critical of him for doing that. You will have to pass judgment on that particular point. But I have never done that for this reason: I have found that there are so many deserving Washington stenographers and secretaries that needed the work that I just didn't feel it was right to put my wife on the payroll. My wife . . . used to teach stenography and she used to teach shorthand in high school. That was when I met her. And I can tell you that she's worked many hours at night and many hours on Saturdays and Sundays in my office and she's done a fine job. And I'm proud to say tonight that, in the six years I've been in the House and the Senate of the United States, Pat Nixon has never been on the government payroll.

Then, with a curious, unchallenged aside about Reds-in-Washington, he said:

> I felt that the best way to handle these necessary political expenses of get-
> ting my message to the American people and the speeches I made—the
> speeches that I had printed—for the most part concerned this one mes-
> sage of exposing this Administration, the Communism in it, the corrup-
> tion in it. The only way that I could do that was to accept the aid which
> people in my home state of California, who contributed to my campaign
> and who continued to make these contributions after I was elected, were
> glad to make.

And, he added, "I am proud of the fact that not one of them has ever asked me for a special favor." (A claim by the columnist Drew Pearson that Nixon once asked the American ambassador in Havana to intervene in be-half of the fund's organizer, Dana Smith, over a gambling debt was never substantiated.)

At that point, Nixon posed yet another question to himself: "Let me say, incidentally, that some of you may say: 'Well, that's all right, Senator; that's your explanation, but have you got any proof?' " And then Nixon got to the audit of his finances by Price, Waterhouse, accompanied by the legal opinion from the law firm Gibson, Dunn & Crutcher, which he called "the biggest law firm and one of the best ones in Los Angeles" and which he said found him blameless. Nixon, though, was far from done with this part of his talk, and moving past the audits and the crash course in political economics and Senator Sparkman, he became steadily more autobiographical:

> But then I realize that there are still some who may say, and rightfully so . . . "Well, maybe you were able, Senator, to fake this thing. How can we believe what you say? After all, is there a possibility that you got some sums in cash? Is there a possibility that you feathered your own nest?"
>
> And so now what I am going to do—and this is unprecedented in the history of American politics—is give to this television and radio audience a complete financial history: everything I've earned; everything I've spent; everything I owe.

At that, Nixon began to talk about some of the difficult circumstances of his childhood, although he did not mention the deaths of two brothers. He told of working in the family grocery store in East Whittier and of supporting himself through college and how, in 1940, "probably the best thing that ever happened to me happened. I married Pat." And he spoke of how, as a young married couple, they struggled, and then of his time in the Navy, where his "service record was not a particularly unusual one . . . but I was just there when the bombs were falling," and he gave details about his scale of living—a 1950 Oldsmobile, an $80-a-month apartment in Virginia—and the size of their mortgage in California and other debts, going to a line that by now he had perfected: "But I should say this, that Pat doesn't have a mink coat. But she does have a respectable Republican cloth coat. And I always tell her she'd look good in anything."

It was then that Nixon came to the part of his speech that is most remembered, quoted, and mocked:

> One other thing I probably should tell you, because if I don't they'll probably be saying this about me too: We did get something—a gift—after the election. A man down in Texas heard Pat on the radio mention the fact that our two youngsters would like to have a dog. . . . It was a little cocker spaniel dog in a crate that he'd sent all the way from Texas, black-

and-white, spotted. And our little girl Tricia, the six-year-old, named it Checkers. And you know the kids, like all kids, love the dog and I just want to say this right now, that regardless of what they say about it, we're gonna keep it.

More important than Checkers, though, was the last part of his speech, at first subtle and then class-conscious and accusatory, wholly unlike the rest of it:

> I believe it's fine that a man like Governor Stevenson, who inherited a fortune from his father, can run for President. But I also feel that it's essential in this country of ours that a man of modest means can also run for President, because, you know, remember Abraham Lincoln, remember what he said: "God must have loved the common people—he made so many of them."

He was proud of coming up with the Lincoln quote, and he followed that by noting that Stevenson had a fund of his own (it was used to supplement the salaries of some Illinois state employees and was considerably larger and less transparent than Nixon's), adding:

> I don't condemn Mr. Stevenson for what he did. But, until the facts are in there, a doubt will be raised. . . .
> I would suggest that under the circumstances both Mr. Sparkman and Mr. Stevenson should come before the American people, as I have, and make a complete financial statement as to their financial history, and if they don't, it will be an admission that they have something to hide. And I think that you will agree with me. Because, remember, a man who's to be President and a man who's to be Vice President must have the confidence of all the people.

From there, after a campaign detour to blame Truman and the Democrats for Communist advances in China and the war in Korea, he arrived at his finale—part plea, part preemptive attack, and, in his suggestion that the ultimate decision rested with the party, impudently circumvented Eisenhower's authority:

But the decision, my friends, is not mine. I would do nothing that would harm the possibilities of Dwight Eisenhower becoming the President of the United States. And for that reason I am submitting to the Republican National Committee tonight, through this broadcast, the decision which it is theirs to make. . . .

But let me say this last word. Regardless of what happens, I'm going to continue this fight. I'm going to campaign up and down America until we drive the crooks and the Communists and those who defend them out of Washington. And, remember, Eisenhower is a great man. Believe me, he's a great man. And a vote for Eisenhower is a vote for what's good for America—.

He'd been cut off in mid-sentence—he'd run out of time—and he was furious at himself for not being able to give the address of the Republican National Committee to whom he had asked people to wire support. Above all, he thought that he had failed to defend himself, and what made him even more despondent was the ominous, continued silence from General Eisenhower. All he'd heard before going on the air was that bizarre conversation with Tom Dewey, and after the speech, all that he heard came in fragments, through wire service accounts. At the Ambassador Hotel, the telephone lines were jammed—it was hard to get through. Marje Acker had been watching TV in Rose Mary Woods's room, but the only way to call the room was to go through the overloaded hotel switchboard.

Nixon at first had no real sense of what he'd just done, because no one had ever done it before, but it did not take long for him to realize that perhaps he needn't despair; as he left the El Capitan, he was cheered by people who'd been waiting outside. And even without a proper address for the Republican National Committee, telegrams were already coming in at the rate of about four thousand an hour. Loie Gaunt, who worked on Nixon's Senate staff, was helping out at the Washington Hotel and, after the speech, she stayed put, answering calls from people who told her that they'd been moved.

A positive consensus quickly appeared, much of it close to the somewhat conditional view of the *Herald Tribune*, whose editorial insisted that the final decision rested with General Eisenhower and, while not affirming full support of Nixon, now said that he "will emerge from this ordeal . . . not only as a better known but as a bigger man than before." But there were dissenters—"this mawkish ooze ill became the role of a man who might become President," one paper said—and even Nixon's allies found something unsettling about the performance. One might have said of him, as Trollope wrote of the lawyer Mr. Samuel Dockwrath, "He talked well and to the point, and with a tone of voice that could command where command was possible, persuade where persuasion was required, mystify when mystification was needed, and express with accuracy the tone of an obedient humble servant when servility was thought to be expedient."

Eisenhower had watched Nixon's performance from a sofa inside the manager's suite of offices at the Cleveland Public Auditorium, where he was scheduled to speak later that night and where the audience had listened to a radio broadcast of the speech. Mamie sat beside him on a couch, and they were joined by about twenty friends and staffers, among them Bill Robinson, who, Bob Humphreys observed, had quickly become an "enthusiastic Nixon supporter." Eisenhower, when he spoke at an outdoor rally afterward, said, "I have seen many brave men in tough situations. I have never seen any come through in such fashion as Senator Nixon did tonight." Then, in an odd digression, he compared Nixon to George Patton. "I had a singularly brave and skillful leader," he said. "He was my lifelong friend. We were intimate. He committed an error"—a reference to when General Patton went briefly mad and slapped a soldier who was suffering shell shock. "It was a definite error: there was no question about it. I believed that the work of that man was too great to sacrifice." Ike continued, "I happen to be one of those people who, when I get in a fight, would rather have a courageous and honest man by my side than a whole boxcar of pussyfooters."

But Eisenhower was not entirely pleased by Nixon's performance. Rather there were things about it that he did not like at all, and his anger was obvious to some of those who watched him while Nixon spoke. Nixon had dodged the question of resignation—he said "I am not a quitter" but didn't add, as his notes had it, "I could insist on stay" [sic]—but Eisenhower did not appreciate Nixon's asking viewers to wire their support to the Republican National Committee, which was no less than an attempt to take the decision away from him; and he had looked distinctly annoyed when Nixon talked about all the candidates revealing their personal finances. *All* the candidates included Eisenhower, and that meant revealing how a special tax decision permitted him to treat the $635,000 he had been paid for his war memoir as capital gains rather than as taxable earnings.

Eisenhower had sent a congratulatory (though still noncommittal) telegram to Nixon, but its entire text had gotten lost among the others, and the part that Nixon saw that night sounded less like congratulations and more like a summons: "Your presentation was magnificent," the general had said, but went on to reassert his authority in the matter: "While technically no decision rests with me, yet you and I know that the realities of the situation will require a personal pronouncement, which so far as the public is concerned, will be considered decisive. In view of your comprehensive presentation, my personal decision is going to be based on a personal conclusion. To complete the formulation of that personal decision, I feel the need for talking to you and would be most appreciative if you could fly to see me at once. Tomorrow night I shall be at Wheeling, West Virginia."

That was just the sort of message to provoke Nixon, who had been on edge for days, into throwing a minor tantrum, telling Murray Chotiner, who had rarely left his side during this period, that he'd had enough—that he'd expected a decisive answer. And if the broadcast hadn't satisfied the general, what was there to do? At that point, he dictated a telegram of resignation to Rose Mary Woods, who had no intention of sending it. She knew her boss well enough to know when he was posturing.

2

By the morning after the speech, Nixon's mood had improved—reflected in a note that he dashed off to the Nixon family friend Helene Drown:

Helene—Tell the sisters they must have been praying for me last night. 5 minutes before it started, I didn't think I could do it. Then I sat down put my head in my hands + prayed. God Thy will be done not mine. Well I guess they came through for me.

He began to feel proud of what he'd done. "It was like before starting in a football game—you're all keyed up, you're praying, your knees are full of water but then they blow the whistle and you get in there and hit the line," he said. "I probably had been preparing to do it all my life." His restored confidence was accompanied by an impulse of insubordination—a determination to head to a previously scheduled stop in Missoula, Montana, rather than follow orders to meet Eisenhower in Wheeling.

Bob Humphreys and Art Summerfield, the Republican National Committee chairman, were afraid that Nixon would do something rash, and at six A.M., they telephoned Chotiner. As Summerfield talked, Humphreys passed him a scrawled note—actually many notes that together made up a single anti-poetical scrawl that looked like haikus strung together:

Art—
tell him
to intercept
Dick before
he says something
to press
Ike's phone number
Superior 1-6979
Dick should
hold at
that airport
until you
have talked
to Ike
He
Must
Intercept
Nixon
They're crappin'
you—
Nixon has
not left
yet

Have a wire
—Main 1504—
opened up
between you
and Dick at
airport while
you get Ike
out of bed—
Tell Dick's
guys to open
the wire

Eisenhower and Nixon were poker players, and Nixon, now that he held a better hand, was prepared to bluff. Chotiner went so far as to tell Summerfield that Nixon had written a resignation letter. As for going to Wheeling, Chotiner said, "Unless you can give us your personal assurance direct from the General that Dick will stay on the ticket with the General's blessing, I think I can persuade him. I know I can't otherwise." Summerfield then arranged for the general and the senator to talk later that day—Eisenhower in Portsmouth, Ohio, and Nixon in Missoula—and when the conversation was over, Summerfield told reporters, "I am certain that Senator Richard Nixon will remain the Republican candidate for Vice President," and an aide let reporters know that Nixon believed he "was not a GI in this war," and furthermore that he was "not going there [Wheeling] to be cross examined any further." It also happened that after the Nixon party got to Missoula the candidate had a chance to read some of the messages that he hadn't seen in Los Angeles—among them the entire wire from Eisenhower that not only began "Your presentation was magnificent" but now concluded, "Whatever personal affection and admiration I had for you—and they are very great—are undiminished."

On the last leg of the flight, from Denver to Wheeling, Nixon fell asleep. His plane arrived at about ten P.M., which marked the first time that a DC-6B had landed on the short hilltop runway at Stifel Field, where a crowd had gathered in the chilly night and where Eisenhower had waited for about forty-five minutes. "We weren't sure who was going to meet us or where we were supposed to go," Marje Acker recalled, "so Murray Chotiner said, 'It's always a tradition that staff get off first and the candidate and Mrs. Nixon get off last.' After they'd cleared the stairs, Murray said he'd go down and see what the situation was. Well, he barely got to the foot of the steps—I was standing near the top, in the plane—and Eisenhower comes bounding up the stairs and he looked straight at me and said, 'Where's Dick?' and I remember those piercing blue eyes."

Nixon, who was standing with Pat at the rear of the plane, asked, "What are you doing here, General? You didn't have to come here to meet us."

Eisenhower put his arm around Nixon and said, "I certainly did, Dick. You're my boy," at which point they shook hands and Nixon, never less than uncomfortable in Ike's presence, made an awkward joke: "This is something new—as though we've never done this before!" he said, almost a shout, apparently referring to their handshake. Then Eisenhower and the Nixons descended the stairs and pushed through the crowd to waiting cars, with Eisenhower saying, "You run interference—I'll follow you." Every detail was scrutinized by reporters—about eighty of them, who had been riding on the general's train.

On the short drive to City Island Stadium, where they were to speak, Sherman Adams, who was in the front seat, heard Eisenhower say, "You've had a hard time, young fellow. It was a hard thing for you to go through and I want you to know I understand that." Eisenhower didn't mention the strain on their relationship or the pressure to drop Nixon from the ticket; Nixon talked about the reaction to his speech. Pat Nixon and Mamie Eisenhower rode in another car where Mamie, after a long silence, finally said, "I don't know why all this happened when we were getting along so well," to which Pat replied, "But you just don't realize what *we've* been through," in a tone that ended the conversation.

At the stadium rally, Eisenhower read a telegram that he'd received in Cleveland which said, "Dear General: I am trusting that the absolute truth may come out concerning this attack on Richard, and when it does I am sure you will be guided right in your decision, to place implicit faith in his integrity and honesty. Best wishes from one who has known Richard longer than anyone else. His Mother." ("Mom trusted Eisenhower to see the light which she believed every man has in his mind if you turn it on," Edward Nixon said.) When Nixon spoke, he said that there were two occasions "when I think that I was prouder to be an American than any other time," adding that both times Eisenhower was present—and that "the chills run up your back, and you realize down deep what a great and good country this is." He told the crowd how he'd first seen the general from a high floor in lower Manhattan during the V-E Day parade in 1945—and even then could sense "the greatness that not only makes him a wonderful candidate, but is going to make him a great President." The second occasion, he said, was that very day, though he did not quite separate his own triumphant moment from the candidate whom he called "a great American." It was cold in the stadium; Mamie Eisenhower shared some of her fur wrap with Pat Nixon, who was wearing her cloth coat.

Nixon then made the surprising declaration that he was pleased that Ike had not simply rushed to his defense. Rather, he said, "there has been too much of that in the present Administration. There is too much of this business of cover-up; too much of this business of clamming up whenever any charges are made against those in high places." He added, "I want you to know that this is probably the greatest moment of my life." After that, Senator Knowland, who was still traveling with Eisenhower, said, "Great speech, Dick," and also, "Everything is going to be all right, Dick," and Nixon said, "Good old Bill," at which point he finally broke down, burying his head on Knowland's shoulder. The photograph of the two men, one of them weeping and the other comforting him, appeared the next day in just about every newspaper in the country.

It was not, though, the greatest moment of Nixon's life; it was more like having been inside a flaming, descending aircraft and surviving, although somewhat scalded. For despite their public scene of reconciliation—despite Nixon's praise for Ike's judiciousness—the two men had no reason to trust one another; in fact, after the speeches, the general summoned Dick and Pat to his quarters on the campaign train, where he quizzed Nixon about fresh rumors concerning his finances. At the not-so-young age of thirty-nine, Nixon had discovered that when it came to presidential politics, he was as disposable as the Ike-and-Dick buttons that strangers wore at campaign rallies and that his future was entirely in the hands of this forbidding figure with the amazing grin and chilly blue eyes to whom he owed everything and who owed him nothing in return. He had said that he would not crawl, yet he had become a supplicant and had come close to being broken by uncertainty and stress.

Ten years later Nixon wrote that the fund episode had "left a deep scar which was never to heal completely," and that it "was the hardest, the sharpest . . . of my public life." His daughter Julie recalled how her father would mark the date each September 23, asking, "Did you know today is the anniversary of the fund speech?" When she asked her mother about that time, Pat Nixon replied, "Do we have to talk about this? It kills me."

While Nixon had learned that he could not rely on Eisenhower—that his supportive words had no meaning—Eisenhower had learned that he could never regard Nixon in the same way. He was still General Ike, adored by crowds and destined to win the presidency. But he had permitted a subordinate to seize control of the campaign's first emergency; and Nixon began to realize that Eisenhower's vulnerabilities included an inability to confront him directly. That absence of certainty could make life harder, but at the same time, in close combat, it might leave him an opening. In any case, after the fund episode, there was no way to pretend that important decisions about Nixon's future belonged to Eisenhower alone.

CHAPTER 5

President Eisenhower

1

Because Dwight D. Eisenhower's victory was so clear-cut (he won 55.1 percent of the popular vote; his Electoral College margin was 442 to 89), it was hard to imagine that anyone had ever doubted the outcome, although fifty political writers polled in September by *Newsweek* had predicted that Governor Stevenson would defeat him. "I just remember him looking very serene—he just knew it was going to go the way it was going to go," the aide Stephen Benedict said. His victory looked especially certain after a speech in which he promised to "forgo the diversions of politics and to concentrate on the job of ending the Korean War." That meant a visit to Korea, and the general appended these three sentences: "I shall make the trip. Only in that way could I learn how best to serve the American people in the cause of peace. I shall go to Korea."

The "I shall go" speech, delivered on October 24 in Detroit, was the inspiration of two men borrowed from the Luce organization: a young, dandyish *Life* editor, Emmet John Hughes—he was thirty-two, and lived in the Hotel des Artistes in an apartment with purple velvet walls—who probably deserves the writing credit; and a crafty "psychological warfare" expert, Charles Douglas Jackson (known as "C.D."), on leave as publisher of *Fortune*. The lines were perfectly constructed for Eisenhower. Even the rhythm—*"I shall make the trip . . . I shall go to Korea"*—bespoke the gravity of the promise and the image of its speaker. This was no shifty politician but a soldier who spoke the way the general had during the war. One of Stevenson's Chicago allies, Colonel Jacob M. (Jack) Arvey, who had been listening on the radio, said to his wife, "That's the speech that will beat us."

Right after Election Day, Eisenhower and Nixon took vacations—the Eisenhowers to Augusta and the Nixon family to Miami Beach. Nixon tried to stay away from politics (he was asked by reporters if a "fund" had paid for his vacation) and wouldn't comment on an idea to limit a vice president's term in case a president died within his first two years in office. That morbid proposal, emerging less than a week after the election, came from two southern Democratic senators, J. William Fulbright of Arkansas and George Smathers of Florida, both of whom insisted that no one should take it personally. "I have long felt that the Founding Fathers intended that the Vice President should be caretaker of the office until the next general election," Fulbright said, imagining a special election at the midway point. If the two senators were actually worried about Eisenhower's health, they didn't say so.

On November 24, Nixon and Eisenhower met in New York—the first time that they'd seen each other since an election eve rally in Boston. They had a two-hour lunch, and afterward Nixon was vague about his role in an administration that was being populated by people who seemed to have much more in common with an illustrious general than with a first-term senator from Southern California, the second youngest vice president in American history. Eisenhower had said that he took the vice president's job seriously; he didn't want him in a Throttlebottom role—someone just "pounding the gavel in the Senate"—and wanted him "to be able to step into the presidency smoothly in case anything happens to me."

Yet Eisenhower still saw Nixon as a political man—not a particularly positive talent in his view. Certainly other professional politicians had joined the administration—for instance Sherman Adams, a former congressman and governor, who was named chief of staff; his title was to be *"the* assistant to the President," with an emphasis on the "the." Henry Cabot Lodge, who had lost his Massachusetts Senate seat to John F. Kennedy, was named ambassador to the United Nations; Herbert Brownell, the attorney general–designate, had been involved in presidential politics since 1944; and former governor Harold Stassen was going to head a disarmament agency. But these men for the most part were another breed. The vice president–elect, who would turn forty on January 9, could look at them and see men from distinguished American families (Lodge, Adams, and John Foster Dulles, Ike's foreign affairs adviser during the campaign, who was named secretary of state); millionaire businessmen (Charles E. Wilson, the head of General Motors, as secretary of defense, and George M. Humphrey, chairman of the board of the M. A. Hanna Company of Cleveland and a former Taft supporter, as treasury secretary), and Ike's military acquaintances (retired Major General Wilton (Jerry) Persons, the designated assistant chief of staff, and Colonel Andrew J. Goodpaster, whom Ike had known at SHAPE, as staff secretary), and think that while he was the second-highest elected official in the land, he was not going to stand out in that sort of company. Even as minor a figure as Bryce Nathaniel Harlow, a thirty-six-year-old Oklahoman with a talent for writing speeches and memoranda, had a special provenance—he'd come from the Pentagon, where he'd been an assistant to General Persons. C. D. Jackson, the émigré from the Luce organization, was asked to take on responsibility for what Sherman Adams called "cold war planning," but he felt comfortable with Ike—he'd known him since the war—and his rambling, highly opinionated memoranda demonstrated a talent as an ingratiating and manipulative bureaucrat; his colleague Emmet John Hughes came on as a speechwriter and, as it turned out, a careful note taker. There was also Eisenhower's beloved brother Milton, an unpaid, unofficial adviser, who was nine years younger but whose career in government predated Ike's and of whom the president said, "I believe him to be the most knowledgeable and widely informed of all the people with whom I deal."

Nixon also saw that the people around Eisenhower tended to be easterners—New Yorkers, in fact, and for that matter New Yorkers with ties to Tom Dewey. Colonel Robert McCormick's *Chicago Tribune* found something approaching conspiracy in the Dewey-centric makeup of the ensemble: Foster Dulles, for instance, had been Dewey's chief adviser on foreign affairs, and Dewey in 1946 had appointed Dulles to a vacancy in the United States Senate—a seat that he lost when he ran against Herbert Lehman two years later. Foster's brother, Allen, another Dewey man, was to be the director of Central Intelligence; C. Douglas Dillon, chairman of the board of the investment bank Dillon, Read and a Dulles associate, would be ambassador to France. The ambassador to Italy was going to be the free-spirited Clare Boothe Luce, whose husband's magazines had supported Eisenhower and who had encouraged his political career since the 1940s. And Jim Hagerty, the press secretary, had been Dewey's press secretary for ten years (and during two presidential campaigns), and before that a legislative correspondent in Albany for the *New York Times*; his deputy, Murray Snyder, had been the chief political writer for the *Herald Tribune*. Ann Cook Whitman, who had been hired as a secretary during the campaign, was asked to stay on. Mrs. Whitman, described by the *Herald Tribune* reporter Robert J. Donovan as a "slender woman with dark eyes and silver hair . . . keen, sensitive, risible, youthful, chic, and distinctly good-looking," was forty-four. Her title of confidential secretary only hints at the range of her duties (correspondent and diarist), her long hours, and her devotion to the president over the next eight years.

Nixon's New York lunch with Eisenhower came on the same day that Ike appointed his secretary of agriculture, the Mormon elder Ezra Taft Benson, and paid a visit to the United Nations. After lunch, Nixon told reporters that Eisenhower "indicated he wanted me to take an active role in expediting legislation," and he added, "I'll do whatever General Eisenhower wants to be done for the success of the Administration." There was nothing asked, and nothing said, about Ike's promised trip to Korea, which had been carefully planned and was to begin soon, and in which Nixon had no role. In fact, the Korean expedition was carried off with great stealth, beginning shortly before dawn on a chilly November 29, and while the president-elect spent only three days there (long enough to see his son, John, an Army major), he quickly decided that the American military position was untenable. As he later wrote, "We could not stand forever on a static front and continue to accept casualties without any visible results."

2

On January 21, 1953, Eisenhower started his White House diary: "My first day at President's Desk. Plenty of worries and difficult problems but such has been my portion for a long time—the result is that this just seems (today) like a continuation of all I've been doing since July '41—even before that!" Even the Inauguration Day rituals felt like a continuation of what had gone before—including the small-bore hostility between Ike and Truman as they rode silently to the Capitol for the swearing-in. Eisenhower and Nixon stayed in the reviewing stand throughout, and students of social Washington could note that Herbert Hoover sat to the right of Mamie Eisenhower and that Speaker Joe Martin sat behind Hoover; John S. D. Eisenhower was home from Korea for the occasion, and was joined by his wife, Barbara, along with Ike's mother-in-law, Mrs. John Sheldon (Elivera) Doud. Close by were Clare Boothe Luce and General George Marshall, and scattered about were relatives, including more than fifteen who belonged to the Nixon clan. Dick's younger brother, Edward, who was twenty-three, was impressed at meeting Eisenhower, and his father, Frank Nixon, was more impressed at being introduced to Herbert Hoover.

The worries to which Eisenhower referred in his diary included the Korean fighting, but also persistent tensions with the Soviet Union, conflicts between Arabs and Jews, and the development by America and Russia of a new, deadlier class of nuclear weapons—the hydrogen bomb, which had just been successfully tested. The president was comfortable facing issues affecting war and peace; finding solutions to domestic politics, however, was a different sort of test, even though Republicans had a narrow majority in the House and a one-vote margin in the Senate. He also had to worry about getting along with his former rival Bob Taft, the Senate majority leader, and Taft was already annoyed with Eisenhower for his choice of secretary of labor, Martin Durkin, who was not only a Democrat but the president of the Journeymen Plumbers and Steamfitters Union. It was, Taft said, "an incredible appointment . . . a man who . . . fought General Eisenhower's election." It was bad enough that Durkin was a Democrat, but what particularly galled Taft, the coauthor of the Taft-Hartley Labor Relations Act, which restrained the power of unions (and which Durkin wanted to repeal), was that no one had warned him.

The Durkin choice gave Nixon the opportunity to defend Eisenhower while also giving him some early instruction in the useful art of the nonsensical apology. "I do not agree with those who criticize [Durkin's] appointment on the ground that he is a labor leader," Nixon said with apparent thoughtfulness. "I believe it is essential for the Administration to avoid the situation that developed in the previous Administration in which the Cabinet was loaded with individuals leaning to one point of view. General Eisenhower, by appointing Durkin, has appointed a man who vigorously represents the point of view of respected labor leaders—and that point of view should be represented in the Cabinet." That Nixon did not believe a word he was saying made no difference; it is impossible to imagine that he would have defended Martin Durkin in any other circumstance. Nixon, though, *did* mean what he went on to say about the regrettable failure to notify Taft in advance. That, Nixon said with all the vagueness at his command, was a "technical matter."

There was a sameness to the cabinet ensemble. But for all the wealth and maleness and middle-agedness in the cabinet, there were great differences in how each was regarded by the president. Eisenhower right away had his eye out for talent and in particular for someone who might be a "logical successor" to himself. So he made lists—the habit would become increasingly pronounced over the years—and informally rated people who, were he still in the Army, would be in line for promotion. What he called the "general field of personality" meant a lot to him. By his fourth month in office, he had concluded that Treasury's George Humphrey had a "splendid personality," and that Cabot Lodge was "well-educated, widely-experienced, quick, shrewd, and possessed of a fine personality." Ike's list included Herb Brownell (he was "perfectly confident that he would make an outstanding President") and (so far without comment) Vice President Nixon. Outside of Ike's list making though, Nixon seemed steadily to be rising in his estimation.

The cabinet meetings, which Eisenhower tried to hold every Friday (the National Security Council met on Thursdays), were an ideal forum in which to judge a person's "presentation"—an environment in which George Humphrey quickly became primus inter pares. Humphrey was the same age as Eisenhower, and his great asset was having a friendly, all-embracing personality that put everyone at ease. Although the president was impressed by Foster Dulles's knowledge of foreign affairs, he found that he was "not particularly persuasive in presentation" and, what was more troublesome, that he "seemed to have a curious lack of understanding as to how his words and manner may affect another personality." Nixon, with his aptitude for synthesis and analysis, did well in the Cabinet Room, where he sat opposite the president, often taking notes. "He was always there, very much quiet," a staff member, Roemer McPhee, recalled. "He would speak if spoken to of course, but as the President went around the table, he always called on Nixon last. And he'd say, 'Now, Dick, what do you think?' And Nixon would make some of the most brilliant summaries of what had been said pro and con and come forth with a conclusion or recommendation which was equally terrific. It wasn't always followed, but it was a master lawyer doing a master lawyer's job. And that impressed the President."

In the first months of 1953, Nixon's quiet ascent was being noticed. The *New York Times* described him as having "youth, amiability, immunity to fatigue, and a knack for getting on with people" as well as a "passion for anonymity." The vice president, it was noted, could be "a catalytic agent"—a person who spent more time at the White House than anyone else from Capitol Hill and more time on the Hill than any member of the administration—a person who had so far "steered a canny course between the threatening shoals." (The vice president had three offices: a suite in the Senate Office Building, a formal room near the Senate chamber for ceremonial duties, and a small, clammy hideaway office—P-55—on the mezzanine of the Capitol.) The Alsop brothers observed that the "able and serious" Nixon was taking "a most active part" in the work of the National Security Council and that he had begun to express careful views on questions of national defense—for instance weighing pressure on the budget (Senator Taft's worry) against the risks of Soviet nuclear superiority (Nixon's concern, which the Alsop brothers shared). The columnist Roscoe Drummond, eager to court a high official, was quick to drop a note to Nixon in which he said "I am riskfully enclosing a column which I wrote this week. I trust that I am not going to discover that I am wrong. I'm not, am I?" The flattering column spoke of the "increasing power, the increasing prestige, and the increasing political potential of Vice President Richard M. Nixon," and went on, "It is evident by now that, without any fanfare and without the creation of any fancy assignment, the Vice-President is being made a significant figure and a significant force in the Eisenhower administration." Very likely some of these judgments originated with Nixon, who, in off-the-record speeches, was saying identical things: "The Vice President is not one who can serve best if he receives publicity," and, "He will do a better job if he can be quietly useful," and moreover, "The Vice President has one very great opportunity which probably exceeds that of any man in the government . . . . He participates in more activities of the government than any other government official."

Nixon at first had no role in foreign policy, and as if to remedy that shortcoming, Eisenhower in midsummer did him the immense favor of asking him to take on his first quasi-diplomatic assignment: to travel with Pat on an extensive goodwill tour of the Far East and Southeast Asia. The suggestion came suddenly. Eisenhower had looked across the table at Nixon, who was in the Cabinet Room with Dulles and others, and asked what he was doing in the fall, to which the vice president replied, "Well, anything you like." In a diary entry on June 1, in which Ike complained about Senator Taft ("His best friends explain his irascibility as frankness, and his blind prejudices as outspokenness"), he added that Nixon by contrast "is not only bright, quick and energetic—but loyal and cooperative."

The vice president was also wise enough in those first months to take up the study of golf, and in the summer of 1953, he worked on his game at the Spring Lake Golf and Country Club in Mantoloking, New Jersey, where he spent weekends with his family. Although he never became fond of the game, he understood its social utility and he was determined to master it. He had even joined the expensive and exclusive all-male Burning Tree Country Club—Ike's club—in Bethesda, which the newspaperman Jim Bassett described as "probably the only place in the world where the President . . . can sit around in his skivvies with his friends" (Ike's locker was identified by a card on which was scrawled, in pencil, "The President, U.S.A.") and where a typical Nixon foursome might include Bill Rogers, Philip Graham, the publisher of the *Washington Post* ("a lean, humorous, satirical sort of guy," in Bassett's view), and Senator Prescott Bush of Connecticut. When a reporter in New Jersey asked Nixon if he hoped someday to play golf with Eisenhower, he cheerfully replied that it would be "quite a while before I am in his class," but he wanted to be ready for that eventual game. Lawrence Radak, a Bronx native who was staying with relatives in nearby Asbury Park, caddied for Nixon that summer and remembered the vice president on his first day at Spring Lake. "It was just like a professional golf tournament where you'd have these hordes of crowds and they would all run down to the green and wait for him to get to the green," he said. Nixon finished third in his foursome and returned the next day in late afternoon, "almost in twilight," Radak said, "when there wouldn't be too many people on the course. He wanted to get some privacy that way so he could just play nine holes."

Nixon and Eisenhower golfed together on September 11, in Denver, at Cherry Hills Country Club, one of Ike's favorite courses. A photograph taken that day showed them wearing identical golf shirts (Nixon in black, Ike in white) and similar newsboy-style golf hats. Nixon, though, appeared to be mildly terrified, his hands clasped together, resting on a club. A newspaper account said that the vice president "quailed when he faced cameramen and reporters." Eisenhower was holding a club, too, but looked ready for action, and in fact said to Nixon, "I think you and I ought to take them on"—referring to the others in the foursome, L. B. (Bud) Maytag Sr., a past president of the washing machine company, and Ed Dudley, the golf pro at Cherry Hills.

Nixon looked around uncomfortably. The first hole was 352 yards away, and Eisenhower drove first, sending the ball more than two hundred yards. "Just get up there and hit like you did this morning," the president ordered Nixon. "Quit worrying." Nixon kept worrying; he knew how seriously the president took his golf and how easy it was to look inept. He took a few practice swings before he teed off, and when he made his shot, the ball went a respectable distance—rolling right next to the president's, two hundred yards away. "Great guns!" Eisenhower said. "What're you doing, driving the green?" Nixon finally was able to laugh, and said, "I think I'll go back to the clubhouse. I'll never hit another one like that."

CHAPTER 6

Diplomatic Vistas

1

Nixon had hoped to spend the end of the summer with his family on the Jersey Shore, but the president in early July had informed him that he, too, was planning to leave town in August and so they needed to coordinate "our respective absences." Or, as Ike put it in a note, he hoped to be gone for five or six weeks and "I think it would be a very fine idea for you to be in Washington during that period, if at all possible."

So although Nixon dutifully made his way to Mantoloking each weekend, it turned out that for him, the summer of 1953, apart from trying to master golf, was pretty much all business. Part of the time was spent with briefing books, as he prepared for his trip to Asia; Eisenhower had also asked him to chair the President's Committee on Government Contracts, which dealt with racial discrimination at the federal level—this at a time when even newspapers like the *Washington Post* would run employment ads for "men" as well as for "colored men." Eisenhower was not comfortable with racial questions, but with Nixon's appointment he meant to signal that he took the issue seriously. The appointment also helped Nixon acquire an early reputation as a champion, although never a fervent one, of civil rights. As a House member, he had voted to abolish the poll tax, but he had opposed a Senate bill to strengthen the Fair Employment Practices

Commission; the civil rights leader Roy Wilkins thought that Nixon's voting record was "not good," but Wilkins would later change his mind.

When Nixon came out to Denver in September, the Eisenhowers were staying with Mamie's mother, Elivera Doud. The eight-room Doud house at 750 Lafayette Street was situated in an upper-middle-class neighborhood about twenty blocks from the city's downtown and the Brown Palace Hotel, where reporters stayed; it was also a short drive to the president's office at Lowry Air Force Base and to the Cherry Hills Country Club. Eisenhower liked his vacations; he enjoyed not only golf and bridge and fishing, but reading western novels and spending time with friends, often members of the gang, or with Milton.

It had turned out to be a busy summer. On July 26, an "armistice"—actually a cease-fire—ended the fighting in Korea. The agreement, signed in Panmunjom after years of haggling dating back to Truman's time, did not guarantee a lasting peace, and the reaction generally was anything but celebratory since no one knew what a victory would have looked like. Yet when a group of photographers and reporters asked the president how he felt, he replied, with a big smile, "The war is over and I hope my son is going to come home soon."

Eisenhower could end hostilities because of who he was; another president might have been called an appeaser, or worse, for having stopped the shooting without being able to claim victory. But Eisenhower believed that there were no acceptable alternatives. If the truce talks had irreparably broken down, there would have been pressure to use atomic weapons against China, which was supplying the North (General MacArthur from the sidelines had been urging that course), with consequences that could not then—and still could not—be imagined. Also, Senator Taft had fallen ill with what was originally described as a "serious hip ailment." The end came rapidly; one day in June he was on crutches, clearly in pain as he tried to get about, and on another he announced that he was turning his leadership duties over to Senator Knowland, which brought to the Senate a more strident tone and a diminished intellect. Taft died on July 31 of cancer, and his Senate colleagues and the president mourned the loss perhaps more than they had expected to; it was as if everyone suddenly realized that there was nothing ordinary in such an honorable and steady career, and that Bob Taft was not at all the reactionary cold fish so often portrayed.

("In some things I found him extraordinarily 'leftish,'" Ike wrote in his diary. "This applied specifically to his attitude toward old-age pensions. He told me that he believed every individual in the United States, upon reaching the age of 65, should automatically go on a minimum pension basis, paid by the Federal government.") With all this, the president found something especially inviting about the chance to head west in August.

The death of Senator Taft only added to pressures on the vice president, who had to negotiate various roles—on the Hill, where he presided over the Senate, as well as at the White House, where his responsibility was less clear. Taft's death also left fewer people who were able to head off the latest provocations from Wisconsin senator Joseph McCarthy, who some years before had discovered that the subject of domestic subversion was a gift to an office seeker. His epiphany came soon after he delivered a speech in Wheeling, West Virginia, on February 9, 1950, and claimed to have a list of 205 people "known to the Secretary of State as being members of the Communist Party." His numbers were fictional—and subsequently amended more than once—but, as Richard Rovere observed, "He was a . . . prospector who drilled Communism and saw it come up a gusher."

Eisenhower viewed McCarthy as a headline hunter and believed that "nothing will be so effective in combating his particular kind of trouble-making as to ignore him." Merely ignoring McCarthy, though, was a chancy tactic; one could never be sure when or how he was going to strike, or who his target would be. A year before Eisenhower's nomination, Mc-Carthy had accused General Marshall of Soviet sympathies and of being part of a "conspiracy so immense, an infamy so black, as to dwarf any in the previous history of man." That had presented a problem for Eisenhower the candidate; Marshall after all was probably the person most responsible for his rapid advancement in the military, and moreover Eisenhower admired him enormously. Yet when he was to deliver a speech in Milwaukee, he gave in to political advisers and agreed to delete a passage in praise of Marshall so as not to vex McCarthy. Its excision was a shameful concession, and Eisenhower never quite faced up to it, although in his memoirs he acknowledged that the episode had allowed people to say that he had "capitulated to the McCarthyites" while adding, untruthfully, "This was, of course, completely untrue." Marshall's wife later said to the columnist Marquis Childs, "George will not tell you but I will. He sat in front of that radio night after night waiting for General Eisenhower to say a word in his defense." Marshall's proximity to Ike at the inaugural parade was above all a form of apology for the surrender to McCarthy.

Dick Nixon and Joe McCarthy were not exactly friends, nor were they twin spirits, although many on the American left tended to regard them as such. McCarthy's indifference to facts and his carelessness about the rules of evidence made the lawyerly Nixon uneasy; he sometimes urged McCarthy to go slow—"Always understate, never overstate your case," he advised—and McCarthy had never taken personally to Nixon, who could be stiff even when he tried to be chummy. When they were Senate colleagues (McCarthy had been elected in 1946), Nixon was still a committed Red hunter, but a prissy and proper Red hunter compared with McCarthy and, furthermore, his active Red-hunting days were pretty much behind him. McCarthy was also protected and surrounded by a circle of friends, sycophants, and sympathetic journalists like the Hearst columnist George Sokolsky, who had the face of a well-fed commissar and whose column appeared in about three hundred newspapers. Those who watched him closely—in particular reporters—found something beguiling and just plain fun about Joe, as they called him, even while they were aware of the distant explosions of lives being ruined. "It was a sort of game for us, as it was for McCarthy," Charles Seib, who covered the senator for Hearst's International News Service, recalled. Yet by 1953 it was becoming more difficult for some of his friends to stand by him; there were signs that he was starting to veer out of control and he'd begun to scare off people like his Senate colleague Jack Kennedy, who had enjoyed his boisterous company. And everyone had heard about the fight at the Sulgrave Club, where McCarthy had either punched, slapped, or kicked the columnist Drew Pearson in the testicles.

In the late fall of 1953, Eisenhower was asked whether Communism would be an issue in the next election and said, "Now, I hope that this whole thing will be a matter of history and of memory by the time the next election comes around. I don't believe we can live in fear of each other forever." McCarthy did not let that slide. "The raw, harsh, unpleasant fact," he said, "is that communism is an issue and will be an issue in

1954." Until then, McCarthy had been content to go after relatively powerless targets, people like Chip Bohlen, appointed ambassador to the Soviet
Union; or Harvard's James Bryant Conant, named as high commissioner
for Germany; or Greek shipowners who did business with China; or General Marshall, who was not going to bother denying that he had been part
of a vast Soviet conspiracy. Nixon got McCarthy to abandon a public fight
against Conant, and along with Senator Taft helped to rescue Bohlen's
appointment. ("I believe I can safely say that at least half a dozen senators
voted for Bohlen who might otherwise have voted against him on the basis
of the information I gave them privately," Nixon said in an off-the-record
talk.) But a showdown between McCarthy and the administration seemed
ever more likely—"This is war and no mistake about it," the Alsops had
written. It wasn't yet war, but the administration needed someone to deal
with McCarthy, preferably someone comfortable in McCarthy's territory,
an assignment for which Nixon was ideally equipped.

2

When the Nixons traveled, Hannah Nixon would come east to stay with
Tricia and Julie and this Asian trip was to be their longest unbroken journey, lasting sixty-eight days. The vice president could not have picked
a better time to be out of town. While Senator McCarthy was stirring
things up, the Nixons' itinerary included Japan, Korea, the Philippines,
Australia, Thailand, India, Pakistan, Iran, and Libya. In Vietnam, Nixon
got fresh views on the guerrilla war with the Vietminh, whom the French
had been fighting since the end of the Pacific war. He met in Saigon with
Bao Dai, the last emperor of the state, who told him that they worried
most about China and that if and when the Chinese came in, "Ho Chi
Minh is finished." In Hanoi the Nixons attended a dinner given by the
French commissioner general, Maurice Dejean, who said, "Indo-China
is not a position to be given up but a place to defend and save," and the
vice president agreed with that, saying that Vietnam needed to remain
within the French Union: "It is impossible to lay down arms until victory
is completely won." The American ambassador in Vietnam told the State
Department that the Nixons' visit was "extremely successful. . . . Their

personalities, their tireless and sincere interest and friendliness in meeting people of all walks of life made a definitely good impression which echoed in the local press." He added that Nixon's many speeches there "added conviction to the general opinion that American desire to aid in winning this war against communism . . . is sincere and continuing."

While the Nixons made their way home, their press notices were excellent. The *New York Times* reported that the vice president demonstrated that "he has a knack for walking into delicate foreign political situations and saying the right things." A summary of reactions recorded by *Times* correspondents along the route was that "the common man of Asia liked this big, friendly, informal, democratic, serious young American, and got the impression that he likes them." In Pakistan, when Nixon was leaving Karachi, a security guard said, "Sahib likes us"; in Indonesia, Nixon charmed the crowds by calling out *"Merdeka!"*—a revolutionary slogan that means "freedom." In Japan, he made an effort to shake hands with policemen and pat the heads of babies. "With this background," the *Times* account said, "Mr. Nixon will be able to influence United States foreign policy as has perhaps no other Vice President," and a story in *Life* went so far as to say that he has "established himself as an 'assistant President,' a mover and shaper of national and world affairs." Another *Times* story, this one with the headline NIXON'S ASIA TOUR ADDS TO PRESTIGE, said that since the fund crisis, the vice president not only filled in during the president's absences, but had repeatedly served as "mollifier to prevent an open breach" between Senator McCarthy and the president.

Eisenhower personally welcomed Pat and Dick on the North Portico of the mansion and seemed so pleased to see them that he held out his hand in welcome even before the vice president was out of his limousine. In a handwritten note, he said, "We . . . have missed your wise counsel, your energetic support and your extraordinary dedication to the service of the country. On the purely personal side, it was fine to see you looking so well after the rigors of a trip that must have taxed the strength of even such young and vigorous people as yourself. I look forward to some quiet opportunity when I can hear a real recital of your adventures and accomplishments."

But that, as it turned out, was more or less that. The president then hurried off to attend a reception for the White House Conference of Mayors.

There were no immediate invitations to a private meal, or even coffee, in the living quarters, where the president always had time to play a rubber of bridge with members of the gang. Nixon, though, did write and deliver a memorandum for the National Security Council in which he made a number of general observations (he seemed almost shocked that "Orientals" couldn't mingle at the racetrack with the British in Hong Kong) and called Afghanistan "a good, tough friend." As for Indochina, he said that "French troop morale is excellent, a lot better than realized," which he probably got wrong, and also that if the French left Indochina, "the only capable leadership at the present time in Vietnam is Communist leadership," which he probably got right. ("Commies only one capable of governing them," his handwritten notes said.) After that, Nixon went back to being a top officer in Ike's private army, assigned to patrol the rogue Joe McCarthy.

CHAPTER 7

The Troublesome Senator

1

The cabinet surprised Eisenhower on January 20, 1954, the anniversary of his swearing-in, by presenting him with a Steuben glass cup, engraved with eight scenes from his life, including one of a boy sitting under a wheat stalk in Kansas and another of the general in charge of the Normandy invasion. The day before, the president observed Richard Nixon's first year in office in much more elaborate fashion: he gave a dinner with music by the Marine band and a guest list that included Edith Bolling Galt Wilson, the eighty-one-year-old widow of President Wilson, along with legislators, businessmen, minor celebrities, and the Slaters—Ellis and Priscilla—who represented Ike's gang. Priscilla Slater in her diary imagined a warm, almost familial relationship between the two families:

> At eight promptly a blare on a bugle and the entrance of the flags announced the Eisenhowers and Nixons, who stood at the door of the room and greeted the guests—eighty of us . . . [Mamie] has an unusual combination of warmth and enthusiasm that is almost girlish, with the dignity befitting the President's wife. . . . She introduced us to the Nixons as two of their best friends. Mrs. Nixon is young and friendly, appallingly thin. Mr. Nixon is a fine-looking, earnest young man. I am sure the friends of

the Eisenhowers hope he will catch the public's imagination and run for the presidency some not too far distant day.

There were no particular Nixon friends present, but there weren't very many Nixon friends anyway. Dick, sometimes accompanied by Pat, was out on the circuit an average of five nights a week—he had mastered the art of changing into black-tie in ten minutes, white-tie in fifteen—but with social obligations and two young children, there was little time, or inclination, to establish the sort of actual friendships that they'd formed in California with people like Jack and Helene Drown, or Robert and Carol Finch. (Bob Finch, who had known and advised Nixon since the 1940s, had an almost younger brother relationship with the vice president.) Dick's closest Washington friend was probably Bill Rogers, who was now the deputy attorney general—the Alsop brothers called him "Damon to Nixon's Pythias." On those nights when Nixon didn't go home for dinner—when, as the newspaperman Jim Bassett put it, "he's in one of his lonesome-lost moods and calls up to go off somewhere for dinner," he might have steak and martinis at Duke Zeibert's or La Salle de Bois. Bassett, who'd taken a job doing PR for the Republican National Committee, was an occasional dining companion. "Darned if I know *when* D. goes home for dinner," he wrote to his wife.

Among the guests were a few people for whom Eisenhower felt nothing but abhorrence, such as Senator McCarthy; the disreputable Indiana senator William Ezra Jenner, who believed that a "secret invisible government" was leading the United States to destruction and that the United Nations had somehow infiltrated the American educational system; and Senator John W. Bricker, who had been Dewey's running mate in 1944 and whose sponsorship of a Constitutional amendment to limit the president's treaty-making power had deeply distressed Eisenhower. Those three senators, particularly McCarthy, were not there by chance. At the end of the year, Nixon and Bill Rogers had spent time with McCarthy in Key Biscayne, where they'd urged him to move away from his obsession with Communism and to explore other topics. McCarthy wasn't interested, and no one by then had much hope that he could be persuaded to change the subject. The president's belief was that the senator's behavior would lead to his own destruction, a view that fit his aversion to confrontation. Nixon agreed with only part of that tack—the part about not confronting McCarthy. He saw the question in political terms—an open conflict with the senator could only damage the party and encourage their opponents—yet he also recognized that McCarthy's tactics raised questions that went beyond partisanship. "There may be a time when as a matter of principle the President may have to become involved in such a fight," he told his occasional confidant, *Newsweek*'s Ralph de Toledano. "But I think it is the responsibility of all of us to avoid it as long as we possibly can. It will give aid and comfort to no one but the Democrats."

There was, though, no way to avoid a face-off—not after McCarthy in the late winter of 1954 began the most difficult fight of his life: a confrontation with Ike's beloved Army, which he accused of attempting to "coddle and promote communists." The origin of this charge was the promotion and honorable discharge of an Army dentist named Irving Peress who had actually belonged to the Communist Party; his papers had apparently lagged behind his advancement, an embarrassment for everyone involved. Eisenhower kept his usual silence while McCarthy, sensing an advantage, tried to humiliate a decorated Army general as well as the secretary of the Army, Robert Stevens. It was clear, though, that the administration needed to break with him, and that was the topic at a semi-secret meeting in Herbert Brownell's office, in January, attended by Cabot Lodge, Sherman Adams, Bill Rogers, Jerry Persons, and Nixon, among others. By the end of February, the situation was beyond repair—even a supposedly secret peacemaking lunch between Stevens and McCarthy in Nixon's hideaway Capitol office just made things worse. The Alsop brothers, trying to describe the mood in Washington, wrote that "the atmosphere suggests Berlin after the Reichstag fire with Stevens in the role of Van der Lubbe, the dull-witted Dutchman, Eisenhower as the aging Hindenburg, and with Hitler played by you-know-who." By then, Nixon was becoming less circumspect about McCarthy, and remarked to Jim Bassett that "It's probably time we dumped him."

But while McCarthy kept getting publicity, his Gallup numbers were declining. He did not help himself when, along with Illinois's senator Everett Dirksen, he suggested in early March that service personnel who were

Reds or who used the Fifth Amendment might be sent to what they called "disagreeable labor camps," seemingly unaware that such language had a Soviet clang. A few days after the labor camps suggestion, Adlai Stevenson, as the titular leader of the Democratic Party, disparaged McCarthy as well as Eisenhower's leadership, and combined his targets as if they constituted one frightful *ism*:

> Where one party says that the other is the party of traitors who have deliberately conspired to betray America . . . they violate not only the limits of partisanship, they also offend the credulity of our people, and they stain the vision of America and of democracy for us and for the world we seek to lead. . . . [A] political party divided against itself, half McCarthy and half Eisenhower, cannot produce national unity; cannot govern with confidence and purpose.

The next day, Edward R. Murrow's *See It Now* program on CBS accused McCarthy of building a career on half truths and congressional immunity—a thirty-minute indictment that hastened the shrinkage of McCarthy's reputation; and Senator Ralph E. Flanders, a Vermont Republican, said on the Senate floor that "one must conclude that [McCarthy's] is a one-man party and that its name is McCarthyism, a title which he has proudly accepted." After that, Eisenhower's silence began to end—he made it clear at his next press conference that he liked what Senator Flanders had said; press secretary Jim Hagerty in his diary noted that Eisenhower in a meeting with legislators had called McCarthy a "pimple on the path of progress" (or had he said "ass" rather than "path"?) and had "really made up his mind to fight Joe from now on." He also knew that if someone was going to answer both Stevenson and McCarthy, there was only one logical choice—the vice president, who, after all, knew the rules of a trade that Eisenhower liked to rise above and who, as a *New York Times* story carefully phrased it, had been investigating "alleged Communist infiltration before Senator McCarthy entered the field in February, 1950."

2

When Eisenhower was asked who had come up with the idea that Nixon should rebut Stevenson and McCarthy, he claimed not to be sure. "There was a meeting at which I participated, and I don't remember that I was the one that suggested it," he said. "I most certainly concurred heartily." He did more than concur; he called Nixon and more or less ordered him to do it, and while Nixon at first was happy to accept the job, he soon began to have his doubts—"in agony," Jim Bassett observed.

Nixon had no objection to answering Stevenson—taking on the Democrats was part of his job description. Going after McCarthy, though, was a particularly sensitive assignment in light of Nixon's history and he felt stuck. "This is one I can't win," he said to de Toledano and others. Once, when he'd talked with Ike about the Bricker Amendment and suggested a political compromise—"As in any battle, you need a second line of retreat"—Eisenhower had replied, "No, Dick, you need two to go ahead, only one to retreat." In McCarthy's case, no retreat was possible, and it did not lift Nixon's spirits when, in the midst of composing a draft, the president summoned him to the White House so that they could go over what he planned to say, a conversation that Nixon remembered:

> He said that first he didn't think I needed advice on a political speech, and that I had his complete confidence in my ability to handle it. He said, however, he felt that he knew what lifted people and he was convinced that it was necessary to get across to them that we had a progressive, dynamic program which benefited all the people. He did advise that I work a smile or two into the program. I told him that was one of my difficulties and some people had suggested that was one thing I should try to do.

Nixon not only knew that he was being used but that he was powerless when it came to warding off suggestions from a man who had few sound instincts when it came to the art of politics. Jim Bassett, who helped with the speech, later told the journalist David Halberstam that he'd rarely seen Nixon so angry. His suppressed resentment could be seen when he recorded his impression of something that was rarely on display—Eisenhower's vanity:

He pointed out that Lincoln and Washington, our two greatest Presidents, were men who were subjected to considerable attack and who never indulged in personalities. He said, "Now be sure and don't put me on the same level, but it might be well subtly to work in that fact as you answer Stevenson." . . .

He said, "Try to get across to the people that we are working for a program for America, and that the little snapping at our heels isn't going to deter us." He suggested I might get in the fact he had commanded 5 million troops in Europe.

Nixon was to speak on a Saturday night from a studio in Broadcast House, the new home of CBS's local affiliate, WTOP, but, because of "equal time" rules, a problem arose: Stevenson's speech had never aired in Washington, which meant that Nixon's rebuttal could not be shown there either. WTOP was owned by the *Washington Post*, and the solution, which was agreed to and then arranged by the publisher, Philip Graham, was to show a kinescope of the Stevenson speech and to follow that with Nixon's live appearance. Graham urged Nixon, his occasional golf companion at Burning Tree, to try to reach the "egghead" audience.

Nixon spent a full day and night in his hideaway office at the Capitol and in a suite at the Statler Hotel, working with his usual thoroughness, writing and discarding drafts on legal-sized yellow paper. "I must confess that this hasn't been an easy talk to prepare," he began, and to show where he stood on the issue of fighting Communism, he said, "Isn't it wonderful that finally we have a Secretary of State who isn't taken in by the Communists, who stands up to them?" He managed to produce the smile that Ike had urged, albeit a tortured one. But no one much cared what he had to say about Communism or the Democrats but rather what he would say about McCarthy. And on that subject, Nixon applied a tested formula—asserting something that was utterly reasonable as if it were in doubt: "Here I want to make a statement that some of you are going to agree with and some of you are not, but should be made," he said, and the "statement," it turned out, was to endorse the idea that "procedures for dealing with the threat of

Communism in the United States must be fair and they must be proper."
Having said that, the vice president employed a weirdly vivid metaphor,
reminiscent of his rodent imagery in the 1952 campaign:

> Now, I can imagine that some of you who are listening will say, "Well,
> why all of this hullabaloo about being fair when you're dealing with a
> gang of traitors?"
>
> As a matter of fact I've heard people say, "After all, they're a bunch of
> rats. What we ought to do is to go out and shoot 'em." Well, I'll agree
> they're a bunch of rats, but just remember this: When you go out to shoot
> rats, you have to shoot straight, because when you shoot wildly it not only
> means that the rat will get away more easily, you make it easier on the rat.

It was hard to listen to this and not imagine dozens if not hundreds of
rodents slithering in all directions as a determined rat killer tried to gun
them down with a six-shooter. But the vice president was using this colorful
language in order to arrive at a civics lesson—making the point that if one
is out to get rid of Communists, it is important to get rid of them in proper,
legal fashion. "You might hit someone else who's trying to shoot rats too,"
he said, as a warning. "And so we've got to be fair. For two very good reasons: One, because it's right, and two, because it's the most effective way
of doing the job." It was then that he began to criticize McCarthy and his
methods, although without actually mentioning the senator's name:

> Well why do we fight Communism in the first place? Because Commu-
> nism threatens freedom and when we use unfair methods for fighting
> Communists, we help to destroy freedom ourself . . . And when through
> carelessness you lump the innocent and the guilty together, what you do is
> give the guilty a chance to pull the cloak of innocence around themselves.

There was nothing inherently interesting in what he was saying—it
was no more than a variation of what Murrow had said and what any civil
libertarian would endorse—but it meant something that *Nixon* was saying
it. By now, there was no mistaking his subject, not when he went from the
general to the specific:

Now in recent weeks we've seen a striking example of the truth of these principles I've just enunciated. Men who have in the past done effective work exposing Communists in this country have, by reckless talk and questionable methods, made themselves the issue rather than the cause they believe in so deeply.

The performance seemed to satisfy Eisenhower, who was watching from Camp David and telephoned to say "It was just right, Dick." But it troubled McCarthy's most loyal supporters, such as the columnist George Sokolsky, who sent Nixon a telegram that referred to "the very delicate circumstances" while suggesting that there was no real need to settle the party's differences. Back at the Statler suite afterward, Jim Bassett found Nixon in a curious mood, heightened by having had two straight Scotches, which he drank quickly—"Hardest speech I ever gave," he said, as if he'd forgotten the fund speech eighteen months earlier. Nixon suggested at one point that they invite the American cabaret singer Hildegarde, who was performing in the Statler's Embassy Room, to their suite for conversation. ("This is the cutest gag I've ever heard," Hildegarde said, declining.)

McCarthy after the speech had no comment, which reflected the care with which Nixon had prepared his remarks. Nixon may not have been immune to a McCarthy counterattack, but he pretty well knew that McCarthy was too smart to try to take him on. In private, though, McCarthy was starting to say things like "That prick Nixon, kissing Ike's ass to make it to the White House." The popular television and radio personality Arthur Godfrey, whose Virginia farm the Nixon family later visited, loved the speech and ruminated about it on his Monday morning broadcast, which had millions of listeners: "Did you by any chance—I hope you did—listen to Vice President Nixon Saturday night? Did you watch him and listen to him? If you didn't you should have," Godfrey said. "I don't know what it was that made me feel about it as I did but it made me feel even a little bit prouder than ever to live in this country of ours." And yet, as with the fund speech, this one left a vaguely sour aftertaste: it increased the antipathy to Nixon among those who were already inclined that way and did nothing to boost him with those whose support he most needed.

CHAPTER 8

"Mr. Nixon's War"

1

Nixon had for years expressed alarm at the advance of Communism, particularly in Southeast Asia, where he believed that the stakes for the United States were high. His interest became even keener after his travels in the fall of 1953, an experience that heightened his sober affect and increased his self-confidence. Not long after his McCarthy speech, in March 1954, a magazine profile described him as a man preparing for the ultimate task—"the sudden day when he might providentially be called upon to serve as a President in his own right"—and what better preparation than a first-hand familiarity with the world's unrest? President Eisenhower, too, was deeply aware of the situation in Indochina, but his view of America's role there was not the view of his vice president, who was forming an idée fixe about the region and who, during his visit, had come close to announcing a new direction in American policy. "We must see to it," he told reporters in Hanoi, "that no supplies are lacking for the Indochina war, which is at present a world front."

World front or not, in March of 1954, after eight years of guerrilla war, there did not seem to be much chance that the French could defeat the armies of the nationalist Vietminh party. The French commander by then had come up with an inexplicably stupid strategy: to draw Vietminh troops to a valley called Dien Bien Phu, close to the Laotian border—a spot smaller than two football fields—with the idea that the enemy could then be crushed with superior soldiers and modern weaponry. But the French needed help, and that is what brought General Paul Ély, the chief of staff of the French armed forces, to Washington, where he found wide acceptance of the idea that a Communist takeover of one Southeast Asian country threatened every other Southeast Asian country, and indeed the future of free nations everywhere.

Nixon would have liked to help the French; so would Foster Dulles, who did not want to be associated with the question "Who lost Indochina?" Nixon and Dulles had grown steadily closer, although they were as far apart in age as Nixon and Eisenhower and although the differences in their experience and social standing were far greater. Dulles's grandfather, John W. Foster, and his uncle, Robert Lansing, had been secretaries of state under Benjamin Harrison and Woodrow Wilson; Dulles's law firm, Sullivan & Cromwell, was one of those that had ignored Dick Nixon's job application when he graduated from Duke. They were both awkward in social situations. Nixon, solemn and attentive, never found it easy to joke or to relax—or made it easy for others to relax—but he found he could do so with Dulles. He was likely comparing him to Eisenhower when he said that sometimes people who are "gregarious and outgoing are not as comfortable to spend time with as a man like Dulles who is quite reserved and sometimes austere and cold, when you first meet him." Dulles had noticeably bad breath and a habit of hunching forward when he spoke, unnerving his listeners with, as his biographer Townsend Hoopes put it, "a palpably physical intensity, fixing the speaker with a steady stare that often rattled him and never failed to put him on the defensive." His speech, as his assistant Roderic O'Connor described it, was painfully slow—"long pauses between sentences, you could just see he was mentally writing it out on the paper. It used to drive some people crazy. They thought maybe he'd just suddenly stopped talking or forgotten or his mind was wandering"—and at dinner parties he was known to absentmindedly nibble on candle wax. But the secretary of state was never less than influential and had almost casually begun to assume the role of mentor and friend to the vice president; on Sunday afternoons, he would sometimes drop by the Nixons' home in Washington's Spring Valley neighborhood, and the two of them would climb the stairs to Nixon's office-study and chat about the world. "I cherished my relationship with him," Nixon said.

Eisenhower found few prospects less inviting than involvement in another Asian conflict. When he was asked in February whether the dispatch of American technicians to the region might lead the nation into war, he replied, "No one could be more bitterly opposed to ever getting the United States involved in a hot war in that region than I am." In case doubts remained, Ike tried to erase them when he said "I cannot conceive of a greater tragedy for America than to get heavily involved now in an all-out war in any of those regions, particularly with large units. So what we are doing is supporting the Vietnamese and the French in their conduct of that war."

The support to which Eisenhower referred was vague. There had been talk of "lending" B-29 heavy bombers to the French, but French pilots didn't have the training to fly them. Nor was Eisenhower inclined to rally his countrymen to the defense of Dien Bien Phu. As Melanie Billings-Yun has argued in her brilliant study of U.S. policy and the Indochina war, Eisenhower in fact was stealthily doing what he could to undermine the chance of American participation—often by proposing conditions that would have been difficult if not impossible to meet.

Nixon, by contrast, was discouraged by what he felt was a lack of spine in the White House. He could not say it publicly—vice presidents didn't do that—but after the National Security Council discussed the Indochina situation on April 6, 1954, he recorded his dejection and his realization that Ike might be trying to sabotage any attempt to draw America into the fighting:

> Dulles presented [a] plan about trying to get united action among the allies. I said that such a plan was all right as far as it goes but that, if it were limited to resisting overt aggression alone, it would not meet the real future danger in Asia. . . . I also said that I didn't think the President should underestimate his ability to get the Congress and the country to follow his leadership. . . . From the conversation, however, it was quite apparent that the President . . . seemed resigned to doing nothing at all unless we could get the allies and the country to go along with whatever was sug-

gested and he did not seem inclined to put much pressure on to get them to come along.

Eisenhower kept acting as if a decision to intervene was in the process of being formed, but, as Nixon intuited, he was only going through the motions of making up his mind during hours of National Security Council meetings when he'd go around a long octagonal table asking for comment while he doodled—sometimes fiercely, often producing perfectly proportioned drawings of cups in saucers, and sometimes the faces of the participants, and occasionally poking his pencil through the paper. The day after the April 6 meeting, he held a press conference and said that "the possible consequences of the loss [of Indochina] are just incalculable to the free world." When he was asked what Indochina actually meant to the United States, he mentioned a "falling domino" principle—"You have a row of dominoes set up, you knock over the first one, and what will happen to the last one is the certainty that it will go over very quickly." But although he may have introduced the "domino theory" to national discourse, he put up a barrier to intervention by adding that "this is the kind of thing that must not be handled by one nation trying to act alone. We must have a concert of opinion, and a concert of readiness to react in whatever way is necessary."

2

The vice president's brimming confidence in his knowledge of Southeast Asia (and his frustration with American inaction) very likely helped to get him into trouble in mid-April, at the annual convention of the American Society of Newspaper Editors, when he was asked, if France withdrew its troops from Indochina, "do you think that the United States should send in American troops to replace them if that were necessary to prevent Indochina being taken by the Communists?" Nixon had already set ground rules: nothing that he said could be attributed to him. So speaking as a "high official," he replied that the question was of course hypothetical, and, with that disclaimer, went on to discuss what sounded not the least bit hypothetical:

The United States is the leader of the free world, and the free world cannot afford in Asia a further retreat to the Communists. I trust that we can do it without putting American boys in. I think that with proper leadership we can. . . . But under the circumstances, if in order to avoid further Communist expansion in Asia and particularly in Indochina, if in order to avoid it, we must take the risk now by putting American boys in, I believe that the executive branch of the government has to take the politically unpopular position of facing up to it and doing it, and I personally would support such a decision.

It took just a day for the "high official" to be identified as the vice president and for confusion and alarm to follow. Was America really prepared to intervene in Southeast Asia—and even send troops? Yes, it was true that Eisenhower had talked about "dominoes" and Foster Dulles had never stopped saying that a Communist political system imposed on Southeast Asia "would be a grave threat to the whole free community," but until Nixon's comments, the administration had only said how urgent it was to defeat the Vietminh while never saying that it was actually prepared to *do* something about it. Furthermore, despite insisting that his response was hypothetical, it was not as though Nixon had accidentally wandered into the issue. Nixon was always well prepared, and before the questioning he had said much the same thing—that he hoped the United States would not have to commit its soldiers but that there might be no choice if the alternative was retreat. And he meant it. "It was not an Administration trial balloon," he said a decade later. "It was mine. Absolutely." His remarks prompted Sherman Adams to call the State Department, where it was decided that Nixon needed to put out a "brief interpretative statement" in which he'd recant once more: He would insist that he had "enunciated no new United States policy with regard to Indo-China" and that he was merely "stating a course of possible action which he was personally prepared to support under a highly unlikely hypothesis."

But even that didn't end the matter. Members of Congress—Democrats particularly—didn't like what Nixon had said; Senator Edwin C. Johnson of Colorado accused him of "whooping it up for war" and used the phrase "Mr. Nixon's war." Dulles, who had accompanied Eisenhower to Augusta, called Nixon and tried to assure him that the president wasn't upset and, furthermore, that it might actually turn out for the best—at least to judge from the positive reaction in France. These attempts to buck up Nixon's morale, though, could not disguise that he'd made a mistake—that he'd violated one of his own rules: that a vice president "is not in the position . . . to make news on his own." He tried to take most of it back in a conversation with James Reston that permitted the *New York Times* reporter to use phrases like "he thinks" and "he regrets," and in any case to tell readers (thanks to Nixon's prompting) that this was no big deal, that Nixon had been saying much the same thing in private meetings with reporters. But the controversy did not subside, and a week later, at a meeting with Republican leaders at the White House, it came up again. "Charlie Halleck [the House majority leader] . . . said that the suggestion that American boys might be sent to Indochina 'had really hurt,' and that he hoped there would be no more talk of that type." Nixon was grateful that Eisenhower tried to deflect the complaint:

> The President, however, immediately stepped in and said he felt it was important that we not show a weakness at this critical time and that we not let the Russians think that we might not resist in the event that the Communists attempted to step up their present tactics in Indochina and elsewhere. . . . He also pointed out that it was not well to tell the Russians everything as to what we would or would not do.

Eisenhower was weary of the problem—and of the French. They probably couldn't hold out at Dien Bien Phu for more than a week, he told the Republican leaders, adding, "They are very volatile. They think they are a great power one day and they feel sorry for themselves the next day." And if the United States were to send even a single combat soldier to Indochina, he said, the nation's prestige would be at stake—not only in Indochina but throughout the world.

Despite the controversy over Nixon's remarks, he continued to get favorable press—from respectful reporters and a number of columnists, among them the Alsop brothers (particularly Joe, whose worries over Vietnam persisted for decades), the moderate Roscoe Drummond, and the conservative George Sokolsky. One of the few to dismiss Nixon's off-the-record comments was Walter Lippmann; what he'd said, Lippmann wrote, almost contemptuously, consisted of "an assortment of ideas and attitudes—things he learned on his trip" and he added that "the more one searched Mr. Nixon's remarks, the more obvious it is that there is no policy behind them."

There was, though, an idea behind Nixon's remarks, and one could hear that idea debated even as Dien Bien Phu was falling. The National Security Council met again on April 29, a stranger than usual session that included the customary briefing by Allen Dulles, the CIA director, who said that a military loss at Dien Bien Phu would be "very serious but not catastrophic," and a report by Admiral Arthur Radford, the chairman of the Joint Chiefs of Staff. Radford had just seen Churchill, who had repeatedly referred to the shrinkage of the British Empire and informed Radford that England had no interest in helping France hold on to *its* empire. The admiral was a proponent of the so-called New Look—putting more reliance on nuclear weapons—and had by then endorsed a Pentagon report (codenamed Operation Vulture) stating that "three tactical A-weapons, properly employed, would be sufficient to smash the Vietminh effort there." Before Nixon could speak again, Harold Stassen, the disarmament adviser, added his own surprisingly warlike thoughts: he argued that even if the French collapsed and the British stayed out, the United States should go it alone. The American people would be supportive, he said, if the president made clear that it had to be done in order to save the region from Communism.

Eisenhower, who at NSC meetings was considerably more direct and blunt than at press conferences, was not impressed by Stassen's diagnosis or assumptions, and in this setting, his views became even clearer. "If the French indeed collapsed and the United States moved in," he said, "we would in the eyes of many Asiatic peoples merely have replaced French colonialism with American colonialism." And if the United States intervened alone, he added, "it would mean a general war with China and perhaps with the U.S.S.R. which the United States would have to prosecute separated from its allies."

Stassen had a stubborn streak, and, for all his innate intelligence, a dim-witted streak, too. The president wanted allies? He was sure that Australia, New Zealand, and Thailand would support the United States. "This is the time and place to take our stand and make our decision," he said. By now, the president was annoyed at hearing Stassen blithely urge unilateral action, and although sarcasm was not Eisenhower's métier, Stassen brought it out in him. "If our allies were going to fall away in any case," he said, "it might be better for the United States to leap over the smaller obstacles and hit the biggest one with all the power we had. Otherwise, we seemed to be merely playing the enemy's game—getting ourselves involved in brushfire wars in Burma, Afghanistan, and God knows where."

After Eisenhower said that he was "frightened to death at the prospect of American divisions scattered all over the world," Nixon spoke in favor of hitting the Vietminh, although not with nuclear weapons. It might not affect the outcome in Dien Bien Phu, he acknowledged, "but the effect of such air strikes on the climate of opinion throughout the free world might well prove decisive." He added, "It would amount to the United States saying to the Communists, 'This is as far as you go, and no further.' "

Walter Bedell (Beetle) Smith, the assistant secretary of state, who had been Ike's chief of staff during the war in Europe, agreed with Nixon, but he made a suggestion that satisfied everyone: he would consult with Australia and New Zealand and let them know that America had not ruled out military action. That would allow Foster Dulles, who was in Geneva for an Indochina peace conference, to say truthfully that no final decision had been made. That oddly passive-aggressive position was fine with Eisenhower—it was no decision at all. But the president also had a warning for this group: if they hoped to win the support of Congress or the public, they needed to stop any more talk about ground forces in Asia. "People were frightened and were opposed to this idea," Eisenhower said. He didn't mention Nixon's name in this connection, but he didn't need to.

3

In late June, Nixon launched the 1954 midterm campaign at Milwaukee Auditorium, picking up a theme that Foster Dulles had introduced in a speech that January—a policy of "massive retaliatory power" as a response to any sort of attack, conventional or nuclear. But Nixon did this without the qualifiers that Dulles had hastened to add when he realized that he had frightened America's allies as much as he had alarmed the Russians. As an overflow crowd passed around box lunches, Nixon said that a policy of weakness leads only to war, and continued:

> The only language the Communists understand is a policy of strength and firmness. To carry out this policy, we adopted a new military program which provides that when overt aggression occurs, we will place our primary reliance on our massive mobile retaliatory power to be used at our discretion against the major source of the aggression where or whenever it occurs.

Harry Truman's foreign policy, Nixon continued, was "characterized by weakness and surrender of principle at the conference table," and furthermore:

> It failed to recognize that Moscow-inspired and -controlled revolutions like those in China and Indochina constituted Communist aggression of the most dangerous type. . . . To sum it up bluntly, the Acheson policy was directly responsible for the loss of China. And if China had not been lost, there would have been no war in Korea and there would be no war in Indochina today.

It is easy to see why Nixon got carried away. The siege at Dien Bien Phu had ended on May 7, and that long, sad battle for a tiny piece of fortified ground pretty well marked the end of France's colonial adventure in Southeast Asia. But his determination to blame this on Dean Acheson, Truman's secretary of state, was not persuasive, and a day later, James Reston wrote that "since his remarkably successful tour of non-Communist Asia" the vice president "has steadily squandered what seemed to be the most promising political reputation in the Republican Party." Because Reston often served as a conduit for whoever was in power, when he wrote that Nixon's remarks "were privately criticized by Mr. Nixon's associates at the State Department and the White House" and went on to cite other Nixon statements "that have embarrassed the Administration," the message to the vice president was hard to miss. "The hatchet boys (and girls) are really at work on RN," Jim Bassett wrote in his journal. If Nixon still had any doubts, they surely vanished after the president sent one of those notes that an employee hates to get from a boss: "Dear Dick: Will you drop in to see me at your convenience? When you figure you can give me a little time, won't you please ring up [appointments secretary] Tom Stephens, who will arrange a date."

Eisenhower had been concerned enough by Nixon's language to have first written a letter in which he said that he understood "the impulse . . . to lash out at our political opponents" but that "in foreign affairs, I am constantly working to produce a truly bipartisan approach, and I rather think that keeping up attacks against Acheson and the others will, at this late date, hamper our efforts." Eisenhower, though, didn't send the letter—it went into his files. Instead, he saved what he wanted to say for their meeting, which he began by talking about Nixon's "castigation" of the Democrats. Foster Dulles, he said, wanted support from Democrats and now they were "smarting" over Nixon's remarks.

Nixon protested—he'd been careful not to attack *all* Democrats, he said; rather, he had just attacked one of them—Dean Acheson. "What we had to do," he said, "was get across to the people, whose memories are very short, that the leadership they are getting now is not to be compared with . . . the Acheson program." To that, the president replied that Democrats may not have supported all of Acheson's polices when he was Truman's secretary of state, but "they feel that any criticism of him reflects in some degree upon them." He asked Nixon to leave Acheson out of his future speeches.

Nixon tried to hold his ground; he argued that the bipartisanship of earlier times applied only to Europe, not to Asia—and hadn't the president himself criticized recent Asian policy? Then Eisenhower said, "The reason we lost China and [are] in trouble today was because the U.S. insisted upon Chiang Kai-shek taking Communists into his government against Chiang's judgment at the time." He also pointed out that Senator McCarthy had referred several times to "twenty years of treason"; no one, he said, should be able to suggest that Nixon was saying the same indefensible thing. He did not point out—perhaps he did not need to—that George C. Marshall had been secretary of state during part of the troublesome revolutionary period that Nixon had lambasted.

Publicly, Eisenhower was more merciful. Nixon had talked to Jim Bassett about planting a question at the president's next press conference, and sure enough, when Ike was asked about Nixon's comments, he said, "First of all, let's recognize this: each individual in this country is entitled to his own opinions and convictions," and furthermore, "I admire and respect and like the Vice President. I think he is a very splendid American. . . . I wouldn't try to excommunicate him from this party if I were you." He continued, "I assume, whatever the talk was, it was made on an individual responsibility. As I say, if he made the speech, I know this: he believes what he said. But I didn't see the speech."

The president may not literally have *seen* Nixon's speech, but he was aware enough of its contents to have summoned Nixon to his office for a dressing-down and to let journalists know that the administration disapproved. Yet he was a master of equivocation; he could praise Nixon and simultaneously pretend that he was like some cocky freelance politician spouting off—the same freelancer who'd made those comments about sending Americans to fight in Indochina; and three days after his press conference, Nixon was once more accusing the Democrats of having conducted a "policy of weakness, a policy of surrender of principle at the conference table." It was a preview of the furious campaign ahead, and there were no more reprimands from Eisenhower.

CHAPTER 9

The Pounding

1

Murray Chotiner had once advised Nixon that "the people like a fighter," and Nixon liked to portray himself as a fighter when he campaigned. In 1952, he helped to pioneer the role of the modern-day vice presidential warrior, or "hatchet man," a part later played with varying degrees of intensity by a line extending from Lyndon Johnson to Dick Cheney. Between September 15, 1954, and Election Day, Nixon reprised that role, traveling more than 25,000 miles and visiting nearly a hundred cities in thirty states—an isolated man in a United Airlines Convair. It did great damage to his reputation and was hard on his family, particularly, as Nixon's daughter Julie put it, when the relationship with Eisenhower was "so delicate and tenuous."

Eisenhower by contrast spent the first month of the 1954 midterm campaign in Denver. "After a few hours of work in the morning he would golf in the afternoon," Nixon wrote later, sounding a little aggrieved. Eisenhower didn't see it that way; he felt that he could never escape the demands of the office. "Sure, I know the Party wants to trot out that great, big, brilliant, baldheaded guy," he had said, grouchily, when it came to campaigning, and he'd told Field Marshal Montgomery that fall that "No man on earth knows what this job is all about; it's pound, pound, pound."

But Nixon experienced the pounding, too; he would typically go at it for ten to fifteen hours a day, giving speeches that included exhortations to "give our great President a *Republican* Congress that will keep us on the road to peace and that will assure our children the right to grow up under American prosperity and not *socialism*." Communism could still excite crowds, and Nixon was always ready to mention Alger Hiss or the atomic secrets that had been passed to the Russians by Julius Rosenberg. There were few mentions of Dean Acheson, although his name was used to make astounding claims, such as "The difference between the Acheson policy and the Eisenhower policy is simply this: one got us into the war, the other got us out of war."

Nixon, though, no longer seemed to take much pleasure in his campaign chores or the exaggerated language that accompanied them. Unlike the statesmanlike vice president who just a year before had traveled the world, trying to get an education in foreign policy, this domestic Nixon was back to shaking hands with strangers and chatting with small-town American politicians. He referred to Republican volunteer organizations as "balloon blowers." There were occasional glimpses of another, temperate Nixon, as when he talked with approval about the Supreme Court's May 17 decision, which, under the heading of *Brown v. Board of Education*, overturned state laws that had established separate schools for white and Negro students. One day in October, at the airport in Wilmington, Delaware, a city where parents were refusing to send their children to integrated schools, he said, "There is no reason why Americans regardless of race, creed, or color, cannot be educated together." He added that his daughters attended public schools and as he concluded these impromptu remarks, he said, "There are six hundred million people in this world who hold the balance of power, and who are not white. They are trying to determine whether they should be on the Communist side or on our side. . . . One of the factors that would be tremendously helpful is for us here in the United States to show by example, by word and deed that the dream of equality— equality of opportunity, of education, and of employment and the like—is coming true." For saying this, he was praised by Americans for Democratic Action, a group that rarely found much to admire in the vice president, and his remarks launched an epistolary friendship with Peter Kihss, a reporter for the *New York Times*, who regretted that most *Times* readers got only a truncated version when his story was reprinted in the Late City edition. "The more I saw of you the more impressed I was with your personality and ability," Kihss wrote to the vice president.

As the campaign moved west, though, it was as if political combat had erased any hint of reasonable discourse. In Butte, Montana, Nixon said, "The Communist party . . . has determined to conduct its program within the Democratic Party," adding that while "millions of loyal Democrats throughout the United States bitterly resent and will oppose this effort on the part of the Communists to infiltrate the Democratic Party," the Republican Party "never has had the support of the Communist party, it does not have its support now and it will never accept it or have it in the future." In Los Angeles, he said, "There is nothing the Communists would like better than a return to the Acheson policy of weakness, inconsistency, and compromise," or a return to "the Truman loyalty program under which Communist agents were cleared and hired." It was as if political combat had suspended the meaning of language.

There were also signs, some of them risible, that even the indefatigable vice president was getting weary. In mid-October, viewers called a Van Nuys, California, television station, certain that they'd heard him swearing off-camera, saying *"Who the hell did that?"* When reporters caught up with Nixon, he unpersuasively denied using what the United Press had characterized as a "profane phrase," saying, "It wasn't I who swore. It was a technician who knocked over a microphone." On the weekend before Election Day, a heckler in San Mateo, California, interrupted Nixon's speech to shout, "Tell us a dog story, Dick!" The heckler, who was described in a San Mateo police department report as being greatly agitated, was being led away until Nixon said, "Bring that man back. I want him to hear this," whereupon the vice president delivered a brief lecture about fair play. When Nixon was done speaking, though, he said, "Throw him out," and the man, who was loudly resisting, was promptly removed by police.

Nixon could later acknowledge how uncivil the 1954 campaign had been but he seemed unable ever to admit how large a part he had played in its incivility. All that talk about Communism and the Democrats was not about "loyalty" but "judgment," he insisted later, and he wanted people to know that "on a number of occasions I categorically dissociated the administration from McCarthy's reckless charge that the Democratic Party was the party of treason. I said, 'There is only one party of treason in the United States—the Communist Party.' " That's true; he did say that. But he said those other things, too, which led Richard Rovere to write that "no matter how difficult it may be to locate the bounds of propriety, he stepped over them." His language remained so vivid for Democrats that the party put up a "Chamber of Smears" exhibit at party headquarters to memorialize his nastiest remarks.

When the president was asked if he approved of calling the Democrats lax on Communism, he again seemed to suggest that his vice president was on his own and that he didn't quite realize what had been going on in full view of the country. "I have not read the speeches," he said, once more coming close to suggesting that he and Nixon inhabited different political universes. "I have listened lately to two or three talks here in town, and I didn't hear the word 'Communist' mentioned."

Nixon was distressed by such criticism. "I was out front, a target of opportunity, and the more effective I was as a campaigner, the more determined many of the Democrats and their supporters in the media became to clobber me," he wrote; he admitted how he "resented being portrayed as a demagogue or a liar or as the sewer-dwelling denizen of Herblock cartoons in the *Washington Post*." It does not take a great leap to see a connection between these things: his dismay at being portrayed as a sewer dweller (a portrayal that for years defined him to his opponents), his inescapable duty to be the administration's front man, and Eisenhower's role at the root of his unhappiness. He knew that if he was going to have a meaningful political future, he needed to create a "new Nixon" to replace the man who had worked so hard for Eisenhower and his party.

2

Although C. D. Jackson, President Eisenhower's "psychological warfare" man, returned to Time Inc. in 1954, he never lost touch with the president, who listened to his eccentric ideas and enjoyed his hyper-jolly personality. He was a natural gossip, an observer of the administration's office politics—who was up and who was down—and he'd send his observations back to Henry Luce. He would also inflict delicate stabs in the back to people who worked for Ike, telling the president "I don't think I have ever seen a worse executive than Sherman Adams" or that Herbert Brownell, who had played such a key role in Ike's nomination and election, had so far "managed to be neither the nation's No. 1 jurist nor a skillful political adviser."

Jackson got a sense of Nixon's standing during a White House political dinner four days before Christmas. By then, the depressing results of the 1954 midterms had sunk in: despite Nixon's exhausting, dispiriting work, the Democrats had won control of both houses of Congress, which gave new jobs to two Texas politicians—Lyndon Baines Johnson, who became Senate majority leader, and Representative Sam Rayburn, who became speaker. After the meal, Jackson reported to Luce, a number of people, including the vice president and Ike's old friend Lucius Clay, proceeded to the Red Room, one of the state parlors on the first floor, and gathered in a small circle. The "focal point," as Jackson put it, was a small couch where Eisenhower sat next to General Clay.

On the question of a second term, Jackson believed that "the mood and tenor [was] such that I would have given odds that if the decision had to be made now, he would say yes." Actually, Eisenhower was telling friends that he was disinclined to run; he had recently gone through his reasons in a private conversation with Clay, not the least of which was a worry that he was getting too old for the job—"the greater likelihood that a man of seventy will break down under a load than a man of fifty." (Ike was sixty-four.) The president worried that the Republican Party was becoming senescent—a recurring Eisenhower theme: "We must present the able, personable *young men* of the Republican Party, on television, on radio, on platforms and forums, and do it right away," the president told the men in the Red Room. "The American people are sick to death of these disgusting old gangster types that the Party puts up, like that goddamn Troast in New Jersey"—referring to a building contractor named Paul Troast, the chairman of the New Jersey Turnpike Authority, who had been decisively defeated in a race for governor. "And by 'young men,' I don't necessarily mean young in years," Eisenhower added. "I guess I mean anybody up to fifty-five who is looking at tomorrow instead of yesterday."

The forty-one-year-old Dick Nixon was sitting right in front of the president when he said this and when Ike went on to single out someone who wasn't in the room—the forty-four-year-old Robert Bernard Anderson, the deputy secretary of defense, for whom Ike had developed unbounded admiration. "Take Bob Anderson, for instance," Eisenhower said. "That man's got Texas in the palm of his hand. I think he is a perfectly wonderful 'young man.' My God, he could run for Pope on the Presbyterian ticket and get elected. That's the kind of Republican face and voice that ought to be seen and heard." Eisenhower, just warming up, continued, "We have got to begin right now, at the state level and at the precinct level, to see to it that the Party puts up the right kind of young man to run in '56. All the programs in the world, and all the Eisenhower prestige, cannot elect some revolting old Republican hack against a youthful, able, and personable Democrat." Yet for all Ike's complaints about getting old and getting tired, and for all his encouragement of youth—and his insistence during private dinners that no one was indispensable—he still believed that none of his potential successors quite measured up.

If Nixon was less than secure about his standing with the president, he was getting another sort of encouragement from one Arnold A. Hutschnecker, a New York internist whom he'd been consulting since the early 1950s. Hutschnecker was no ordinary internist; his focus was psychosomatic illness and his 1951 book, *The Will to Live,* explored his belief that endocrinology was a key to health. He also had a special interest in psychotherapy—in 1960, he converted his practice to full-time psychoanalysis—and Nixon undoubtedly found him to be a sympathetic confidant, someone with whom he could discuss more than his physical well-being; together, they addressed such weighty questions as the role of chance and destiny. Hutschnecker did much to boost the vice president's self-esteem. He told Nixon that he not only had the "strength and ability, but also the imagination and idealism which are prerequisite attributes for a man of destiny."

The "pounding" of Eisenhower reached an acute phase in March of 1955 after Foster Dulles returned from a visit to the Far East and reported that the Red Chinese "were much more virulent" than he'd previously thought and that he had sensed a "fanatical determination to obliterate any U.S. influence in that part of the world." It was an alarming briefing, but then

China—or the idea of Red China—was a subject to excite not only active anti-Communists like the vice president but the "China Lobby," whose cause was the preservation of the Nationalist regime of Chiang Kai-shek and whose adherents included people like Bill Knowland (sometimes called the "Senator from Formosa") and Henry Luce and his magazines. Eisenhower viewed the Chinese as "completely reckless, arrogant, possibly over-confident, and completely indifferent as to human losses," so within the administration there was something close to unanimity on that subject, along with what seemed at times an almost casual attitude by Eisenhower, Nixon, and Dulles, among others, toward the use of nuclear weapons.

The immediate issue was the fate of two islands held by the Nationalists, Quemoy and Matsu. The United States was committed by treaty to defend Formosa (Taiwan) and the Pescadores islands to the west, but beyond that, the treaty was vague, and purposely so. Chiang, though, resisted pressure to downgrade the importance of Quemoy and Matsu, which meant that whenever the islands were threatened, as they were in the spring of 1955, the United States was placed in a ridiculous position—at risk of being drawn into war with China to defend territory that was neither defensible nor of any strategic importance.

The question of *how* one might defend the islands raised the central issue, and Dulles, on Eisenhower's orders, declared on March 15 that in the event of war in the Far East, America would probably employ "tactical" atomic weapons, which he described as "new and powerful weapons of precision." At the president's news conference the next day, Charles S. von Fremd of CBS asked about Dulles's remarks, and Eisenhower said much the same thing:

> We have been, as you know, active in producing various types of weapons that feature nuclear fission ever since World War II. Now, in any combat where these things can be used on strictly military targets and for strictly military purposes, I see no reason why they shouldn't be used just exactly as you would use a bullet or anything else.

By saying that, Eisenhower did something that he did rarely—he alarmed the nation. Whatever was meant by "tactical" nuclear weapons, the public was not likely to discern much difference between the bomb dropped on Hiroshima and a thermonuclear device capable of obliterating entire cities, particularly when nuclear apocalypse was already part of the national imagination; it was gathering strength in movies like Roger Corman's *Day the World Ended*, and would become stronger in serious futuristic novels such as Nevil Shute's *On the Beach* (1957), in which the human race dies out in a cloud of radioactive dust. The threat also had currency in the real world. Foster Dulles in the fall had been told by Prime Minister Churchill, in a Strangelovian moment, that the Soviets "were in a position where, by a sudden sneak attack, they could kill perhaps ten million of our people. However, the Soviets should know that if within four hours they could kill ten million of us, we could kill, in the next four hours, twenty million of them." (Churchill had also told Cabot Lodge that he'd wanted to demand a Soviet retreat from Eastern Europe in 1948 and would have liked to drop three or four atomic bombs on depopulated areas in order to demonstrate their power. "The failure to have this showdown when we had the monopoly was a catastrophic error," he said.)

Nixon managed to sound more warlike than Dulles when he gave a speech to the Chicago Executive Club on March 17. "It is foolish," he said, "to talk about the possibility that the weapons which might be used in the event a war breaks out in the Pacific would be limited to the conventional Korean and World War II types of explosives. Our forces could not fight an effective war in the Pacific with those types of explosives if they wanted to." He continued, "Tactical atomic explosives are now conventional and will be used against the targets of any aggressive force." Nixon did not specifically endorse the idea of using nuclear weapons to defend Quemoy and Matsu, but as if to erase any doubt as to what he meant, he said, "Today, one tactical bomb has the power of ten thousand bombs of the kind used in World War II. That will give you an idea of what the Chinese Reds, or any other aggressor, will be facing if they decide to war." By the time of his next press conference, on March 23, Eisenhower recognized that this national conversation was getting out of hand, and when he was asked to clarify the assertion that nuclear weapons had the same utility as a bullet, he said:

Well . . . when you get into actual war, you have resorted to force for reaching a decision in a particular area; that is what I call war. And whether the war is big or not, if you have the kind of a weapon that can be limited to military use, then I know of no reason why a large explosion shouldn't be used as freely as a small explosion. That is all I was saying last week.

The president knew that he was saying a good deal more than that and that he still needed to say something less disturbing; and so he added, "[T]he concept of atomic war is too horrible for man to endure and to practice, and he must find some way out of it. That is all I think about this thing." But not quite all. Now and then, Eisenhower would offer a bit of military wisdom disguised as double-talk, and he did so at this news conference: "The only thing I know about war are two things," he said. "The most changeable factor in war is human nature in its day-by-day manifestation; but the only unchanging factor in war is human nature. And the next thing is that every war is going to astonish you in the way it occurred and in the way it is carried out." Nixon paid close attention when the general talked about war, which no doubt led him to jot down Ike's remark that the "only thing you *know* about war is that you *don't* know how it will come or be fought."

CHAPTER 10

Mortal Man

1

In late summer of 1955, the Eisenhowers returned to Denver and stayed, as always, at the Doud house. In a "letter" for *The New Yorker* that was never published in the magazine, Richard Rovere wrote:

> For six weeks now, the President has been in and around Denver, most of the time putting in a one-hour work day in his office at the Lowry Air Force Base where he arrives about 8:00 in the morning and signs whatever papers have been sent out from Washington. In the late mornings and early afternoons he is at the Cherry Hills Country Club playing not less than eighteen holes of golf and more often twenty-seven. After golf, he naps and visits with Mrs. Eisenhower and other members of his and her family in the late afternoons, and spends his evenings dining and playing contract bridge at stag gatherings in his suite on the eighth floor of the Brown Palace Hotel.

It sounded either like a summer idyll or a caricature of a part-timer—an imaginary president who didn't have real-world worries.

After Labor Day, Nixon went to Denver to see the president. Jim Hagerty met him at the airport, and delivered him that night to a suite on the ninth floor of the Brown Palace Hotel. Eisenhower was there, too—seeing friends on the eighth floor—but the president made no effort to greet him; they didn't see each other until the next day, when they spent about an hour together. Nixon suffered from hay fever and his eyes were swollen, but he appeared to enjoy talking to reporters after seeing Ike; their back-and-forth covered several subjects, even the neutered Joe McCarthy, who at the end of 1954 had been censured by the Senate. ("When you make a frontal assault on somebody bigger, you'd better be sure you win," Nixon said. "If you lose, you're through.") As for Eisenhower, Nixon said, "I never saw the President look better than he looked this morning. I feel he's in tip-top shape physically and in his attitude toward his job."

Eisenhower was still acting like an unenthusiastic candidate. A few days after Nixon's visit, he wrote to his brother Milton to complain about the pressure to run again and the tendency of party leaders "to lean on one frail mortal"—himself. "Personally I have felt better during the past ten days than I have for a long time," he continued. "But through a fairly long life, I have seen so much of a sudden and unexpected collapse of personal competence especially after a man has passed the three score mark—that I am practically appalled by the attitude I see so prevalent among Republican spokesmen." He revealed much the same existential apprehension when Leonard Wood Hall, the Republican National Committee chairman, and a delegation of state chairmen came to Denver and urged him to commit to a second term. When the president on September 10 spoke to the group, he said, "Humans are frail—and they are mortal. . . . You never pin your flag so tightly to one mast that if a ship sinks you cannot rip it off and nail it to another."

Two weeks later, the president went to Aksel Nielsen's ranch in Fraser for several days of fishing, painting, and eating well. He returned to Denver on September 23, a warm, sunny Friday, and there he followed the dreamlike routine that Rovere had sketched out—a little work at the office and, using an electric golf cart, twenty-seven holes at Cherry Hills. At the Doud house, the Eisenhowers and Mrs. Doud had dinner with Mary and George Allen (George had been with Ike in Fraser and was doing double duty as a bridge player). At about ten o'clock, the president went to his bedroom on the second floor. He seemed all right, although he had complained earlier of slight indigestion, blaming it on some raw onions that he'd had for lunch. At 1:30 A.M., he woke up with severe chest pains, and an hour later he went to Mamie's room and put his hand on his chest to show where it hurt. On the assumption that it might be a recurrence of indigestion, Mamie gave him milk of magnesia, but she was worried enough to telephone his doctor, Major General Howard McCrum Snyder, who was staying four miles away.

Snyder was a gentleman "of very easily recognized gentility," an acquaintance said, "with a full head of beautiful, gray-white hair, and so distinguished looking that you'd turn around and look at him two or three times." His competence, though, was a matter of concern; General Clay had advised the president that Snyder, who was almost seventy-five years old, "is really not capable of providing the medical care and advice that a president of the United States should have." But there was no one else to call at that place and at that time of night, and Snyder, who arrived a few minutes later, listened to Ike's heart with a stethoscope; he took the president's pulse, which was rapid, and tested his blood pressure, which had gone up, and gave him a shot of morphine to ease the pain. At about 3:45 A.M., he gave Eisenhower a second shot of morphine in the belief that he needed rest. By then, as the *Herald Tribune*'s Robert J. Donovan later put it, Snyder, sitting alone in the hours before dawn, was the only man in the world who knew that the president had suffered a fairly major heart attack.

2

On most Saturdays, Richard Nixon would go to his office on Capitol Hill, often meeting informally with wire service reporters, leaning back, his feet on the desk in an approximation of relaxed sociability. But on this Saturday, Dick and Pat had been at the wedding of one Miss Drusilla Nelson (though they'd skipped the reception) and when they got home to 4801 Tilden Street, he started to read the city's afternoon paper, the *Evening Star*. A front-page brief said that the president was suffering from indigestion and Nixon recalled a conversation with the governor-general of Australia, William Slim, whom he'd met on his Far East trip. Slim had served with Eisenhower during the war and had greeted Nixon by asking "How's

Ike? How's his tummy? Ike always used to have trouble with his tummy." But then the telephone rang, and Jim Hagerty without preliminaries told Nixon all that he knew, after which Nixon said, "My God!" and asked what he could do. He also said, "I don't think we should announce it as a heart attack until we are absolutely sure."

Everyone was absolutely sure, Hagerty said, and, furthermore, the press was about to be informed. He was going to hurry out to Denver—he'd been on vacation—and promised to keep Nixon up-to-date. "Let me know where you can be reached at all times," Hagerty said, and Nixon assured him that he'd "stay by the telephone throughout the day and night." He asked Hagerty to call whenever he could. Nixon just sat in his living room for a few minutes. "For quite a while I didn't even think to tell Pat, who was upstairs," he said later. As someone who was acutely sensitive to the politics of every act, Nixon above all understood his new position. So did Murray Chotiner, who asked Rose Mary Woods to pass on his thought that "This is really going to be a wonderful opportunity for Dick to show the country what he is made of—to help put down some of the sniping that has been going on against him." Lou Guylay, the press aide for the Republican National Committee, said that the vice president needed to "Watch every syllable he utters. Every move should be watched. All eyes are on him . . . and he certainly doesn't want to give the impression that he is trying to move in."

For much of that Saturday, Hagerty was on the phone. He talked to the president's four brothers, and tried to get word to senior officials who were on late-summer vacations, some of them quite far away. Sherman Adams, for instance, was fishing in Scotland, and got the news when he arrived at the airbase at Prestwick as he was on his way home. Herbert Brownell was in Spain, where, he later recalled, "We had just arrived at the beach near Torremolinos and changed into our bathing suits when a message from the ambassador called me from the beach." William Rogers, the acting attorney general, had been at a Saturday football game when the phone calls started coming in from Denver. Ann Whitman reached him at a little after five, and three minutes later, Nixon got through to him: Could Rogers come over? he asked. By then, reporters had surrounded the Tilden Street house, and when they spotted Rogers, they asked him to arrange a press conference with Nixon. As soon as he got inside, Rogers could see why Nixon had wanted to avoid the press: "I realized that, while he was trying to keep his composure, he was in semi-shock. His eyes were red and his face was drawn and pale."

The Rogers family lived a few miles away, in Bethesda, and Rogers suggested that Nixon hide out there. "We had to employ a strategy to get out unnoticed," he said. "I had my wife drive over and park behind the house and, while the Nixon girls"—Tricia and Julie were nine and seven—"were used as decoys to engage the reporters and correspondents in small talk, the two of us slipped out through the back door." Soon after they arrived in Bethesda, Nixon asked Rogers what the Constitution had to say about a president being incapacitated. "I'm sorry—I don't have the vaguest idea," Rogers replied.

Nixon did not sleep well, and not just because of the president's illness. The pollen count on that warm September night in the Maryland suburbs was high and his hay fever was back, with its swelling and discomfort. He didn't go to bed until about 2:30 A.M., and was sneezing most of the night. Then there was the noise: on the third floor, just above Nixon's temporary bedroom, the Rogerses' fifteen-year-old son, Anthony, a ham radio enthusiast, was busy. "There was an all-night ham radio contest where I was trying to talk to as many people around the world as I could. And it was all Morse code," Tony Rogers recalled. "I would come down periodically to get something to eat just to get out of my room. I became aware at some point in the evening that Nixon and my father had come over."

Nixon on the second floor heard "the high-pitched dots and dashes of the Morse code penetrating the ceiling overhead," but many things were keeping him awake. "During the three years I had been Vice President, I had not consciously thought of the possibility of his becoming ill or dying," he later wrote, to which he added the improbable assertion that he doubted "if any Vice President allows his mind to dwell on such a subject." During the night, Tony Rogers hardly saw Nixon, who was using the phone in his parents' bedroom. "My father was on the kitchen phone which was a wall phone, so he was standing up most of the time," he said. "And every time I went down, my father was still on the phone. It was one of the times I just realized what was at stake and that Nixon wasn't just a guy who came over after playing golf, he was really doing something really serious. It was a very tense night."

Nixon returned home on Sunday morning and took the family to the Westmoreland Congregational Church, about a mile away. The president's illness dominated the Sunday news, some of it fanciful: There was a story that plans had been drawn up for Nixon to take over the presidency; the *Chicago Tribune* went so far as to report that Ike was planning to resign. Nixon spoke to the press for the first time after church, and said, with assured banality, "The business of government will go on without delay. . . . Under the President's administration a team has been set up in Washington which will carry out his well-defined plans."

The change in Nixon's status was obvious; everyone could see the presence of the Secret Service in all those cars that were taking parking spots on Tilden Street. The vice president's security had previously consisted of two Secret Service men who began work at eight-thirty in the morning and left at five in the afternoon (although they tagged along if he went out at night). He had an up-to-date alarm system but, as his military aide, Air Force Major James (Don) Hughes, said, he "was not particularly apt at handling machinery, so I don't think the machine was turned on that much." Now, as Pat Nixon wrote to her friend Helene Drown, it had become "a madhouse around here . . . security are with Dick constantly—consequently there is no peace."

Foster Dulles and Nixon conferred early that Sunday afternoon—the first of many conversations they had during Ike's illness. One of the first things that Dulles had done was to ask his staff to research the most celebrated case of presidential incapacity: Woodrow Wilson's disabling stroke in 1919. Dulles was familiar with much of it, not only because his uncle, Robert Lansing, had been Wilson's secretary of state, but because Dulles as a thirty-year-old had been legal counsel to the American delegation at the Versailles Peace Conference. Dulles knew that Lansing had been forced out by Mrs. Wilson when he tried to transform the cabinet into a governing body, so Dulles not surprisingly told Nixon that he was deeply concerned about who was going to do what—and, more immediately, who was going to be in Denver with the president. Dulles thought—and Nixon agreed—that it ought to be Sherman Adams, who was returning the next day from Scotland. Later that day, Nixon, Rogers, and Adams's deputy,

Jerry Persons, met at the Rogers house, although they didn't accomplish much—they didn't even act on Nixon's suggestion that they schedule a cabinet meeting.

On Monday, with Adams back in Washington, Nixon went to the White House to have lunch with the senior staff; he stayed on afterward to talk with Adams, with whom his relationship was usually correct and never friendly. That night—again at the Rogers house—Adams, Persons, and Nixon were joined by the political people, Leonard Hall and Lou Guylay, who wanted to discuss what was already on everyone's mind: whether Eisenhower would be able to run again. "My own guess is that the President is pretty much out of it," Guylay said. "I imagine, I don't know, he is going to feel that his few remaining years of life should be spent in tranquility." They talked for about four hours, going over what to do and how to go about doing it, getting nowhere. Adams, who was exhausted after a transatlantic flight, was acting strange. When someone asked what he thought about the situation, he looked lost in thought and then said, "Fellows, I never had such fishing in my life." He talked about fishing in Scotland for eight or nine minutes, Len Hall recalled—"He never mentioned Ike's situation and the next day he packed his bag and went to Denver." The stock market that Monday fell by nearly 32 points—about 8 percent of what had been a long-term bull market—its biggest single-day drop since October 1929.

Nothing quite functioned as it should. The cabinet, which even in the best of times was split between conservatives and moderates, was leaderless, and a week after Eisenhower's coronary, the group met for the first time. Nixon, who wore a dark double-breasted suit, took his usual chair, with Treasury's George Humphrey on his right and Attorney General Brownell on his left; the president's chair opposite Nixon stayed empty. Because there was no formal agenda, the table was uncluttered, but the room was crowded—by one estimate, there were more than thirty officials in addition to cabinet officers. At 9:30 A.M., Nixon asked for a moment of silent prayer, a ritual that Eisenhower had established, and read the morning medical bulletin from Denver. He also had a few things that he wanted to say, and spoke from notes: he thought that they shouldn't delay decisions that needed to be made, and that they shouldn't let routine decisions pile up. In short, he said, they needed to "keep the business of government going sans interruption." He also warned people in the room that divisions would be played up by outsiders.

The session went on for two and a half hours and for all that time, as they discussed plans for running the government in the president's absence, Nixon was uncomfortable. He wasn't the acting president—he was just a presiding officer in the absence of the president—and yet he was next in line to the presidency. As the meeting ended, Dulles spoke up, praising Nixon for the way that he'd conducted himself: "I want you to know we are proud to be on this team and proud to be serving in this Cabinet under your leadership," he said. The compliment meant a lot to Nixon, and when he talked later in the day to Dulles he thanked him for the gesture. "Dulles was my major adviser as to what I should do and the role I should play," Nixon said. "He knew this was a hard period for me."

In Denver, there was a sense of improvisation; in just thirty-six hours, Russell Baker wrote, "the summer White House has changed from a thing of golden, indolent tranquility to a cold gray chaotic nightmare." Even the weather changed, from autumn sunshine to fog, rain, and cold winds. Journalistic reinforcements rushed out to Denver; the wire service reporters began working in shifts, with some spending nights on bunk beds at Lowry, staying close in case the president, who was in critical condition, took a bad turn.

Medical reinforcements arrived, too—notably Paul Dudley White, a fifty-nine-year-old cardiologist from Mass General, who was recruited by some of Ike's friends. White was the author of a textbook on heart disease and was perfectly suited to the celebrity he was about to acquire—he was soon popping up regularly on TV and radio and dispensing advice to the nation—but while he was no doubt a hound for publicity, his arrival was a great relief to those who had worried about the quality of care that the president was getting from Howard Snyder. Clarence G. Lasby's definitive study, *Eisenhower's Heart Attack*, tells a story of good luck, serendipitous decisions, and a possible cover-up of the medical record by Dr. Snyder, starting with his inexplicable delay in summoning outside help.

Nixon and Dulles thought that the president ought to put something in writing to guide them, and Eisenhower from his hospital bed dictated a "Dear Dick" letter, saying, "I hope you will continue to have meetings of the National Security Council and of the Cabinet, over which you will preside in accordance with the procedures which you have followed at my request in the past during my absence from Washington." As Eisenhower got stronger, Adams arranged brief appointments with the president in order of cabinet rank, although Adams insisted on being there too. Nixon saw Eisenhower (with Adams present) in the late afternoon of October 8, and again the next day. Each visit lasted about fifteen minutes, and the scene was striking: the vigorous, forty-two-year-old Nixon and the bedridden, sixty-four-year-old Eisenhower, who, Nixon later recalled, "looked startlingly thin and pale." (One of Nixon's handwritten notes included the phrase "a crippled old man"—inside quotation marks and without elaboration—and the most likely explanation is that it was a depressed remark uttered by Ike himself.) Eisenhower apologized for Nixon's having to make the trek to Denver and he told him what it was like to suffer a heart attack—Mamie still had no idea how much it had hurt. He even broached the idea—instantly abandoned—of delegating authority to Nixon for six months. He'd clearly been engaged by the question of presidential incapacity and this was a roundabout way of addressing the subject. Eisenhower knew some of the history but hadn't realized—and this surprised Nixon—that Wilson's secretary of state, Robert Lansing, was Foster Dulles's uncle.

Afterward, Nixon met with reporters, to whom he said, "from the time I went in the door" he could see that the president was eager to hear how the government was functioning and that he'd told Ike that "he needn't rush to get back to his office." He said that he'd also told the president that "there had not been one iota of jealousy there had only been dedicated effort" from the team. That was not true. Sherman Adams, who never forgot that he was *the* assistant to the president, still wondered who was going to be the boss in the absence of the boss. He understood Nixon's dilemma— that the vice president had to be wary of "appearing to assume presidential prerogatives before he became constitutionally eligible for them"—and he believed that Foster Dulles, who was surprisingly territorial about his job, was worried about Milton Eisenhower's influence. Adams also informed Nixon that Dulles didn't trust Harold Stassen, the disarmament adviser; he thought that Stassen was bright enough but lacked stability, a sentiment with which Nixon, who'd had his own Stassen problem during the fund episode, surely sympathized.

This, then, was not a mutually supportive and trusting band of public servants, but they nevertheless carried on. "Everyone was so conscious of the influence that Mrs. Wilson had during the illness of President Wilson that everybody was exceedingly careful to see to it that the normal procedures of government functioned," Milton Eisenhower said. And they all agreed that "there must be no implication, no hint that anyone was trying to take over the responsibilities, or to have an undue influence."

For the next two months, the government was run by a sort of ad hoc committee—Walter Lippmann called it a "council of state"—consisting of Nixon, Dulles, Brownell, Humphrey, Adams, and Jerry Persons, although, as Adams put it, they were "never recognized as a formal governing council." The president's illness had come when Congress was in recess and there were no foreign crises, yet each of these "committee" members was aware that he might have to deal with something serious—the sort of domestic or international emergency that would make this "community of understanding" inadequate. When Herbert Brownell came to Denver, the president asked the attorney general, "What happens under the Constitution if my illness is prolonged and emergencies arise requiring immediate action?" and Brownell, like Bill Rogers, didn't know.

3

From the moment that Eisenhower fell ill, his future—political and corporal—was a consuming topic among politicians and journalists, most of whom assumed that he didn't have much of one. James Reston set the tone by writing almost immediately that "it was generally agreed that physicians would be extremely hesitant to recommend that a man of 64 who had a coronary thrombosis should attempt to carry on the burdens of the Presidency for another five years," and the broadcaster Eric Sevareid, a master of solemnity, said that "the chances of his candidacy were about 100-to-1 against." In early October, Clare Boothe Luce took time out from her ambassadorial duties in Rome and some cultural kibitzing (she had managed in the summer to get *Blackboard Jungle* withdrawn from the Venice film festival) to give the vice president ("Dear Dick") some personal and political advice in the form of a rambling, wildly flattering, and wholly inappropriate letter:

> Like half the world I thank God that our beloved President is out of danger. And I pray that he will soon be able to return to his great labors. But I also know what everyone takes for granted here—that he will not run again. Nor must he be persuaded to, for if he did those who had persuaded him would seem to be urging him to death, for the sake of party advantage.
>
> I know that you already are aware that the Luces believe only one man in America has the ability, the intelligence, the courage, and the possibility to be President in '56—yourself. It will not be easy for you to win either the nomination or the election. The forces arrayed against you are very very heavy. But they are certainly not insuperable, and I for one am confident that you will surmount them—unless the Republicans show themselves really capable of the stupidity of which the Democrats have so often charged them. If they wrangle among themselves over a prize that only you can possibly pluck . . . they will NOT succeed. . . .
>
> And above all do not compromise or lose your greatest strength vis-à-vis the voting public—the fact that the Commies, and the many friends they have all around the world—including in America, fear you and hate you, because they know you see the world—or rather their roles in the world clearly. In short, don't try to be popular with Khrushchev—or even the sappy minded liberals, who will never forgive you, tho' you kissed the ground before them, for the Hiss story. . . .
>
> Again, be confident that many others feel as Harry and I do. Don't let yourself get too tired and be prepared with a serene spirit, if you can manage it, for much bitterness and unkindness not only from enemies but even from those you may have counted as friends. The cruelest storms rage around the highest mountains.

Nixon was dourly amused by the flattering class in Washington—"Men who had hardly cloaked their antipathy before now paid me courtesy calls or sought to give me sagacious advice about my brilliant future," he wrote. Mostly, though, Nixon tended to view his altered outlook with sensitivity and political sharpness. He was extra careful about what he said to reporters, even those he trusted, such as Clint Mosher, the political editor of the *San Francisco Examiner,* with whom he spoke (knowing that it was being overheard and transcribed by Rose Mary Woods) on October 10:

> *Nixon*: As you know, my attitude and it is a very honest one. I am one of a few who are named who at least is actually concerned with one thing and that is that the top guy (1) recover and (2) that his program continues. Who continues it is not as important as that they continue.
>
> *Mosher*: I know that Dick.
>
> *Nixon*: Stassen this morning said he was available. . . . Incidentally, you noticed that I said I was not going to engage in any political speculation until the President returns.

Eisenhower left Fitzsimons Army Hospital on Veterans Day, November 11—about fifty days after his heart attack—and returned briefly to Washington before heading off for ten days to the farm in Gettysburg, Pennsylvania, that he'd bought in 1950 for $23,000. He convened National Security Council and cabinet meetings ten days later. He thanked everyone for a "perfect" performance during his absence, but didn't single out any individual—notably not Nixon. "This was characteristic of Eisenhower," Nixon later wrote. He'd been thanked for other chores— for instance his travels and campaigning. "But after this most difficult assignment of all—treading the tightrope during his convalescence from the heart attack—there was no personal thank you," he said, adding, "Nor was one needed or expected. After all, we both recognized that I had only done what a Vice President should do when the President is ill." Despite these cloying disclaimers, Nixon could not conceal his hurt feelings. Even at Camp David, he was something of an outsider. After the NSC met and after an evening session that included Dulles, Nixon, George Humphrey, and the Defense Secretary Charlie Wilson, the president played bridge with Humphrey, Dulles, and Wilson. Nixon, who was excluded from the foursome, left and did not return until morning.

Eisenhower *had* been grateful in his fashion, but his gratitude had done nothing to erase his doubts about Nixon, who had been an occasional topic of conversation in Denver. One day he'd told Adams that his illness had made people far more aware of the vice president—"He is a darn good young man," he said, to which Adams replied that the president's absence was making *everyone* "sharpen their wits." Eisenhower then said that the country as a whole still considered Nixon "a bit immature," but on the other hand he respected his judgment. Adams didn't disagree, but said that Nixon lacked the sort of experience that Eisenhower had—of being able to take a group like the cabinet, hear them out, and say, "This is what we are going to do"—and have everyone accept his judgment. "He has not quite reached a maturity of intellect," Adams said, and the President didn't object.

Inside the White House, Nixon had won no new friends. His admiring biographer Bela Kornitzer wrote that the senior staff "had a hard time controlling their aversion to someone they considered a lone wolf," and took another look at this man with "the jutting jaw line, the ski-jump nose, and the shadowy complexion which always appears unshaven." Reporters, he said, looked for a smile, "a cocky command. . . . But Nixon was Nixon: he looked grim, and he looked tired."

He had every reason to look grim and tired, and not just because he might suddenly find himself in charge. If Eisenhower decided not to run again, as almost everyone assumed, Nixon's hold on the vice presidency would vanish. And although he would be a contender for the nomination, he knew that he, more than any competitor, would need the president's support. He wasn't helped by stories such as one that appeared on the front page of the *New York Times* two days after Ike's heart attack, under the headline NIXON IS CONSIDERED IN FOREFRONT FOR '56, saying that he had fallen "heir to one of the greatest responsibilities and political opportunities ever presented to so young a man in the history of the Republic." It sounded like praise, but it was an early alarm for every potential Republican aspirant—Knowland, Stassen, Dewey, Warren, persons yet unknown—as well as for the Democrats who hated Nixon and couldn't wait to see the last of him.

CHAPTER 11

Survivor

<u>1</u>

The eleven months between Eisenhower's heart attack and the 1956 Republican National Convention were excruciating for Nixon, a period far more difficult than the fund episode. Although the pain was never as intense as it had been in 1952, it lingered much longer, and the question of his fate came in two stages: Would Eisenhower run, and if he did, would he want Nixon to run with him?

No one knew better than Nixon that he was never first in any of those lists of "logical successors" that the president enjoyed making, as if General Ike were reviewing top officers who would drop on and off the manifests. And while these personal shopping lists regularly changed, Robert Anderson's name tended to remain at the top. In fact if the president's wish could have been granted in the months after his heart attack, Bob Anderson would have moved into the Oval room as soon as he could pack his things. "He is just about the ablest man that I know anywhere," Eisenhower wrote to his childhood friend Swede Hazlett toward the end of 1954.

The two men appeared to have little in common. Anderson was a Democrat, an oil man, and a lawyer; because he'd had paralytic polio as a boy, he had never served in the military, though he had been an adviser to the secretary of war. And while Eisenhower usually felt most comfortable among men of his own generation, Anderson was nearly twenty years his junior—just three years older than Nixon. But there was that personal chemistry that meant so much to Ike, and which drew him to all those businessmen after the war. Anderson, who had a slight stoop and looked older than his age, was viewed by some of his colleagues as exceptionally bright and likable. One White House assistant said that he could "delve into the deepest of subjects and describe it with such terms and explain it with such examples that every man present was with him all the way." Others who spent time with Anderson, though, were mystified by the attraction. Eisenhower's son, John, thought that Anderson's chief talent lay in his ability as a briefer, a gift that shined during cabinet meetings. There was also a political basis for Eisenhower's affection: Anderson, a Texan, had a good relationship with the two most important Democrats in Washington, Sam Rayburn and Lyndon Johnson, both Texans.

Leonard Hall, the Republican National Committee chairman, was not enthusiastic about the cultivation of Bob Anderson, but then Hall was a realist. In his years as a party boss, he was highly visible (literally, at 230 pounds) and a persuasive, gregarious presence, a man fond of magic tricks and silly songs. To outsiders, as *Time* once put it, he was like "a bald and bouncy glad-hander, as carefree as a prankster at an American Legion convention." He was also a through-and-through party man—a former New York assemblyman and a seven-term congressman (he had served with Nixon), and for three years the sheriff of Nassau County. He had grown up with the party; his father, Franklyn Hall, was the coachman at Theodore Roosevelt's Oyster Bay estate, Sagamore Hill. So not only did Hall have little enthusiasm for a southwestern Democrat like Bob Anderson, he was a fairly reliable supporter of Richard Nixon.

Eisenhower regularly expanded his catalogue of latent presidential talent. In a letter to the investment banker George Whitney, he mentioned other "relatively young men" who might have a bright future, among them Senator Clifford Case of New Jersey, Governor Leo Hoegh of Iowa, and the House minority leader, Charles Halleck of Indiana. Most of these men have faded speedily into historical obscurity, but the president discerned a spark in each of them, often one that no one else had spotted. "I hear a great many good things about a man named [Albert] Cobo, Mayor of Detroit," his letter to Whitney continued. "I understand he is really a wonderful fellow. We should instantly start bringing him up." Not stopping there, he mentioned more "very fine men that should be brought forward," including two congressmen and "quite a number of others who have a great sense of dedication and plenty of brains." Eisenhower was in many ways a natural politician (that was obvious to anyone who had watched him deal with Churchill, de Gaulle, and Field Marshal Montgomery during the war), but he was astonishingly naive about the business of politics.

He could also be evasive, as he was when Leonard Hall drove up to Gettysburg on November 28, hoping to talk about 1956. When Hall mentioned that reporters were waiting outside for some word, the president informed him that he wasn't ready to say anything—he'd leave that up to Hall. "Len, you're looking at an old dodo," he said at one point, as if to suggest that years and illness had caught up with him. When Hall talked to the press, he came close to winging it; he said that he believed Eisenhower would run again and that Nixon would run with him. Hall was described with some accuracy as being "sent away uninformed but hopefully glowing."

2

Nixon did not get many invitations to see the president, and later said that he had no idea something was afoot when he was asked to come by the Oval Office on the day after Christmas, a place where it was hard to miss such furnishings as a framed photograph of Ike with Bobby Jones and other golf partners and a pen set on the desk with the raised five stars of the General of the Army. As it turned out, the president had a definite agenda. In fact, without much preamble he informed Nixon that he wanted to discuss his future. It was "most disappointing," Eisenhower said, that Nixon's popularity was no greater, an apparent reference to a recent Gallup survey that showed Nixon losing a presidential match-up to Adlai Stevenson by a margin of five to four. "I want you to come in from time to time to discuss the situation with regard to yourself," the president said. "We might have to initiate a crash program for building you up."

Yet even as he delivered this unwelcome guidance—and there was no mistaking that more bad news lay ahead—Eisenhower tried to appear sympathetic. Sounding not unlike a human resources counselor, he continued, "There has never been a job I have given you that you haven't done to perfection as far as I am concerned. The thing that concerns me is that the public does not realize adequately the job you have done." Nixon, who didn't yet know where this was going, said that he would do whatever the president wanted him to do, and it was then that Eisenhower came up with a suggestion that left Nixon feeling rattled: although the president's own political plans were uncertain, he proposed that Nixon take a cabinet job in a new administration—just about any position he wanted, with the exception of attorney general, which Ike ruled out owing to Nixon's lack of legal experience, and secretary of state, which, if Dulles stepped down, he said would go to the undersecretary, Herbert Hoover Jr., the ex-president's son. That seems hard to believe. Hoover's views were considered ultraconservative and were often at variance with Eisenhower's; they brought him into frequent conflict with another Eisenhower aide, Nelson Rockefeller, who had worked at the Department of Health, Education and Welfare with Oveta Culp Hobby and moved to the State Department in late 1954, where he took C. D. Jackson's job as the "psychological warfare" expert.

Nixon, who very much wanted to keep his current job, was not only unnerved by this suggestion but didn't know how to respond. He saw no way simply to say that he wanted to stay put. He understood that no matter what the rationale for taking a cabinet job, there would be a perception that he had been "dumped." Eisenhower also revealed that he was going to convene a political dinner and that Nixon would not be invited. "Ordinarily you would be the first one I would ask," he told his vice president. "Since you are going to be so much the object of conversation, it would be embarrassing to you. I have no secrets from you." Nixon was quick to agree that it would be embarrassing, and they talked a little more about Nixon's aspirations—another human resources moment. He had to wonder: Was he being fired? He was prepared to believe that the president simply wasn't himself; Foster Dulles thought that Ike had been brooding since his heart attack. There was also, Nixon realized, the possibility that Ike was being straightforward—that he thought Nixon needed executive experience and that if he ever wanted to be president, he needed to run a large agency like the Defense Department.

• • •

Eisenhower's "political dinner" was devoted to whether he should run for a second term. The invitations, delivered by Ann Whitman by telephone, came with instructions that it was a "top secret" affair; the attendees, who met on January 12, included Foster Dulles, George Humphrey, Herbert Brownell, Sherman Adams, Jim Hagerty, Cabot Lodge, Len Hall, and Milton Eisenhower. Mamie Eisenhower stayed for cocktails and a dinner, after which the group went to the president's sitting room on the second floor. Eisenhower appeared to be in a good mood, and said, "Now, listen, I want each one of you fellows to tell me why I should run for President. Then I'm going to sit down with my adviser, my brother here, and I'm going to make a decision." The group then talked for hours, starting with Dulles, the senior cabinet officer, who flattered the president: Eisenhower, he said, "was where he was and what he was because of his wisdom and dedication to public service"—and Dulles made the implicit argument that the president was indispensable "at a time when humanity faces its greatest physical danger through the development of nuclear weapons which could destroy life on this globe." Eisenhower then went around the circle, asking in no particular order for more opinions, and when they were done, everyone but Milton wanted the president, if he felt able, to run again.

Eight days later, Republicans across the country held Salute to Eisenhower events, which raised $5 million for the party. Nixon spoke in Chicago and said, "The Truman-Acheson policy got us into war and the Dulles-Eisenhower policy got us out of war," this time without an objection from Ike. Eisenhower, in Washington, sounded almost Stevensonian: "I would devoutly wish there were some method by which the American people could, under the circumstances, point out the path of my true duty." C. D. Jackson was at the Washington "salute," and while he thought that Ike and Mamie looked splendid, he didn't think he sounded like a candidate, and reported that to Henry Luce. In the morning, Jackson saw the president, who told him, "You know, I used to think that I was indestructible. Well, I wasn't, and you are not, and neither is anybody else— and in this job, fatigue is a central problem."

Then Jackson paid a call on Foster Dulles, whose general pessimism about the world was not likely to ease the president's fatigue. He told Jackson that "within not more than two years the Russians would be able to knock out U.S. industry and also knock out our overseas bases." Dulles was also worried about his boss: "The President is the kind of person who has got to get emotionally involved in order to move. He has got to get excited first, and then his outgiving personality surrounds his inner excitement and he carries tremendous weight." Dulles continued, "Now, the doctors tell him that getting excited is just exactly what he should not do, so that I am very much afraid that we are just going to stagnate for the rest of the year, as we have been stagnating since his heart attack."

Yet Dulles, unlike Jackson, believed that the president was going to run again even though he still tossed out the names of unlikely successors. One day in February, Dulles told Eisenhower that if he quit after one term, he'd support Nixon. When Eisenhower suggested that Nixon ought to take a cabinet post, Dulles said, "You might want to make him Secretary of State," which made the president laugh. You can't get out of your job that easily, he said, but suddenly he wasn't joking: he doubted that Nixon was qualified to be secretary of state, which was the same as saying that he doubted Nixon's aptitude for the presidency. Ike, in his indirect fashion, had just made it clear that he really did want to replace him.

Nixon was not only habitually suspicious, but his personal antennae were preternaturally sensitive; while he was sure that Eisenhower had been having conversations about his future, he didn't know what was being said—by whom or to whom. He thought that he'd done everything right; Murray Chotiner saw it the same way, and he tried to cheer up Nixon, praising him for his conduct after the president fell ill. "There was no effort . . . to make political capital out of a national loss; or to assert authority beyond the minimum called for by the emergency," Chotiner wrote. "Such gestures as visiting Cabinet officials in their offices, unobtrusive comings and goings, and both courtesy and restraint in dealings with the press—all these paid off." There were constant intrigues. Someone unnamed had left a note for Rose Mary Woods that said "General Clay is a mysterious figure," along with a warning that friends of Lucius Clay were promoting Dan Thornton, the Colorado governor, for vice president. But Nixon was used to that. What he did not suspect was that Len Hall, his steady supporter—perhaps the only one around whose political instincts matched his—was being less than loyal.

In fact, one morning in early February, Hall met with the president and began to brainstorm about the vice presidency, veering off on to tangents that one would not have expected from a Republican national chairman. At one point, Hall suggested replacing Nixon on the ticket with Frank Lausche, the governor of Ohio—a surprising proposition because Lausche, like Bob Anderson, was a Democrat. The very thought excited Hall, who pointed out that Abraham Lincoln, too, had shown an ecumenical spirit by choosing the Democrat Andrew Johnson in 1864. It would be a turning point in history, Hall continued—not only was Lausche a Democrat, he was a Catholic; and if the Republicans did not pick a Catholic this time, he said, the Democrats would do it next time. Hall mentioned Senator Kennedy of Massachusetts, whom he called "an attractive guy."

Eisenhower, getting into the spirit of turning points, mentioned Spessard L. Holland, the Florida senator and onetime governor—another Democrat. Holland was then in his mid-sixties, so he was not precisely representative of the new, young people Eisenhower always talked about bringing up. Hall did not like that idea at all; he gently reminded Ike that Holland was still in favor of segregated schools, having signed the so-called Southern Manifesto, drafted by Senator Strom Thurmond of South Carolina, which vowed to resist the *Brown* decision.

Their conversation became increasingly odd. Eisenhower undoubtedly wanted to make a change, but rather than simply uttering a declarative sentence to that effect, he kept on making outlandish suggestions, and the next name he came up with was Allan Shivers, a three-term Texas governor. Shivers, too, was a Democrat; like Oveta Culp Hobby, he had helped Ike carry Texas in 1952. And, like Spessard Holland, he was another opponent of the Supreme Court's desegregation ruling. So Hall came back to his first choice: "The one that would be the shocker would be Lausche," he said.

When the conversation turned to Nixon, Hall suggested that he could be a "hero and drop out of the race," and for a moment the chairman of the Republican National Committee seemed to be entertaining the fantasy that "there should be a new alignment of party, people should not just be voting labels." It would be easy enough to get Nixon out of the picture, Hall said; the question was whether to "build him up some way in doing it." Eisenhower said that when Hall talked to Nixon—it was understood that he was assigning this woeful task to Hall—he should say, "What do you want to do? If the President doesn't run, you have just as wide open a field, and the friendship of the President, you have the knowledge that the President believes in you. But what is the best thing for you to do? For yourself, and that means the good of the party." Having now disposed of Nixon, Eisenhower then returned to a familiar topic, saying, "I think that at this moment if I could have my favorite fellow, my first choice would be Bob Anderson," although he was willing to entertain the idea of Lausche. Then it was back to Nixon, and he said, "Well all right, you see him and talk to him, but be very, very gentle."

Given the president's wishes and authority, that ought to have settled the matter: Eisenhower would run with someone else in 1956 and he'd offer Nixon a cabinet post. But Hall, who had been a willing co-conspirator, had been a Nixon friend after a fashion since 1946, when they'd both served in the House; and, in his own recollection, despite his burst of enthusiasm for Lausche, he'd been a deeply troubled friend. "I didn't sleep that night—I couldn't because I knew I had been given a hot potato," he recalled. In the morning, he called Bob Humphreys, the campaign director of the Republican National Committee and Nixon's champion during the fund crisis. Hall and Humphreys had breakfast, during which Hall told Humphreys about his conversation with the president; he asked Humphreys to accompany him when he talked to Nixon—an encounter that Hall recalled vividly: "So I went up there and gave it to Nixon blow by blow. I didn't pull anything out at all. Nixon just said, 'So, he doesn't want me on the ticket.' I remember again how that cloud came over Nixon's face, those eyebrows came down and you didn't see whites of eyes or anything. Here was a fellow who had just been hit in the solar plexus." The news so affected Nixon that he briefly hospitalized himself; or, as Eisenhower was told on February 8, "Len Hall called, said he was 'supposed to do a little checking with the Vice President.' Says that the Vice President hasn't been feeling well and has now gone to Walter Reed . . . so he is a little handicapped."

But Eisenhower, true to form, never actually insisted that Nixon take another job; he could hint, and discuss the future using the subjunctive mood, but even during the war, it was the sort of chore that he tried to hand off, as when he ordered General Omar Bradley to tell Patton that he was losing command of the 10th Armored Division. By turning it over to Len Hall, for whom delivering a blunt message was almost as difficult as it was for Eisenhower, he left a small escape hatch for Nixon; it let him keep talking intermittently with the president, as if nothing had been settled. On one occasion, Eisenhower thought aloud about a campaign to which he'd not yet committed. "I consented to four years only," he told Nixon. "Now I find myself almost under greater pressures than originally to continue another four years, in spite of four extra years on me, in spite of a heart attack, and knowing that I am going to have to defend myself against certain remarks such as, 'See he is an invalid' and all that—it's going to be really a tough campaign this fall." Nixon, trying to sound both sensitive and kindhearted, thought a few TV speeches would suffice; for that moment, it sounded as if they were still a political team. But usually Ike would drop ever more unsubtle hints: no vice president since Martin Van Buren had been elected president, he said in one chat, and in another pointed out that Herbert Hoover had used his position as Calvin Coolidge's secretary of commerce to build his pre-presidential reputation. In early February, Eisenhower broached the subject of his life expectancy and simultaneously belittled Nixon's job: "I would personally think that if we can count on me living five years, your place is not serving eight years as Vice President—because people get the idea the Vice President does nothing," adding that he'd be much better off taking "one of the big departments, HEW, Defense, Interior, any one of which is entirely possible." Then he added, "However, if you calculate that I won't last five years, of course that is different."

The longer this went on, the more Nixon felt that he'd been "thrown into another period of agonizing indecision"—Bryce Harlow called it a time of "absolutely indescribable anguish." But he hung on. It was like an awkward dance in which the music keeps playing and the partners keep bruising one another's toes. But after nearly three years, Nixon had almost gotten used to those times when, as he had phrased it four years earlier, Eisenhower was neither going to shit nor get off the pot.

Eisenhower waited until Leap Year Day to reveal that he'd seek a second term, a decision that was not surprising and yet led the editors of *The New Republic* to observe that "No man elected President at 65 has lived out his term in the White House. No man with a damaged heart has accepted his party's Presidential nomination." He made the announcement in the Indian Treaty Room at the old State Department building, his arms behind his back, his left hand occasionally clenching and unclenching as he said that he was following "the path of duty." When he was asked about Nixon, he had a convoluted answer ready:

> As a matter of fact, I wouldn't mention the vice presidency in spite of my tremendous admiration for Mr. Nixon, for this reason: I believe it is traditional that the Vice President is not nominated until after a presidential candidate is nominated; so I think that we will have to wait to see who the Republican convention nominates, and then it will be proper to give an expression on that point.

In other words, Eisenhower, although he called Nixon "a loyal and dedicated associate," insisted that he was going to wait for the Republican National Convention nearly six months hence before having more to say about Nixon's future. That was a ridiculous statement—as ridiculous as the idea that his renomination was in doubt—and it only made reporters more curious than usual, especially because Nixon recently had gotten into trouble by talking about the *Brown* decision and saying that "President Eisenhower's great Republican Administration has registered the greatest advance for the rights of racial minorities since the Emancipation Proclamation itself." He'd added that *Brown* ought to be counted among the administration's accomplishments because it came from "a great Republican Chief Justice, Earl Warren."

That politicization of the Court brought forth a barrage of negative editorial comment—some of the harshest coming from Nixon's constant critic Walter Lippmann, who now called him a "ruthless partisan . . . a politician who divides and embitters the people" and in addition a man who "does not have within his conscience those scruples which the country has the right to expect in the President of the United States." Far worse for Nixon than Lippmann's intemperate flare-up, the comment annoyed the president, who, when he was asked about it, said, "Once a man has passed into the Supreme Court, he is an American citizen and nothing else in my book until he comes out of that Court." He was angrier in private; to Len

Hall, he said, "What kind of a man is he? Doesn't he think of anything but politics?"

All of this made Nixon miserable; Eisenhower's real wishes couldn't be clearer, and Nixon began jotting down ways to be manly, to say that he'd had enough—that he was renouncing any interest in renomination—while trying not to sound resentful. "The field is wide open to many good candidates," he scrawled on notepaper, and then several variations of "So that there will be absolute freedom I announce now that I am not a candidate for renomination and will neither engage in, encourage, or approve any activities in behalf of my renomination."

Nixon's supporters believed that the enemies he had accumulated since the 1940s, mostly on the left, were aligning against him. The columnist George Sokolsky wrote that the efforts "of powerful forces inside and outside the Republican Party to kill off" Nixon are "so aggressive and gangster-like as to be suitable for an Erle Stanley Gardner murder." Within the administration, Jim Hagerty was doing his part to undermine the vice president, telling Eisenhower about a trip he'd taken to the South where he found "not one person was for Nixon for Vice President for a second term." As Ann Whitman summarized it, Hagerty had learned that "Nixon is in some way connected in Southerners' minds with the Negro difficulty."

The cabinet offer was leaked to *Newsweek*, which published an item saying that "The President didn't ask Nixon to withdraw—only to consider it," and which repeated Ike's idea "that a place in the Cabinet might be more advantageous than the Vice Presidency as a stepping stone to the White House." That naturally prompted the first question at Eisenhower's news conference on March 7:

> *Q: Mr. President, there have been some published reports that some of your advisers are urging you to dump Vice President Nixon from the Republican ticket this year; and, secondly, that you yourself have suggested to Mr. Nixon that he consider standing aside this time and, perhaps, take a Cabinet post. Can you tell us whether there is anything to those reports?*
>
> A: Well, now, as to the first one, I will promise you this much: if anyone ever has the effrontery to come in and urge me to dump somebody that I respect as I do Vice President Nixon, there will be

more commotion around my office than you have noticed yet. Second, I have not presumed to tell the Vice President what he should do with his own future. . . . The only thing I have asked him to do is to chart out his own course, and tell me what he would like to do. I have never gone beyond that.

The "chart out his own course" phrase along with Ike's mild fibbing brought Nixon to a new level of dejection. And while he said nothing publicly about disavowing another term, he continued his private exercise in the theoretical obliteration of his political self. *My decision = what is best for Party? What is best for Ike?* he jotted down on notepaper. *Believe now is time to stop speculation. . . . I have appreciated opportunity to serve. Have appreciated the President's friendship and support. . . . He has stood by me—the decision is mine. . . . I have reached the conclusion that best interest of party, President, country will be served by my withdrawing. . . . There must be free choice.* And he offered at least one clear-sighted insight: *As long as I am potential candidate—there is a natural tendency to limit choice.*

But for all that, and for all his hypothetical willingness to abjure the executive branch, he never meant it, just as he'd never meant to send his "resignation" letter during the fund crisis; his political cunning didn't desert him. The New Hampshire presidential primary was just a week away, on March 13, and although Eisenhower easily won it, with 56,464 votes, second place went to a noncandidate, Nixon, who got nearly 23,000 write-in votes. It was not a spontaneous outpouring—the conservative New Hampshire senator Styles Bridges, a Nixon ally, had helped instigate and organize the write-ins—but the results were a reminder of Nixon's popularity with the Republican base and they prompted Eisenhower to prepare a response for the next round of questions about Nixon. The plan was for Ike to say "The idea of trying to promote a fight between me and Dick Nixon is like trying to promote a fight between me and my brother. I am happy to have him as a personal friend, I am happy to have him as an associate and I am happy to have him in government." During the run-through before the news conference, Eisenhower also said:

That still doesn't make him Vice President. He has serious problems. He has his own way to make. He has got to decide whether he puts his eggs into the basket of the improbable future four years from now. I don't know exactly what he wants to do, and I don't think he knows himself. I am not going to say he is the only individual I would have for Vice President. There is nothing to be gained politically by ditching him. He is going to be the "comer" four years from now. I want a bevy of young fellows to be available four years from now. Nixon can't always be the understudy to the star.

At the actual press conference on March 14, Eisenhower not only kept to the original script, but slightly embellished it:

> Anyone who attempts to drive a wedge of any kind between Dick Nixon and me is—has just as much chance as if he tried to drive it between my brother and me. We are very close. . . . I am very happy that Dick Nixon is my friend. I am very happy to have him as an associate in government. I would be happy to be on any political ticket in which I was a candidate with him. Now if those words aren't plain, then it is merely because people can't understand the plain unvarnished truth.

As this all dragged into April, Eisenhower told Lucius Clay that he was perplexed by what he saw as Nixon's inability to be straightforward: "I suggested to our friend the very great value of finding a way to say 'Yes,' if it was indeed his intention to remain in the same slot . . . but in this one field he seems to have a shyness or a bewilderment that I do not understand." In fact, Eisenhower had made it almost impossible for Nixon to simply say "yes"—not after he'd kept urging him to say "no"; and Nixon seemed willing to suffer uncertainty as long as Eisenhower was willing to prolong things. This lack of resolution could not continue, though, and when a reporter in late April reminded the president about his "chart out his own course" comment and asked if Nixon had reported back, he said, "Well he hasn't reported back in the terms in which I used the expression that morning, no," and he added, "He hasn't given me any authority to quote him, any answer that I would consider final and definitive."

It was then that Nixon realized he had won this latest tug-of-war with Eisenhower, who now had no second line of retreat. Early the next morning, he called the president's office to ask for an appointment, and

Eisenhower agreed to see him that afternoon. When they met in the Oval Office to discuss what would be Eisenhower's capitulation—as awkward as any encounter between them had ever been—Nixon spoke with utter insincerity, saying "The only reason I waited this long to tell you was that I didn't want to do anything that would make you think I was trying to force my way onto the ticket if you didn't want me on it," even though they both knew that he'd taken precisely the path that he just claimed to have rejected. Jim Hagerty came into the room, and when Eisenhower asked how he thought they should make the announcement, Hagerty suggested letting Nixon do it himself. "Jim, you go with him," Eisenhower said, "and after he finishes his announcement, you say I was delighted to hear this news from the Vice-President." At that moment, Nixon was like a spurned suitor whose object of desire had finally agreed to a marriage of convenience.

Even then, Ike was searching for a way out; he suggested that when Nixon spoke to a cluster of reporters, he should say, "If they want me, I would be happy and delighted. If the Party found any reason to have me serve in any other capacity, I would be perfectly willing." Once more, Nixon did not quite follow orders, and a few minutes later, in a singularly joyless press conference, Nixon and Hagerty stood outside the White House, where Hagerty, with no apparent gusto, said, "The President has asked me to tell you gentlemen that he was delighted to hear that the Vice President would accept the nomination." When Nixon was asked who had requested the meeting with Eisenhower, he replied, laboriously, "I would say that it was a mutual thing. The President has indicated that he would like to talk to me about this matter at any time it was convenient, and when I had something to report to him. Consequently, the meeting was arranged in accordance with his wishes." As for when he had made his decision, Nixon said, "Well, I announced it today."

The president a little later went to the South Lawn to hit golf balls and kept at it for about an hour. The only genuine enthusiasm that day came from Foster Dulles, who called Pat Nixon at home to say that he was pleased. "Dick always says that you're the first to call," she said. Nixon naturally thought that the matter was settled, but he couldn't have been more wrong.

3

On the evening of June 8, Eisenhower attended a White House News Photographers Association banquet at the Sheraton-Park Hotel. He joked with Bob Hope, one of the guests, and talked to Sam Rayburn and Lyndon Johnson. He didn't get back to the White House until ten-thirty or so, and not long after that he didn't feel well.

Mamie Eisenhower wasn't terribly worried; she supposed it was a flare-up of an old digestive problem. When she telephoned the president's doctor at a quarter to one, Howard Snyder recommended milk of magnesia—a reliable remedy that had worked before. Not this time, though, and when Mrs. Eisenhower called again, she asked Snyder, who lived a couple of miles away, at 2101 Connecticut Avenue, to come to the residence. Snyder had many shortcomings as a doctor; when Ike in the 1940s smoked three and a half packs of cigarettes a day, Snyder had advised him, "Cut it down to one pack. That won't hurt you," and he had come close to improvising in the first hours after the heart attack. But he knew the president's medical history—he'd been his physician during the war—and he stayed by Eisenhower's side during the night. Early in the morning, he informed Hagerty that the president still wasn't feeling well and Hagerty called Nixon at about seven-thirty, telling him that it was probably nothing serious. Then Hagerty talked to the press, and although he said, "It's not an illness—it's an upset stomach," reporters nonetheless came running. At a little past noon, after a team of doctors examined the president, Hagerty revealed that the problem was more than a stomachache: "The President has an attack of ileitis"—a gastrointestinal obstruction—he explained, and soon after that an olive drab Army ambulance appeared at the mansion's ground-floor entrance. Tourists at the Southwest Gate wondered what was going on, especially with all those reporters milling around. At about one-thirty, Army corpsmen carried the president out on a stretcher; the ambulance passed through the Southeast Gate, away from the reporters, on its way uptown to Walter Reed Army Hospital.

The rest of the day was filled by medical bulletins—some excruciatingly technical. There were assurances that the illness had no connection to the president's heart condition and that there was no malignancy; in early reports, it was said that an operation might not be necessary. But doctors quickly abandoned this hopeful prognosis and concluded that they had no choice, that if the obstruction was left untreated, the intestine might become gangrenous. At about three the next morning, a surgical team performed an ileotransverse colostomy, an operation that bypassed about ten inches of the president's small intestine.

Doctors had been nervous about having to perform major abdominal surgery just nine months after the coronary, but the procedure not only solved an immediate problem, but remedied an old one—Ike's recurring indigestion. At a fairly jovial press conference the next day, Hagerty and Ike's surgeon, Major General Leonard Heaton, answered questions about when, and with what vigor, the president might resume playing golf; and the cabinet and White House staff like an army in waiting took up many of the roles that they'd taken up after the heart attack.

But while the public was reassured and the government functioned, it was also true that the president by any reasonable definition was an invalid. It took several weeks of convalescence in Gettysburg before he approached full strength, and some Democrats began to suggest, in the columnist Stewart Alsop's words, that the president was no more than "an amiable but aging and ailing man, trapped into running against his will by ruthless politicians and big businessmen, determined to use him for their own purposes." Lippmann weighed in, too, and asked, "Who is in fact likely to exercise the powers of the Presidency during the next four years—the President in the full vigor of his capacity, the President having to spare himself and to depend on his staff, or the Vice President?" He added that the "discussion of these things is a horrid duty," but Lippmann understood that such horrid duties are often the lot of a Washington columnist; he managed to reach the end of his eight hundred words with the unsurprising thought that "much will almost certainly depend" on whether Ike is able to display "a convincing vigor in the conduct of this office." When Nixon was asked if there was any change in Ike's decision to run for a second term, his response was unusually stilted: "The man who should speak concerning the President's future plans, the man who knows best what the requirements of leadership are in the national field and in the international field, and who knows the burdens of this office, and who knows his own physical condition best, is the President of the United States."

Ike's latest illness also reawakened the presidential ambitions of Harold Stassen, who was interviewed on the CBS radio program *Capitol Cloak-room,* and said that Eisenhower would run "if his health permits," but if not, "I do not believe that either Earl Warren or I would sit by and see the Republican Party move toward defeat." He did not mention a similar guardian's role for Richard Nixon. But by then he was plotting to get Nixon off the ticket.

4

The Stassen plot was revealed in mid-July, when the president invited Len Hall and Jim Hagerty to Gettysburg so that they could begin to make plans for the convention, just a month off. They decided that Charlie Hal-leck, the House minority leader, should nominate Ike and Hall suggested that they might as well pick someone to nominate Nixon. They settled on Governor Herter of Massachusetts, who had been both an early Eisen-hower supporter and a Nixon friend since they'd served in the House.

But when Hall called Herter, "I got a reaction—it wasn't a gasp but, by God, I knew something was wrong." Indeed something was. Although Herter said that he "probably" would be happy to do it, he wanted time to think—and for a good reason: Stassen had already reached Herter and had proposed that he take Nixon's spot on the ticket. He told Herter that he'd commissioned a poll (methodology unknown), showing that an Eisen-hower-Herter ticket would poll 6 percent more than Eisenhower-Nixon, which was possibly the difference between winning and losing. In fact, Stassen said, the situation was so dire that he needed to warn the president, and on July 20, four days after Eisenhower returned to the White House for the first time since his operation, Stassen came by for what he called "political purposes." Their conversation lasted fifteen minutes, but it gave Stassen time to tell the president what he'd told Herter.

It was, to say the least, unorthodox for a cabinet-level official to call for replacing a vice president. It was also strange timing for a "dump-Nixon" campaign. Not only was the convention just a month off, but hadn't Eisenhower settled the question in April? Eisenhower, though, did not act particularly concerned, and he let it be known through Hagerty and others that Stassen was free to speak as a private citizen "so long as he did not purport to speak in my name." Eisenhower then set off for Panama to attend the Inter-American Conference, a trip that had been on his schedule long before he fell ill. While Ike was out of town, Stassen called the first of several news conferences and told reporters about his Herter–for–Vice President campaign. He also tried to inform Nixon face-to-face, but after Nixon began to duck him, he wrote a letter—it was delivered by hand to Rose Mary Woods—in which he said that he hoped Nixon would "join in supporting Chris Herter" and that he had reached this decision "notwithstanding my long and continuing personal friendly feeling toward you."

Herter, though, was not particularly eager to run for vice president and was a little nonplussed by the attention he was getting. His chief interest was foreign policy, and, after talking with Sherman Adams, he believed that he had a good chance of becoming undersecretary of state, replacing Herbert Hoover Jr. Len Hall moved swiftly to undercut Stassen—he asked Herter if he'd be willing to nominate Nixon and Herter agreed. "We have been close friends for many years," he said in a press release. But while that ought to have stopped Stassen for good, it didn't; nor was Stassen stopped by the virulent criticism that he was getting from fellow Republicans or the mockery from publications that referred to him as Childe Harold. Nor had anyone inside the White House tried to stop him. Rather, he was given a short leave of absence to pursue his seemingly hopeless quest. The next time Len Hall saw the president, he had every reason to believe that he was enjoying Stassen's theater, perhaps too much; no one needed to say what was obvious—that Ike was sorry to have Nixon on the ticket again. Hall, though, liked his politics without surprises and was counting on an untroubled path to another Ike-and-Dick ticket. "So I walked into the President's office," Hall recalled. "He was sitting there with a sort of a smirk on. He looked at me and all he said was, 'Len, you're holding the reins a little tight, aren't you?'"

Eisenhower had more than politics on his mind that summer—in particular the nationalization of the Suez Canal on July 26 by Colonel Gamal Abdel Nasser, the Egyptian president. The Washington press corps, though, found the Stassen-Nixon story more interesting than an impend-

ing Middle East crisis; Russell Baker pointed out helpfully that just before
FDR dropped Henry Wallace from the ticket in 1944, he had said, "I like
him and I respect him and he is my personal friend. For these reasons I personally would vote for his renomination if I were a delegate to the convention." To stir up more theories of anti-Nixon plots, Drew Pearson reported
that Milton Eisenhower was the real motor behind the Stassen drive. True
or not, seeing it in print was too much for Milton—and embarrassing to
his brother. Milton quickly wrote Nixon to tell him "I want to say to you
with directness and finality that it has never occurred to me that anyone
but you should be considered for the vice-presidential nomination. . . . It
happens I think Harold Stassen's action was unforgivable, harmful, and
childish." That sounded fine, but Nixon, having suffered for months, could
not stop worrying. Pearson also reported that during Stassen's private crusade a Republican operative kept track of his movements and watched his
office to see who came and went. This interlude of political espionage was
certainly commissioned on Nixon's behalf, but Pearson did not tie the effort directly to the vice president; it ended at about the time Stassen arrived
in San Francisco on the Friday before the convention, still insisting that "a
man can be drafted at any time."

Stassen asked for another meeting with the president, but enough
was enough. Herbert Brownell suggested that Eisenhower needed to tell
Stassen—order him, actually—to close down his oppositional campaign,
and what better way than by telling Stassen to second Nixon's renomination? Stassen saw the president for eleven minutes, after which Eisenhower
said that he would rejoin the administration as an arms negotiator; that
was followed by a Stassen telegram to Nixon saying, "I have concluded that
I would like to second your nomination . . . and join wholeheartedly and
cheerfully in support of the nominees." To reporters, he looked haggard
and beaten, and when he was asked again if Nixon would hurt the national
ticket, he said, testily, "Any comment as to what lies behind instead of
where we go from here has no real point."

It is hard to know what made Stassen behave as he did. In the summer of 1956, he was not yet the perennial and increasingly ridiculous
presidential aspirant of his later years (the phrase "to Stassenize," probably
coined by Stewart Alsop, is still used to describe what happens to someone
who repeatedly pursues hopeless candidacies), although he was certainly

motivated by the ambition that had driven him since the 1930s and the elimination of Nixon would mean one fewer competitor for the presidency. According to his son, it was personal. Glen Harold Stassen, who became a minister and a teacher of theology, said that his father had an abiding distrust of Nixon. When the younger Stassen was twenty and the Herter gambit was in progress, "Dad came home one day and said, 'Richard Nixon has a moral blank where other people have their morality.' " Harold Stassen never said that publicly, though. "I have the feeling that this is something Dad said just to me," Glen Harold Stassen said.

Nixon did not get to enjoy this victory; he had just learned that his father was mortally ill and he hurried to his parents' home in La Habra. It was a last chance to show Frank Nixon how far he had come, and he did so when his father said, "You know, I'd really like to talk to Fulton Lewis Jr." The vice president quickly arranged a telephone conversation between his father and the popular conservative radio commentator. "Dad was in tears really at finally having the pleasure of talking to Fulton Lewis Jr.," Edward Nixon said. "It was good to have Dick's influence—because he *had* influence."

5

Eisenhower always claimed to have been puzzled by Nixon's torment— "Hell, I offered him anything in government he wanted," he told William Bragg Ewald Jr., a former White House aide who assisted with his memoirs. "My readiness to accept him as running mate in 1956 was evident, or should have been," he wrote, and he continued, disingenuously, "Years later I learned from a book of his [*Six Crises*] . . . that he regarded that period as one of agonizing uncertainty, apparently believing that I might be thinking of dropping him and hoping that I would personally make the final decision. To do so did not occur to me. I had placed the question completely in his hands, where I thought it properly should be." Eisenhower may have remembered it that way, but he wasn't struggling to be truthful—in fact he was making it up. He had told Len Hall that he wanted to replace Nixon, and he told his brother Milton that Nixon had forced himself back onto the ticket—and that he couldn't find a good way to block him. Eisenhower very likely gave passive encouragement to Stassen's plot. Republican leaders were sure that Stassen "at least had the President's acquiescence," James Reston reported, and Reston felt confident enough to assure readers of his "personal knowledge" that Stassen would never have gone forward "if the President had told [him] that he was determined to have Mr. Nixon on the ticket, or even that a public move on behalf of Governor Herter would embarrass the President." That is not quite the same as actively egging Stassen on, but for a president who liked his office politics to go undetected it's almost the same thing. When Stassen years later was asked whether Eisenhower knew in advance of his plan to replace Nixon with Herter, he said, "Oh, certainly. Certainly. Thoroughly." But then he had nothing more that he wanted to say.

CHAPTER 12

The Liberation of Richard Nixon

The 1956 campaign began with a post–Labor Day picnic at the Eisenhower farm, an occasion that brought together both Eisenhower and Nixon as well as other officeholders and cabinet members (though not Harold Stassen) and portly, ebullient Leonard Hall, who could look around at the crowd of five hundred men and women—most of them bused up from Washington—and take some satisfaction in knowing that after months of doubt and illness and intrigue, the Ike-and-Dick ticket was intact.

Earlier that day, Eisenhower telephoned Nixon and issued the day's orders: "I think today you ought to take notice of some of these attacks that have been made on the Administration and on me," he said. "I think that when Stevenson calls this Administration racketeers and rascals, when they say we are heartless in dealing with the problems of the people and the problems of the farmers, when they say we have no peace and no prosperity, I want them to be called on it. I would like for you to do so." And, the president continued, his vanity showing, "If you have to praise me that will be okay. I, of course, will be a little embarrassed by that but I know you have to do it to answer. I suggest something along the lines: 'Do you want to go back to war in order to have prosperity under the Democrats?' After all, there were nine million unemployed in 1939 before World War II, and also a great number before the Korean War. 'Do you want to go back to the casualty lists?' "

Nixon was not at all happy with this assignment. He wanted to run an elevated campaign this time, more in the style of Adlai Stevenson. He wanted to nurture a less partisan image—he was thinking of his future and of his diminished reputation—and said that he wanted to emphasize "the peace and prosperity that they're saying we don't have." The president, though, was annoyed by Stevenson's patronizing insinuations about his general alertness, as when he said things like, "Everyone shares in sympathy for the circumstances which have created a part-time presidency." It made him all the more eager to strike back with his weapon of choice: Nixon. "Of course, it isn't necessary to attack [Stevenson] personally but we should point out that he is wrong," Eisenhower said.

At the farm, Nixon spoke first and his praise of the president was, as usual, fulsome; Eisenhower, he said, "is leading the most massive assault on misery, poverty, disease, and hate that the world has ever seen." Eisenhower's speech was unfocused, but he was generous to Nixon, as if making amends for what he'd put him through in the winter and spring, or perhaps trying to persuade himself. "There is no man in the history of America who has had such a careful preparation as has Vice President Nixon for carrying out the duties of the Presidency if that duty should ever fall upon him," he said. Before the speeches, he took Nixon and Len Hall to see his Black Angus cattle; reporters and photographers rushed after them. Afterward, Eisenhower went off to the farmhouse, joined by a couple of pals. An unnamed Nixon friend told the journalist Theodore White that as Nixon watched them disappear inside, he said—bitterly, as the friend recalled it— "Do you know, he's never asked me into that house yet."

Outwardly, the 1956 campaign was remarkably free of substance; the comedian Mort Sahl's routine that year included the observation that "Eisenhower stands for 'gradualism.' Stevenson stands for 'moderation.' Between these two extremes, the people must choose." Eisenhower never doubted that he'd win and was happy to leave most of the campaigning to Nixon, who, soon after the Gettysburg event, was dispatched on a thirty-two-state, fifteen-thousand-mile tour. In the general's eyes, the vice president was like Patton on the hustings, and at forty-three, Nixon seemed to have plenty of stamina for what was the first presidential campaign to make extensive use of air travel—which meant more stops and more speeches. Airplanes also gave Nixon more time alone, which he appreciated.

Nixon followed orders; he even dipped into his trusty campaign satchel and once more found Dean Acheson, whose very name was shorthand for the purported softness of a Stevenson who "quailed" when Dulles took a "strong stand" on Quemoy and Matsu. And he always tried to describe Eisenhower lovingly as either "a man who ranks among the greatest of the legendary heroes of this nation" or "a man of destiny, both at home and abroad."

But no matter what Nixon said about Eisenhower, there was no way for him to escape being Nixon; in fact, what he said about the president only emphasized that he wasn't Eisenhower. Stevenson tried to make Nixon—his personality, his alleged sneakiness, his heartbeat-away-ness—the only real issue facing the voters. He would come up with other topics in due course; in one speech, talking about the French failure at Dien Bien Phu, he sounded like vintage Dick Nixon: "The free world suffered a severe defeat in Asia and lost a rich country and more than ten million people in Indochina." But most of what Stevenson said—whether it concerned Eisenhower's golf holidays or the threat of the hydrogen bomb—was tied in some way to Nixon. When he conjured up Nixon with his "hand on the trigger of the H-bomb," he called him someone who "has no standard of truth but convenience and no standard of morality except what will serve his interest in an election." Over four years, Stevenson had come to dislike, probably even to hate Nixon, and in private conversations described him as "sly," "slippery," and "ruthless."

But Nixon could also act infuriatingly high-minded—not the creature depicted by Stevenson. In Houston at the end of September he revealed that he was an "honorary member" of the National Association for the Advancement of Colored People—a group that many southerners were eager to smother—and that he planned to talk about civil rights in Louisville, which had integrated its public schools without violence. (The *New York Times* headline: NIXON DISCLOSES LINK TO N.A.A.C.P.) When he was asked in Minneapolis how he felt about the policies and programs of the NAACP, he said, as he did consistently, that he believed people needed to work together for "a country in which there is an equal opportunity for education, for employment, and in which all the good things of this life are guaranteed all citizens, regardless of race, creed, or color."

Stevenson never gave up. Nor was he willing to lose with grace. On election eve, in a nationally televised speech, he said that Nixon "has put away his switchblade and now assumes the aspect of an Eagle Scout," and that "presidential negligence on questions of peace and war may plunge the whole world into the horror of hydrogen war." That shrillness no doubt came from the heart, but Stevenson took it a step beyond: he introduced the supposition that Eisenhower would not survive his second term: "And distasteful as this matter is," Stevenson said, looking grave, "I must say bluntly that every piece of scientific evidence we have, every lesson of history and experience, indicates that a Republican victory tomorrow would mean that Richard M. Nixon would probably be President of this country within the next four years." He continued, "I say frankly, as a citizen more than a candidate, that I recoil at the prospect of Mr. Nixon as custodian of this nation's future, as guardian of the hydrogen bomb, as representative of America in the world, as Commander in Chief of the United States armed forces."

It was odd to hear a candidate for president make an issue of his actuarial anxieties, and the speech was in every way counterproductive and somewhat illogical, too. It was as if Stevenson was telling people not to vote for Eisenhower because of his wrongheaded policies but that it would be disastrous if Eisenhower was not at the helm.

For Richard Nixon, the 1956 election was liberation. Perhaps his future could not be separated from the administration's record or from the affection that the country felt for Eisenhower, who got ten million more votes than he had in 1952, but at least he no longer had to depend on the president to keep his job; he had tenure until 1961. Also, Nixon's influence within the administration was bound to grow; that was clear to anyone who looked at who was left over from the first term. Dulles's health was not good—he was in the early stages of colon cancer and had such intense back pain that when he traveled he took along a board; in early December, Christian Herter as expected was named undersecretary of state, making him the presumptive successor to Dulles. Attorney General Brownell wasn't going to stay much longer, and his deputy—and replacement—would be Nixon's friend Bill Rogers. Eisenhower might have dreamed of a Bob Anderson presidency, but that was no more likely than a Milton Eisenhower presidency, and Nixon, so much cleverer than Ike when it came to the political long view—so much quicker to understand what was possible—could not yet see any strong competition in the contest for the 1960 nomination, which he already had his eye on. The idea that a vice president was an heir to the presidency probably vanished during the administration of Thomas Jefferson, when Aaron Burr and then George Clinton held the job, but it had gained considerable currency during Ike's two major illnesses.

Nixon kept private his dissents over foreign policy, in particular the administration's response in the Middle East, where Egypt's Nasser in July had nationalized the Suez Canal and intended to block Israeli shipping through the canal and the Gulf of Aqaba. That set off, in slow motion, a plot by three of America's closest allies—England, France, and Israel—to reverse the situation. Israel invaded Egypt in late October, an action that France and Britain used as a pretext to mount their own joint invasion—to serve as "peacemakers" as they forcibly took back the canal. Eisenhower then stepped in, putting pressure on the combatants to agree to a cease-fire and pull back, a policy that succeeded in stopping the fighting but also precipitated the fall of Prime Minister Anthony Eden's government. (On September 2, 1956, Eisenhower, with anticolonialist fervor, wrote to Eden, saying, "I do not see how the economy of Western Europe can long survive the burden of prolonged military operations, as well as the denial of Near East oil. Also the peoples of the Near East and of North Africa and, to some extent, of all of Asia and all of Africa, would be consolidated against the West to a degree which, I fear, could not be overcome in a generation and, perhaps, not even in a century.") Nixon at the time was an obedient follower—"Because we took the position we did, the peoples of Africa and Asia know now that we walk with them as moral equals," he told *U.S. News & World Report*. But a decade later, he told an interviewer, "I want to make clear, I did not participate in those decisions because I was on the road and carrying the brunt of the campaign," and he only expressed his real view—that the American position was wrong—long after Eisenhower had left office. He did so in a 1983 letter to the British M.P. Julian Amery; to his biographer Jonathan Aitken; and in casual conversations taped in the Oval Office during his presidency, during which he also claimed that Eisenhower had his own late regrets—an assertion that is hard to substantiate. The Alsop brothers regarded the administration's policy as "a positive orgy of smarmy self-righteousness."

Eisenhower later said that the three weeks leading up to the election were "the most crowded and demanding" of his presidency, and what he faced was all the more difficult because Foster Dulles had undergone emergency surgery on the weekend before the election. The Suez crisis exacerbated tensions between Russia and the West (even while it put the Americans and Soviets briefly on the same side); and so did a revolutionary mood in Eastern Europe, in Poland and particularly in Hungary. Rebels who were defying the Soviet-sponsored regime thought that implicit promises had been made—on Radio Free Europe, by Dulles, who had often used the word "liberation," and by the vice president, who on October 29 in a speech at Occidental College said that the uprisings in Eastern Europe showed the "rightness of the liberation position." These views came close to defying Eisenhower, who had ruled out using force in the region and was feeling pressure from some of the administration's prickliest personalities, such as Clare Boothe Luce, who had pleaded with the president to intervene.

Mrs. Luce, whose charm and connections usually got her time alone with Ike, stopped by after the election and suggested in all seriousness that the United States ought to launch a preventive nuclear war against Russia. This so unnerved the president (one aide thought that Mrs. Luce seemed on the "verge of a nervous breakdown") that he immediately wrote a confidential note to Henry Luce in which he said he was "quite certain that the implications . . . of an all-out war have not sufficiently impressed themselves upon her"—that the "inescapable results on the civilization of the northern hemisphere would be something almost beyond the comprehension of the normal individual." Mrs. Luce recalled the conversation somewhat differently, as one in which Eisenhower confessed to her how he worried about a nuclear war—he no longer believed (if he ever had) that atomic missiles were interchangeable with bullets. "I cannot sleep at night," he told her. "I think of nothing else, trying to limit the range of weapons.

But this is not possible. . . . How do you tell when they are getting ready for the great attack? This is the horror of the whole situation. . . . Every day this question is <u>the</u> question. . . . There must be some other way. What liberties could we enjoy in smoking ruins?"

In the aftermath of the Hungarian uprising, some 200,000 refugees crossed the border into Austria; on December 19, the vice president flew there to see things for himself, and when he returned, he made their cause his own. Nixon appeared on a Christmas night television program to benefit the refugees and was joined by a number of performers who were then appearing on Broadway, including Julie Andrews (*My Fair Lady*) and Charles Laughton (*Major Barbara*). He spoke about the "incredibly courageous" Hungarian people who had "helped expose Communism for the gigantic failure it is."

He seemed emotional about what he'd seen. During a meeting in the president's office, he said that the United States should admit more of the refugees. When Eisenhower said that it might be less expensive if they stayed put and the United States paid for their upkeep, Nixon disagreed; if people had to linger in those camps, he said, their morale would suffer. In fact, he continued, those Hungarians offered a chance "to get needed flexibility into our immigration law." Throughout the meeting, one heard Nixon arguing for quick decisions and open doors, and Eisenhower, while not quite opposing this approach, sounding far less enthusiastic, even a little chilly. In a meeting with legislative leaders a few days later Nixon spoke with continued passion of the "high quality of these refugees," people that Ike was willing to help but preferred to keep at a distance.

At the end of the year, Eisenhower wrote another "Dear Dick" letter and seemed to acknowledge a change in his estimation of Nixon: "In these past four years you have brought to the office of Vice President a real stature that formerly it had not known; you have proved yourself an able and popular 'Ambassador' to our friends in many parts of the world." It may have been boilerplate Ike—and no one understood the ephemeral quality of his words better than Nixon, who over the past twelve months had watched his own fortunes change and nearly disappear. But for once, if not for very long, he could take a deep breath, look Eisenhower in the eye, and, when he felt rested again, really begin to chart his own course.

CHAPTER 13

"Once an Oppressed People Rise"

1

E. Frederic Morrow, a lawyer and a senior manager at CBS television, was the first African American to hold an executive position in any White House—after two years of awkward silences, he was appointed a presidential aide in 1955—and while he liked Eisenhower personally, he later said that Ike's "lukewarm stand on civil rights made me heartsick." It was, Morrow confessed, "the greatest cross I had to bear in my eight years in Washington," and it was made no easier inside a White House that was not particularly friendly to the cause of civil rights or to African Americans. Morrow felt a visceral hostility from Jerry Persons, Sherman Adams's deputy, an Alabamian whom he regarded as unambiguously anti-black (Joe Alsop described Persons as a "sly, morally sinuous man with deceptively agreeable manners"), and he endured many unintentional slights and insults even from people who meant well.

Morrow admired the vice president and was impressed by what he judged to be his sensitivity on racial issues. Nixon was one of the few who had taken the time to encourage Morrow in his career—"He felt that I must continually break through into new areas, achieve goals and help blaze a trail that would make it easier to integrate other Negroes into top Government echelons"—and he agreed with Nixon that it was a bad idea to keep naming black Americans to jobs that dealt with race relations. It was "rather pathetic to see a Negro laboring on something that consistently points up race or color," Nixon had said to him, and he promised Morrow that if he ever had another position in government—meaning the presidency—"he would utilize it to permit Negroes greater opportunities to serve their country in positions of prestige and influence." In private, Nixon's views on race were more paternalistic than he let on, but his sympathy for the aspirations of American blacks was real and during the Eisenhower years Negro leaders saw him as an ally—the administration's most important advocate for equal rights.

In January 1957, Foster Dulles telephoned Nixon at home during the dinner hour to ask what he thought about making a trip to Africa, where Nixon had never been. He urged him to head the American delegation to the Gold Coast in March, when the nation, now Ghana, was to get its independence from England. Africa was "the coming continent," Dulles said, and the administration was eager to be involved. Fred Morrow was invited to join the delegation by Sherman Adams, who called him over to his table in the White House mess and said, "Fred, how would you like to go to Africa with Dick? Maybe you'll find some of your relatives over there." Morrow replied with good humor—he liked Adams—and said that he had problems enough with his American relatives.

Dick and Pat Nixon seemed particularly comfortable among the world's outsiders, and the visit on a personal level was as successful as their trip to Asia in the fall of 1953. Morrow recalled a stop in Morocco where "the Vice-President and his wife, in typical American fashion, left the stands to mingle with the people. . . . Mrs. Nixon patted babies on the head and finally picked up a very dirty infant to cuddle on her lap. The crowd literally went crazy over this display of friendliness on the part of the 'VP' and his wife." By the time they reached Ghana, the vice president, who at home was often a portrait of shuddering reserve, had become the personification of spontaneous physicality. A reporter for the *Pittsburgh Courier* wrote, "Oft-times . . . [I] had heard that Mr. Nixon lacked warmth, soul, sincerity . . . that everything he did was motivated by cold, calculating logic. The Nixon I observed does not fit this stereotype," and the writer, his enthusiasm growing, continued: "I can't forget the sight of Dick Nixon kissing the upturned faces of little black babies. I can't forget the sight of Dick Nixon getting out of his car to reach for the hands of those who would clasp his, in a spirit of brotherhood which symbolizes a universal language of friendship." Gold Coasters gave him the title "American Show Boy," an expression of admiration for a rousing speaker.

The Negro press, which worried with good reason about Eisenhower's views on race, took note of Nixon's outwardly congenial relationship with the Baptist minister Martin Luther King Jr., whom he met for the first time at the Ghanaian independence ceremonies. "At the celebration," the *Atlanta Daily World* reported, "two great Americans met. . . . Both are young and vigorous and each possessing the sense of modern liberality, let it be hoped that more will become of this cordial meeting on African soil." Dr. King, a slightly chubby man standing about five foot eight, was twenty-eight years old and already famous for having led a boycott to desegregate buses in Montgomery, Alabama. He had been trying for some time to meet the vice president without much luck, and had tended to see him as something of a hopeless right-winger. So it was a happy coincidence to run into him in Accra, Ghana's capital, where, in the course of an amiable conversation, he urged Nixon to speak out in behalf of civil rights and blacks who were being terrorized in the South. King came away from their encounter liking the vice president, not least because he sensed in him a man "with no basic racial prejudice," which he attributed to Nixon's Quaker background. "He has a genius for winning people," King later observed to the *Herald Tribune*'s Earl Mazo. "He is a superb diplomat. He knows what to say, when to say, and where to say." Before they left, Nixon invited King to call on him in Washington. "It will be a pleasure to see you and talk with you again," the vice president wrote after they'd agreed upon a date in June, and King replied, "I am looking forward with great anticipation to a most profitable afternoon together." King was particularly eager for an audience with President Eisenhower, and meeting Nixon would mark progress toward that goal.

2

Eisenhower was a little squeamish when it came to civil rights. Ann Whitman would sometimes bring up the topic, and he would say, "Ann, you would feel differently if you had been raised in the South like I was," a curious statement from someone who had been reared in Kansas, a border state. The president did support the 1957 civil rights bill that was making its way through Congress (it was part of Nixon's domestic portfolio), but three years after the *Brown* decision he was still doubtful about the ruling. "I think that no other single event has so disturbed the domestic scene in many years as did the Supreme Court's decision of 1954 in the school segregation case," he wrote to his friend Swede Hazlett that summer, and once told Ann Whitman that the Court should have started with graduate schools and gone from there to college, high school, and then the lower grades. He knew that the prospect of racial integration discomfited northerners too, even people like his friend Arthur Hays Sulzberger, the publisher of the *New York Times*, who agreed with Eisenhower that using the law—or force—"only increased the problems." Ann Whitman noted that Sulzberger "shamefacedly admitted, for private use only, that even he would not want his seven or eight year old granddaughter to go to school with Negro boys just older than she is."

The vice president and Dr. King had their talk in Nixon's Senate office on June 13, 1957, a couple of months before the Senate began debate on the civil rights bill. Labor Secretary James Mitchell accompanied Nixon; the Reverend Ralph David Abernathy was with King, who had no illusions about American attitudes: the majority of whites, King said, don't favor integration, but they're willing to accept it. He also said that he and Abernathy had voted for Eisenhower, that Negroes were eager for the president "to talk calmly and rationally on the issue," and that blacks in general were disappointed because Eisenhower wasn't being more aggressive—"speaking out would help." And while they stressed nonviolence in voter registration drives, they didn't know how long violence—"a blow-up"—could be avoided. At one point, King said, "Once an oppressed people rise—they cannot be stopped." Nixon, who was taking notes, jotted that down, along with the phrases *Negro determined to gain dignity. . . . This is part of world problem—quest for human dignity all over the world.* The visit with Nixon lasted nearly three hours and King afterward told reporters that while it was not a substitute for a session with Eisenhower it was "a step in that direction."

King came out of the meeting still impressed by the vice president. "I . . . feel that Nixon would have done much more to meet the present crisis in race relations than President Eisenhower has done," he later told Mazo, who was writing a biography of Nixon. "He has one of the most magnetic personalities that I have ever confronted." Then he added, "When you are close to Nixon he almost disarms you with his apparent sincerity. You never get the impression that he is the same man . . . who made a tear-jerking speech in the 1952 campaign. . . . And so I would conclude by saying that if Richard Nixon is not sincere, he is the most dangerous man in America."

The 1957 Civil Rights Act, which passed the Senate in August, went further than any such legislation since the Reconstruction era; the debate was notable for, among other things, a record-breaking filibuster by Strom Thurmond, a mad theatrical feat that lasted for more than twenty-four hours and embarrassed even segregationists like Richard Russell of Georgia, who was an almost cinematic embodiment of southern Bourbonism. While considerable credit for the bill has gone to Lyndon Johnson and Sam Rayburn, when it came to voting rights, they were willing—even eager—to settle for something weaker than what administration sponsors wanted. In particular they went along with an amendment that guaranteed a jury trial for officials accused of violating voting rights—a provision that would very likely have nullified its effect in southern courtrooms.

Nixon, although limited by his role as the nonvoting president of the Senate, was more than willing to take on LBJ, who at one point accused the vice president of heading a "concerted propaganda campaign" to misrepresent the Senate version of the bill; Nixon replied epigrammatically that the Johnson version of the bill was "a vote against the right to vote." When Nixon was photographed with King, conservative Republicans complained; Nixon, they said, should try to appeal to conservatives in the South as well as the North. Nixon, though, said that doing so would only divide the Republican Party in much the way that Democrats were divided by the racial issue. His assertion that Republicans should be steadfast about civil rights made him a target for senators like Russell, who reminded Nixon of the price he might have to pay in the South if he ever became a presidential candidate and he slyly referred to Nixon as "the most distinguished member" of the NAACP. The politics behind the bill—presidential and regional, from Nixon, Lyndon Johnson, the southern bloc and northern Republicans—were complex and ever-shifting. When the final vote was taken, supporters of the bill knew that it was far from perfect but agreed with King, whose political instincts were as fine as anyone's, "that it is much better than no bill." As for voting rights, the legislation in its final form permitted a federal judge in a criminal contempt case to impose fines and jail sentences for up to forty-five days, even without a jury—another compromise, but an improvement over the original. After it passed, Jackie Robinson wrote to Nixon, saying, "I and many others will never forget the fight you made and what you stand for." King also wrote to say, "I will long remember the rich fellowship which we shared together and the fruitful discussion that we had," and he continued:

Let me say before closing how deeply grateful all people of goodwill are to you for your assiduous labor and dauntless courage in seeking to make the Civil Rights Bill a reality. This has impressed people all across the country, both Negro and white. This is certainly an expression of your devotion to the highest mandates of the moral law. It is also an expression of your political wisdom. More and more the negro vote is becoming a decisive factor in national politics.... History has demonstrated that inadequate legislation supported by mass action can accomplish more than adequate legislation which remains unenforced for the lack of a determined mass movement.

There were certainly many motives behind these expressions of mutual flattery. King, in a P.S., said, "I hope you will see your way clear to speak to the President" concerning their discussions and Nixon recognized the importance of the black vote in a national election. His public rhetoric later changed, especially in his 1968 campaign for the presidency, but he never really wavered on this issue. Unlike two of his eventual successors, George H. W. Bush and Ronald Reagan, Nixon supported the 1964 Civil Rights Act. In the summer of 1957, he replied to Dr. King in much the same spirit that King had shown:

I am sure you know how much I appreciate your generous comments. . . .
My only regret is that I have been unable to do more than I have. Progress
is understandably slow in this field, but we at least can be sure that we are
moving steadily and surely ahead.

About a year later, on June 23, 1958, King got his audience with Eisenhower. Rocco Siciliano, a young presidential assistant, had helped to
arrange the meeting with several Negro leaders, among them A. Philip
Randolph, vice president of the AFL-CIO and founder of the Brotherhood
of Sleeping Car Porters, and Roy Wilkins, the executive secretary of the
NAACP. Because the group had been allotted just thirty minutes, they
decided to speak in sequence, with each man taking about five minutes.
When it was King's turn, he asked for an executive pronouncement that
the law concerning desegregation "will be vigorously upheld" and also
asked Eisenhower to conduct "a White House conference of constructive
leadership."

"Throughout the meeting," Siciliano recalled, "the president sat absorbed by these speakers—his eyes and posture showed that intense concentration," but Ike was baffled by the implicit complaint that "bitterness
on the part of the Negro people was at its height." This get-together accomplished nothing specific—Eisenhower wasn't interested in setting up
a conference on race relations—and King's biographer Taylor Branch considered the meeting "an empty still life, framed but devoid of substance."
But Siciliano, who was present throughout, along with Fred Morrow and
William Rogers, believes that Branch missed what he called the "epochal
nature" of the event. "No black group," Siciliano said, "had ever met with
a President of the United States on business."

3

At the end of the summer of 1957, Foster Dulles and Nixon discussed ways
to enlarge Nixon's role within the administration. The attachment between
Nixon and Dulles had grown deeper since the president's heart attack; they
recognized each other as allies when it came to the Soviet Union, Indo-

china, Formosa, "liberating" Eastern Europe, and the political liquidation of Harold Stassen, who was still serving as an arms negotiator. Dulles knew that Nixon was—although Dulles never used the word—a little bored by the vice presidency. He was eager for another foreign trip—no goodwill tours, please, but perhaps he could receive an honorary degree? And, oh yes, didn't it make sense for him to have a more active congressional role, considering his unique job as part of the executive as well as the legislative branches? Dulles told Nixon that he'd talk this over with Sherman Adams and Herb Brownell and, if it seemed appropriate, the president.

Dulles soon did just that, and about a week later Eisenhower dictated a rambling "Dear Dick" letter (copies went to Dulles and Sherman Adams), in which he vaguely sketched out ways to expand the vice president's responsibilities. "My basic thought is that you might find it possible—and intriguing—to be of even more help in our whole governmental program dealing with affairs abroad than you have been in the past," he said. "By your extensive travel, you have been of inestimable assistance to the Secretary of State and to me. In addition you have gained an understanding of our problems that is both unusual and comprehensive . . . supplemented by your special position of having one foot in the Executive Branch and one foot in the Legislative Branch." It sounded plausible enough, but Eisenhower had not fully thought it through and in any case outside events soon intruded.

It had been a hard summer for Eisenhower. He hadn't even managed to get out of town, unless one counts an occasional golf excursion to the Burning Tree Country Club, in suburban Maryland; there were no trips to Denver or Augusta or even Gettysburg. But right after Labor Day, he flew to Newport, Rhode Island, where he stayed at a favorite spot, a house overlooking the water near the Naval War College, which offered access to the excellent golf course at the Newport Country Club, a short boat ride away. He was not, however, going to get much rest there. On September 4, the governor of Arkansas, Orval Faubus, ordered the Arkansas National Guard to surround Central High School in Little Rock in order to prevent nine Negro students from enrolling—to avoid violence, he said. The situation presented Eisenhower with precisely the dilemma that he'd been dreading since the *Brown* decision—how, as he put it to Swede Hazlett, to consider both "the customs and fears of a great section of our population, and . . . the binding effect that Supreme Court decisions must have on all of us if our form of government is to survive and prosper." Nothing, though, had prepared him for Little Rock, which was not just a challenge for the courts but a problem for the State Department as images of mobs who yelled "go home, niggers" were shown around the world. Nixon saw the disturbances through the eyes of a world traveler, alert to anti-American propaganda; when he'd reported to the president after his Africa trip, he noted that "Every instance of prejudice in this country is blown up in such manner as to create a completely false impression of the attitudes and practices of the great majority of the American people," adding "We cannot talk equality to the peoples of Africa and Asia and practice inequality in the United States." Nor, Eisenhower understood, could the governor of Arkansas be permitted to nullify a ruling of the Supreme Court. On September 24, determined to put an end to it, he called in the 101st Airborne Division, in battle array. A day later, the "Little Rock Nine" were safely escorted to their classes at Central High School. "In my career I learned that if you have to use force, use overwhelming force," he told Attorney General Brownell.

Georgia senator Richard Russell compared the "invasion" of Little Rock to the tactics of Hitler, an extraordinary insult to the general who had helped to liberate Europe from the Nazis, and extraordinarily obtuse when it came to a president who had considerable sympathy for the South. Nixon during and after the standoff tried to reprise his role as the in-house champion of equal rights, a part that he played with muted fervor; he wrote to southern editors in support of the administration's stand, yet he knew that whatever he said was likely to further alienate the South. As for himself, there were rumors that he was unhappy with the president's leadership—that, as one newspaper put it, he believed that Eisenhower's "vacillation" on civil rights was "unfortunate from the Republican point of view," but he was never quoted directly. "Nixon had a full realization of the need for change," Rocco Siciliano said. "Most everybody there under Eisenhower was just the status quo. It wasn't that they didn't recognize in an abstract, intellectual sort of way that civil rights was something that should happen, but it was going to happen on the next person's watch."

CHAPTER 14

Worn Down

1

About ten days after federal troops restored order in Little Rock, on October 4, 1957, the Soviet Union, using a two-stage ballistic missile, launched the world's first artificial satellite, Sputnik (Russian for "traveling companion"), and if there was a moment when Richard Nixon's public allegiance to everything Eisenhower began to wobble, it was then, after Sputnik. It was not as though the launch should have surprised anyone who'd been paying even casual attention. Three years earlier, the Alsop brothers informed their readers that the Soviets would send up a satellite within the decade—in their best alarmist style, they called it "another military development almost as decisive as the H-bomb itself." But if not quite that, Sputnik was nonetheless a jolt; its passage around the earth—its *beep-beep* recorded by ham radio enthusiasts—came to stand for Soviet superiority in rocketry and one could only imagine what else. "It is a grim business," Walter Lippmann wrote, "because a society cannot stand still. If it loses the momentum of its own progress, it will deteriorate and decline."

Richard Nixon agreed with those who saw it as a grim business, in contrast to the president, who seemed almost relaxed about the subject; Sherman Adams recalled Eisenhower's little joke during a National Security Council meeting: "Any of you fellows want to go to the moon? I don't. I'm happier right here." Adams, too, seemed unable to grasp why this Russian achievement was so disturbing or why it so quickly came to represent a society's destiny. He tried in a speech to make fun of "Soviet satellites that sail over our heads and land on the front page of every American newspaper," and added even more lamely that "the serving of science, not high score in an outer space basketball game, has been and still is our country's goal." Eisenhower at his next press conference said that he saw nothing "significant in that development as far as security is concerned," while conceding that "it does definitely prove the possession by the Russian scientists of a very powerful thrust in their rocketry, and that is important." He mentioned—and probably shouldn't have—that the United States planned to launch its own satellite in December.

After Nixon heard all this, including the president's confident assessment, he found it hard to suppress his bafflement and impatience with what he saw as almost willful shortsightedness by Eisenhower and some of his advisers. Nixon viewed Sputnik as a matter of national destiny as well as preparedness; he was excited by this sort of thing, and attracted by the romantic idea that "when a great nation drops out of the race to explore the unknown, that nation ceases to be great." On the day after Sherman Adams's "basketball" quip, Nixon spoke to businessmen in San Francisco and said, "We could make no greater mistake than to brush off this event as a scientific stunt of more significance to the man in the moon than to men on Earth. We . . . must never overlook that the Soviet Union has developed a scientific and industrial capacity of great magnitude"—of a capacity to make war against the West.

Nixon would have liked to blame the Democrats. Before speaking to editorial writers in Oklahoma City, he asked Foster Dulles for some confirmation that missile development had, as he said to Dulles, "been almost wholly neglected by the Democratic Administration after World War II." Dulles assured Nixon that this was true; in fact, he said, when he'd visited Moscow after the war, he'd seen German missile scientists getting "VIP treatment." And he'd been told that "there was practically nothing done during the early postwar years." But after nearly five years in office, it wasn't easy for a Republican administration to blame Harry Truman and his party for military apathy. So on this subject, the fault line between Eisenhower and Nixon threatened to widen. Eisenhower was surprisingly uninformed when he talked about space, or rocket technology, which had not advanced much beyond what Nazi scientists like Werner von Braun had accomplished at Peenemünde. He knew that it was much harder to reach a small target with an intermediate-range ballistic missile than to reach earth orbit with a multi-stage rocket carrying a 184-pound satellite, but the thing itself—the actual Sputnik—seemed to flummox him. At a National Security Council meeting on October 10, he said that he'd recently learned that "two so-called intelligence people" were saying that the Russian satellite was taking photographs of the United States. Donald Quarles, the deputy secretary of defense, had no idea who was saying such a thing, but he doubted it—although he conceded that a Sputnik camera *might* be taking pictures of some kind. Eisenhower worried that America's prospective satellite would orbit at a lower altitude than the Russian one and that a lower trajectory might somehow lower the nation's prestige. Quarles tried to reassure the president by telling him that the American satellite (which would weigh less than twenty-two pounds) would have "more refined equipment" than the Soviet model.

It was a dispiriting session. Allen Dulles acknowledged that the Russians had managed a sort of propaganda hat trick by combining the Sputnik launch with successful tests of a hydrogen bomb as well as an intercontinental ballistic missile. When Nixon asked if the CIA had any idea how much the United States spent on basic research compared with the Soviet Union, Dulles replied that there were no good estimates, although he could say what was obvious: that the Soviets since 1945 had put considerable emphasis on missiles.

Minutes from the meeting don't say that the vice president was shaking his head at this back-and-forth, but Nixon's political intuition didn't fail him. He understood how vulnerable the administration might be to the charge—fair or not—of being inattentive to the nation's security. Democrats like Stuart Symington of Missouri, a member of the Senate Armed Services Committee and a presidential aspirant, were already accusing Eisenhower of not being alert to the Soviet threat, and Nixon warned his colleagues around the table that Congress would want to know what the administration had been doing about a missile program. The president sounded ill at ease at this prospect, and unusually defensive. Yes, he said, they all might be obliged to testify before congressional committees, but he reminded them that the earth satellite program had been adopted by this very same National Security Council after due deliberation. In short, "we should answer inquiries by stating that we have a plan—a good plan—and that we are going to stick to it." The five-star general was suddenly not infallible. "I . . . have a feeling," Stewart Alsop wrote to Lyndon Johnson, "that Sputnik has finally killed the 'Ike knows all about defense' myth."

In this atmosphere, people who were disinclined to see much good in Nixon were beginning to look again. As James Reston put it, the vice president "was frankly facing the facts and furnishing some leadership, particularly among the new young men now assuming executive authority." The *New York Times* columnist Arthur Krock suggested that Nixon in San Francisco had, unlike Sherman Adams, expressed "what is or will be the sober second thought of the administration." No one was yet writing about the so-called missile gap, which was to become an issue in the next election, but Nixon could anticipate it. So could Lyndon Johnson; two days before Eisenhower's State of the Union address, the majority leader said, "Control of space means control of the world."

There was, though, no missile gap (as opposed to a rocketry gap)—a significant difference. A nation with an intercontinental ballistic missile capable of carrying a small thermonuclear warhead to a precise target would possess the ultimate murderous weapon—what the nuclear physicist John von Neumann, who had urged the administration to move ahead quickly on both fronts, called "the thermonuclear breakthrough." Two years before Sputnik, in the summer of 1955, von Neumann had briefed Eisenhower, Nixon, and others, using phrases like "nuclear blackmail," "thirty minutes en route," "fifteen minutes warning," and "no known defense against it," while also describing what a single hydrogen bomb could do to Manhattan. Von Neumann himself was an early-warning system, and Nixon was among those who believed the warning. In an unpublished memoir, "Twenty-Four Minutes to Checkmate," Vincent T. Ford, who served on the staff of the Department of the Air Force, recorded some of this discussion and singled out the vice president for praise: "Thank God Mr. Nixon was made of stern stuff. He knew we weren't trying to sell the President another service package." He quoted Nixon as saying, "This project must be given a highest national priority above all others and a separate budget and anything else it needs to get the job done"—much the same language adopted by the NSC.

By early 1957, the Defense Department could report that missiles with mythological names like Jupiter, Thor, and Atlas had been successfully fired and that the Air Force expected to have a working ICBM by early 1959. And while it was supposed that the Russians had been making progress, too, there was no solid intelligence about their advances—not until Sputnik. In November 1957, less than a month after the first Sputnik, the Russians launched a second one: Sputnik 2 weighed more than a half ton, and carried a twelve-pound mixed-breed dog named Laika, who died quickly—probably from the intense heat—but became the first living organism to be sent into space. After that, pressure on the United States to get *something* into orbit became more intense, and the president felt the pressure. He came close to publicly confessing his exhaustion when CBS's Charles von Fremd took note of the difficulties of recent weeks—most obviously Little Rock and Sputnik—and asked, "Do all of these great problems sap your strength physically or mentally in any way, sir?" To that, the president said: "Well, I will tell you, Mr. von Fremd. If you will go back to July 25th, of a year ago, when the Egyptians seized the canal . . . if you can point out a day since then that there hasn't been some critical problem placed upon my desk, I can't remember when it was. And I will say this: I find it a bit wearing, but I find it endurable, if you have got the faith in America that I have."

2

Something meanwhile was happening to Vice President Nixon. He wasn't changing, really, but circumstances continued to change him—letting him become more independent, untethered. These national defense questions had something to do with it, and with his willingness to oppose Eisenhower—openly, in meetings, and even in a few off-the-record conversations with journalists, which was a little risky for someone in his position.

In early December, when a Navy Vanguard rocket carrying a tiny satellite took off from Cape Canaveral and reached a height of only four feet before falling back and exploding, it was as if Russia's two artificial moons were there simply to mock the Eisenhower administration's progress in science and missile development. On the day of the Vanguard's crash landing, Dulles told Nixon that he had rarely been so despondent. Nixon said that he'd been "screaming about it too," and added, "We failed to realize the psychological importance of it. We have to get something up." Nixon was also concerned about who would be in charge of an American space program. Eisenhower had told legislative leaders that any new space agency—and it was agreed that America needed a space agency—ought to be established within the Department of Defense. But James Rhyne Killian, the former president of MIT and Eisenhower's adviser on science and technology, had his doubts; so did Nixon, who favored a separate office for "peaceful" research. Simply in terms of world opinion, Nixon argued, wouldn't it be much better "if non-military research in outer space were carried forward by an agency entirely separate from the military?" He pointed out that if all space projects fell under the auspices of the Defense Department, the military would then have little incentive to pursue anything that *didn't* have a military purpose. Eisenhower seemed to bend a little. He noted that the Pentagon would inevitably have to be involved— after all, the military possessed all the hardware—but he did not rule out what he called an eventual "great Department of Space."

When Killian at the legislative leaders meeting said that a lunar probe would probably be Russia's next act, Eisenhower said that these space ventures needed a "rule of reason"; they couldn't just pour funds into them "where there was nothing of value to the Nation's security." He added, "I'd rather have a good Redstone than be able to hit the moon" because "we didn't have any enemies on the moon!" Despite Ike's scorn, Senator Knowland said that he liked the idea of sending a rocket to the moon. Knowland may not have had much imagination or critical intelligence, but like Nixon he understood how world opinion was affected by such feats. "If we are close enough to doing a probe," he said, "we should press it." Eisenhower didn't object—but only as long as it could be done with a missile that was ready to go; he didn't want to "rush into an all-out effort on each one of these glamour performances." Killian thought that the United States could send an unmanned rocket to the moon by 1960 or, in a rush effort, by

1959. But as it turned out, America would have finished in second place; the Soviet Union accomplished it in January 1959; and the following October, the Luna 3 spacecraft was the first to take photographs of the dark side of the moon and beam them back to earth.

America at the end of January 1958 finally sent up its first successful satellite, Explorer 1, using the Army's modified Jupiter C rocket—a variation of the German V-2. But in this period, and on this subject, Nixon felt undervalued and unappreciated—an underling who wasn't taken seriously on the big questions that concerned the president and his top people. That led him to talk with surprising frankness and fairly raw language in an off-the-record conversation with the journalist Stewart Alsop, starting with a complaint about a lack of toughness at the Pentagon, where Neil McElroy, the former president of Procter & Gamble, was now in charge. McElroy's specialty at P&G had been brand management—the relatively new idea that a brand such as Tide could be treated and managed like a separate business inside a company that also manufactured Cheer. "I tell you one thing—there just aren't enough sons-of-bitches about now," Nixon said to Alsop. "You know what I mean? That's an impossible job anyway, but you need a son-of-a-bitch in it. Like Tom Dewey. Dewey's not going to get the Secretary of Defense or any job in this Administration. You know the way he talks, the way he'll say 'That's a lot of horseshit,' or something like that. The President doesn't like him." The vice president, apparently referring to what he regarded as the administration's relatively relaxed approach to defense issues, continued, "This 'togetherness' bullshit. I don't believe in that. I think the time will come when we'll look back at this era and ask ourselves whether we were crazy or something."

When it came to the military budget, Nixon believed that his opinions were more tolerated than respected and that the president saw him through a reductive lens. "Now, you have to understand my position," Nixon said. "The President, with his military training I suppose, tends to put people in a category. He listens to me, he respects my judgment, on political matters, he regards me as a political expert only—if I try to speak up on defense matters, say, from a strict military point of view, he says, 'What does this guy know about it?' So I put the case on a political basis."

When Alsop suggested that it might be politically beneficial for Nixon to speak out on defense questions, Nixon reminded him that he was "still a part of this Administration," meaning that he was bound by the rule that a vice president always defers to a president. When Alsop asked straight out if Eisenhower would turn against him, Nixon replied, "I don't think Eisenhower is going to try to dictate the candidate in 1960, but I think he will use his power to prevent any candidate he doesn't want from getting it." Nixon had always found it hard to gauge what was on Eisenhower's mind, but people close to the president could see that, as he admitted to Charles von Fremd, the job's physical demands were wearing him down. "When I wake up in the morning," he wrote to his oldest brother, Arthur, in November, "I sometimes wonder just what new problem can possibly be laid on my desk during the day to come. There always seems to be an even more complex one than I could have imagined."

CHAPTER 15

Should He Resign?

1

On the afternoon of November 25, 1957, President Eisenhower attended to his ceremonial duties as head of state, a task far less strenuous than having to deal with artificial moons or southern governors. The king of Morocco, Mohammed V, was in town for a state visit, and during the welcoming rituals at National Airport, people noticed that Eisenhower, who was bare-headed, had several times pulled out a handkerchief and blown his nose. By the time of the twenty-one-gun salute, he had begun to look as if he was suffering more than mere sniffles, and when he got back to the White House after a long procession, he told Mrs. Eisenhower that he felt a chill coming on.

Later that afternoon, when Eisenhower picked up a pen to sign some papers, he began to experience a strange dizziness. That lasted just a mo-ment, but when he reached for a sheet of paper, he found it difficult to hold on to it. That was frustrating, then a little alarming, and finally bewilder-ing, especially when he found that the words, as he put it, "seemed literally to run off the top of the page." He dropped his pen—then wasn't able to pick it up. When he tried to stand, he found that he had to grip a chair, and soon enough he buzzed for his interim appointments secretary, Robert Keith Gray, who gathered his folders and hurried in. Gray noticed that

Ike had removed his glasses and that, in a jerky motion, he folded them and tried to put them in his breast pocket. "These . . . darned . . . glasses," he said, as they slipped out of his hand and onto the carpet. When Gray asked if he could do anything, Eisenhower, speaking very slowly, said, "No no . . . not . . . now . . . thanks." Gray realized that he'd been dismissed when Ike picked a paper from the stack in front of him and appeared to read it. When the president called Ann Whitman, she came at once, but then she couldn't understand what he wanted to say.

The president refused to leave his desk, and Mrs. Whitman heard him say, or try to say, "Go away from me." Then Andrew Goodpaster, the president's staff secretary, arrived and was able to persuade Ike to accompany him to the living quarters. Whitman called Howard Snyder, the president's doctor, and went to Sherman Adams's office; she looked to Adams as if she were about to cry. "The President has gone back to the house," she said to Adams. "He tried to tell me something but he couldn't express himself. Something seemed to have happened to him all of a sudden." She added, "I can't imagine what's wrong with him."

Eisenhower didn't know, either, but he knew that he was speaking gibberish. Colonel Goodpaster told him, "Mr. President, I think we should get you to bed."

The always attentive Dr. Snyder, after a quick examination, thought that Ike might have the flu, and recommended rest. But after a nap, the president's speech difficulties hadn't gone away. And there were matters that had to be attended to, starting with the state dinner that night. These dinners were elaborate affairs, with toasts and a heavy meal, plus music and sometimes dancing afterward; and it was obvious that Eisenhower was in no shape for this one. Leonard Heaton, the commandant of the Walter Reed Medical Center (he had overseen the president's operation for ileitis), hurried to the White House, accompanied by specialists in neurology and internal medicine. The doctors quickly decided that the president was not in mortal danger; his temperature was normal, and his pulse and blood pressure and outward signs were regular enough. But something was seriously wrong, that was clear, and it did not take long to conclude that he had suffered a cerebral occlusion—a stroke.

Adams, Goodpaster, and Snyder talked with Mrs. Eisenhower, who was deeply upset by what was happening to her husband. They discussed what to do about the dinner for the king. Should Mrs. Eisenhower go alone, should Dick and Pat Nixon take over, or should it be canceled altogether? By then, the president's son, John Eisenhower, had joined them, and as they were talking, the president materialized in a doorway, dressed in a brown-checked bathrobe, and took a seat in an easy chair as if nothing were out of the ordinary. "What are you doing up, Ike?" Mamie asked, with something of a gasp. He started to say something, "I suppose you are dis—" but he struggled with the rest of the sentence: "—talking about the dinner tonight." The president was becoming increasingly annoyed at this novel problem. "There's nothing the matter with me!" he insisted. "I am perfectly all right!" But he wasn't all right, which only made him more impatient, particularly as he kept saying words that had no relation to the words he was thinking of. "We can't let him go down there in this condition," Mamie said.

Adams agreed, and so did Dr. Snyder, who tried to persuade the president that people would notice his speech impediment and exaggerate its import. Adams said that the king would understand his absence and that the Nixons would be happy to fill in—which was not what Eisenhower wanted to be told. His face reddened—that characteristic angry flush—as he shook his head and said, "If I cannot attend to my duties, I am simply going to give up this job. Now that is all there is to it." After that, he walked out of the room, and one could hear that he was muttering something about a NATO conference in Paris, which he was scheduled to attend and which was just two weeks off.

Nixon learned about Ike's latest illness when Sherman Adams called his Senate office late that afternoon. When Nixon asked how serious it was, Adams said, "We'll know more in the morning." Then Adams, who so often was abrupt, became surprisingly emotional. "This is a terribly, terribly difficult thing to handle," he said. "You may be President in the next twenty-four hours."

At 6:20 P.M., the country was informed that the president had a chill and wouldn't attend the dinner for the king of Morocco or deliver a speech the next day in Cleveland. At the dinner that night, Mamie Eisenhower greeted her guests without showing any sign that something was wrong. But when she spoke to Nixon, who was standing in for the president, she mentioned her husband's heart attack and the ileitis operation and then, for just an instant, her voice broke and she said, "This really is too much for any one man to bear." Nixon tried to reassure her—he had mastered the art of the solicitous comment, the comforting truism: Ike after all had made rapid recoveries in the past; he was a strong man. But Nixon was worried on several levels. Unlike the autumn of 1955, the international situation this time was not so calm—not with two Russian satellites circling the earth—and doctors had said that this episode might be the first of many strokes, the next ones far more debilitating.

Jim Hagerty, Eisenhower's press secretary, had gone to Paris in advance of the NATO meeting, so a deputy told reporters on Tuesday morning that the president was "progressing very well," but did not say from what, a mysterious statement that wasn't clarified until that afternoon when the press was informed that Ike had suffered a stroke and that "while the present condition is mild and is expected to be transitory in nature, it will require a period of rest and substantially decreased activity estimated at several weeks." There were reassuring reports that the president's reasoning powers were unaffected, and not a hint of what family members and doctors had witnessed that morning when he had pointed to a favorite watercolor, a Turner depicting Culzean Castle in Scotland, and, as John Eisenhower described it, "Dad began to burble, trying to name it. The more he tried, the more frustrated he became. He thrashed on the double bed, beating the bedclothes with his fists."

"This third sickness further reduces a vigor, a capacity to lead that had already been grievously impaired," the *Reporter* magazine's editorial said; inside the White House, the staff didn't know what to make of it. "It was a very—a sad time—we were all just holding fire, waiting," the aide Rocco Siciliano recalled. The public had a quite different reaction to the stroke than it had had to the heart attack. "Nobody in official circles really accepts the pretense that all will soon be well," the columnist Doris Fleeson wrote, adding ominously, "What is in the offing is a struggle for power such as this capital has not seen since the Civil War." Almost immediately, there were suggestions that Ike ought simply to resign. The *New York Post*, a friend of neither Ike nor Dick, published an editorial saying, "The issue is whether the U.S. is to have Richard Nixon as President or no President. We choose Nixon." James Reston went so far as to suggest that Ike was getting stupid: "We are in a race with the pace of history. We are in a time when brain power is more important than fire power, but in the last five years the President has gradually drifted apart from the intellectual opinion of the country, filled up his social hours with bantering locker-room cronies, and denied himself the mental stimulus that is always available to any President." Others did not take so drastic a view. Walter Lippmann wanted Nixon to have "temporarily and only for the period of his convalescence . . . the powers and duties of his office, but not the office itself." Perhaps sensing the arrival of a new regent, Lippmann now described the vice president—whom he had regarded for years as one regards a poisonous insect—as someone "who has been maturing successfully" and recently has shown that "he has the vigor and boldness to go in the direction that Mr. Eisenhower himself would go, if he had the necessary vigor of mind and body." The editorial writers at the *New York Herald Tribune*, as if facing the worst, wrote that "No President since Washington has been more beloved by the American people."

Ann Whitman thought that Eisenhower's condition had improved remarkably in less than twenty-four hours, although that was worrisome, too—he was suddenly *too* eager to do things and his doctors wanted him to rest. On the Wednesday before Thanksgiving, he told Mrs. Whitman that he might just head over to his office and hold a press conference. He spoke on the telephone, signed papers, and met with Nixon, Adams, and Goodpaster; in the afternoon he spent ten minutes with King Mohammed, the king's son, and their interpreter. He said that he not only might attend the NATO meeting but perhaps even deliver that speech in Cleveland.

Jim Hagerty, who had hurried back from Paris, tried to answer questions about the president's condition. Did he have trouble speaking? ("Slight difficulty on long words.") Did he shave himself, or was it done by his valet? (Ike did it himself.) There were questions about anticoagulants and spinal taps and possible paralysis. (There was none.) Later, with Hagerty at his side, the vice president spoke with reporters.

Nixon by then had gotten used to stepping in—this was the president's third medical emergency—but this was the first time that he had stepped *forward* in this way, and with a White House backdrop, too. To be sure, the press had asked for him and Hagerty had encouraged him to do it, but Nixon was sensitive about conducting a formal Q-and-A in that place. He insisted that the president was still in charge while knowing that he was not; in fact, although he did not say it, the government was again being run by a committee. (*The New Republic* thought that Congress ought to make this government-by-committee an official body, much like the National Security Council.) Yet even though the team was in place, Nixon could neither explain how decisions were being made nor even who was presiding at meetings. "I think that the question is perhaps a rather difficult one to answer with proper description," he said, and continued:

> There is actually, I would say, no presiding in the sense we think of it. We gather around the table and the—in Governor Adams's office, and the Secretary of Defense knows why he is there and he says "this is the problem." He presents it. And there is no problem of recognition as to this person speaks and then this person, in deciding, which requires a presiding officer.

When Nixon was asked to define his own role with the president, his answer was both tortured and deft:

> My role at the present time I think is best described by my title. I am the Vice President. I don't mean to be facetious, but I would emphasize that the—in a situation of this type, it is true that the Vice President does assume some additional duties. Most of those duties are ceremonial, as for example, my attendance at the dinner for the King of Morocco. . . . Some of those duties involve consultation with the Cabinet officers and others in clearing away non-essentials and in preparing subjects for presentation to the President, which he must decide. And preparing those in such a way that he can decide them in a limited time.

Someone finally dared to ask the question that was on everyone's mind:

Q: . . . Now I realize this may be a somewhat embarrassing question to put to you—
NIXON: No questions are embarrassing.

Q—but do you have any reason to believe that the President may be considering resigning?
NIXON: I have no reason whatever to believe that the President is considering or will consider resigning. After having seen him, after having talked also to his doctor, I am convinced that, one, that his recovery is sure, and that it very well may be even sooner than would normally be the case, although no one can give a prognosis in these cases. . . . I would like to scotch once and for all if I can any rumors to the effect that the President, first, is in a condition which would make it necessary for him to consider resigning, and second, that the President himself or anybody in the President's official family have discussed or are considering the possibility of resignation.

Nixon also declared that "the President is champing at the bit. He is very anxious to get back over to the office," and while Nixon was not actually fibbing, neither was he being forthright. He had heard the president say "window" when he meant to say "mirror," and say "ceiling" when he meant to say "floor." The truth was that Eisenhower's determination to hurry back was beginning to alarm his aides as well as his doctors. Foster Dulles had even telephoned Nixon to complain about Ike's bursts of energy and said that they were going to tell him that "he could not go to NATO unless he behaved."

Nixon's press conference in any case had gone well—"without a bobble," as James Reston put it. Nixon knew it, too. In a handwritten note to himself, he wrote, *'55 [heart attack]—had to prove self with Cabinet; '57 position recognized.* It was as if Reston, like Lippmann, had witnessed a complete Nixon transformation; moreover, Reston declared that the vice president "even looks different. He seems to have lost a little weight. His hair is cut closer on the sides and on top. His speech is more vivid and articulate and his manner more patient and courteous."

• • •

On Thanksgiving morning, Hagerty told reporters that the president was going to church, and the Eisenhowers drove the half mile from the White House to the National Presbyterian Church, where they sat in a fifth-row pew, joined the congregation in singing hymns, and heard the Reverend Edward L. R. Elson offer a special prayer for the president. That would not have been easy on an ordinary day; Ike regarded Elson as "a complete phony," according to Mrs. Whitman, and complained generally about going to church. On this Thanksgiving, when the president left the church (he was wrapped in a heavy overcoat) a crowd of about three hundred standing outside applauded him. He smiled, but it was not the usual broad Eisenhower grin. That evening, he had turkey with Mamie, his son, John, his daughter-in-law, Barbara, and his four grandchildren. On Friday, the Eisenhowers were driven to Gettysburg for the weekend.

The next day, Foster Dulles called Nixon to talk about plans for a cabinet meeting that had been scheduled for Monday. They needed to give the agenda more thought, Dulles said, and Nixon agreed, saying that he'd like to shorten it—make it a little more "punchy"; he told Dulles that Eisenhower might insist on being there, at least to open the meeting. As for a congressional leaders meeting that was set for Tuesday, Dulles thought it would be fine if the president wanted to make a brief appearance; no one liked coming in from the Hill unless the president was present. Nixon said that he didn't care if the congressional delegation stayed away—he wasn't going to urge the president to make an extra effort for their sake. Hagerty meanwhile was telling reporters that the president was making excellent progress—that on Saturday, for instance, he had watched the Army-Navy football game. But Hagerty's cheerful bulletins bore no resemblance to what was being said in private, even among Ike's friends, such as gang members George Allen and Cliff Roberts, who had hurried to see him in Gettysburg. Roberts thought that there was something different about Ike: his eyes appeared to him "a little stare-y" and his speech was more deliberate than usual—"when he speeded up he would occasionally have to stop and grope for the right word." The president told his golfing companion that he couldn't decide whether to go to the NATO meeting or to send Nixon—that, as Roberts noted, "his big problem was whether to resign or not, that on domestic problems he felt someone else could do just as well as he could, that on foreign problems he felt that he was possibly better equipped to keep things from breaking out into open warfare than anybody else."

Dulles could not get his mind off what had happened when Woodrow Wilson had his stroke, and on the Sunday of Thanksgiving weekend, he telephoned the vice president again. He said that they were liable to run into a situation where the president was incapable of acting and didn't realize it. Nixon replied that he was worried, too; he thought that Eisenhower's judgment was not good and that no one around him "would be able to exercise judgment or control." Dulles brought up something else—something that concerned Nixon directly: for the first time, Dulles had gotten the impression—there was nothing specific—that Eisenhower was sensitive about Nixon's conduct as vice president. Such misgivings were in the air; General Lucius Clay, whose animus toward Nixon was easily awakened, later confessed his suspicion that Nixon was preparing to take over some presidential duties. "I can't say that I had any foundation for it," Clay said, "but this was a concern that I had." For his part, Dulles said, Nixon had "handled this thing to perfection," but he still couldn't help worrying that the situation might turn into a "reproduction of the Wilson problem, jealousy and usurpation of power." Dulles also worried about Eisenhower's disposition—for instance his eagerness to return to Washington and his sharp flare of temper over an editorial in the *New York Times*. The upsetting commentary was undoubtedly one entitled "To Carry the Load," which said that a "shifting committee of government officials and Cabinet officers appeared to be exercising power in the President's name," and that illness would likely prevent his attendance at the NATO meeting—a decision that "apparently was reached without consulting the President." It was time, the newspaper said, for Congress to "clarify the disability provision in the Constitution." Dulles called Dr. Heaton at Walter Reed to ask if there might be a way to "control him medically."

But the president had taken charge of his own case and on Monday, December 2, he returned to Washington to preside at the cabinet meeting. After that, he tried to keep up his schedule, and attended meetings with congressional leaders on Tuesday and Republican congressmen on Wednesday.

When Eisenhower saw the legislators, there was a surprise guest: Adlai Stevenson. His attendance was a result of an unusual exercise in bipartisanship, beginning that October when Dulles had asked Stevenson to help prepare the agenda for the upcoming NATO meeting. Bipartisanship was nothing new in the administration, but after Sputnik and Little Rock, it made particular sense to offer a role to top Democrats; and no Democrat, with the possible exception of Harry Truman, was Stevenson's rival in prestige or influence. Even Nixon, according to Dulles, "expressed enthusiasm for the idea and hoped that it would work out."

Dulles and Stevenson had a fairly easy relationship—they had friends in common, and their views, when one stripped away their personal tics (witty Adlai, dour Foster), were not all that dissimilar. Eisenhower had never much liked Stevenson, and the feeling was mutual, but he respected him, apart from what he felt was Stevenson's over-fondness for "phrase-making." Mutual affection was not required for a working relationship, but Stevenson was especially alert to slights, or signs of disrespect, and when the *New York Times* in mid-November reported that he had accepted the role of "consultant" in preparing for the Paris talks, Stevenson made it a point to describe himself only as a "temporary tenant" at the State Department.

These careful arrangements were shaken by the president's illness. Dulles had immediately informed Stevenson that Eisenhower might require weeks of rest, which would prevent his going to Paris. If that were the case, Dulles continued, the vice president would probably attend. Publicly Stevenson said that he prayed for the president's recovery and planned to stay on to help. Privately, he advised Dulles that it would be unwise to dispatch Nixon rather than, say, senior members of the cabinet, and that he personally would be reluctant to go if he had to be together in Paris with the vice president, whom he had never stopped loathing.

After the legislators meeting, Stevenson, accompanied by Dulles, saw Eisenhower privately—the first time in four years that they'd met. They had a friendly talk, but something that was said—some ambivalence about his role—disturbed Stevenson. *Had* the president invited Stevenson to accompany him to Paris? he was asked by reporters. "I don't know whether I've been invited or not," Stevenson said, uncomfortably. Even though Stevenson agreed with many administration policies, he had worried about inadvertently endorsing all of them; in addition, members of his party were uneasy at this collaboration, and later that day, it all unraveled. On Department of State stationery, Stevenson told the president that "unless there were compelling and unforeseen developments," he wasn't going to the NATO conference. Eisenhower was startled by Stevenson's quibbling over language. "He said 'I have not been invited, but I've been asked to go,' " he said to Dulles. "What the hell does that mean? I think the man is fuzzy."

Then it was Nixon's turn; he asked Ann Whitman for an appointment with the president that afternoon. It was a rare request—Ike usually initiated their meetings—but these were unusual circumstances, and much of what they said, directly and not, had to do with Eisenhower's health. Nixon by then had already heard from Dr. Arnold Hutschnecker, who informed his occasional patient that "precise clinical data alone are not sufficient to determine an individual state of health nor to predict an impending illness." Hutschnecker proposed sending the president a copy of his book, *The Will to Live,* and soon did so. Ike knew what people were saying about him—those suggestions that he ought to resign, or take what amounted to a medical leave, those gratingly solicitous editorials and columns. He had already told Dulles that if he was unable to go to the NATO meeting, people would question whether he should continue in office or "abdicate," and when he saw Nixon, he told him that he'd regarded the week's various meetings as a sort of trial run, if he'd needed to skip them, he would have had to do some "very hard and tough thinking about the future." Nixon was solicitous, too, but he could overdo it, and he urged the president not to confuse his difficulty finding the right phrase or word (Ike said that he couldn't remember the word for "thermostat") with the common experience of being at a loss for words.

Dulles had forewarned him, but now Nixon sensed that something wasn't quite right between them. Nothing was said directly, but when the president said that he thought he'd return for a few days to Gettysburg— that it didn't seem important to schedule any more meetings right away—he added, "this is in your best interests too because of the possible impression of stepping in and exerting authority." In a memo to himself afterward, Nixon wrote, "This was the only point in the conversation where I sensed that he may have had some feeling of resentment that we had called the Cabinet meeting and Security Council meeting and undertaken other activities in his absence. This was true even though when Adams and I had seen him a few days ago Adams told him that we planned to have meetings and the President indicated for us to go ahead and 'maybe he would try to stop by.' "

Nixon had reckoned on staying for ten minutes, but they talked for an hour and ten minutes, and when he emerged, he told Mrs. Whitman that the president would not let him go. Eisenhower's thoughts seemed to be racing. At one point he came up with a meta-Constitutional suggestion concerning a new sort of role for Nixon: if the vice president could just be relieved of his duties of presiding over the Senate, he could move to the East Wing with his own personal staff and see people when there was no reason for the president to see them. It wasn't just a stray thought, either, although it vanished almost as quickly as it was introduced. Eisenhower said very much the same thing to Bill Rogers, who had succeeded Herbert Brownell as attorney general in late 1957. Rogers, like Dulles and Nixon, also sensed that Eisenhower was not pleased that decisions of any sort were being made in his absence.

The president the next day sent an "Eyes Only-Personal" cable to Prime Minister Harold Macmillan, in which he basically denied his illness— "The earliest symptoms of my indisposition were sufficiently slight that the doctors did not class the difficulty as a 'stroke,' " he said, although he did admit having suffered "a marked 'word confusion,' with, also, some loss of memory of words alone." He concluded, "All this means, as of this moment, that I am planning to be at the NATO meeting in mid-month." What Ike did not say was that he saw the conference in Paris as another test: he had decided that if he carried it off successfully, he would finish his second term; if not, he would resign.

About fifty people—diplomats and government officials led by Nixon— waved goodbye when the president on December 13 boarded the Columbine III for the twenty-two-hour flight to Paris. It was cold and getting dark and the scene was improbable; few had expected that Eisenhower, two and a half weeks after suffering a stroke, however minor, would make this journey; onlookers called out "Good luck." People were worried about how he'd hold up; in Paris, there was a brief panic in the press corps when he skipped a scheduled dinner at the Elysées Palace, but the next day he was attending meetings again. When he returned to Washington a week later, his color was good, and one had to listen closely for any hesitancy in his speech. Yet a more general worry—that he would be a part-timer for the remaining years of his presidency—was not dispelled even when he delivered the State of the Union address on January 9, speaking for nearly forty-five minutes and only rarely stumbling over a word. The House chamber provided its usual divided applause, but there was general cheering at the sight of an apparently vigorous president and one could see that Mrs. Eisenhower never took her eyes off her husband. It was an oddly constructed speech—defensive when the president conceded that "we are probably somewhat behind the Soviets in some areas of long-range ballistic missile development." And was he blaming the Democrats when he said, "When it is remembered that our country has concentrated on the development of ballistic missiles for only about a third as long as the Soviets, [America's] achievements show a rate of progress that speaks for itself"?

Back at work, the president didn't ignore what he'd just been through, and when he sent Nixon his usual birthday greeting, he did something altogether uncharacteristic: he thanked him for carrying on, writing, "May I say once again how grateful I am for your understanding and help over these last difficult weeks?" A week after the State of the Union, he held a press conference—his first since his stroke—where he was asked about his health and said, "I feel very well indeed. If I had sunlight this afternoon and had two hours, I would like to be on the golf course right now, and that is what I would like to do. But no one can tell what the physical future is." Yet he was never quite the same; an aura of frailty never went away. His aide Bryce Harlow recalled that "for a period of some weeks and months after the stroke, the President went through a period of great difficulty in going through a press conference, to have any sureness that what was in his thinking would come out saying precisely what he wanted to say." More reporters were ordered to travel with him, even on routine trips. Robert Novak, who was then with *The Wall Street Journal*, said, "After that stroke, he was a death waiting to happen."

CHAPTER 16

Dirty Work

1

Eisenhower was not one to dwell on the transience of human life, but he was deeply aware of how his death or disability might affect the nation. The question of presidential succession was often on his mind; it was a subject of conversations with his two attorneys general—Herbert Brownell and William Rogers—after his heart attack in September 1955, and if anything he became more fixated on it after his stroke, when he brought it up with Nixon and Rogers.

Little more than two months after that episode, he sent Nixon a carefully worded memorandum on the question of presidential inability: it discussed what was to be done if he couldn't perform his job or, what was more delicate, if he was unable to recognize his own incapacity. Eisenhower did not like to think about the prospect of turning the presidency over to Nixon, but he never believed that his vice president would actually try to usurp him, and on the central question of transferring power Eisenhower used the language of a trusting colleague; rather than a general set of guidelines with all their accompanying Constitutional questions, he chose to propose some specific ones "so far as you and I are concerned . . . particularly in view of our mutual confidence and friendship" and continued,

... you will be the individual explicitly and exclusively responsible for determining whether there is any inability of mine that makes it necessary for you to discharge the powers and duties of the Presidency, and you will decide the exact timing of the devolution of this responsibility on you. . . . I will be the one to determine if and when it is proper for me to resume the powers and duties of the Presidency.

As for the more sensitive question—that "I might, without warning, become personally incapable of making a decision at the moment when it should be made"—the memorandum continued,

The existence of this agreement recognizing your clear and exclusive responsibility for deciding upon the inability of the President to perform his duties and exercise his powers will remove any necessity or desire on the part of friends and staffs to impede the right and authority of the Vice President in reaching his decision on the matter.

The memorandum, which was dated February 5, 1958, was shown first only to Nixon and a few others, but a month later the gist of it was made public. When Eisenhower at a news conference was asked about "this pact between yourself and the Vice President," he replied, "No, this isn't a pact. . . . We are not trying to rewrite the Constitution. We are trying just to say that we are trying to carry out what normal humans of good faith having some confidence in each other would do in accordance with the language of the Constitution." When he was asked whether power being transferred back and forth between president and vice president might lead to "a sort of musical chairs," he replied, "I think it means when the inability is removed he resumes his duties," and added, "I admit this: if a man were so deranged that he thought he was able, and the consensus was that he couldn't, there would have to be something else done." But the administration *was* trying to tinker with the Constitution, and Congress had separately begun to study the question, too.

Eisenhower and his advisers had tried to anticipate the major problems. One Justice Department memo looked at what might happen if the president, having temporarily surrendered his office, then disagreed with the vice president over his fitness to resume it. It cited the case of Governor

Henry Horner of Illinois, who, after a series of illnesses in 1938, had a disruptive struggle for control when his lieutenant governor assumed the office. Attorney General Rogers got so interested in this untested question that he consulted a Supreme Court justice, Felix Frankfurter, who believed that the Constitution ignored the issue because of a "realization by the Framers that almost any means created its own problems and that therefore the matter was to be left to the pressure of events whenever the contingency arose." Rogers's suggestion that the Committee on Style had ducked its responsibility seemed almost to offend Frankfurter, who wrote "I need hardly add that there were no keener, more resourceful draftsmen than Hamilton and Madison"—two of the committee's five members—and repeated his belief that they had purposely "concluded to leave the matter in the undefined form in which it now stands."

Rogers, though, had something far more specific in mind, namely how a presidential incapacity might affect Nixon or his eventual successors. Because of "uncertainty as to whether the office or the powers and duties of the office devolve on the Vice President in case of inability of a President," he wrote to Frankfurter, until it's "clearly established . . . that the devolution involves only the powers and duties of the office and is temporary," it was going to be a difficult problem. Frankfurter conceded the point, but seemed to take it less seriously than Rogers; after all, he pointed out, there had been only two cases in which it might have been an issue: after the attempt in 1881 to assassinate President James Garfield, who lingered for eleven weeks before dying of gunshot wounds, and in the aftermath of Woodrow Wilson's disabling stroke.

This was relatively new legal territory (it led to what became the 25th Amendment, which was passed by Congress in 1965 and ratified two years later), and the discussion raised issues that are still relevant, such as what role the Supreme Court ought to play in a political dispute. The idea that the Court might become involved in an issue like presidential succession horrified Assistant Attorney General Malcolm Wilkey, whose memorandum, as if anticipating *Bush v. Gore*, argued that "Once you convert the Court to deciding political questions, you identify the character of the Court as a political rather than as a judicial body," adding that when the Court gets into the political arena, "it may inflict upon itself a fatal wound." A president's incapacity, Wilkey believed, should be determined by the vice president and the cabinet; and Congress if need be could safeguard the process. In certain cases of presidential incapacity—say an enfeebled president who clung to his office—the legislature could act just as it would in cases of impeachment, although without the "odium" of an actual impeachment. It all seemed improvised, and was, but without a law or precedent to guide them, Eisenhower, Nixon, and their legal kibitzers had probably arrived at a design that would have worked.

Perhaps it was the uncertainty over the president's health, or simply that he was nearing the midpoint of his second term, but the succession issue led to more questions as to whether, in a vague, what-lies-at-his-core sort of way, Richard Nixon was ready—would *ever* be ready—to be president. For Democrats in particular, there was that "we do not like thee Doctor Fell" problem, but Eisenhower did not seem eager to embrace the idea, either; he sometimes sounded as if he thought that Nixon was scratching at the White House door. At press conferences, the vice president was sometimes the subtext—and for mischievous reporters the unnamed text, as during this colloquy in April:

> Q: *I think it fair to say, Mr. President, I think there is some dissatis-faction in both major political parties with the obvious candidate to succeed you as President. I wonder, do you think that the President has any responsibility to encourage those not in political life to seek the Presidency?*
> A: I don't know exactly what the purport of your question is.
>
> Q: *That is not a loaded question, Mr. President.*
> A: Well, I mean this: I don't have any responsibility for trying to groom any successor.
>
> Q: *Not "groom," Mr. President. I had in mind, in a general sense, to suggest that perhaps the parties themselves might go outside what we might call professional politicians to seek possible candidates.*
> A: . . . Now remember this, with respect to the case between Mr. Nixon and me: we are warm friends. I admire him and I re-

spect him. I have said this dozens of times. . . . Now, when it comes
to the successor, as far as I am concerned, the candidates will be
named by the Republican Party and I submit that I think there is a
lot of darn good men that could be used.

Eisenhower's remarks could be—and were—interpreted as exhibiting
a certain coolness toward his vice president. Who knew? It was a good
moment for Nixon to leave town for what was meant to be a short goodwill tour of South America, although there was never a way to escape the
eruptions of domestic politics. In Argentina, Nixon carefully said that
Eisenhower had taken the "proper and only position" in avoiding any early
commitment for 1960, and two days later, in La Paz, Bolivia, he went into
a rambling discussion about the office, this dilation possibly abetted by
the altitude. (Although La Paz is more than thirteen thousand feet above
sea level, the Nixons refused the offer of oxygen tanks.) "Those who seek
the Presidency seldom win it," Nixon said, adding that it "is one office in
which circumstances, rather than a man's ability, usually determine the
result. If it is the right man at the right time, he will be chosen."

There were not many reporters on the tour; Nixon had said that he
didn't expect it to be newsworthy. As it turned out, he was wrong about
the newsworthiness of a trip that ended abruptly in Caracas, Venezuela,
when cars carrying the vice president, Pat Nixon, and their party were surrounded by a stone-throwing mob that seemed intent on murdering them.
A frequently recounted moment came when Jack Sherwood, one of six
Secret Service agents on the trip, drew his revolver and said, "I guess we're
going to have to kill some of these sons of bitches," to which Nixon was
quoted as saying, "If you do, they'll tear us to pieces." A last-minute intervention by Venezuelan soldiers allowed the motorcade to make its escape
to the hotel where the Nixons were staying and where Nixon, in a cold
fury, went to his room and demonstratively lay down as if to nap; he made
the new junta wait for nearly an hour before he listened to their apology.

The experience was as politically beneficial as it was fearsome; the Caracas mobs were on television and in newspapers, and when the Nixons
returned to Washington, they were welcomed at National Airport by the
president, cabinet members, leaders of Congress, as well as their frightened
daughters. People stood along the streets, too, a reception that Bob Hum-

phreys, Nixon's ally since the fund episode, had planned even before the Nixons got to Venezuela. But as Humphreys put it later, "Needless to say, what had started as a reasonably good bonfire was turned overnight into a roaring conflagration."

Nixon had come a long way since 1954, when he was called into Eisenhower's office and scolded for his intemperate language; now, unlike Eisenhower, he had a political future that might include the presidency. Over the summer, he was present when real issues of war and peace were at stake, such as Eisenhower's decision to send in the Marines, with supporting air and sea power, to Lebanon when the region was roiled by the murder of the Anglophile Iraqi royal family. Dulles and Nixon had opposed the intervention, and at one point Nixon said, "You cannot allow it to appear that the Mideast countries are simply a pawn in the big power contest for their resources"; Eisenhower, though, saw the region's oil reserves as pretty much the whole point. In mid-August, when the Chinese Communists started shelling Quemoy and Matsu for the second time in three years, it again seemed possible that a "small" nuclear war might ensue if the offshore islands were attacked. During a discussion in Eisenhower's office, which was not declassified until the spring of 2011, General Nathan Twining, the chairman of the Joint Chiefs, expressed confidence that the Communist bloc wouldn't drop atomic bombs on Taiwan even if the United States dropped them "on a few of their air bases." Nixon at the meeting sounded just as uneasy as Eisenhower and endorsed a vague statement about regional peace that had been issued by the Nationalist foreign minister. But the shelling stopped, just as it had four years earlier, and the second Taiwan Strait crisis, like the first one, ended quietly and a little mysteriously.

2

Nixon and Sherman Adams, the White House chief of staff, never grew fond of each other, but their duties rarely overlapped, their offices were at opposite ends of Pennsylvania Avenue, and they tended to stay out of each other's way. So of all the tasks assigned to Nixon by Eisenhower, none was quite as onerous as being ordered to fire Adams, whose secret life was first uncovered in May 1958, in several installments, by the muckraker-columnist Jack Anderson. The wire service stories that followed contained many of the phrases that alarm officeholders everywhere: Adams's bills for a "plush Boston hotel" had been paid by a "millionaire industrialist," a man named Bernard Goldfine who was accused, furthermore, of "obtaining government favors," namely interceding with federal regulatory agencies. The idea that Adams was a man on the take seemed completely out of character or—which was not the same thing—the character that Adams played: a New Englander of brusqueness, rectitude, and stern loyalty.

The Eisenhower years had been pretty much free of scandal, and one reason for that was the presence of Adams, whose uprightness seemed unassailable. By modern standards, Adams's lapse seemed barely to cross the scandal threshold. Goldfine, the "millionaire industrialist," was an Adams friend and former constituent; the hotel bills that he paid amounted to little more than $2,000 over a four-year period. The next round of disclosures—that Goldfine had given Adams an oriental rug worth $2,400 and a vicuña coat with a market value of $700—was more damaging, but that appeared to be about it. What no one then appeared to know—and what Robert F. Kennedy's Justice Department apparently discovered a few years later—was that Adams may have accepted as much as $400,000 in unreported cash payments during his White House years. Adams in any case conceded that he'd been imprudent, but insisted that there was nothing wrong with accepting gifts from a friend and that there had been no quid pro quo.

Democrats thought that these revelations sounded very much like the "mess in Washington" that Eisenhower in 1952 had promised to clean up. Vicuña coats and Persian rugs and "plush" hotel suites were, come to think of it, not unlike freezers and mink coats and five percenters. Ike expressed his concern about Adams at a news conference on June 18, when he said that "the utmost prudence must necessarily be observed by everyone attached to the White House," while saying of Adams, "I admire his abilities. I respect him because of his personal and official integrity. I need him." Those last three words were quoted repeatedly in the weeks and months that followed.

The removal of Sherman Adams did not go quickly or smoothly; it was hard for Eisenhower to fire anyone—no one knew that better than Nixon, who had the same difficulty—and the last person that Ike wanted to get rid of was Adams. It turned into a chore that presented a kind of historical symmetry: if Nixon during the fund crisis was a potential drag on the presidential ticket, Republicans, who had already begun to stare into the abyss of the post-Eisenhower era, believed that Adams could damage them in the 1958 midterms.

Nixon's errand was to nudge Adams to resign while not actually saying that Eisenhower wanted him to quit. He certainly felt a shock of recognition at getting this assignment, but he knew Ike's style. The first time that he talked to Adams in mid-July, he tried to follow instructions. He told him that the president felt such loyalty that he didn't even want to consider a resignation; but then, like a gentle prosecutor, he began to present all the reasons why Adams should decide for himself to quit. After Nixon mentioned the Goldfine matter, which Adams agreed had been "pretty bad," Nixon noted that most Republicans in Congress wanted him to leave, and on top of that, there was the problem that he was creating for Eisenhower. Personally, Nixon continued, he knew that no one worked as hard—or as quickly or as efficiently and decisively—as Adams, and that it would be very difficult to replace him. And yet the "clamoring" for his resignation was bound to get worse in the fall, with the impending election.

Nixon proceeded with this operation with almost surgical precision, especially when he said "I would be less than candid if I did not say it was a very distressing situation and would continue to be so for a long period of time." When Nixon said that Adams needed to decide his fate for himself and Adams replied that it was up to the president, the dialogue sounded familiar to someone who not so long before had been asked to chart his own course. Nixon hated being forced to do this. After talking with Adams, he called Foster Dulles. He was sick of the Adams affair, he said—Eisenhower simply had to tell Adams himself what he wanted him to do.

In the latter part of August, the four Nixons went to White Sulphur Springs, West Virginia, to the Greenbrier, a two-hundred-year-old resort that offered just about everything from golf to horseback riding to fishing, none of which particularly appealed to Nixon but gave his wife and daughters a chance to escape the mugginess of a Washington summer. "Every vacation we had planned since coming to Congress in 1947 had been cut short," Nixon thought, "but this time it would be different." Yet the vice president had a restless boss. On the very morning that the Nixons checked in at the Greenbrier, Eisenhower telephoned with a request—Adams again: "I wonder if you could talk to Sherm now that the Congress is out," the president said. He mentioned that the Republican National Committee was about to meet in Chicago, and "I was really hoping that we could get the matter resolved before then."

Nixon obediently hurried back to Washington, arriving in late afternoon, and when he saw Eisenhower the next day, the president told him "to talk bluntly to Adams about the political realities of the situation we faced." As Nixon understood it, he still wasn't being ordered to ask for Adams's resignation, although Eisenhower wanted that result—again, it had to be said and yet not said directly. So this time, when he spoke to Adams, he talked about how Adams was hurting Republican candidates. "Who will take my place?" Adams asked. "I've never heard anyone suggested." He also asked, "What do you think is the President's view?"

"He hasn't told me to tell you this, Sherm, so I am only expressing my personal view," Nixon said. "But I believe that the President thinks you are a liability and that you should resign." (The lawyerly Nixon showed much the same proficiency that Dewey had demonstrated during the fund crisis when Nixon had asked if Eisenhower wanted him to resign and Dewey had replied, "I don't want to imply that the General approves of the decision, but our group would not have asked me to make this call unless we all felt we represented his view.")

Adams saw Eisenhower that afternoon, but the president still couldn't bring himself to tell Adams that he was being dismissed. When Nixon returned to the White House, he saw Ike on the South Lawn, hitting five-irons—taking a golfer's full swings, as if to vent. There was no mention of Nixon returning to his family in White Sulphur Springs; rather, the president said, "I'm going to play some golf this afternoon, Dick, and I wonder if you would like to join me."

So on this August afternoon, Nixon and Eisenhower were driven to the Burning Tree Country Club to play a game that Nixon would never learn to love. To further diminish the fun of the excursion, Ann Whitman had warned Nixon that the boss was in a "sour mood," which became evident during their game; Eisenhower told Nixon that it was the worst round he'd had in months. Then, on the ride back, the president said, "Sherm won't take any of the responsibility. He leaves it all to me. Still, I can't fire a man who is sincere just for political reasons. He must resign in a way I can't refuse." Ike continued, "I think Sherm must have misunderstood what you said. You had better write me an aide-mémoire on your conversation."

When Nixon mentioned that Adams had raised the question of a successor—that he didn't know who could replace him—this self-assessment of indispensability did not improve the president's mood. As Nixon remembered the moment, "Eisenhower's face flushed, and he said curtly and coldly, 'That's my problem, not his.' He looked out the car window for a minute and then said, 'He has a heart condition. He might use that as a reason for resigning.' " Eisenhower then told Nixon to ask Meade Alcorn, who had succeeded Leonard Hall as Republican National Committee chairman, to confront Adams: "I want Alcorn to really lay it on the line with him."

That ended Nixon's immediate responsibility—he could hand it off to Alcorn and return to the Greenbrier, where the Nixon family's mood was not chipper. "My mother would remember always that particular episode, not only because the vacation plans were ruined, but also because she foresaw that for her husband it was a no-win proposition," the Nixons' daughter Julie recalled. The president then left for Newport, and Adams flew to New Brunswick for salmon fishing. At the end of August, a *Washington Post* headline read, ADAMS STILL IN JOB DESPITE FORECASTERS.

Meade Alcorn's involvement in the Adams affair began with a call from Newport, where Ike had just left the golf links. "You've got to get his resignation. I'm not going to ask for it," the president said. "And I think this ought to be moved right along."

"Well, Sherm is fishing," Alcorn informed the president. "He's in Canada somewhere, fishing."

"Well, get him. You've got to get hold of him and get him. I think that this thing can't wait. I'm very disturbed about how this is striking people." He said that the Adams case was jeopardizing those with a political future—people like Nixon, Bill Rogers, and Cabot Lodge.

Adams and his wife were at the Miramachi River, in New Brunswick, one of the great rivers for Atlantic salmon, when word came that he was wanted back at the office; by the next day, he was meeting with Meade Alcorn. "I told him this was probably the unhappiest thing that had ever occurred to me in my whole political career," Alcorn recalled. "He looked at me as only Sherm Adams can look at somebody and said, 'What's the President think?'" And Alcorn told him. Adams met with the president in mid-September to work out the particulars of his resignation and was quickly replaced by his deputy, Jerry Persons.

Years later, when Nixon was president, he often referred to the Adams case. He would say that Adams was treated too harshly and he'd complain at having to do Eisenhower's dirty work. In the midst of the Watergate scandal, he said that unlike Ike, he had personally fired his two top aides, H. R. (Bob) Haldeman and John Ehrlichman. (Haldeman in his diary disputes this, saying that he got the word from Nixon's press secretary, Ron Ziegler, and that he was the one who told Ehrlichman.) Nixon sometimes claimed that it was he who got Adams to quit, but when he said that during a television interview with David Frost, Alcorn finally objected. Nixon then promised to correct the record in *RN*, the memoir that he was writing, and he kept his word.

The Adams firing prompted Nixon to recall a conversation with Walter Bedell Smith, Ike's chief of staff during the war. "We were sitting having scotch and soda, and Bedell got very emotional," Nixon told Frank Gannon, who helped with *RN*. Nixon wrote: "Tears began to stream down his cheeks and he blurted out his pent-up feelings. 'I was just Ike's prat-boy,' he said. 'Ike always had to have a prat-boy, someone who'd do the dirty work for him. He always had to have someone else who could do the firing, or the reprimanding, or give any orders which he knew people would find unpleasant to carry out. Ike always has to be the nice guy. That's the way it is in the White House and the way it will always be in any organization that Ike runs.'"

CHAPTER 17

Unstoppable

1

Moments before President Eisenhower arrived to deliver the State of the Union message on January 7, 1960, one could hear a certain swelling of applause as the vice president entered the House chamber and took his place on the dais next to Speaker Rayburn, who detested Nixon and who referred to him privately as "that ugly man with the chinquapin eyes." It was quite a contrast from the year before, when the Adams-Goldfine scandal was still fresh and the midterms had not gone well. The elections, though, had left Nixon with a serious rival: while Republicans in 1958 were losing forty-eight House seats and fifteen Senate seats, the former Eisenhower appointee Nelson Rockefeller, a natural politician brimming with bonhomie and vitality, was elected governor of New York by beating another rich man, the incumbent Averell Harriman.

Yet the vice president, as if magically, seemed to have grown, to have become a more consequential figure in an administration that was losing its consequential figures—first Sherman Adams and then John Foster Dulles, who had died the previous May of colon cancer. Nixon had learned a lot from Dulles, with whom he grew closer after Eisenhower had his heart attack, and who had encouraged his interest in foreign policy. When the new Cuban leader Fidel Castro visited the United States in early 1959,

Nixon was the highest-ranking official to see him and afterward produced a perceptive aide-mémoire in which he said that Castro "has those indefinable qualities which make him a leader of men," though adding, "He is either incredibly naïve about Communism or under Communist discipline—my guess is the former." Nixon was impatient to taste more of this world, and Dulles had been an ideal coach. Nixon in turn gave Dulles political advice, such as urging him to keep the delegation to the 1955 Geneva disarmament conference to a manageable size and telling him, "Don't take anyone about whom the columnists can say, 'Look who has the President's ear.'"

Nixon went to see Dulles several times at Walter Reed, and Dulles was grateful; his secretary, Phyllis Bernau, later told Nixon that "He loved you and I hope you realize how much you helped him fight his noble battle." But Nixon usually had many things on his mind, and it was no different this time. The nominating conventions were more than a year off, but it was not too early to enlist the mortally ill Dulles in the early stages of his presidential campaign. Nixon never did so directly; rather, he used such intermediaries as Leonard Hall and the former undersecretary of state Herbert Hoover Jr., who passed along the message that Nixon "might like a letter from the Secretary telling of his great admiration etc." Dulles went along with it, up to a point; direct involvement in domestic politics made him uneasy. He suggested using an interview that he'd given to Earl Mazo in which he'd said "I don't know anybody who so effectively represents abroad the best qualities of America," which Nixon thought was "fine and all that was called for and all that could be expected." Dulles's support for Nixon's candidacy was genuine; privately, he'd said that "after looking everybody over I think Dick is the man the future of the country depends on."

Nixon also seemed transformed by a trip to Russia the previous July, which brought him more attention than anyone, including Eisenhower and Nixon himself, had anticipated. In fact, before he'd left the country, Eisenhower had made clear that any meeting with the Soviet boss, Nikita Khrushchev, would be a "goodwill gesture"—nothing more. "We should be careful to understand one thing about the Vice Presidential position in this government of ours," he told reporters, and went on to point out that a vice president was "not a part of the diplomatic processes and machinery of this country." Nixon, he added, "knows all about government, he knows about the attitudes, he can impart information, but he is not negotiating anything." Eisenhower may not have intended to firmly undercut Nixon, but he hadn't said a word to enhance his stature—in fact the opposite. Nixon tried to shrug this off, telling a reporter on the flight to Moscow, "There is always the potential that we will make some yardage," but he knew that he would have to gain yardage on a field of his own making.

The most vivid images of Nixon's visit originated at the U.S. Trade and Cultural Fair in Moscow's Sokolniki Park, where he stood face-to-face with Khrushchev, arguing about the benefits of capitalism and Communism in front of an American model kitchen, a scene that became known as the "Kitchen Debate." Nixon jabbed with a finger and Khrushchev gesticulated in reply, his short, round body moving whenever he looked angry—which was much of the time that he spent with the vice president. Beneath the surface, the two didn't seem to like one another very much and Nixon in one of his memoranda to Eisenhower said that their conversations sometimes "got so ridiculous that . . . on several occasions I jocularly needled him by saying 'You are always right and we are always wrong. Is there ever a time when you can say you might be wrong?' " A decade later, Nixon had inflated this confrontation to epic proportions, telling an interviewer, "I felt like a fighter wearing sixteen-ounce gloves and bound by Marquis of Queensbury rules, up against a bare-knuckled slugger who had gouged, kneed, and kicked." Nixon also gave a speech to the Russian people, and afterward, at a dinner at Spaso House, he went through the sort of unwinding that others had witnessed at moments of high tension. Milton Eisenhower, who was present, told the historian Michael Beschloss that he "came back terribly upset, terribly nervous and high-strung. . . . So he drank about six martinis before we sat down to dinner. As soon as we sat down, he started going around the table to see what everyone thinks about the speech. And he'd keep interrupting the person: 'Did you hear me say this? Did you hear this?' And then he began using abusive—well, not abusive, but vulgar swear words and everything else in this mixed company." But while the Moscow trip on a personal level was a diplomatic fiasco, on the political level it was a triumph.

• • •

Nixon's view of Rockefeller had been a mixture of mistrust and wary dislike (the feeling was mutual) from the time that Rockefeller won the governorship. Rocky (even the nickname made the grandson of John D. Rockefeller sound like a member of the peasantry) seemed always to be lurking, or so Nixon believed. His suspicions got the better of him when Khrushchev made his first visit to America, in September 1959, and Nixon's office heard "several reports, the last one from a 'totally unimpeachable source,' that Nelson Rockefeller is being very critical of the Khrushchev visit," and furthermore—purportedly quoting Rockefeller—"that the 'Vice President is totally responsible for the visit.'" The reports probably weren't accurate, and it's hard to understand why it mattered anyway, but it plagued Nixon to the point that he asked Rose Mary Woods to call Ann Whitman to set things straight with the president; and Woods did so with gusto, telling Whitman that it was "a dangerous thing to have a Governor playing politics with anything as important to the entire Free World and the Captive world as well." When Mrs. Whitman passed all this on to her boss, she appended the thought that "it just didn't sound like Nelson at all."

The tone of Whitman's note suggests that she was mildly amused by both men, who were portrayed by her as squabbling schoolchildren—one suspicious, the other dismissive—who needed a grown-up to arbitrate. ("I am resigning from politics," she wrote at the bottom of the page.) Eisenhower did step in, first in a conversation with Rockefeller and then in a letter to Nixon, in which he said that Rockefeller had "stated clearly and without equivocation that the story that disturbed you is without any foundation in fact," and that "Nelson branded it as a 'complete lie.'" The president added that he'd given Rockefeller a full account of his correspondence with Khrushchev and "told him that you had been informed of my invitation just before you went to Russia and therefore you were obviously innocent of any purpose of your own in urging a visit."

Ike's displeasure was obvious; and even if he'd meant to sound evenhanded, his letter was addressed to only one person—to Nixon. "My concern about the matter," Ike said, getting to the heart of it, "is that two people—even if they should both become candidates for the same nomination—who have supported me so long and faithfully through the years I have been in this office, should find themselves publicly at odds about an issue that in fact does not exist. My own opinion is that people can be politically ambitious if they so desire without necessarily becoming personal antagonists." Ann Whitman had heard some of this before. A few weeks earlier, after a breakfast with Nixon, the president had remarked, dismissively, and disingenuously, "It is terrible when people get politically ambitious—they have so many problems."

Khrushchev's designated escort in America was Henry Cabot Lodge, still the U.S. ambassador to the United Nations, who took him to a supermarket, a midwestern farm, a Hollywood soundstage, and more, including, at the end, a private visit with Rockefeller. Lodge never quite admitted it, but during their travels he developed a liking for Khrushchev. This fondness between a party boss and a Boston aristocrat, to whom Khrushchev referred as *"moi brat"*—my brother—was like a clichéd screwball comedy. In contrast to Lodge, Nixon's role during Khrushchev's visit was pretty much limited to showing up from time to time, more as an onlooker than a participant, a painful semi-exclusion for an overly sensitive politician. Because Nixon feared a loss of face if he wasn't present at an Eisenhower-Khrushchev session at Camp David, he asked Rose Woods to remind Ann Whitman that the president had asked him to be in town. "Delicate question," was how Whitman's note to her boss began. "Will you be wanting him to come up to Camp David next Saturday? As the story was put to me, it would get him off the hook because—in view of your request—he cancelled dedication of a dam for next Saturday using the K. visit as an excuse. So if he is not included in talks, it looks bad. All this from Rose." Eisenhower checked the box that said "Tell him," and added a scribbled line that said *"State asking him up on Saturday."*

Eisenhower was weary of such hypersensitivity. In March, when Harold Macmillan visited America, Nixon was eager to take part in talks at Camp David. Eisenhower, though, didn't include him and, as Nixon recalled, the president told him "that he was irritated at the way people raised this question because he was constantly trying to give me every opportunity to not only do things that were constructive but also to appear in a favorable light." A crueler version of this episode was related with gossipy amusement by President Kennedy: Eisenhower, after noting how eager Nixon had been to spend that weekend at Camp David, told Macmillan "I wouldn't have him on the place."

2

Nixon by early 1960 had also begun to seem more substantial thanks to a Rockefeller surprise: just after Christmas, he'd declared that he wasn't going to be a presidential candidate, a disappointment for enthusiasts of political combat. His announcement came almost immediately after a page-one *New York Times* story described his embryonic campaign apparatus as "fabulous and fantastic," adding that in its "size, complexity, cost and separation of functions," it was comparable to an organization set up after a party's nomination. The declaration left Nixon as "the certain nominee," or so the *New York Times* columnist Arthur Krock wrote the next day. People who knew Rockefeller, though, didn't believe it, and a few days after Eisenhower delivered his State of the Union speech, Nixon had lunch with the perpetually suspicious C. D. Jackson and others from Time Inc., during which Jackson brought up the possibility of open hostilities. Jackson predicted that Rockefeller would first send up "a cautious anti-Nixon trial balloon," and if that went well, it would "lead to more and stronger stuff until Nelson would find himself committed as the Republican anti-Nixon champion." Their former colleague the speechwriter Emmet John Hughes, who had gone to work for Rockefeller and disliked Nixon, had a "mesmeric effect" on Rockefeller, Jackson said.

The *Time* lunch broached a delicate subject: Nixon himself and his image, which, as Jackson put it bluntly—as if Nixon wasn't in the room— "arises not out of his alleged vices, but out of his evident virtues. He is too perfect; he never makes a misstep; the image is of an antiseptic man, not a warm man—like the perfect hospital nurse, beautifully starched, doing everything exactly right, but not a woman. . . . There is an aura of contrivance about even the best things he has done." Jackson had no remedy apart from telling Nixon that he needed to "forget himself for a minute and do something spontaneously even though it might not be to his best interest—preferably something involving principle." Nixon accepted this criticism and even demonstrated some morose wit, managing a smile as he said, "It is a little difficult to contrive to be uncontrived. But I understand what you mean."

Nixon assured this group that Eisenhower was prepared to support him. That was overstating it, but it did seem as though Ike was ready to accept the unavoidable. At a press conference on January 13 (right after Nixon's lunch with the Time Inc. crowd), the president was asked what he thought about Rockefeller's withdrawal and said, "I would just say that I was just as astonished as anybody else, but I just take his statement at face value and that's that. I do agree that it does give a certain atmosphere of no competition, you might say, on the nomination." But as usual, Eisenhower was not going to make it easy for Nixon, and when the question was put to him two weeks later, he sounded much as he always had:

> . . . we're all human, and we don't know what is around the next corner. I maintain that there are a number of Republicans, eminent men, big men, that could fulfill the requirements of the position; and until the nominations are in as a matter of history, why, I think I should not talk too much about an individual. I have so often, because of his close association with me, had opportunity and the occasion to express my admiration and respect for the Vice President. I am quite sure at least he is not unaware of my sentiments in this regard.

That declaration, although encased by words like "admiration" and "respect," was startlingly negative, but that was how the president talked when he talked about Nixon. People knew what he meant by "eminent men, big men"—that he was eager to welcome another contestant for the nomination—just as they knew that he would not name names. And yet when he talked about his regard for the likely nominee, he was still casting about for alternatives, such as Bob Anderson, for whom his admiration had never slackened. "Would it get some Republican interest started up in Texas if the organization there should name Bob Anderson as a 'favorite son'?" he wrote to Oveta Culp Hobby, his former secretary of health, education and welfare and a Texan. Eisenhower, like Anderson, surely realized how fruitless this idea was but it didn't stop him from promoting it.

But no other eminent or big men were actively seeking the Republican nomination, and then, in mid-March, Eisenhower finally acknowledged, perhaps even endorsed, the inevitable candidate—first in an "off-the-record" remark at the annual dinner of the Gridiron Club, one of Washington's self-congratulatory media-political events, and then at a press conference, where he said, although still without mentioning Nixon's name, "But if anyone is wondering whether I have any personal preference or even bias with respect to the upcoming Presidential race, the answer is yes, very definitely." Yet it took one more question to absolutely corner Ike:

Q: Mr. President . . . Were you also speaking there of Mr. Nixon?
A: Was there any doubt in your mind?

Q: No, sir. (Laughter)

Yet while Rockefeller had announced his removal from competition, he could not, as C. D. Jackson had predicted, quite abandon the race. The Republican National Convention was to begin in late July, and as the date approached Rockefeller was like a man who had emerged from the sea and still felt an irresistible undertow. In June, he came to the White House for breakfast, and what he most wanted to discuss was Richard Nixon; as Eisenhower recalled, "Inherent in his comments was criticism of what he felt was Nixon's failure to make known his convictions on a number of problems."

That was a nice way to put it. When Rockefeller returned to New York, he issued a ten-point statement three thousand words long, most of it aimed directly at Nixon. The statement, as Eisenhower put it, and not happily, showed the "fine hand of Emmet"—Emmet Hughes—by which he meant that its inflated language and signature lines would have been more at home in a candidate's stump speech: "We cannot, as a nation or a party . . . march to meet the future with a banner aloft whose only emblem is a question mark," or "The path of a great leadership does not lie along the top of a fence." Apart from its Nixon fixation, Rockefeller's ten-point "platform" dealt with everything from health care to labor arbitration to the defense budget—which, as Nixon knew, was an especially sensitive subject. (The Tennessee newspaperman Frank van der Linden said that the only time he saw Eisenhower turn bright red and lose his temper was when a reporter challenged him on the military budget.) Rockefeller had asserted that America's missiles were "dangerously vulnerable to Soviet attack" and that the nation's forces for limited war were "inadequate." These views had been influenced by an ambitious young Harvard professor, Henry A. Kissinger, who for the past couple of years had been expressing them—in the quarterly *Foreign Affairs*, in the *New York Times*, even on Mike Wallace's interview program—along with his thoughts that fighting a war with small nuclear weapons could make sense. When Kissinger expressed such opinions—or said that he would favor total war as "the last resort if the freedom of Berlin cannot be defended otherwise"—he sounded simultaneously rational and insane.

Oveta Culp Hobby telephoned Eisenhower after the Rockefeller breakfast and called the whole business "sad"—saying that Rockefeller, who had worked for Mrs. Hobby at HEW, had great potential. About Nixon, she said, "The other one is not easy," to which Eisenhower replied that he believed the vice president was growing in stature and that people respected him. Mrs. Hobby, referring to an upcoming Nixon speech, said that she hoped he would not "make the kind of talk that will drive intelligent independent voters away."

Rockefeller tried to get in touch with Eisenhower after their breakfast—he wanted advice on whether to become "an avowed candidate" after all. When Eisenhower returned the call, he sounded out of patience, but this was not the first time that Rockefeller had annoyed him. In 1954, when he replaced C. D. Jackson, the exuberant Rockefeller used his family fortune to hire a personal staff of nearly fifty people, accompanied by a baffling organizational chart, and managed to alienate any number of people at the State Department, notably Foster Dulles, who had complained about him to the president. Eisenhower had once remarked that Rockefeller "was too used to borrowing brains instead of using his own," and now he advised Rockefeller that he was in danger of becoming an "off again, on again, gone again, Finnegan." It was hard to understand Rockefeller's hesitant reemergence in the 1960 campaign when he had no delegates and no tangible support beyond New York, but the fifty-year-old Rockefeller was a complicated figure, someone with enormous wealth who, as one person observed, "howled like a stuck pig when he found a traffic tag on his itty-bitty English car," an Austin. It was as if he believed that he was owed the nomination simply for being governor of New York or being born a Rockefeller—or for not being Richard Nixon.

In fact the biggest question that Rockefeller raised in his declaration had little to do with issues and nearly everything to do with, in Joe Alsop's phrase, "haunting doubts about Nixon's character and capabilities." No one was more aware of this than Nixon—the lunch with C. D. Jackson in January had focused on how he was perceived—and the subject was not about to go away, not when people were still writing things like "There is always a new Nixon, as he shuttles back and forth between polar positions that seem diametrically opposed," and it came up in mid-May, when he appeared on *Open End*, a television program moderated by the movie and TV producer David Susskind and named for its theoretical freedom from time limits. Susskind had a minuscule audience—fewer than twenty stations carried *Open End*—and his political opinions were no secret; he was a Democrat, a Stevensonian to boot, and his program was notable not only for its length but for its tone. The Susskind Q-and-A with Nixon went on for three and three quarter hours, past two a.m., during which Susskind asked his questions in an amiable voice as he chain-smoked and drank coffee while Nixon remained, as usual, ploddingly earnest and deeply informed, with occasional moments of dry wit, a grating personality for the Nixon-loathing Susskind audience. Nixon dealt with such subjects as the recognition of Red China, Khrushchev's goals, the recent shooting down of an American U-2 spy plane over Russia, and the role of a vice president, always speaking carefully, never making a slip, even though at around the three-hour mark he sounded weary and once even lost his train of thought. It was a way for Nixon to show his mettle and to deal with the personal issues that his antagonists liked to bring up ("You have been . . . labeled as a deeply partisan man who in the crux of political combat as you have been a good part of your career goes to extremes. . . . Do you wish you could call back some of that extreme partisanship and extreme vitriol?"), as he did some months later with CBS's Walter Cronkite, when he said, with an almost Zen-like cadence, "When people say there is a new Nixon that must mean that people who did not like the Nixon that they knew before now like the one that they know now. I happen to believe, myself, that perhaps many of those who discover the new Nixon may not have known the old one."

But although Nixon could make even some of his supporters uncomfortable, it was no longer easy to regard him merely as the pitiless bastard who had befouled Helen Gahagan Douglas in his 1950 Senate campaign and seemed suspiciously in league with the party's McCarthyite wing. He could also be understood as the dutiful protégé who had traveled the world for Eisenhower, including that harrowing visit to South America—the constant voyager, the steady hand when the president's health failed him, someone with empathic impulses when it came to domestic issues, which he demonstrated when Susskind asked him what he thought about the "sit-down strikes" then taking place in the South:

> I would say that these strikes should not be looked at as primarily consti-tuting a legal problem . . . to me the problem is not legal. . . . The problem is essentially moral. For example, I've often thought, How does a mother of a Negro child tell him or her as he's growing up when he first goes to a store that you can buy something but you can't go and buy a Coca-Cola? Or you can get a Coca-Cola, but you have to stand up while the others get to sit down?

As for Rockefeller, Nixon was prepared—he was always prepared—for a counterattack, and at a June press conference, in Camden, New Jersey, he wanted it known that he had already subjected himself to forty-seven "no holds barred" Q-and-A sessions in the past five months, and so he wanted to point out that while Rockefeller liked to ask questions, he did not seem eager to answer them. When asked if he was willing to debate Rockefeller, his reply dripped with sarcasm and insincerity, the sort of smug, logical tone that could drive his opponents batty:

> The Governor has suggested that he does not know where I stand on these basic issues. I know, of course, he is a busy man and he hasn't had an opportunity to read my press conferences, and I have not had the op-portunity to read his. On the other hand, he is the man who is entitled to know where any candidate for the Presidency stands on any issue. So it occurred to me that one way we could resolve this problem would be for the Governor to meet with me and to question me on all the issues in which he thinks, one, he disagrees with me, or, two, on all the issues where he believes my position to be not clear.

A couple of days later, Nixon got a note from the president, who was in Newport. Ike could see that Rockefeller was outmatched and wrote,

"Last night some of us heard the tape recording of your press conference in Camden. We all thought it was excellent. Congratulations!" There was still a little time to relax. In late June, the Nixons celebrated their twentieth wedding anniversary—a surprise party at the Columbia Country Club, where he went to the piano and played "California, Here I Come."

3

Nixon had known John F. Kennedy, the Democratic front-runner, since they'd both won House seats in 1946; he liked him, and counted him among his Democratic friends. They had both served on the House Labor Committee, and he had sponsored Kennedy's membership at Burning Tree in early 1954. When Kennedy was hospitalized for back surgery later that year, Nixon made sure that his absence did not affect the reorganization of the Senate—a gesture for which Mrs. Kennedy thanked him, writing, "I don't think there is anyone in the world he thinks more highly of than he does you—and this is just another proof of how incredible you are." Their office suites in the Senate Office Building faced each other across a corridor; the lettering on 361 read "Mr. Kennedy, Massachusetts," and on 362, which had a small, starry seal, were the words, "The Vice President." Now and then they would exchange greetings with a "Hi, Dick" and a "How are you, Jack?" Nixon's military aide, Don Hughes, often saw them chatting in the corridor, and one of Nixon's secretaries, Dorothy Cox Donnelly, sometimes accompanied Kennedy when he walked to the Senate floor. In November 1950, Kennedy told a group of Harvard students how pleased he was that Nixon had defeated Helen Gahagan Douglas in his Senate race—she was not, he said, "the sort of person I like working with on committees."

Eisenhower didn't think much of Kennedy—he had "no real stature" he told a visitor—but he didn't think much of Kennedy's rivals, either, apart from Stevenson, who, although he didn't like him, thought that he "might make a pretty good President." Harry Truman for reasons of his own didn't think much of Kennedy either. When the Democrats met in Los Angeles in mid-July and chose him on the first ballot, Truman stayed in Missouri, having said beforehand that Kennedy should withdraw and wait until he reached the maturity of a candidate like Stuart Symington, another Missourian, whose views on defense had led Eisenhower to consider him "a sort of an idiot." Kennedy's choice of running mate, Lyndon Johnson, disturbed liberals, although it was thought that he could help the ticket carry Texas and, perhaps, becalm those southern voters who worried about a papist president and the civil rights planks in the platform.

The Republicans returned to Chicago, where Eisenhower was chosen in 1952, and where, as speakers always liked to point out, Lincoln was nominated in 1860. In the days leading up to the convention, Nelson Rockefeller kept testing the boundaries of party loyalty, as when he dismissed the idea of accepting the vice presidency and turned down a request to second Nixon's nomination. In saying—and not saying—what is usually expected of a party man, Rockefeller was developing a reputation as a spoiler, an obstructionist, a mischief maker; neo-Taftians in particular had already discovered—and been stirred by—the personal charm and ideological originality of Arizona senator Barry Goldwater, and they had long memories. The offstage combat between Rockefeller and Nixon reached its peak on the weekend before the convention, when they met at Rockefeller's twenty-three-room triplex apartment at 810 Fifth Avenue, and worked out what appeared to be an accommodation. The meeting went on from early evening until three in the morning, and after it was over it became clear that not much was accomplished. But what was labeled the "Compact of Fifth Avenue" did succeed in getting Rockefeller's public endorsement and the illusion of party unity. It also made Nixon squirm because it had the whiff of surrender—Goldwater called it "the Munich of the Republican Party"—and because the "Compact" implicitly criticized the president's defense budget, which Rockefeller thought was undernourished. That put Nixon in a vise, not only squeezed by the Rockefeller and Goldwater wings of the party but by Eisenhower's sensitivity on defense questions. When Nixon telephoned the president in Newport to fill him in on the meeting with Rockefeller, he apparently omitted the defense part—it was too uncomfortable—but as soon as Eisenhower learned about it, he called Congressman Melvin Laird, who was in charge of the platform committee, and told him to straighten out Nixon—or else. "This is a disaster!" Eisenhower said to Laird. "I want you to go over and instruct that young man that he's not going to have my support if he stands by that agreement."

Laird solved the problem by simply cutting the offending language out of the platform.

Eisenhower received a hero's welcome in Chicago. He stood in an open limousine and the crowds covered him with confetti. Inside the convention hall, he spoke with some heat about certain unnamed people who had dared to belittle America's preparedness and strength. Rockefeller, having gotten his way, wore a toothy grin and a Nixon button on his right lapel; he called the vice president "a man of courage . . . a man of vision and of judgment" and "the man who will succeed Dwight D. Eisenhower next January—Richard E. Nixon." Perhaps getting Nixon's middle initial wrong could be blamed on the dyslexia that had always plagued him, and while many thought that he'd done it maliciously, he looked enthusiastic, as if to drive away any suspicion that it was deliberate. Rockefeller even invited Nixon to stay with his family at the Rockefeller vacation home in Seal Harbor, Maine, an invitation surely issued with the certainty that it would not be accepted.

Nixon like Kennedy won on the first ballot and then he chose Henry Cabot Lodge (Eisenhower had recommended him) as a running mate. There was nothing obviously wrong with Lodge, who someone described as having "the look of a playboy who has had to go to work"; he had a first-rate résumé and looked good on television. But he also possessed the politically deadly qualities of arrogance and obtuseness and proved himself to be a hopeless candidate, someone who couldn't even help Nixon carry Massachusetts, his home state. Nixon then made the mistake of asking Leonard Hall to manage his campaign although he wasn't willing to surrender control. "I have never had a manager in my life in politics," Nixon told Hall. "I can't have that. I don't like it, don't like the title." So, he continued, "If it's all right with you I'm going to name you and Bob Finch"—the longtime aide and friend—"directors in my campaign." Hall said, "You can do as you please," but he wasn't happy about the arrangement.

The day that he was nominated—July 22, 1960—was the peak of Dick Nixon's political life, though not the most joyful moment, nothing like winning his first race for Congress, in 1946, when, as he later wrote with melancholic sentiment, "Pat and I were happier . . . than we were ever to be again in my political career." His demeanor was solemn, his speech humble, his themes elevated; he was determined to avoid sounding like the jowly cartoon partisan who followed the flesh-and-blood Nixon around. In part it was an echo of Kennedy's speech two weeks earlier at the Democratic convention, which is not to suggest that he borrowed from Kennedy, but rather that, like Kennedy, he used the word "sacrifice" and spoke of the "supreme satisfaction which comes from working together in a cause greater than ourselves." Right after the convention, the evangelist Billy Graham, a Nixon friend—they occasionally played golf at Burning Tree—told Nixon that he'd just spent three days with Martin Luther King Jr. in Rio de Janeiro, at the Baptist World Alliance, and he warned him that Kennedy was working hard to get King's support. "King was greatly impressed and just about sold," Graham said. "I think I at least neutralized him. I think if you could invite him for a brief conference it might swing him. He would be a powerful influence."

CHAPTER 18

"If You Give Me a Week, I Might Think of One"

1

President Eisenhower sometimes acted as if politics was something distinct and separate from the business of governing, and when it came to the 1960 election, he could even sound as if he didn't much care who won. When he was asked if he planned to campaign for the Nixon-Lodge ticket, he said, "Whatever I can do to promote it, and its success . . . I shall do," but then added, "Now this doesn't mean that I possibly should be out on hustings and making partisan speeches." Sounding almost as if he was too busy to be bothered, he said, "I've got a lot of other responsibilities and I've got a lot of other commitments around the country." Nixon would have loved to win without having to rely on the president's almost mystical popularity. "The first reaction of the Nixon people was, 'We don't want anything from Ike,' " William Ewald, an Eisenhower aide who worked on the Nixon campaign, said. Nixon started traveling right after the convention and he slowed down only because of some bad luck in Greensboro, North Carolina, where he banged his knee against a car door, an accident that his military aide, Don Hughes, who was by his side, knew right away was more severe than a mere bump. Nixon tried to ignore the knee even when the soreness lingered and it began to swell; what he did pay close attention to was something that Eisenhower said a week later, on August 24, in response to a question from Charles Mohr of *Time*:

> Q: . . . one of the issues in this campaign is seeming to turn on the question of Mr. Nixon's experience, and the Republicans to some extent almost want to claim that he has had a great deal of practice at being President. . . . Many people have been trying to get at the degree that he has—I don't want to use that word "participated"—but acted in important decisions, and it is hard to pin down.
>
> A: . . . Every commander that I have ever known, or every leader, or every head of a big organization, has needed and sought consultative conferences with his principal subordinates. . . . So the Vice President has participated for eight years, or seven and a half years, in all of the consultative meetings that have been held. And he has never hesitated—and if he had I would have been quite disappointed—he has never hesitated to express his opinion, and when he has been asked for it, expressed his opinion in terms of recommendation as to decision. But no one, and no matter how many differences or whether they are all unanimous—no one has the decisive power. There is no voting. . . .
>
> Q: We understand that the power of decision is entirely yours, Mr. President. I just wondered if you could give us an example of a major idea of his that you had adopted in that role, as the decider and final—
>
> A: If you give me a week, I might think of one. I don't remember.

If a single Eisenhower comment is remembered from the 1960 presidential campaign, it's that: *If you give me a week, I might think of one. I don't remember.* That remark at the end of a desultory press conference and accompanied by laughter from reporters was a particularly unfortunate moment for Nixon, who had wanted to emphasize not only his experience but the contention that he had played a major part in decision making—an exaggerated claim that made its way into a May interview with *U.S. News & World Report* in which he described his "executive" role ("I get a picture not only of what is happening around the world, but, in addition to that, every morning I receive an up-to-date summary report of all actions being taken by various Government agencies affecting domestic affairs"). It was also incorporated into the Republican platform with references to various "Nixon-Eisenhower" initiatives. That language annoyed Eisenhower almost as much as the implied criticism of his defense budget.

Eisenhower "immediately knew that it had come out wrong," Nixon later wrote, and telephoned his regrets. Aides recall the president referring to "that damn I'll-wait-for-a-week quote," and saying, "I wish to hell I'd never said it." And it *may* just have been something that came out wrong in an unfocused news conference that skipped from the campaign to farm policy to the postwar conference held in Potsdam. Also, it had ended—those sessions ended punctually—and since the president tried to hold them every week, it made perfect sense to say "give me a week." But he did not rush to clarify the remark, and Jim Hagerty, who could have helped to repair the damage, said nothing. (Eisenhower's grandson, David, said that Nixon was so angry at Hagerty for his inaction that when he became president "his entire communications operation was organized in such a way to avoid a Hagerty.") For Senator Kennedy, who was already making fun of Nixon's experience—his 1958 trip to South America "provoked a riot" and he'd told Khrushchev during the Kitchen Debate that "while we may be behind in space we were certainly ahead in color television"—the remark was a gift. Eisenhower may have been "facetious," as he told Nixon, but William Ewald, who worked with Ike on his memoirs, has noted that whenever he used a word like "jocular" or "facetious," he usually meant something else—"he was often concealing a wound or an irritant." Ewald is sure that the reporter's question about Nixon's role "had struck a nerve: the allegation that Eisenhower didn't run the government."

Nixon could not just ignore "give-me-a-week" and yet it would have been strange for him to call a press conference to discuss it. So he chose another sort of forum, one with a much larger audience: a television talk show. The star of NBC's *Tonight Show* then was the affable and emotional Jack Paar, who could be funny, but ran his program less like a comedian and more like the host of an ongoing late-night conversation—his broadcast was not so much dominated by celebrities as by characters who became far more interesting in Paar's engaging company. So it made strategic sense for Nixon, facing his first campaign embarrassment, to want to chat.

Senator Kennedy had been on the program and Nixon tried to be as jaunty as any Kennedy—parting the curtains himself after Paar introduced him, as if he were coming out to sing or tell jokes rather than attempt to brush away his discomfiture.

Paar tried to be amusing. He observed that running against the Kennedys was like "running against beavers," and continued, "They are everywhere, I am telling you. Little Bobby Kennedy is in New York and he was in the Puerto Rican section yesterday eating tamales. How are you on Spanish food? This may be a case of how many foreign foods you can eat. Rockefeller beat Harriman on a couple of blintzes."

Nixon, who was not comfortable in this environment, made a stab at drollness: "All I can say is this: That I can eat anything." Then, sensing that the line had not quite worked, he continued, "I was going to say as far as food is concerned, I will tell you I happen to like Mexican food"—at which point Paar cut him off to say that that might help in Texas, but what about Puerto Rico? When Paar tried another joke—asking Nixon if he would refrain from mentioning his opponent's age—Nixon seemed about to wilt: "As a matter of fact, I don't think age is an issue, Jack. Your name is Jack—that's a little embarrassing to me, at the moment. That wasn't in the script was it?"

"No, it wasn't," Paar replied.

But Nixon was prepared when it came to the point of his appearance—Eisenhower's comment. Paar feigned embarrassment, as if he was being unpardonably rude simply by bringing it up; ingratiating awkwardness was Paar's style: "Forgive me for asking that, but they want to make me really powerful, and I don't want to be, really."

And then Nixon tried to close the subject for good, having clearly rehearsed his most important comments: "Jack," he said, "actually the President stated the case exactly and correctly from the standpoint of both his Administration and I would hope any administration, Democratic or Republican, because only the President of the United States can make the great decisions affecting our country." Having said that, he went on to say that his own experience "has been in sitting in councils of the Administration, in the Cabinet and Security, being asked—and that, incidentally, is a very great privilege, being asked my opinion on matters where I have experience."

The Paar show did not erase what Ike had said, but the appearance helped push it into the past; and it began a friendly relationship with Paar that gave Nixon some rare, lighthearted moments when he most needed them. It also introduced Nixon to Paul Keyes, described by Paar's onetime sidekick Hugh Downs as "the majordomo—the foreman, of Paar's writing staff," who would play an important, albeit peripheral role in Nixon's future. James Reston, writing with faux bafflement about Paar and the presidential candidates, managed entirely to miss the point: "Just who gains from all this and why these two deadly serious and tense young men want to prove that they are funny and relaxed is not quite clear." It was almost as if Reston had gotten a glimpse of a low-rent future in which solemn politicians unashamedly went on comedy shows and could only close his eyes.

When Nixon visited the Paar program he had a physical problem as well as a political one. The knee that he'd bumped in Greensboro was acting up and by the end of August had become so infected that he checked into Walter Reed, where he was treated with a heavy dose of antibiotics and warned by doctors to stay put. Among his visitors was the president, and it was startling to see them together: there was Nixon confined to bed, his infected limb held motionless by a traction weight, and there was Eisenhower standing at his bedside, pink-faced, wearing a big grin. Ike was about to turn seventy—then the oldest president ever to serve—and he looked terrific. It was almost the reverse image of Nixon's visit to Ike in Denver after the heart attack.

It appeared to be a happy moment, but it wasn't, in part because Pat Nixon, who hated campaigning, was in a bad mood; her husband wanted her "cheered up," perhaps taken for a swim by Rose Mary Woods and other staff members. Ann Whitman wrote in her diary, "Later, the President intimated that while the Vice President was 'all right' when he visited the hospital, there was some lack of warmth. He mentioned again, as he has several times, the fact that the Vice President has very few friends. Of course the difference to me is obvious," Mrs. Whitman continued, in an editorial aside, "the President is a man of integrity and sincere in his every action. . . . But the Vice President sometimes seems like a man who is acting like a nice man rather than being one."

That lack of warmth no doubt had something to do with Ike's "give-me-a-week" remark, and when Nixon left the hospital after a twelve-day stay, the president tried to be helpful. On a steamy mid-September day—Hurricane Donna was headed up the East Coast and gusts of rain and wind had already arrived—he was driven to Baltimore's Friendship Airport (the only local airport able to handle passenger jets) to help launch a national campaign trip for the ticket. Ike called Nixon and Lodge, who were there, "the finest team an American could choose," and impressed the Nixon aide Jim Bassett by "grinning and perspiring with the rest of us mere mortals in a low-ceilinged airport waiting room . . . pinkfaced and so damned human looking." But two more weeks went by before the president held another press conference and more than a month—at a fund-raising dinner in Chicago on September 29—before he made what he called an "unequivocal statement" that "Dick Nixon has the broadest and deepest preparation and experience of any man I know." That compliment was urgently needed. Four days earlier, Nixon and Kennedy had held the first of four televised debates, and a question about Nixon's experience was posed by NBC's Sander Vanocur, who managed while asking it to quote Ike's give-me-a-week remark verbatim for anyone who might have missed it the first time. Nixon not only sounded wooden and uncertain ("Well, I would suggest Mr. Vanocur, that uh—if you know the President, that was probably a facetious remark") but he still had a hospital pallor and even looked a little undersized. Moreover, he was on edge; he believed that most journalists favored the seductive, scarily handsome Kennedy, and he got that right. Vanocur for instance was a Kennedy friend.

Prime Minister Harold Macmillan remembers watching the debate with Eisenhower, who had flown to New York for a United Nations session. When the president asked the prime minister what he thought, Macmillan said, "Your chap's beat." When Ike asked what he meant by that, Macmillan replied, "One of them looked like a convicted criminal and the other looked like a rather engaging young undergraduate. Well, you know, Nixon had that curious sort of furtive, dark face."

2

Then there was the religious issue—Kennedy after all was the first Roman Catholic to run for president since Al Smith in 1928—although Nixon knew that it might be unwise to attempt to exploit it; as he told Clare Boothe Luce, a convert to Catholicism, doing so would likely "drive the small percentage of Catholic voters who are still on our side to vote for Kennedy." And there would have been something risible in making an issue of anyone's religion. Eisenhower, the Mennonite—or Jehovah's Witness–turned–Presbyterian, disliked going to church, although he was usually ready to invoke God in a speech or at a cabinet meeting or give the deity a permanent place in the Pledge of Allegiance. Nixon, who was reared as a Quaker, was never comfortable with public expressions of faith; Billy Graham worried about the depth of his friend's beliefs, once telling him that "throughout Protestantism there is running a question as to your religious convictions." The forty-year-old Graham had been giving Nixon unsolicited political advice since the mid-1950s and as early as 1957, like an amateur pundit, he had written to inform him that "Senator Kennedy is getting a fantastic build-up in certain elements of the press" (Kennedy by then had appeared on the cover of *Life*), adding that, "when the chips are down, the religious issue would be very strong and might conceivably work in your behalf." A month before the 1960 convention, Graham pointed out that "Since the Protestant voters out-number the Catholics three to one, you must concentrate on solidifying the Protestant vote." At least he was more discreet than Norman Vincent Peale, an author (*The Power of Positive Thinking*) and the pastor of the Dutch Reformed Marble Collegiate Church in New York, a man who combined the look of a middle-aged bank executive with the declamatory talent of a super-salesman. Peale headed a group of ministers and laymen who, after insisting that "Romish influence" should be discussed "only in a spirit of truth, tolerance and fairness," said that a Roman Catholic president would be under "extreme pressure from the hierarchy of his church" to align American foreign policy with the Vatican's. This moment of bigotry embarrassed not only Nixon, but Peale who rapidly withdrew from national politics. When Eisenhower was asked for his opinion, he said, "Mr. Nixon and I agreed long ago that one thing that we would never raise, and never mention, is the religious issue in this coming campaign."

By October, Eisenhower was becoming ever more pessimistic about Nixon's chances, remarking one day that if he had "taken the job I wanted him to in 1956"—secretary of defense—"he would be in a lot better position today." At the end of October, he invited the vice president to a strategy lunch with Len Hall, who was attempting to run the campaign, and a few others. The day started badly. Before the meal, Nixon and Hall talked to Ike about California, which was suffering from layoffs in the aviation industry. If the administration could just do something to spur hiring—say a federal contract to build fighter planes—it might help Nixon carry the state. At that suggestion, Eisenhower sounded offended. "As long as I'm President," he said, "not one dollar of defense money will be spent to get a vote for a Republican or a Democrat." When Nixon and Hall were alone, Nixon let loose. "That goddamned old fool," he said to Hall. "If I had been sitting in that chair and wanted to keep my successor there I'd spend the whole goddamned treasury."

It got worse during lunch. Eisenhower said, "Tell me how I can help," and offered to campaign in the New York City area, as well as Cleveland, and Pittsburgh, and possibly Illinois. It was about then that Nixon said, "Mr. President, you've done enough." Eisenhower immediately looked at Hall. "His face was screwed up and you could see he was mad," Hall recalled. "He flushed. We broke up. It was like somebody had thrown cold water over him." After the meeting, Eisenhower telephoned Hall. "What the hell's the matter with that guy?" he asked. "Doesn't he want me?" Then he added, "Did you watch us at all when we were walking back to the Oval room?" When Hall said he hadn't been watching, Eisenhower said, "Well, by God, he was walking, his shoulders were hunched forward, his head was down between his shoulders. If I'd seen an officer up at the front in World War II, out in the field like that, I'd have fired him on the spot." The president added, "He doesn't look like a winner to me, Len."

It had, as it turned out, been like a comedy of errors without the comedy. A few years later, Eisenhower said, "Well, I carried out exactly what he asked me to do. We of course did not want to make it look, neither did he nor I, that I was naming him as President, that I had pushed him out in front and that I was—he was just a papa's boy, he was just a figure on his own." But Ike's role, or lack of it, was more complicated than that. In fact, with the vote just a few days away and the polls showing a very close race, Nixon was more than willing to let the president help—to be a "papa's boy." What had complicated matters was a telephone call earlier that day from Howard Snyder, Eisenhower's loyal doctor, who told Nixon that he was worried about Ike's health—and that Mamie was worried, too. He hoped that Nixon would do what he could to limit the president's campaign schedule (Mrs. Eisenhower had made the same appeal to Pat Nixon—"almost in tears"). And that seems to have been what Nixon was thinking when he told Eisenhower that he'd done enough. Some are skeptical of a story that shows Nixon being selfless, but Eisenhower himself seemed to acknowledge its veracity in an interview with *Saturday Review* in 1966, where he said that he hadn't learned about this wifely intervention for several years.

Eisenhower's observation, though, was correct: the Nixon campaign and Nixon himself had lost their buoyancy. He still sounded like a rock-'em, sock-'em campaigner when he called Kennedy rash, immature, and impulsive, or a man who could be manipulated by Khrushchev, or someone who would take the country down "a road paved with glittering promises that leads to disaster." But the tough language sounded almost mechanical and joylessness permeated the campaign. Len Hall, who was frustrated enough by the candidate, was also annoyed by the presence of a new arrival, H. R. Haldeman, a chilly thirty-three-year-old advertising man without any obvious ideology. Haldeman had first worked for Nixon in 1956 as an advance man; he was taken on after writing several fawning letters ("I believe completely in Richard Nixon") to the vice president's office manager, Loie Gaunt, who informed Nixon that Haldeman came from a wealthy Los Angeles family and that he "would be a good worker." Hall suspected that Haldeman, who was running the advance team and was far more influential than he'd been four years earlier, was trying to encroach on his role.

It didn't help that the country was in a mild recession and that the economic conservatives who dominated and advised the administration were opposed to the tax cuts that Nixon wanted. And Nixon, who took pride in staying cool, was finding it hard to control his temper as the pressure on him increased. A White House aide, who briefly worked on the Nixon campaign, was on the Nixon train as they traveled down the western side of the Mississippi River and recalled, "We were in Iowa I think, and I was astounded. He was swearing in four-letter words right and left in his discourse. And that bothered me because I had never heard Eisenhower use a scatological four-letter word, though he used plenty of four-letter words—'goddamn it to hell.' So Nixon was swearing as he spoke, and I was so stunned by that, because of course I had seen him in action, in those leadership meetings, in the cabinet meetings."

On another occasion, the campaign was crossing Iowa by car with plans to stop in small towns where Nixon would speak. It turned out that there weren't many towns and not much point to the drive; it was a waste of a day and Nixon's irritation grew steadily. Major Hughes was in the front seat, directly in front of the candidate, and, as Haldeman recorded the moment, "Suddenly—incredibly—Nixon began to kick the back of Hughes's seat with both feet. And he wouldn't stop! Thump! Thump! Thump!" The seat and Hughes jolted forward as Nixon kept kicking until the car stopped and Hughes, silently, got out and started walking down the road. Hughes, who recalled that day years later, said, "We were all tired, lack of sleep. Something went wrong. He just kicked the back of the seat. He didn't mean anything by it. It was just frustration. I'd had enough and I just started to walk. I got about a hundred yards and Haldeman got hold of me. It was a temper tantrum." Even the devoted Rose Mary Woods was subject to Nixon's bad humor, and when it got too much for her, Len Hall would take her to dinner and let out his own frustration at trying to run the campaign, saying, "Well, I don't know how you stand this man, and I can't stand it any longer." But then they'd go back to work.

Nixon was also burdened with Cabot Lodge, who could barely keep up with the rigors of the campaign and at one point sounded close to quitting—a threat that Nixon took so seriously that he sent Fred Seaton, the interior secretary and a Nixon political adviser, to handle Lodge. Lodge also embarrassed Nixon—and risked alienating white southerners—by promising to put a Negro in the cabinet, a pledge that he made without checking with Nixon.

Despite the Negro-in-the-cabinet vow, there was a worrisome shift in the attitude of black voters. Martin Luther King Jr. had been arrested after a sit-in demonstration in DeKalb County, Georgia; the presiding judge said that Dr. King had violated an earlier probation (for driving without a license) and sentenced him to four months at hard labor at the Georgia State Prison in Reidsville, where King was transported in chains, in the back of a paddy wagon with a police dog. Coretta Scott King was terrified; she believed that her husband would be killed—not a groundless fear considering the appalling history of police crimes against blacks in Georgia—and she made panicked telephone calls to, among others, the Nixon and Kennedy organizations, asking someone, please, to intercede. Both campaigns were worried about losing white southern voters, but Senator Kennedy called Mrs. King, and his brother Robert telephoned Georgia's governor, a call that helped to free King. Nixon apparently tried to reach Attorney General Rogers or someone at the White House, but, as an aide put it, "some hang-up occurred someplace."

It was a cautious, even cowardly response by Nixon, not only because the proper choice was clear but because King was no stranger; they had been on friendly terms since they'd met in 1957. It was a little puzzling, too, because Nixon was the one major administration official who went out of his way to meet regularly with black leaders—people like John Johnson, the publisher of *Ebony*, the Jackie Robinsons, and reporters from the Negro press; in fact, after the Nixons moved into a new house in Wesley Heights, their first big social event included the black journalists and officials who had been with him during his 1957 trip to Africa. The Eisenhower aide Frederic Morrow had joined the Nixon campaign (although he felt that he was kept out of sight) and had pleaded for a statement deploring the arrest. Billy Graham had urged Nixon to stay in touch with Dr. King, and polls suggested that Nixon was going to do about as well with Negro voters as Eisenhower had—why put that at risk?

Nixon told Jackie Robinson (who was campaigning for the Nixon-Lodge ticket) that he had "frequently counseled with Dr. King and have a great respect for him," but wanted to avoid what he called a "grandstand play." Yet he seemed unable to distinguish between a grandstand play and doing nothing. The Kennedy organization knew just how to exploit his silence: in the last week of the campaign, two million copies of a pamphlet called " 'No Comment' Nixon Versus a Candidate with a Heart, Senator Kennedy" were distributed to the voters who would most appreciate them.

Just before Election Day, the Nixon camp came up with the suggestion that Eisenhower should ask both candidates to make public their health records (a way to expose Kennedy's rumored Addison's disease). That idea did not go over well. Jim Hagerty, his hostility to Nixon rising to the surface, called it a "cheap, lousy, stinking political trick" and the president said, "I am not making myself a party to a thing that has to do with the health of the candidates." If that scheme had gone forward, Nixon might have had to confront the persistent, though not quite correct rumors that he was seeing a New York psychiatrist—Arnold Hutschnecker. Although Hutschnecker was still identified as an internist, their relationship surely extended well beyond that, to a sort of mutual confidence and professional friendship, one that allowed the doctor to tell his patient with "a heavy heart" that during the campaign he had "watched certain developments which I felt would or could become fateful and about which I could do nothing." And Hutschnecker was confident enough in his knowledge of Nixon to later pronounce that the campaign's loss of energy stemmed not only from fatigue and the knee injury, but from the fact that Nixon had "suffered a debilitating, painful and depressing rejection by an authoritative father figure." Then there was a suggestion from the Nixon campaign that Nixon, if elected, would invite Communist bloc leaders to the United States and ask President Eisenhower to make reciprocal visits. Eisenhower, as Ann Whitman put it, "was astonished, did not like the idea of 'auctioning off the Presidency' in this manner . . . and felt it was a last-ditch, hysterical action." He went along with it, however, only to learn that Nixon had modified the proposal: he would ask *all* the former presidents— Truman, Hoover, and Eisenhower—to participate. Ike had never agreed to that—Ike and *Truman?*—and came close to asking Nixon to retract it. But by then, it was just about Election Day and all was forgotten.

The Nixons as Election Day approached were exhausted, and it showed. Just a day before the vote, during a stop in Detroit, the candidate threw a punch at an advertising consultant, Everett Hart, who had set Nixon off by refusing to run an errand. "I was really mad," Hart later told Rose Mary Woods, "because I had had a rib removed when I had had open heart surgery and that is where he hit me—in the ribs." Nixon eventually apologized, but Hart left the campaign. The pressure on the candidate was only increased by a promise to visit all fifty states; he had just managed to squeeze in Alaska before arriving in San Bernardino at one in the morning, where he spoke to a small crowd. At a little past seven, Pat and Dick voted, in Whittier. But after posing for pictures and shaking hands, the vice president turned to Herbert Klein, his perpetually weary-looking press secretary, and said, "I'm going to try to get away from you and the damn press. I want to be away from everything today. Understand?" Then to Major Hughes he said, "C'mon, I'm going to show you guys around Southern California," and the next few hours were among the oddest ever spent by a candidate on Election Day.

The entourage included the Secret Service agent and Caracas veteran Jack Sherwood, who sat in the backseat with Nixon; in the front were Hughes and a Los Angeles policeman who drove the car, a white convertible. "I don't want the radio on," Nixon said to his three companions as they pulled out. "I don't want any talk about the election. I'm just going to show you where I grew up."

Nixon seemed elated as they headed south. They made a stop in La Habra, where Nixon spent about fifteen minutes with his mother; in Yorba Linda, his birthplace; and in East Whittier, the site of the family grocery store. Hughes had thought the excursion would not last long, but after a while, Nixon suggested that they all go someplace for a drink. When Hughes reminded him that the bars were closed on Election Day, the vice president said, "Oh yeah, well, tell you what—let's go to Mexico."

It had been at least twenty years since Nixon had been across the border, in Tijuana, but as he'd told Jack Paar, he was fond of Mexican food and here was an opportunity to consume some. Hughes by now was concerned that no one knew where they were; he suggested that they ought to stop and call someone—Herb Klein, perhaps, or Bob Finch, whose nominal title was still campaign director. "No calls," the vice president said, so they kept driving. After a while, Hughes relieved the driver and Nixon moved to the front seat. Driving south with two aides and an L.A. cop, Nixon was so relaxed by the time they reached the outskirts of San Diego that he'd fallen asleep.

The party of four arrived in Tijuana at about eleven in the morning, and stopped at a bar and restaurant called Old Heidelberg, on Tijuana's main street. It was closed—it was still early—but someone recognized Nixon, and soon enough, they were drinking margaritas and German beer and eating tacos, enchiladas, and beans; then the mayor of Tijuana showed up and joined them. Nixon waited until one o'clock before he told Hughes to call Finch.

They started north at about two in the afternoon, making a stop at the eighteenth-century Spanish mission at San Juan Capistrano, where Nixon said to Hughes, a Roman Catholic, "I'm going to take my favorite Catholic into chapel." (Rose Mary Woods, also a Catholic, remembers Nixon once saying, "I think I'm more Catholic than some of you people.") In a chapel near the ruins of the old mission, Hughes and Nixon knelt together and Nixon said a prayer. Then, after Nixon stopped for a pineapple milkshake, they drove directly to Los Angeles where the returns were soon coming in from the East.

3

At about midnight on the West Coast, it was clear that the vice president needed to say something. Both Nixons came down to the ballroom of the Ambassador Hotel and Nixon came close to acknowledging his defeat: "if the present trend continues, Senator Kennedy will be the next President of the United States." He managed an approximate quick grin and talked about how Americans, after a hard-fought contest, always unite behind the victor. Pat Nixon looked miserable and tried to smile—sometimes a little out-of-sync with what her husband was saying. It had been a rough campaign; she had lost weight, which gave her an emaciated look.

A few minutes later—at 3:25 A.M. in the east—Nixon called Eisenhower. "He seemed controlled, not downcast particularly," Ann Whitman thought after speaking with him. Eisenhower urged him to concede (Nixon said that he'd already done that, although he hadn't, quite) and added that "if by some miracle the vote could be upset, conceding would not be harmful." He told Eisenhower that he still thought they would win California (he was correct) but also that Illinois and Minnesota could be his—which might be enough to close the popular vote margin. It was a short conversation. Eisenhower told Nixon to get a good rest and to send his love to Pat. "We can be proud of these last eight years," Eisenhower said, and Nixon said—it's unclear whether he was referring to the campaign or to Ike's presidency—"You did a grand job."

Nixon formally conceded the next morning in a telegram to Kennedy, which Herb Klein read to reporters. The closeness of the election—the closest of the twentieth century—provided no consolation; rather, it only tempted some Nixon operatives to challenge the result. Out of 69 million votes cast, Kennedy led Nixon by only 118,000, with an electoral vote margin of 303 to 219. In Illinois and Texas, Kennedy's margins were suspiciously thin—or thin enough to set in motion the theory that Nixon had been cheated. After all, electoral fraud was nothing new in the Chicago of Mayor Richard Daley, and who the hell knew what went on in the Texas of Lyndon Johnson?

Nixon always insisted that others encouraged him to appeal the outcome and that he rejected the idea; he didn't want to create a "constitutional crisis," it was said, and he didn't want to be viewed as a sore loser. Nixon may have behaved admirably, but perhaps not quite as admirably as he wanted others to think. The historian David Greenberg has pointed out that while Nixon would say that Eisenhower encouraged him to challenge the result and that he refused, Ike quickly came to believe it was a bad idea; and while Nixon personally never got involved in trying to create ad hoc groups like the Nixon Recount Committee, he did not do much to discourage them.

The president was not on hand to welcome the Nixons back from the West Coast—he had left the next morning for Augusta, along with gang members Slats Slater, Bill Robinson, and Cliff Roberts. "Well, this is the biggest defeat of my life," Eisenhower said when he sat down at the bridge table inside the Columbine, a baffling assessment of his career. He complained about the campaign's management, saying, "Dick never asked me how I thought the campaign should be run. I offered him Montgomery"—the television director Robert Montgomery—"who would never have let him look as he did in that first television debate. Cabot Lodge should never have stuck his nose into the makeup of the Cabinet—promising a Negro cost us thousands of votes in the South, maybe South Carolina and Texas."

As for not staying around long enough to greet Nixon, the explanation for that came eighteen months later in a letter to Nixon from John S. D. Eisenhower, who explained that his father had been "more tired and discouraged than any of us had seen him in his career" and that he had begun to "develop physical symptoms, such as heart flutters and the like." So, John Eisenhower wrote, "you can see why all his associates practically shoved him on the airplane, the morning of November seventh."

However, before he boarded the plane Eisenhower found a moment to write a note to the Nixons in which one false note followed another: "While it seems ridiculous for me to be speaking of fatigue when I know what you and Pat have been through these many weeks, I am nevertheless feeling a great need to get some sunshine, recreation and rest," he said. "I want to express to you both the fervent hope that the two of you will not be too greatly disappointed by yesterday's election returns," he continued, almost as if he were speaking about a round of golf. "I know that whatever disappointment you do feel will not be for yourselves but for our country and for the jeopardy in which our great hopes and aims for the future have been placed." The letter finished up in this bland spirit:

> On the personal side, you will unquestionably have a happier life during these next four years, especially because of your closer contact with your two beautiful daughters. Of course I have no indication of what your future plans may be—possibly you do not know yourselves. But wherever you go or whatever activities in which you may be engaged, you will have my best wishes. I assure you that my official confidence in you, Dick, has not been shaken for a moment, and of course all four of you may be certain that the affection that Mamie and I feel for you will never grow less.

Nixon never asked what Eisenhower meant by "official confidence," and Eisenhower might not have known the answer if he had.

A month later, Eisenhower discussed the election with Nixon and a small group that included his outgoing chief of staff, Jerry Persons, the new Republican National Committee chairman, Thruston Morton, and his aide Bryce Harlow, who took notes. Eisenhower repeated some of the second-guessing that he'd been hearing: debating Kennedy was a mistake; Nixon should never have gone to New York to see Rockefeller. Nixon remarked that, you know, everybody makes mistakes in a campaign but Lodge's statement "just killed us in the South." On that subject, Eisenhower said that his administration had made civil rights a priority—as if it had been *his* priority—and had still lost black support; Negroes, he added, "just do not give a damn." Nixon corrected him on his statistics; he pointed out that the Republican ticket actually got *more* black votes than it had in 1952, so the administration's record probably did help some. But then he added, a little bitterly, that the 1960 black vote was a "bought vote, and it isn't bought by civil rights," which prompted Thruston Morton to say of Negro voters, "the hell with them."

A month later, it was reported that the Justice Department had looked into ways to free Dr. King when he was jailed and that the White House staff had even drafted a statement for Eisenhower. The president would have said, "It seems to me fundamentally unjust that a man who has peacefully attempted to establish his right to equal treatment, free from racial discrimination, should be imprisoned on an unrelated charge, in itself insignificant," and then added that he'd asked the attorney general to work for his release. The statement, though, was never issued. King later said:

> I always felt that Nixon lost a real opportunity to express . . . support of something much larger than an individual, because this expressed support of the movement for civil rights in a way. And I had known Nixon longer. He had been supposedly close to me, and he would call me frequently about things, getting, seeking my advice. And yet, when this moment came, it was like he had never heard of me, you see. So this is why I really considered him a moral coward and one who was really unwilling to take a courageous step and take a risk.

Nixon wasn't in a mood to relive missteps. His family was about to be uprooted after fourteen years; they were going to sell their Wesley Heights house and move back to California. Nixon tried but sometimes failed to hide his resentment over the outcome of the election, even turning down a request to participate in an NBC broadcast titled *Tribute to a Patriot*—a softhearted farewell to Ike, with appearances by, among others, Harold Macmillan, the West Point Glee Club, Bobby Jones, and President-elect Kennedy. His absence would have been viewed as a public sulk (Jerry Persons told Len Hall that Nixon had seemed to him "completely irrational") and Nixon changed his mind after Hall told him that his absence would be seen as proof of a breach with the president. Eisenhower in the end thanked Nixon and told him how sorry he was that "such a hassle arose about your participation," but nothing was going to improve Nixon's mood. The Ewalds—Bill and his wife, Mary—got a sense of that at a farewell party at the Nixons' during the holidays. The vice president's words of greeting to the Ewalds were "We won, but they stole it from us."

CHAPTER 19

The Good Life

<u>1</u>

It would have been natural for Nixon and Eisenhower to go their separate ways after January 20; that was the custom of the men who held those jobs. The Eisenhowers intended to live on the farm in Gettysburg and, during the cold months, in Palm Desert, California; Ike would have an office in nearby Indio at a ranch owned by the aviatrix Jacqueline Cochran and her husband, Floyd Odlum, an investor who had made his fortune during the Depression. There he would work on his memoirs (two volumes were planned for Doubleday) and otherwise sort out life as one of America's three surviving ex-presidents—a distinction that didn't seem to mean all that much to him. He hadn't had much to do with the other two; he hadn't spoken to Harry Truman, now seventy-six, since the 1953 inaugural (not counting a brief handshake at George C. Marshall's funeral in the fall of 1959), and Herbert Hoover, who was eighty-six, was becoming ever more calcified. At Eisenhower's request, Congress passed a special bill that restored his rank as a five-star general, and that was how he preferred to be addressed for the rest of his life. He intended to stay connected with his circle of friends and looked forward to playing more golf and bridge in Gettysburg, Augusta, and California at the Eldorado Country Club in

Indian Wells (where he now socialized with people like Bob Hope, Freeman Gosden, and Lawrence Welk), and having the time simply to live the way many retired Americans lived, although Eisenhower, at seventy, was considerably better off and better connected than most retired Americans.

The future was not so clear for Nixon, who, on January 9, observed his forty-eighth birthday and who, at that point, could only count on practicing law again, probably in Los Angeles. He'd been a lawyer when he'd run for Congress in 1946, but he'd also been thirty-three years old and returning to that life in middle age was not an inviting prospect. His annual birthday greeting from Ike could not have helped his mood:

> I am sorry that as I send you my warmest felicitations . . . I could not have the privilege of addressing you as "Mr. President." But all that is past and done, and I hope that you and Pat and your lovely daughters will find Southern California much to your liking. I hope, too, that I shall see you when Mamie and I are there. With warm regard, and Happy Birthday!

Nixon had wanted nothing more than to stay in public life at the national level, and yet suddenly, although his résumé was most impressive, he appeared to be blocked. Kennedy would surely run again in 1964, and incumbents tended to win unless, like William Howard Taft in 1912, they got into third-party difficulties or, like Hoover twenty years later, they were blamed for a nation's economic collapse. Eight years hence, Nixon could seem like used, unwanted goods. It is easy to see why he was tempted by a suggestion from Del Webb, then the owner of the New York Yankees, that he become commissioner of Major League Baseball.

Nixon wasn't planning to sit in an office drafting wills and contracts. He was in demand as a speaker and he wanted to write. When he paid a courtesy call on Kennedy, the new president encouraged his literary aspirations—telling him, in Nixon's recollection, that "every public man should write a book at some time in his life, both for the mental discipline and because it tends to elevate him in popular esteem to the respect status of an 'intellectual,' " a tenet of self-help that it is impossible to read without smiling.

The Nixons, considering their status, had lived relatively normal lives.

Their daughters had first attended Washington public school and then the more select Sidwell Friends School, and they had lived in their own homes, on Tilden Street in Spring Valley and then on Forest Lane in Wesley Heights. (There was no vice presidential "mansion" until 1974, and the first vice president actually to live at One Observatory Place, next to the Naval Observatory, was Walter Mondale.) Pat Nixon had been photographed wheeling a shopping cart through the aisles of a local supermarket, and claimed to do many of her own household chores, such as sewing curtains, although she had turned over the cooking to a housekeeper. "Honest to Pete, I'm no gourmet," she once told *Look* magazine. The Nixons had little or nothing to do with Georgetown society, but they had become, in every sense of the word, Washingtonians.

By contrast, Dwight and Mamie Eisenhower had never lived the way most Americans live. As Stephen Ambrose has pointed out, Ike never learned how to do many of the things that other people regard as routine, such as paying tolls on a turnpike, or mixing frozen orange juice, or adjusting the picture on a television set. He'd grown up in the Army, and then he'd gone into politics, after a brief detour as a college president. He could not even use a rotary telephone—that was what secretaries and aides were for—and on the evening of January 20, 1961, when he wanted to call his son, he shouted for a Secret Service agent: "Come show me how you work this goddamned thing!"

So while it would have been natural for the Eisenhowers and Nixons to fall out of touch, something else happened. As the Eisenhower era ended, one could see both men tapping into pools of—if not affection, then whatever it was that they alone shared. Five days before the Kennedy inaugural, Nixon wrote a two-page letter to Eisenhower that went far beyond a pro forma appreciation of what the past eight years had meant to him although he also needed a way to express that—and more:

> At the end of the last Cabinet meeting Friday, I was trying to think of something to say which would sum up the feeling all of us had in our hearts without being overly sentimental. Incidentally, like you, I always feel that expressions of affection and sentiment between two men who work together are embarrassing and should, whenever possible, be avoided! But in this case, two words would have done the trick—thank you.

Nixon then did become sentimental. He wrote about the "mountain-top experience" of working with Ike and the cabinet, and said that "never in this nation's history has one man in public life owed so much to another as I owe to you." He mentioned "countless gestures of friendship which Mrs. Eisenhower and you have extended to us through these years," as if the fund crisis, Ike's maddening runaround in 1956, the "give-me-a-week" remark had been packed up and shipped off to another dimension. His letter concluded with the hope that "the sun will always shine on your life in the years ahead as warmly and brightly as it will in your stay at Palm Springs."

It was not a note that called for a response, but Eisenhower, on his next-to-last day in office, wrote back in nearly the same spirit, making clear that he was not "putting a period to our long and satisfying association and friendship." Rather, he said, "I am sure that you and I will find many reasons, in addition to the personal, to confer together from time to time. I believe we not only should but will want to keep our contacts on a fairly frequent basis." As for the election, it was as if Ike now saw the loss as his, too: "I am not an individual who accepts defeat easily," he said, adding that "the future can still bring to you a real culmination in your service to the country."

A month later, after Nixon had moved to Los Angeles, living at first in a hotel, Eisenhower sent him a short note from Palm Desert. This one, though, had a personal, almost intimate quality; just as unusual, there was an invitation to socialize. One might almost have concluded that Ike was getting bored:

> If you come out this way, or should you find it possible to visit the desert area during the next six weeks or so, I hope you will come to see me.
> I have been having difficulty with my back and haven't played golf for ten days, but maybe I will improve enough to have a game if you come out.

Nixon did come out—in early March, he and Pat made the drive from Los Angeles to Palm Desert to have lunch at the Eisenhowers' new cottage, with palm trees on the lawn and situated on the eleventh fairway of the Eldorado Country Club. It was their first get-together since the Kennedy inaugural and while the agenda was private, their apparent goodwill—the two couples posed for pictures—was on display. Soon after, in a birthday note to Pat Nixon, Eisenhower commiserated on the hassles of house hunting—he knew it "must be pretty hectic for you."

The transition into private life certainly was hectic and the house hunting was tedious; the Nixons looked at Hancock Park as well as Pacific Palisades, Beverly Hills, and Flintridge—"wherever that is," Nixon said. (La Cañada Flintridge was about an hour's commute from downtown L.A.) In mid-March, he announced that he was joining a downtown Los Angeles law firm, Adams, Duque and Hazeltine, under an arrangement that would give him time for outside activities. He did not disappear (when he reported for work on the tenth floor of the ornate Pacific Mutual Life Insurance Building, on West Sixth Street, he was met by flashbulbs), but the headlines naturally went to Kennedy—even a report that Warner Bros. was going to make a movie called *PT-109*, about Kennedy's wartime adventures in the Pacific.

At the start of what Nixon and historians would call his "wilderness years," the former vice president lived almost like a hermit. While his family was in Washington (the Nixons wanted Julie and Tricia to finish the school year at Sidwell), Nixon recalled, "Relatives and friends wanted me to stay with them, but I preferred to be alone." He rented a small apartment on Wilshire Boulevard close to his downtown office where, he said, he learned how to fix his own meals and "actually learned to enjoy heating a TV dinner and eating it alone while reading a book or magazine." But he wasn't enjoying it much. During one of his first weekends in California, Nixon called an old friend and said, "My God, what do you do out here? There's nothing to do, nobody to talk to. What am I supposed to do? Go out and garden in the yard? I can't take this."

The Nixons soon found temporary and deluxe lodging at 901 North Bundy Drive (a house that they rented from the movie director Walter Lang), but even a luxurious Tudor-style house in Brentwood with neighbors like Alfred Hitchcock, Jascha Heifetz, and Kim Novak gave little pleasure to someone who'd come within 118,000 votes of being president and who for the time being had no real idea what to do next. "He is bored out of his mind, he misses Washington," Stephen Hess, who had been on the White House speechwriting staff, said. "It's all he's ever known since he got out of the Navy." Not so long before, his biggest problem was Nelson Rockefeller; now he was stuck in a West Coast law firm and Rockefeller was the governor of the most populous state in the union. So it was natural for Nixon to be drawn to the idea of becoming governor of the second-largest state, and at the end of March, he returned to the Eldorado Country Club for another lunch with Ike—this time without their wives present—and once again they kept the subject of their talks entirely to themselves.

When Nixon got another letter from Eisenhower, in April, the general had returned to Gettysburg and the personal tone had reverted once again to somewhat chilly formality—in this case, even to reproach—over Nixon's apparent ingratitude toward his 1960 supporters. "There is one thing—a small thing if you will—that has come to my attention periodically in connection with your campaign," Eisenhower wrote. "A number of substantial contributors to your campaign have told me that they have received no word of thanks from you, or, indeed, from anyone in your organization." He continued, "All of the people to whom I have talked have professed that they themselves wanted no expression of gratitude. Nonetheless, I think that most people do."

Such niceties didn't much interest Nixon. When young Steve Hess left the White House, he was asked by his former boss, Bryce Harlow, to help Eisenhower and Nixon with their mail—a profitable job because the Republican National Committee was willing to pay Hess on a piecework basis. "Every time I see something that involves an Eisenhower or a Nixon friend—somebody in their Cabinet, a social friend, their daughter got married, they got an honorary degree—I'd draft a note," Hess said. "I'd go around town and people would say, 'I got the nicest note from the General.'" Nixon mostly wanted to stay in touch with Washington, with what was going on in the only part of the country that really interested him. "I'm in a sense writing a newsletter for one person—what are your friends doing?" Hess said. As for the correspondence, "I go into Nixon and he said, 'Don't send those letters. I don't want to be remembered as someone who remembers somebody's birthday.' So Eisenhower, who spends his life claiming he's not a politician was innately a politician. Nixon, who's picked because he's the politician of the match, says, 'Don't send the letters.' "

After a while, Hess got other assignments. The former vice president was potentially a valuable commodity for publications like the *Los Angeles Times,* which paid him to write political commentary. "And he says, 'Well, you'll do this for me,' " Hess said. Nixon was generous. "Let's say he got ten thousand dollars from the *Saturday Evening Post*—he'd give me half the money. I'd say, 'Dick, you don't have to do this,' and he'd say, 'It'd just go to the IRS anyway.' " In April, Nixon agreed to write the book that he'd thought about—it would be a sort-of memoir for Doubleday in which he'd recount various "crises," such as the Hiss case, but also Eisenhower's heart attack and the scare that he'd had with that mob in Caracas, as well as the Khrushchev encounter and the 1960 campaign. And of course he would relive the fund episode and his state of uncertainty in 1956. Nixon's chief assist for the project came from Alvin Moscow, a young New Yorker who had been recommended by the writer and Nixon family friend Adela Rogers St. Johns.

Even with these projects, it did not take Nixon—still bored, out of his element—very long to start thinking about a return to politics, if he'd ever stopped. By the spring of 1961, if he gave a speech it focused mostly on foreign policy and, soon enough, the failings of the Kennedy administration. He wrote to Bryce Harlow, saying that after a hundred days, "no fair-minded person would question my right to give my appraisal of the administration," and it was time to break his "self-imposed silence." But he didn't speak with the heat that he'd shown when he was younger; there was, rather, an almost judicious tone, with remarks about the need for a "mature" foreign policy; he did not, for instance, rush to criticize Kennedy after America's inept attempt in mid-April to overthrow Fidel Castro with an unsupported invasion at the Bay of Pigs, an adventure that appalled Ike (who privately called it a "very dreary account of mismanagement, indecision and timidity at the wrong time"). When Nixon joined Eisenhower at a Pennsylvania party rally in June, Eisenhower stayed with domestic politics, saying that the Kennedy administration was transforming the government "into a gigantic federal Santa Claus," while Nixon, in reference to the Bay of Pigs, said, "It is essential that you act just as big as you talk."

Nixon never stopped missing his old life, the time when he didn't have to fly commercial and when he was surrounded by partisan crowds rather than by curious onlookers. On a plane from Chicago to Des Moines, a passenger approached Nixon, who was trying to nap, and said, "I want to say hello. I thought I recognized your face." Nixon replied, "I guess it's a hard one to miss."

By the late spring of 1961, speculation about Nixon running for governor of California had begun. It made sense; here was a former vice president, perhaps the most eligible candidate in America, and an election was coming up in 1962. The *Los Angeles Times*'s Kyle Palmer, a political editor and writer whose worshipful affection for Nixon extended back to his 1946 congressional race, guessed that the "likeliest immediate turn of fate" would be Nixon's seeking the governorship. "Whatever the disappointment and sadness of his amazingly close defeat last November, the warmth and almost mystic acclaim he gets wherever he goes are a most inspiring and sustaining influence upon his thinking and his planning," Palmer wrote. In mid-July, Nixon wrote to Eisenhower about it and sounded dubious— "It is a very difficult decision but I continue to lean strongly against the idea of entering the race if we can find another candidate who will have some reasonable chance of being successful," he said. He promised to send along his own detailed analysis of the pros and cons.

By now, the newspapers had gotten hold of the idea that there might really be a contest between Nixon and Governor Pat Brown, who had defeated Senator Knowland in 1958; from a journalist's standpoint, the prospect was delectable. Nixon, though, sounded genuinely torn, and the person to whom he turned for advice was Eisenhower, whose opinion still mattered enormously; it was as if he was willing to suspend his doubts about Ike's political aptitude when he sketched out his own clear-sighted assessment of his prospects: on the "pro" side, those in favor of a run argued that he could win, and that the office would provide him with a staff and a forum. But the "con" arguments struck Nixon as equally persuasive, and perhaps more so—starting with the worry that if he lost, "I would be virtually finished as far as public influence is concerned," and even if he won, he might have to deal with problems that could "require some action which could be very unpopular both in the state and in the nation." There was also, simply put, the geographical imperative: in California, he would be "so far away from the centers of national and international news media that I simply do not believe it would be possible for me to continue to speak at all constructively" on the issues he cared about. That point appeared to shift the balance against making the race. General MacArthur and Herbert Hoover, both of whom lived in the Waldorf Towers in New York, urged him to run for Congress, which would bring him to Washington, his natural home, rather than to the alien desert of Sacramento.

Eisenhower waited a couple of weeks to get back to Nixon; and when he did, he seemed to take a nonposition: "Since I gather you have almost completely made up your mind for reasons which I would not dispute for an instant, I shall not venture any opinion of my own." Furthermore, any opinion that he did venture "could be totally wrong from your viewpoint." And yet, wasn't there something a little reproving between those lines? The former president continued in this tone:

> Over the years I have wrestled with many decisions. But somehow or other, when the chips were down, the decision seemed to come by itself and without a conscious thought process. Suddenly something seems inescapable or right and any other course unthinkable. So I am sure the answer—whatever it is—will come to you.

At the end of August, Nixon came east—for a quick business trip, he said—and made a detour to see Eisenhower in Gettysburg. They played golf, but mostly Nixon was there to talk more about the gubernatorial race; and this time Ike had the unequivocal advice that he had previously withheld: he urged him to run—a conversation that continued in Washington, where they played another round at Burning Tree (a foursome that included Bill Rogers and John S. D. Eisenhower). "I can find no alternative to an affirmative decision," Eisenhower wrote to Nixon a few days later, and set forth his argument:

> None of our other Republican "friends" would stand a chance in my opinion, of defeating the incumbent. If [former governor Goodwin] Knight, for instance, should run and be defeated (assuming you backed him, as

assuredly you would have to), then in effect you have suffered a defeat. If you run and win, as I believe you can, you offset to a large extent the razor-thin margin by which you lost the Presidential race last November. Finally, I see no reason why, if you are elected Governor, you cannot, if you wish, make the 1964 Presidential race—and I think you would be in a far more powerful position as Governor, controlling a large delegation, than otherwise.

The general concluded by saying that "whatever it is worth, I have added my two cents' worth," but it was certainly more than "two cents' worth"—it was more like a hard shove. Had the advice come from almost anyone else, Nixon might not have taken it seriously. After all, why would a defeat for Goodie Knight be a defeat for Nixon? Knight had been soundly beaten when he ran for Knowland's Senate seat in 1958, which was no reflection on anyone but Knight. Nor was Nixon at that point thinking about 1964 and, what was more important, he had minimal interest in local issues. Even though the polls suggested that Nixon had only to show up in order to win, and the governorship of California was a major prize, would he have gone ahead if Ike's letter had begun by saying, "I can find no alternative to a *negative* decision"?

So Nixon did it. On September 27, in front of cameras at the Statler Hilton in Los Angeles, he not only announced for governor, but declared that he would not be a candidate for president in 1964. He also said that the only person to whom he'd confided his plans beyond his family was General Eisenhower. Nixon's family was not happy about this turn, coming less than a year after the presidential race. Adela Rogers St. Johns told Fawn Brodie, an unsympathetic Nixon biographer, that she'd overheard a quarrel between Nixon and his wife during which Pat, in the heat of domestic battle, said, "If you ever run for office again, I'll kill myself."

CHAPTER 20

The Obituary Writers

1

In the late fall of 1961, Nixon was both running for governor and writing his memoir *Six Crises*. Alvin Moscow, his collaborator, had set up an office in the garage at North Bundy Drive, and every morning they would talk for about two hours—about Alger Hiss, about politics, about Eisenhower—while Moscow took notes, a routine interrupted on November 6, 1961, when a brushfire swept through parts of Bel Air and Beverly Glen, destroying several houses—including Joe E. Brown's, across the street—and forcing the evacuation of about three thousand residents, including the movie stars Red Skelton and Burt Lancaster; when an aide hurried up into the hills to help, he saw Nixon carrying framed photographs to his car. The Nixons spent the night at the Biltmore Hotel, but apart from some burned trees and shrubs, their place suffered only minor smoke damage. "Quite a number of large homes are now nothing but rubble," Nixon wrote to a friend. "A little further up the street there is an area that looks as though a bomb had been dropped."

Dwight and Mamie Eisenhower meanwhile had taken the train cross-country to their winter home in Palm Desert and during the next few weeks it was as if the Nixons and the Eisenhowers were becoming closer, if not exactly close. For one thing, the Eisenhowers, who during Ike's presidency had never invited the Nixons inside the Gettysburg house—or for that matter the living quarters of the White House—sometimes sounded eager to see more of them. Perhaps it was the informality of California, or the relative proximity of Los Angeles, or perhaps Ike was enjoying a vicarious involvement in Nixon's gubernatorial campaign, but there it was— gestures, spontaneous and otherwise, of friendship.

Nixon by then could use all the friendship he could get. The California campaign was already a nightmare; it was as if he had stepped into the dysfunctional past of an unloving family. It had awakened dormant animosity between Nixon and the former governor, Goodwin Knight, who decided that he, too, wanted to enter the June primary. Then Nixon not only had Knight to face, but two additional opponents: a liberal Republican, the former lieutenant governor Harold J. (Butch) Powers, and a conservative Republican, the Assembly leader Joseph Shell, a local hero who had led USC to the Rose Bowl in 1939. So there promised to be lots of time for acrimony and general ill will, which started when Knight accused Nixon of offering an unethical deal—to appoint him chief justice of California's Supreme Court if he would stay out of the race. Nixon called the story "false and libelous"; Knight said he had witnesses, and Nixon said he had witnesses, too. The accusations that they exchanged left no room for mere misunderstanding; someone had to be dissembling and to judge by all the details provided by Knight, it was probably Nixon.

Then, in mid-January, Knight quit the race, pleading bad health—he was suffering from infectious hepatitis. ("I know this is a difficult blow to a man who has been such a vigorous and tireless campaigner," Nixon said.) Harold Powers dropped out, too, saying that the "kingmakers" had made sure that state Republicans "shall take a discard from the rubble heap of national politics and like it."

Nixon started out in much the way he had a dozen years earlier, when he ran for the Senate. But the state had changed. Californians suspected Nixon's motives—40 percent thought that he planned to run for president in two years. Mark Harris, who wrote about the campaign for *Life* magazine, got the impression that Nixon was bored by "the repetition of things: every day was not different to him." Even those on his staff felt that his heart was never in it.

Nixon also had to deal with the far right that, in its milder form, took shape in organizations like the Christian Anti-Communist Crusade, led by Fred C. Schwarz, an Australian doctor who had emigrated in 1953 and whose supporters included most surprisingly C. D. Jackson, who was now the publisher of *Life*. More preposterous than Schwarz was the John Birch Society, founded by Robert Welch, an eccentric candy maker from Boston, whose book *The Politician* called Eisenhower a "dedicated conscious agent of the Communist conspiracy." Nixon saw them as "the nuts . . . you could just hear them crackling there in the head," but he knew that he would have to deal with them. Nixon also had to deal with the decidedly rightward drift of his party. Ideological shifts in both parties worried him; in 1959, when he spoke at the Commonwealth Club in San Francisco and was asked how he'd feel about a realignment of the two major parties—a sharp liberal-conservative division—he replied, "I think it would be a great tragedy," and continued, "I think one of the attributes of our political system has been that we have avoided generally violent swings in Administrations from one extreme to the other. And the reason we have avoided that is that in both parties there has been room for a broad spectrum of opinion." Therefore, he added, "when your Administrations come to power, they will represent the whole people rather than just one segment of the people." Not only Birchers but conservatives like Joe Shell had little sympathy for that sort of view and had every reason to be suspicious of Nixon's search for a middle ground.

At the start of 1962, the Nixons sent flowers to welcome the Eisenhowers to a new house in Indian Wells and Mamie Eisenhower wrote back with chatty exuberance: "I have rarely seen as beautiful an arrangement—great big white chrysanthemums and smaller white pompoms, and white Christmas bells mingled with the flowers." As for their new house, "the walls are white" and "the kitchen is an electronic marvel."

The Nixons had a new house, too, in a new affluent enclave, Trousdale Estates, situated north of Sunset Boulevard in Beverly Hills. This one, at 410 Martin Lane, was large even by California standards—sixty-five hundred square feet with seven baths, four bedrooms, three fireplaces, a library, and a huge living room. "Its interior, at entry, was of a solid, soft color tending toward white, immediately leading not farther inward but instantly outward, opening swiftly onto a patio," one visitor wrote. "I had no sooner entered than I was out again, as if it were a trick house. Beyond the patio was a swimming pool."

The Nixons saw the Eisenhowers' house on a Saturday in February when the whole family was invited to stay at a cottage nearby. Ike was looking forward to golf on Sunday; and if Dick could stay for another game on Monday, "so much the better." A few days before the visit, Eisenhower got an advance copy of *Six Crises* and although he hadn't yet read it, he told Nixon how impressed he was by the speed with which it was written.

Mamie took Pat, Tricia, and Julie shopping in nearby Palm Springs, while the two men played golf from eight in the morning until nearly noon, persisting even when they got soaked by rain. The next day, after the Nixons returned to Los Angeles, Eisenhower wrote to admit that "There seems to be a great residue of political fever left in me," and, with a surge of warmth, he complimented Nixon on his knowledge of politics in California and throughout America. "Despite the unexpected body blow the rainstorm gave our golf game yesterday morning, I, for one, had a wonderful time during our twenty-four hours together," he wrote. "I shall surely see you before we go back East. . . . And whenever you get a moment, do call or drop me a line."

Nixon had written in much the same spirit, saying, "I can't tell you how much Pat and I enjoyed our visit with you and Mrs. Eisenhower. It was a welcome respite after a week of campaigning in some of our smaller Northern California towns." As for *Six Crises*, Nixon added, "This was my first effort in the literary field and probably my last. I spent all of October, November and December in writing the final draft of the book. It was the hardest work I have ever done from the standpoint of concentration and discipline required."

On March 1, Nixon and Joe Shell appeared at the convention of the California Republican Assembly, where Nixon intended to denounce Robert Welch and the John Birch Society. But it was one thing to attack someone like the retired Major General Edwin Walker—an out-and-out Bircher, who was running for governor of Texas as a Democrat—and another to alienate conservatives who would certainly choose him over Pat Brown. At the convention, Nixon handed out a statement saying that the organization needed to "once and for all repudiate Robert Welch and those who accept his leadership and viewpoints," adding that no Republican organization can "compromise with the demagoguery and the totalitarian views of Robert Welch."

Nixon sent his statement to Eisenhower along with a note: "I thought it was time to take on the lunatic fringe once and for all." Ike replied the next day and praised Nixon for "in large measure [getting] the Assembly to take what you said—and like it." Both of them knew, however, that Nixon had not gotten what he'd asked for; the resolution passed by the Assembly condemned Welch but not his followers—it only urged members of the John Birch Society to get out of it "forthwith." It did, though, remind Californians that there was indeed a lunatic fringe and that the Republicans were the ones who found it necessary to deal with it.

2

With the publication of *Six Crises*, Nixon had to once more relive some of his worst moments. "I interviewed him on all the five crises," Alvin Moscow said, but not the sixth—the 1960 campaign, a chapter that was nearly half as long as the other five sections combined. Nixon wrote that one alone, working in the desert town of Apple Valley, dictating tapes that Don Hughes, his former military aide, would pick up and send by bus to Rose Mary Woods, who had moved to Los Angeles to work for Nixon. The first draft of that last chapter, Moscow said, "was really awful," but they cut it back. "We would go line by line, and he'd say 'I like this line,' and I'd say 'It just doesn't ring right.' I'd say, 'You made this point before—you don't have to say it again.' "

In its final version, Moscow said, the book "was basically as it came out of his mouth." It often seems more revealing than it really is, but its flashes of candor and emotion made it unusual for a politician and the not-quite-suppressed anger directed at Eisenhower is sometimes startling. Nixon never directly criticized Ike, but there was no way to separate episodes like the fund crisis, or the way the 1956 nomination kept being pulled from his grasp, from the man who "had a quality of reserve which, at least subconsciously, tended to make a visitor feel like a junior officer coming in to see the commanding General."

"Tell me about Eisenhower, what kind of man was he?" Moscow asked at one point, and Nixon said, "Well I'll tell you. Eisenhower was one of the most devious men I've ever met." Moscow knew right away that the "devious" quote was a ghostwriter's jewel; Nixon understood the same thing, but with less pleasure. "When he was going over the book," Moscow recalled, "he said, 'I can't call Eisenhower devious.' And I said, 'You're really giving him character, everyone thinks he's a superficial smiling guy with no brains, and here you're . . . ' So he said, 'Well, let's call him "the most devious man I ever met in the best sense of the word.' " In the published version, it read, "He was a far more complex and devious man than most people realized, and in the best sense of those words," and as if to bury any hint that Nixon meant that critically, he added, "His mind was quick and facile. His thoughts far outraced his speech and this gave rise to his frequent 'scrambled syntax' which more perceptive critics should have recognized as the mark of a far-ranging and versatile mind rather than an indication of poor training in grammar."

The memoir reached the *New York Times* best-seller list on April 8, at number 14, and appeared there every week for the next four months, once reaching number 4. (Its nonfiction competition included Louis Nizer's *My Life in Court*, Barbara Tuchman's *The Guns of August*, and Theodore White's celebratory account of the 1960 campaign, *The Making of the President*.) The book sold more than a quarter million copies and earned more than $200,000 in royalties. But it was not an ideal campaign book; something about Nixon tempted people to try to analyze him, and here was a memoir of self-analysis.

Perhaps because he was so busy with the early stages of the campaign and book promotion, Nixon didn't attend the dedication of the Eisenhower Library in Abilene in May. "I do wish you and Pat could have been with us," Ike wrote, sounding almost hurt. "A lot of our old friends turned up," he added, as if he'd suddenly thrust Nixon into the old-friend category.

• • •

In early October, Eisenhower campaigned alongside his former vice president in San Francisco. As the motorcade passed, many onlookers, holding transistor radios, were paying more attention to the fourth game of the World Series, in which the San Francisco Giants were beating the Yankees 7 to 3. When Ike spoke, it was as if he wanted to make up for all that he'd never quite managed to say two years earlier. In fact, he informed Californians, "one of the biggest mistakes of my political career was not working harder for Dick Nixon in 1960," and his praise was effusive: "Richard Nixon is one man so intimately and thoroughly known to me that without hesitation I can personally vouch for his ability, his sense of duty, his sharpness of mind, and his wealth in wisdom." To that, Nixon said, "All that I have been through becomes worthwhile to hear that tribute from the greatest living American."

By then, though, the campaign—it was being run by Nixon's former chief advance man, H. R. Haldeman—was probably doomed. Leonard Hall wrote to Nixon to say, "I read, with some surprise that Bob Halderman [sic] has been named your campaign manager," adding that among people he knew, "The general comment in regard to it is, 'This means that Dick is going to run his own campaign.' This is not good." Nixon got some volunteer coaching from Jack Paar's onetime producer Paul Keyes, but that didn't prevent him from saying things like, "If I have any greater interest than politics, it's sports," and in late October, when it looked as if tension between the United States and Soviet Union over Russian missiles in Cuba might bring on an annihilating nuclear war, there was a burst of patriotic affection for President Kennedy that helped Pat Brown. Just before the vote, Paar dashed off a note to Nixon—"Dear Dick—I pray you'll win!" This time, though, it wasn't even close. Brown defeated Nixon by a 53-to-47 percent margin.

People watched Nixon's moody, angry farewell to politics—his "last press conference"—with disbelief, fascination, and mirth. There was Richard Nixon at his rawest, scolding the press: "But as I leave you I want you to know, just think how much you're going to be missing. You won't have Nixon to kick around anymore." Alvin Moscow, who had been standing next to Rose Mary Woods, knew that Nixon, who could tolerate only small amounts of alcohol, had been drinking (one beer, according to Haldeman, would "transform his normal speech into the rambling elocution of a Bowery wino") and like others in the Nixon entourage, Moscow feared the worst. He never saw Nixon again. "I got a copy of the book," he said. "I got a number of nice cards. I was on a list."

Nixon was met outside by two old friends, Murray Chotiner and Jack Drown, who drove him to Martin Lane, where Pat, Julie, and Tricia had been watching TV. As Julie recalled, they were waiting in the hallway at the front door when the defeated candidate came into the house; Pat spoke first, her voice breaking: "Oh, Dick." Nixon hurried past all of them and went to the backyard. The Nixon daughters had never seen their parents behaving like that—their emotions so obvious, their unhappiness so powerful, and they found it bewildering. This was a real defeat—humiliating, unequivocal. That evening, Helene and Jack Drown came by and took Julie and Tricia to their house in Rolling Hills, about thirty miles south of Los Angeles, where they stayed for several days. There were rumors that Nixon had struck his wife—and those who knew Nixon best knew that he was susceptible to rages—but the sources for that story were at best second- or third-hand. After a few days, when the family was reunited, Julie thought that her parents seemed like themselves, although the subject was rarely discussed at home. "There was a sadness," Tricia Nixon said, "and the sadness went on for years."

On the following Sunday, the American Broadcasting Company aired a program titled *The Political Obituary of Richard M. Nixon,* put together and moderated by Howard K. Smith. The broadcast featured allies and foes of Nixon and, in a category all his own, Alger Hiss. ABC's news director then was Jim Hagerty, Eisenhower's former press secretary, and at Bryce Harlow's outraged urging, Ike called Hagerty to say that Smith ought to be fired; Hagerty said that he had no regrets about including this "chapter in Mr. Nixon's history." As for Nixon, Eisenhower told reporters, "He's too able a man. . . . It's not possible to say his career is ended"; he also wrote to Nixon to say, "I shall never understand why the voters, either now or in 1960, should deny themselves such an opportunity, but I'm sure that in the future they will come to regret their ill-considered action." One can never know if Eisenhower meant it or if he just meant to be kind, but he was one of the few who said that he could imagine a political future for Richard Nixon.

Even Murray Chotiner could only envisage him in the role of a party elder, someone who would speak out on major issues without worrying about the political consequences. Nixon was being written off, and he surely felt a certain *et tu*-ness when former allies like the conservative columnist George Sokolsky, who thought that Nixon had abetted Joe McCarthy's downfall, turned on him. Far more hurtful was something attributed to Eisenhower by Emmet John Hughes, who had written a mildly unfriendly book, *The Ordeal of Power,* about his years as a speechwriter. An excerpt in *Look* recalled how Ike in 1956 had urged Nixon to take a cabinet post; then, it continued, the president said to Hughes, "The fact is, of course, I've watched Dick a long time and he just hasn't grown. So I just haven't honestly been able to believe that he is presidential timber." Eisenhower was upset by Hughes's memoir—he regarded him as a turncoat— and worried how his words would strike an already despondent Nixon, but he said nothing about it until early December, when the editor of the *Augusta Chronicle* tracked him down. He conceded that he might have said Nixon wasn't ready for the presidency in 1956, but that was not the same as saying that Nixon wasn't ready for the presidency, period.

CHAPTER 21

Easterners

1

Some four months after the gubernatorial election, on a Friday, the Nixons drove to Palm Desert and spent another evening with the Eisenhowers. The former president and vice president played golf the next day, and when reporters asked what they'd talked about, they had nothing to say about golf, politics, or Nixon's future. Saturday was St. Patrick's Day, Pat Nixon's fictitious birthday (she was actually born on the 16th, but the family had invested the day with Hibernian sentiment), and the Nixons left after lunch to celebrate at what the newspapers called their "eyrie-like" home at Trousdale Estates. It had been about two years since the Nixons' first trek to Palm Desert, when Nixon was trying to shake off the defeat to Kennedy. Here they were again, and although the news was not yet public, beginning their goodbyes to California, with Nixon demonstrating his almost spooky capacity for resilience.

Rose Mary Woods and Bryce Harlow were worried about Nixon. Harlow thought that he needed to "recover his equilibrium" and that "some foundation type of thing" might be a good next step. "It's difficult to see how he is going to find lasting satisfaction in strictly mercenary life," he told Woods, adding that that "would mean he has thrown over his lifelong ambition of public service." Yet the mercenary life was where

Nixon seemed to be tending that March. Just before his stopover at Palm Desert, he had visited the Baltusrol Golf Club in New Jersey, where he played a round with Elmer Bobst, the CEO of the giant pharmaceutical company Warner-Lambert, and a couple of lawyers from the Wall Street firm Mudge, Stern, Baldwin & Todd. Nixon and Bobst had met during the 1952 campaign and a friendship had taken hold when Nixon spoke at Bobst's country club, in Mantoloking, New Jersey, the town where the Nixons spent part of the summer of 1953.

As the foursome walked the course, one of the senior partners, John Alexander, said, "Dick, are you really going to practice law?" to which Nixon replied, "John, if you knew anything about politics, you'd know that a politician doesn't give up his base. My base is California. When I come to New York, all that's behind me—I intend to do what I can for the firm." That was not quite true. He was invited to join the firm as a name partner (he just needed to pass the New York bar), but he certainly was not about to abandon public life. He knew that his "last press conference" had raised doubts about his temperament and that he had appeared a little unhinged compared with the average defeated candidate, but also that what he'd said—in particular his complaints about press partiality—had found sympathetic agreement around the country. Eisenhower in *The Saturday Evening Post* had recently written that the press was habitually unfriendly to his former vice president. "Whether or not it was wise of Dick to lay down this bitter indictment of the press is a question which I shall not discuss here," Eisenhower wrote. "But he did have a point. Throughout his public career, it seemed that a considerable segment of the press was on his back. I suppose," he added, as if he'd never heard of such a thing, "it was an extension of the curious 'I don't like Nixon' cult, which I never could really understand."

Nixon tried to erase that incident by showing up in different venues. In March, he appeared on Jack Paar's new prime-time program, an event that he treated as if it were a presidential debate. He became so obsessed with preparations that he wrote to his new friend, Paul Keyes, who was now producing the Paar show, to try out some hypothetical questions and answers:

Paar might say . . . What is the hardest work you ever did? (I would an-swer this question by saying picking string beans as a youngster and writ-ing a book in my older years.) . . .

What person who is not in politics would have the best chance of being a success in politics had he chosen that as a career? (My answer would be—Billy Graham—with reasons I could give that might be of interest.) . . .

Who is the bravest man you have ever met? (Here I might answer by describing Dulles's last days in his bout with cancer. It is a rather moving story, providing it isn't considered to be too unpleasant for the television audience.)

Getting into the spirit of this, Keyes suggested that Paar might ask "What Washington executive do you think is doing the best job at his post today?" and that Nixon's answer ought to be J. Edgar Hoover. In the end, though, Nixon took another tack: he played the piano. After Paar said, "The funny thing is, we have hired about fifteen Democratic violinists," Nixon laughed. Paar also said, "And Jose"—Jose Melis, the program's bandleader—"has made a concerto arrangement of this hinky-dinky song," a remark that didn't seem to faze Nixon, who then walked to a grand piano and played a wholly unremarkable composition that he'd en-titled "Piano Concerto #1," which was remarkable only for being his own.

Nixon's next public appearance came in April, in Washington, at the convention of the American Society of Newspaper Editors. He talked about something he called the "freedom doctrine," said that he had no intention of seeking political office, and was happy to suggest that the Republicans' strongest ticket in 1964 would be Nelson Rockefeller and Barry Goldwater. "If Jack and Lyndon could get together, Barry and Nel-son can," he said with the magnanimity of someone who believed that Kennedy was bound to be reelected. As for his "last press conference," he wanted to "extend" the record after his remarks in California: he raised an invisible glass "to the working press of America, the most underpaid and skilled craftsmen in America." The newspaper executives applauded.

The *New York Times* reported his speech on page one, and the syndi-cated columnist Roscoe Drummond a couple of days later announced that Nixon, having declared that he was no longer running for anything, was "emerging as the clearest and most constructive voice in the Republican opposition." The column evidently pleased Nixon, for he soon granted Drummond an interview in which he made several interesting claims and promises, almost none of which turned out to be true.

2

Walter Cronkite, on his CBS news program, broke the news that the former vice president was moving to New York to join a Wall Street law firm and that he'd already started looking for a place to live. That search ended with a twelve-room cooperative apartment at 810 Fifth Avenue, situated in the building where Nelson Rockefeller lived, although Rockefeller had a bigger place on a higher floor which was reached by another elevator. The governor's circumstances had changed, too; at the age of fifty-four, he had divorced his wife of thirty-two years and married Margaretta Fitler (Happy) Murphy, a thirty-six-year-old mother of four, whose name was often accompanied by the word "divorce" or, perhaps, "home-wrecker" when the subject was Rockefeller's future in politics.

Ten days after the move was reported, Nixon's conversation with Roscoe Drummond was published in two successive columns, and in the first of them, he said, "I will not again be a candidate for anything. Under no circumstances whatever. That is categorical." If that wasn't categorical enough, Nixon went on to make it super-categorical, saying, "I want to make it clear that under no circumstances do I contemplate at any time entering New York politics. That means not as a candidate for governor, not as a candidate for senator, not as a candidate for Congress, not as a candidate for anything, not now and not in the future."

Not that he was giving up public life—just public office. "I have made the determination that that contribution can better be made in the area of ideas than in the area of elective politics." It was an astonishing avowal, this self-transformation from rocking, socking campaigner into philosopher-pol. His new role, he said, wasn't that of a party leader but rather "that of being a conscious leader of thought in the party and in the exposition of policy and philosophy."

Drummond made one more stab at pinning Nixon down—and again

Nixon was unequivocal. "I say categorically that I have no contemplation at all of being the candidate for anything in 1964, 1966, 1968, or 1972. . . . Anybody who thinks I could be a candidate for anything in any year is just off his rocker." He had a full-time job at Mudge, Stern, Baldwin & Todd; he was going to be practicing law in the big leagues.

Two days later, Drummond related the "human story" behind Nixon's "final decision" to remove himself from elective politics—that it was Pat Nixon's choice. In this version, after Nixon told his wife about the offer from Mudge, Stern, "It took her half a second to say yes. She wanted me— all of us—to be out of the line of fire politically" and "to be sure we stayed out." He may even have meant what he said, but the idea that a move to a Wall Street law firm was equivalent to giving up politics was preposterous. Thomas Evans, who was a senior partner at Mudge, Stern, has observed that no single sector has produced as many presidential candidates— among them Franklin Roosevelt, Thomas Dewey, Wendell Willkie, John W. Davis, and Samuel J. Tilden—so it was hard to imagine that Nixon's visibility would be diminished by this new habitat and career turn. One person who seemed to view this with complete seriousness was General Eisenhower, who wrote to thank the Nixons for sending a shipment of ice cream to Mamie, who was in the hospital (like her husband, she also suffered from digestive problems), and also to "wish you every success in your new venture and hope that it will be the beginning of a most satisfactory life for the Nixon family as 'Easterners.' "

As for himself, Nixon could read the polls and while he saw that the public still had a positive view of him, it was not wildly positive; and no group— not even his Republican base—wanted him to run for president in 1964. As a New Yorker, he could insist that his affection for California was undiminished by his loss there. "If it were a question of where to live, it would be California," he told Drummond. "We like the life there; we have our family there, our friends." He said that he intended to take vacations in California and that he was buying a house there for his mother, but the truth was that the Nixon family couldn't wait to leave—not least because the children of John Birchers had been making life miserable for Tricia and Julie in their private school.

He said his formal goodbyes to the state in June, at a luncheon at the Biltmore Hotel in downtown L.A., where more than a thousand people paid $6 a ticket, with some of the proceeds going to buy a combination color TV–phonograph for the Nixons' New York apartment. The master of ceremonies was the reality show pioneer Art Linkletter, who said that Nixon "now at last relieved of burdens and pressures can do what every young man dreams of—make some money." And then the Nixons were gone—all four of them—first on a vacation with their old friends, Jack and Helene Drown, and then to New York where Dick would start work at Mudge, Stern's offices in the financial district, on 20 Broad Street.

The vacation lasted seven weeks, and for the younger contingent—Julie, who was turning fifteen; Tricia, at seventeen, and the Drowns' daughter, Maureen, at twenty—it was a rare family getaway. For Nixon, who almost never was seen without jacket and tie, it was a chance to behave like a former vice president, still holding forth on large issues in distant places. In Paris, he met with General de Gaulle, who gave him a friendly welcome for which Nixon was always grateful. (De Gaulle admired Nixon, and regarded him as "One of those frank and firm personalities on whom one feels one could count for great matters, if it fell to him, one day, to be responsible for them.") In Cairo, as the rest of the party traipsed to the pyramids, Nixon saw Colonel Nasser and for good measure told reporters that he supported President Kennedy's civil rights proposals—"I am not a Johnny-come-lately in this field," he reminded them.

Eisenhower had also been traveling—to Normandy, where CBS was filming a documentary for the twentieth anniversary of the D-Day invasion—and when he returned to New York, the press sought his opinions on several matters. What about the treaty to ban nuclear testing in the atmosphere? (America, Russia, and England had agreed, but the Senate had yet to ratify it; Ike was tentatively in favor.) Did he have a personal choice for a Republican presidential nominee in 1964? ("As of this moment," he replied, "not a one. I want to see what everyone has to say.") Then he offered the names of a dozen potential candidates for 1964, including such familiar ones as Barry Goldwater, Nelson Rockefeller, and Michigan's governor, George Romney, along with such lesser known ones as General Lucius Clay and even Gabriel Hauge, his former economic adviser, whose name was unknown to the general public. Nixon was not on

The presidential ticket at the 1952 Republican convention: "I sensed when I held the General's arm up that he resisted it just a little," Nixon said years later. *Dwight D. Eisenhower Presidential Library*

Soon after the convention, the two candidates got together in Fraser, Colorado, where the general tried without success to teach the senator the art of fly-fishing. *Dwight D. Eisenhower Presidential Library*

Eisenhower and Nixon, in two open cars, campaigned in Los Angeles on August 6, 1952. Governor Earl Warren is seated to Ike's left. *Dwight D. Eisenhower Presidential Library*

On September 18, 1952, the *New York Post* reported that Senator Nixon had been receiving money from a "secret" fund supported by an unnamed group of millionaires.

Five days later, Nixon spoke to the nation in what became known as the Checkers speech.

After the speech, Nixon was summoned to meet with Eisenhower in Wheeling, West Virginia. While the two men spoke at an outdoor stadium, Mrs. Eisenhower shared her fur wrap with Mrs. Nixon. *Getty Images*

John Foster Dulles and Eisenhower in Morningside Heights. During the campaign, Dulles advised Ike on foreign policy; he was named secretary of state soon after the election. *AP Photo*

The four Nixons managed a truncated family vacation on the New Jersey shore in August 1953. *Nixon Photographic Collection*

A month later, Eisenhower and Nixon played golf at Denver's Cherry Hills Country Club. Nixon had just begun to learn the game. *AP Photo*

Nixon, Eisenhower, and the Republican National Committee's Leonard Hall often discussed politics. *Dwight D. Eisenhower Presidential Library*

Nixon and his friend Billy Graham at Yankee Stadium, during the evangelist's four-month New York crusade in the summer of 1957. *AP Photo*

Nixon as well as Eisenhower sometimes got unsolicited advice from Clare Boothe Luce, the wife of the Time Inc. publisher Henry Luce. *Getty Images*

Eisenhower and Nixon toasted coffee mugs on January 20, 1957. *Dwight D. Eisenhower Presidential Library*

During the second inaugural, Ike's grandson, David, stared intently at Julie Nixon, who had gotten a black eye in a sledding accident. (Tricia Nixon is on Julie's left; David's sister Barbara Anne is on his right.) *Dwight D. Eisenhower Presidential Library*

On May 15, 1958, the president welcomed the Nixons back from South America, where a mob had attacked their motorcade. Julie and Tricia were there, too. *Dwight D. Eisenhower Presidential Library*

Eisenhower met with some of the nation's leading civil rights leaders on June 23, 1958. On the president's right: Lester Granger, National Urban League; Martin Luther King Jr.; and E. Frederic Morrow. On Ike's left: A. Philip Randolph, president of the Brotherhood of Sleeping Car Porters; William Rogers; Rocco C. Siciliano, who arranged this meeting; and Roy Wilkins, president of the NAACP. *Dwight D. Eisenhower Presidential Library*

Three weeks after Eisenhower suffered a mild stroke, he went ahead with plans to attend a NATO meeting in Paris. Nixon was among those who saw him off at the airport on December 13, 1957. *Dwight D. Eisenhower Presidential Library*

Shortly before the 1968 convention, candidate Nixon chatted with his daughter Julie and her fiancé, David Eisenhower, in the den of the Nixons' New York apartment. *Getty Images*

A mostly bedridden General Eisenhower marked his seventy-eighth birthday at Walter Reed Army Hospital—the last time he was seen in public. *Dwight D. Eisenhower Presidential Library*

On March 30, 1969, in the Rotunda of the Capitol, President Nixon placed a wreath on General Eisenhower's casket. *Corbis*

the list, and when Ike was asked if he thought that Nixon might seek the nomination, he said, "He's told me he positively cannot be so considered" and added that Nixon had told him that one reason for moving to New York was to take himself out of the running.

On the day that Ike's comments appeared, Nixon reported to the general about his own journey, much as he might have done when he was vice president. But now, as a New York lawyer, his tone was almost that of an old friend if one overlooks the underlying stiffness. "Welcome back!" he began. "Your visit . . . must have brought back many unforgettable memories." He told Eisenhower that it had been a treat for him to spend time with Pat and their daughters, but "I have one word of advice for others who take teenagers abroad—don't waste any money taking them to expensive restaurants! They prefer the simple things they are used to such as hamburgers, hot dogs, malted milks, provided you can find them."

He managed to let Eisenhower know that he was still someone who could open doors: "I had some interesting conversations with several of the European leaders all of whom—and particularly Adenauer, De Gaulle and Franco, sent their best to you." As for the test ban treaty, "While I believe that we probably have to go along . . . I certainly do not share the gushing attitude of the columnists who see in it the beginning of the end of the cold war. And on the political front," he continued, "if some of our Republican candidates cannot better control their cannibalistic instincts whatever chance the nominee will have in 1964 will be completely destroyed." When Ike wrote back a couple days later, he said, "The only difference I have found between the habits of your children and my grandchildren is that for some reason [mine] seemed to like all the expensive cuts of steak while we were traveling in Europe." He agreed with Nixon's cautious view of the test ban treaty and also on the need for Republican candidates to "forgo cannibalistic tendencies."

Nixon didn't mention Eisenhower's list of potential candidates, and may not yet have seen it—his letter to Ike was written on the day that a wire story appeared in a few newspapers. But soon it began to irk him, and word of his injured feelings slowly made its way to Gettysburg. Someone had sent the general a newspaper clipping that, as Ike put it in a letter to Nixon in late September, "quotes you as saying at a private gathering that you thought it strange that I had not included you." Eisenhower, though, doubted that Nixon had said "any such thing," because after all, he reminded him, "you had frankly told me that you were not available even for consideration," and furthermore he never meant to limit his list to just those names. "Actually," he continued, "I could, without pausing for breath, name at least 30, any one of whom would be much better than we now have," a diminishment not only of President Kennedy but of Nixon, and he concluded by writing, "It appears that the newspaper people are never going to cease their attempts to make it appear that you and I have been sworn enemies from the very beginning of our acquaintanceship."

Then in October, the general told the Associated Press that he wanted a "good, lively fight" at the 1964 Republican convention, by which he really meant that he was worried about the ascent of Barry Goldwater. When he was asked yet again if he'd like Nixon to run in 1964, he tried to put it all to rest, saying, "I don't think he wants it. He is still a very highly qualified man for the job. He didn't win and that, of course, people would remember. But he is very well, you might say, 'atmosphered' in the duties and the tribulations and the trials and the tests that come to the top man."

Doubleday in November published *Mandate for Change,* the first of two volumes covering Eisenhower's White House years. He had resisted appearing on television to promote the memoir, but Doubleday persuaded him that along with such popular radio shows as Casper Citron, Barry Gray, and Martha Deane, it was an excellent way to sell books. On CBS's *Face the Nation,* Eisenhower was asked yet again about Nixon. Some reviewers had sensed a "coolness" toward his vice president in the memoir, but Ike acted baffled at the question: "Strangely enough that impression has just persisted throughout the years and I never have known why." He pointed out that he'd campaigned for Nixon in California the year before, and "put these, my favorable opinions, into the most emphatic language I possibly could and I have done it more than once in front of press conferences." As for 1964, he said, "If there should be one of those deadlocks . . . I think he would be one of the likely persons to be examined and approached because he is, after all, a very knowledgeable and courageous type of person."

Nixon the next day said that he "naturally appreciated [Eisenhower's] generous comments," but if he were to come up as a possible candidate in the early primaries, he would "do everything I can legally to get my name out." For that matter, he added, "deadlocks are a thing of the past." And that, in mid-November of 1963, really seemed to be that.

3

For many Americans, Vietnam remained a far-off tributary of the Cold War, although about sixteen thousand military personnel had been sent there by President Kennedy as "advisers." But the last few years had been marked by increasingly violent and highly publicized protests by the Buddhist majority against the regime of President Ngo Dinh Diem, a Catholic—protests that included the sickening sight of monks drenched in gasoline setting themselves on fire. On November 1, 1963, in a coup supported by the Kennedy administration, Diem and his younger brother, Ngo Dinh Nhu, were killed. A prime mover had been the inexperienced American ambassador, Henry Cabot Lodge, which was enough for Clare Boothe Luce to telephone her friend Dick Nixon to say, "What the hell does your running mate Henry Cabot Lodge think he's doing there? *Someone* should let him know the score! . . . You should send him a message to get the hell out of there and come home now and put everyone on the spot. . . . This whole thing stinks with murder."

Nixon tended to agree with Mrs. Luce; he drafted a letter to Lodge, which began with his disdain not quite concealed—"I hesitate to bring a discordant note into the plaudits you must be receiving"—and then got quickly to his point: that "the heavy-handed participation of the United States in the coup which led inevitably to the charge that we were either partially responsible for, or at the very least condoned the murder of Diem and his brother, has left a bad taste in the mouths of many Americans." Nixon finally did not send the letter (he said it might be intercepted), but he did send a copy to Mrs. Luce, who replied that "JFK has bungled it like the Bay of Pigs!"

Eisenhower was also disturbed by the coup, and said so to Nixon. "I rather suspect the Diem affair will be shrouded in mystery for a long time to come," he wrote. "No matter how much the administration may have differed with him, I cannot believe any American would have approved the cold-blooded killing of a man who had, after all, shown great courage when he undertook the task some years ago of defeating communist's [*sic*] attempts to take over his country."

On November 22, 1963, three weeks after the murders of Diem and his brother, a column by James Reston discussed the 1964 race. Like many of his press colleagues, Reston viewed the rise of Goldwater as a threat and seemed to be imploring *someone* to come forward to stop him—if not Rockefeller or Romney or even Nixon then perhaps Cabot Lodge or Governor William Scranton of Pennsylvania, a wealthy, attractive man— one could almost call him a "Republican Kennedy." His column, though, appeared on the day that President Kennedy was murdered, an event that gave commentators a chance to start afresh and which forced Richard Nixon to reconsider his categorical statements of the recent past.

CHAPTER 22

The "Moratorium"

1

General Eisenhower had meetings in New York with, among others, U Thant, the secretary-general of the United Nations, and after that with General Lucius Clay and other old friends, to discuss the worrying rise of Senator Goldwater. Shortly after one-thirty, he was informed by his military aide, Brigadier General Robert Schulz, that President Kennedy had been shot. There was still something about General Eisenhower, now seventy-three, that made people turn to him for reassurance. A reporter asked, "General, will the nation be all right in the months ahead?" and he replied, "I'm not going to predict anything like that. I'd just say this: that the American nation is a people of great common sense. And they are not going to be stampeded or bewildered."

Eisenhower was in fact terribly worried; in those first hours after the assassination, there were rumors of larger killing plots, of world war. The news from Dallas was hard to absorb; one could not quite imagine Jack Kennedy, that picture of middle-aged vigor, growing older, much less dying. "In the civilized countries of the world it doesn't happen so often," Eisenhower told the reporter, morosely, "and you remember, in the starting of World War I, the murder of the Archduke Ferdinand . . . why this itself almost was one of the contributory causes to that war. But here I just don't know what happens."

Nixon had been in Dallas on business, and in the morning, on the way to the airport, Love Field, he had noticed the flags along the motorcade route. Back in New York, when his taxi from La Guardia Airport let him out at the 62nd Street entrance to 810 Fifth Avenue, a doorman ran toward him, weeping.

Stephen Hess, who was still doing chores for Nixon, happened to be meeting his client in New York. "I'm the first person he's seen who's a friend, not something else," Hess recalled. "He's shaken. He opens his attaché case, and he takes out the *Dallas Morning News* to show me the front page, and Adlai Stevenson had been there several weeks before and been spat upon. And he's saying to me, 'Look, I'm not to blame' "—that is, the political opposition could not be faulted. "Because he's worried about who killed Kennedy. And he sits down and he makes two calls. The first call is to Eisenhower, who's at the Waldorf Towers, and he speaks to Bob Schulz, who says he's taking a nap and can't be disturbed. His next call is to J. Edgar Hoover, and Hoover says he was killed by a guy who was handing out Castro literature and been in the Soviet Union. And Nixon is now very relieved." The assassin, Hoover told Nixon, was a Communist. Nixon had been about to sign a contract for a book about the 1964 campaign, which would have given him a large advance and would have been another factor removing him from politics. With the news from Dallas, Nixon's meeting with the publisher was canceled; it was never rescheduled.

Nixon's feelings about Kennedy, toward whom he'd once felt something like affection, had changed since 1960; he had become increasingly critical of his presidency (more intensely, perhaps, because he never stopped believing that the election was stolen), and Kennedy for his part rarely spoke about Nixon with anything but contempt. But Nixon wanted to say *something*, something comforting, to Jacqueline Kennedy, perhaps because, as he later said, he remembered how desolate he'd felt decades earlier after the deaths of his brothers. Whatever the motive—and Nixon was often lifted by bursts of empathy—he went to his library, which had a working fireplace, and stayed up late working on a letter:

Dear Jackie,

*While the hand of fate made Jack and me political opponents I always
cherished the fact that we were personal friends from the time we
came to the Congress together in 1947. That friendship evidenced itself
in many ways including the invitation we received to attend your
wedding.*

*Nothing I could say now could add to the splendid tributes which
have come from throughout the world to him.*

*But I want you to know that the nation will also be forever grateful
for your service as First Lady. You brought to the White House
charm, beauty and elegance as the official hostess for America, and
the mystique of the young in heart which was uniquely yours made an
indelible impression on the American consciousness.*

*If in the days ahead we could be helpful in any way we shall be
honored to be at your command.*

Sincerely,
Dick Nixon.

Mrs. Kennedy's handwritten reply was sent a few weeks later and addressed more formally, and yet, despite her sorrow and the awfulness of
having seen her husband murdered at her side, she already understood
what Nixon was not ready to acknowledge: to an extraordinary degree,
Jackie Kennedy's note dealt mostly with the political future of Richard
Nixon:

Dear Mr. Vice President,

I do thank you for your most thoughtful letter.

*Two young men—colleagues in Congress—adversaries in 1960—
and now look what has happened—Whoever thought such a hideous
thing could happen in this country.*

*I know how you must feel—so long on the path—so closely missing
the greatest prize—and now for you, all the question comes up
again—and you must commit all you and your family's and hopes and*

efforts again—Just one thing I would say to you—if it does not work out as you have hoped for so long—please be consoled by what you already have—your life and your family—

We never value life enough when we have it—and I would not have had Jack live his life any other way—though I know his death could have been prevented, and I will never cease to torture myself with that—

But if you do not win—please think of all that you have—With my appreciation and my regards to your family. I hope your daughters love Chapin School as much as I did—

> *Sincerely,*
> *Jacqueline Kennedy*

Nixon canceled all his appointments on that Friday. "But before I go home, on Saturday," Stephen Hess recalled, "I drop by his home, and a lot of the politicians are there, Len Hall, and they're talking about the political consequences of what happened." Republicans asked for a month-long moratorium on politics, but not everyone observed it—certainly not the press. If it seemed callous to be discussing the next campaign as soon as Kennedy was dead, that hadn't stopped anyone from saying what was obvious: that a Goldwater candidacy was a lot less appealing when the Democrats would, presumably, nominate Lyndon Johnson, a southwesterner all their own. No one knew how to gauge Johnson's strength—he was relatively unknown to the country—although at that moment he had the nation's goodwill.

The service for President Kennedy on Monday, November 25, was held at St. Matthew's Cathedral and attended by such world leaders as Charles de Gaulle and Harold Wilson, the head of the British Labour Party, as well as just about every important American political figure. The Richard Nixons were there (they were among the last to stop at Kennedy's bier at the Capitol), and so were the Nelson Rockefellers and Governor Scranton, who had been a friend and had once dated a Kennedy sister, and Martin Luther King Jr. Two journalists who were Kennedy friends, Benjamin C.

Bradlee of *Newsweek* and Hugh Sidey of *Time,* acted as ushers. In a front row, the Dwight D. Eisenhowers sat next to Harry Truman and his daughter, Margaret.

Eisenhower had no intention of observing anybody's moratorium on politics. He was restless, worried about the Goldwater phenomenon, and one day in early December he came up with the suggestion that Cabot Lodge should seek the nomination. That—and Ike's latest informal appraisal of the Republican field—was announced in the *New York Times* by Felix Belair Jr., a former White House reporter to whom Eisenhower often spoke for stories that contained no direct quotations.

Ike's enthusiasm for Lodge seemed to have grown in proportion to his lack of it for other Republicans, among them Nixon and Scranton. As it was delicately phrased by Belair, "General Eisenhower continues to regard Mr. Nixon as well qualified for the Presidency, but he acknowledges that [he] is a twice-defeated candidate who may have limited appeal to Republican voters." And he seemed to believe that Scranton had promised the voters of Pennsylvania that he would serve his full four-year term, which ended in 1966. But Ike saw Lodge "as the one potential Republican candidate who comes as close to any to his own thinking about large public questions and about how a President of the United States should approach them."

Lodge, who was still in Saigon and having to deal with the messy aftermath of the coup in which he'd had a semi-visible hand, was nonplussed by this sudden attention to political plans that he didn't have. But while he insisted that he had no intention of running for anything, he also said that he would "consider seriously anything the General asked of me. He's an old friend and I have the highest regard for him." Certain parallels were noted between Eisenhower's entreaty to Lodge, who said that he had a duty to stay in Saigon until summer, and the pressure by Lodge and others to get Ike to run in 1952 when he was at SHAPE.

Then it was Scranton's turn: yes, of course he had said that he *expected* to serve his full four-year term, but that was not the same as *pledging* to do so. Scranton was in any case not eager to get into it—he had been a semi-reluctant candidate for Congress and for the governorship, and he favored Nelson Rockefeller for president. But neither was he going to let the former president, no matter how much he liked and admired him, take him out of contention. Later that month, Eisenhower's westbound train stopped in Harrisburg, where he talked with Scranton. "It was not a deep discussion about national politics," Scranton told reporters. "But he did point out that a great many people that he had talked with felt that I should be a major contender for the nomination. And he thought so too." Scranton knew many of the people with whom Ike had talked, including their mutual friends at the *New York Herald Tribune*. At the end of the month, on the precise day that the "moratorium" on politics ended, the *Trib* published a full-page editorial titled "Calling Governor Scranton," a comment which began by summoning Scranton to respond to a "call to duty."

Nixon, too, had observed the moratorium, and if Ike's dismissal of his chances in 1964 bothered him, what was to be done? After all, he had already—categorically—taken himself out of the race. He was also about to be admitted to the New York bar, a step that would make him one of four senior partners in a reorganization of Mudge, Stern, which was about to be renamed Nixon, Mudge, Rose, Guthrie & Alexander. There had been some internal opposition to hiring Nixon. Democrats at the firm didn't like him, and furthermore he brought with him a faint smell of defeat. But others saw him as a fascinating, even mysterious character, bearing little or no resemblance to the man so often described by unkind journalists. Even physically, he was unlike what one expected—he had an unusually large head and a smile that seemed at least in the moment of its emergence to erase his jowls—a "radiant smile," one partner said, joined by the physiognomic flaw of his nose. How would it look if he seemed eager to abandon his new firm? Yet there was no escaping it: simply by being Nixon, he was already a candidate, someone who, like Scranton, might stave off a nasty fight between the Goldwater and Rockefeller factions.

Although Nixon wasn't ready to reopen discussions about his own political future, in mid-December he went to see Eisenhower in Gettysburg where, during their conversation, Lodge's name came up: "Now both of us agreed that we'd like to see him back here because he is a vivacious man, a leader type," the former president said; Nixon didn't want to comment on Lodge's plans—or his own, although, despite his disclaimers and his professional obligations, he was giving the race ever more thought; Kennedy's murder had changed everything. In the days before Christmas, things began to return—if not to normal, then to something that resembled normality if you didn't look too closely at the sadness beneath the surface, the sense that the Kennedy assassination had made the 1964 race somewhat beside the point.

At the end of 1963, the Nixons were living well; their daughters, as Mrs. Kennedy had noted, went to the Chapin School, and their fifth-floor cooperative apartment, for which they had paid about a hundred thousand dollars, overlooked Central Park. Visitors noticed certain furnishings that set it apart from other apartments—a snowscape painted by Dwight D. Eisenhower, a painting of a mountainside done by Mrs. Chiang Kai-shek, and a Buddha with a Grecian face, which had been a gift from the king of Afghanistan. "I came to New York to practice law and not to practice politics," Nixon said, as if he meant it, to Peter Kihss, the *New York Times* reporter with whom he had exchanged friendly notes nearly a decade earlier, when Kihss had written sympathetically about a Nixon speech on the *Brown* decision.

"Richard M. Nixon is a happy New Yorker," Kihss wrote, and described his life as a successful Manhattan lawyer, although one who traveled a lot. He would arrive at 20 Broad Street next door to the New York Stock Exchange at eight-thirty (he was driven in his 1963 Oldsmobile by Manuel (Manolo) Sanchez, a Cuban refugee who had worked for two years for the Nixons) and leave the office at six. He claimed to miss many things about California—a miniature lime tree ("we picked our own limes to make limeade"), outdoor barbecues, and the sunshine—but it was hard to take seriously this gushy view of a place where he had felt separated by distance and intellectual engagement from the world in which he thrived. He found New York a "very cold and very ruthless and very exciting and, therefore, an interesting place to live," he told the journalist Robert Donovan four months later, and frequently used the phrase "fast track" in conversations, saying "Any person tends to vegetate unless he is moving on a fast track. . . . You have to bone up to keep alive in the competition here." To Kihss he stressed the importance of an urban culture. "Urban blight is the No. 1 domestic problem in America," he said. "The disease of the cities is a great tragedy."

He tried to blend in, but one could hardly be Richard Nixon and be anonymous. He joined the Metropolitan Club and the Blind Brook Club, near Rye, where Eisenhower had played golf when he was at Columbia, and the Deepdale Club on Long Island. He had a regular lunch at the Recess, which was situated on the thirty-eighth and thirty-ninth floors of 60 Broad Street, and whose members included Tom Dewey, Herb Brownell, Bill Rogers, and a future treasury secretary, Henry Fowler. People noticed the Nixons—at the movies, at football games, at restaurants like Luchow's, "21," the Stork Club, and Chez Vito, or at the theater, which the family enjoyed, particularly musicals like *Man of La Mancha* and *How to Succeed in Business Without Really Trying.* Jack Paar's daughter, Randy, invited Tricia and Julie to see the Beatles when they made their debut on *The Ed Sullivan Show.* The four Nixons were sometimes spotted walking along Fifth Avenue, accompanied by two dogs, one of them the black-and-white cocker spaniel Checkers, who was now twelve. The Nixons had not joined a church in New York, but, with the church-state politics of 1960 now behind them, they liked to attend services at Norman Vincent Peale's Marble Collegiate Church, which Lieutenant Commander Nixon had occasionally done in 1945 when he was stationed in New York and an anonymous congregant. He was earning a great deal of money and would not have felt out of place among the wealthy middle-aged men who had surrounded President Eisenhower.

One night during the Christmas season, the Nixon family ran into the Truman family at the Shubert Theatre, at a Meredith Willson musical called *Here's Love.* The Truman party consisted of Harry and Bess; their daughter, Margaret; her husband, Clifton Daniel, a *New York Times* editor; and Mrs. Truman's sister-in-law. The Nixons sat a few rows behind them, and before the night was out, they met backstage, where Harry Truman and Dick Nixon shook hands. It all seemed cordial enough, but it was not like Truman's conciliatory encounter with Eisenhower after the Kennedy funeral, when the two former presidents had sandwiches and coffee at Blair House. When photographers in New York asked Truman and Nixon to shake hands again, Truman, who still believed that Nixon had once called him a traitor, refused.

CHAPTER 23

Private Agendas

1

On January 4, 1964, the day after Barry Goldwater announced that he was running for president, a Gallup Poll reported that the first choice of Republican voters was Richard Nixon. That began a year that would bring out the worst in a number of people, including General Eisenhower, who would never quite say what he really thought about Goldwater and his rivals, and Nixon, who would never quite come clean about what he wanted for himself.

Eisenhower thought that Goldwater was a ridiculous figure. "You know, Goldwater's quite a nice guy," he remarked to a former aide. "He's got everything but brains." But that was not something he would say publicly; and he was not ready to support Nelson Rockefeller, Goldwater's chief competitor, whom he did not regard as a nice guy. Not only had Rockefeller once questioned his defense policy, which was bad enough, but he had hired that arch-betrayer Emmet John Hughes.

The New Hampshire primary on March 10 was supposed to help measure the strength of the two leading candidates, but it was also a way to help the country return to life as usual. It was the first political event since the Kennedy assassination, and diversions, whether the sort provided by the Beatles on February 9 (an audience of 73 million watched them on

The Ed Sullivan Show) or the sort provided by presidential politics, were welcome. The 1964 race was a perfect topic for "Inside Report," the political column that the *New York Herald Tribune* had invented by teaming its well-mannered congressional correspondent Rowland Evans with the Chicago-born *Wall Street Journal* political reporter Robert Novak. Evans and Novak believed that neither Goldwater nor Rockefeller could win the nomination and that the real contest would end up being between two men who appeared to be watching the competition from a distance, Nixon and Governor Scranton.

The winner in New Hampshire turned out to be the noncandidate Henry Cabot Lodge, whose plurality was accomplished with write-in votes. It had been a snowy day and the tallies were not large; the results could be—and were—explained by Rockefeller's remarriage or by Goldwater's suggestion that Social Security ought to be voluntary or possibly by actual affection for Lodge, a Massachusetts neighbor, who seemed all the more attractive because he was thousands of miles away in Saigon, and whose organizers had worked hard and stealthily. When Nixon talked over the results with Fred Seaton, the political strategist and former interior secretary, he did not try to hide his private agenda. He said that the primary had "killed Rockefeller" and that Goldwater "was hurt but not mortally, because if he could carry the California primary he would still be in the ballgame." He had nothing but scorn for his former running mate—Cabot Lodge, he said, was a "gutless wonder." When Seaton described Lodge as a "knuckleheaded gutless wonder," Nixon laughed, and they both agreed that Lodge wasn't going to go very far. What Nixon really wanted to talk about, though, were his own prospects for winning the nomination. Seaton told him that he had played it "very cagily"; he advised him to make clear that he was available but not actively pursuing the nomination. When Nixon mentioned becoming a write-in candidate in Nebraska's April primary—though without leaving a trace—he sounded as if he could taste it.

Nixon's timing was close to impeccable. Just days after New Hampshire voted, he left the country on a three-week "business" tour of East Asia. Seaton called it "another gold star" for Nixon, but in fact the trip had been arranged well in advance. He had invitations to meet with, among others, the king of Thailand and Chiang Kai-shek, and during his preparations he had approached Eisenhower, sounding almost hesitant and shy when he asked if he could drop his name ("I know it would mean a great deal to all of these officials if I were to be able to extend personal greetings from you to them"), and sensitive enough about seeking even that small favor to add, "The last thing I want to do, of course, is to put you on the spot in any respect." The trip in any case was bound to remind people that Dick Nixon was comfortable with foreign policy and foreign leaders, and that Lyndon Johnson, a Texan who could look and sound like a rube, was not.

Eisenhower meanwhile was feeling pressure to say something negative about Goldwater and was trying to avoid it. When CBS's Walter Cronkite asked him about the 1964 field, he mentioned Nixon, Scranton, Romney, and Lodge, but added, "not one of them will admit he's a candidate. . . . As someone said, Walter, 'If you're going out for a canter you've got to have a horse.' " George Humphrey, his former treasury secretary and a Goldwater supporter, urged silence, but the general's East Coast friends wouldn't give up and their plot was hatched at the very heart of eastern Republicanism— the 41st Street offices of the *Herald Tribune,* which was bought in 1959 by the sportsman and philanthropist John Hay (Jock) Whitney, Ike's occasional golfing partner and his ambassador to the Court of St. James. In the belief that Goldwater would indeed be out of the "ballgame" if he lost the June California primary to Rockefeller, the newspaper's role was to persuade Eisenhower to write an essay in which he would describe his beau ideal for 1964, a theoretical entity who would presumably bear no resemblance to Senator Goldwater.

The *Trib*'s editorial page editor, Raymond K. Price, saw Eisenhower in Gettysburg and then ghostwrote the article, which ran on the newspaper's front page on Monday, May 25, eight days before California voted. Eisenhower did not actually endorse anyone in his call for a candidate who represented "the responsible, forward-looking Republicanism I tried to espouse as President," but it was hard to miss the point as he came out in favor of just about everything that Goldwater was against, such as the Interstate Highway program, increased Social Security coverage, "loyal support for the United Nations in its peace-keeping efforts," and the "obligation to be vigorous in the furtherance of civil rights." If there was still any doubt about Eisenhower's meaning, a Roscoe Drummond column that abutted his essay began, "If former President Eisenhower can have his way, the Republican Party will not choose Sen. Barry Goldwater as its 1964 Presidential nominee." Rockefeller and Goldwater each insisted that Eisenhower was describing them, but when a reporter asked the general, "My editor wants to know if [Goldwater] fits your specifications," Ike replied, "Let him try to fit that shoe to that foot." Goldwater meanwhile kept saying things that didn't sound quite right, such as suggesting that it would not be particularly deadly to use nuclear "devices" for defoliation in Vietnam. "You might kill a lot of monkeys and animals but would do it at a time of day so it would not kill humans," he said.

None of this was helping Goldwater, and he seemed almost done for when Rockefeller won the Oregon primary and pulled well ahead in the California polls. No one anticipated that Nelson Rockefeller Jr. (weighing seven pounds, ten ounces) would be born on the Saturday before California voted and in that way remind voters that his parents had ended two marriages and committed adultery—which probably cost Rockefeller Sr. a victory. After that, moderate Republicans, a shrinking contingent, could only hope that when delegates arrived in San Francisco in mid-July, they would come to their senses. The panicked *Herald Tribune* began at once to promote Governor Scranton—a natural alliance. Jock Whitney and Scranton were Yale graduates and served together on the Yale Corporation, and Scranton also had ties to the Luce publications: Scranton's brother-in-law, James Linen, was president of Time Inc. Whitney and the *Trib*'s president, Walter Thayer, as Robert Novak later observed, had some memory of how the great press lords had maneuvered Wendell Willkie into the Republican nomination of 1940; in 1964, Scranton was their Willkie.

Most important, it looked as if Eisenhower might actually support Scranton. Earlier that year, the general had met with the governor and, as if speaking for the Republican establishment, told him "It's between you and Nixon," adding, "You will have to make up your mind soon." Scranton, who got the clear impression that Eisenhower favored him and wanted him to fight Nixon for the nomination, said only that he would give "deep thought" to the question. Then in June, after California voted—a month before the Republican convention—Scranton saw Eisenhower in Gettysburg and left with a hope that the general would finally endorse him.

But as Nixon knew, Ike often had a way of not quite saying what people thought he'd said.

Scranton went from Pennsylvania to Cleveland for the annual Governors' Conference, and about the first thing he did when he reached his hotel was telephone Eisenhower. "The essence of his statement then was a sentence: 'I don't want a cabal against Goldwater,' " Scranton recalled. "And I knew right then that he wouldn't come out for me. And that was a hard one to handle because I knew I was supposed to go on television"—on CBS's *Face the Nation*. When he showed up at the studio, he was still so rattled by his conversation with Eisenhower that he could barely reply when he was asked "What is your position with regard to the Republican Presidential nomination?"

Someone watching this maneuvering from a distance might have arrived at the theory that a hidden force was at work. That would be overstating the subtle role that Nixon was playing. But he was still mulling the idea of being a phantom write-in candidate in the Nebraska primary, and he had never stopped thinking of ways to block Goldwater—and of improving the odds of a convention deadlock, at which point the delegates would turn to him as the Great Unifier. Goldwater, who knew what Nixon was up to, said, "I still feel Nixon is my final hurdle, as I have felt all along"; so did Evans and Novak, who were writing an article for *Esquire* in which they would describe Nixon as "a political ghost," and a "political schemer." Nixon meanwhile once more left the country—this time flying to London, where he said, "My role will be one of neutrality."

Eisenhower had been hired as a commentator for ABC (Jim Hagerty's network), and when he got to San Francisco, he said that while "things didn't develop in the way I hoped they would" he wasn't out to stop anyone in particular and had never tried to push Scranton into the race. Neither statement was true, and Ike not long before had attempted to explain his political timidity in a somewhat self-important letter to John D. Rockefeller III, saying "Because Dick Nixon has never been really accepted by the rank and file of Republicans as the 'titular leader' of the Party, this rather 'fuzzy' title has been literally forced upon me . . . I felt I had to 'stay above the battle' and so provide one common contact for all factions of the

Party." But as a politician, Ike was still an amateur and was bound to lose the occasional struggle to accommodate both his party and his conscience. He spoke at the Cow Palace on the convention's second night, but no one paid much heed until he talked about "sensation-seeking columnists and commentators ... who couldn't care less about the good of our party," which set off a roar, followed by more of the same when he said, "And let us not be guilty of maudlin sympathy for the criminal who, roaming the streets with switchblade knife and illegal firearm, seeking a helpless prey, suddenly becomes, upon apprehension, a poor, underprivileged person who counts upon the compassion of our society." It was not Eisenhower's finest hour, but he fared a lot better than Rockefeller, at whom the Goldwater delegates let loose a prolonged shout of pure hatred.

Goldwater, who was nominated on the first ballot, uttered the most famous words of his career toward the end of his acceptance speech: "I would remind you that extremism in the defense of liberty is no vice," he said, and followed that thought by saying "And let me remind you also that moderation in the pursuit of justice is no virtue." The speech thrilled many people inside the Cow Palace, but it did nothing for the party unity that Eisenhower had been talking about. "I felt almost physically sick," Nixon recalled, adding that if Goldwater ever had a chance at winning the White House, "he lost it that night with that speech."

2

After the convention, Nixon made the transition from office seeker to Republican elder, and assigned himself the role of intraparty peacemaker; he helped to arrange a "unity" meeting in Hershey, Pennsylvania, not far from Gettysburg. First, though, Goldwater had to retroactively repair that speech of his, and Nixon called upon his lawyerly talents to help Goldwater refresh his recollection of what he had meant to say rather than what had actually come out of his mouth. In the letters that they exchanged, released through Nixon's law office, Nixon wrote:

> *I have received several inquiries as to the intended meaning of two*
> *sentences of your acceptance speech. . . . I have assured all of those who*

*have raised this question with me that you would be the first to reject
the use of any illegal or improper methods to achieve the great goals of
liberty and justice we all seek.*

*I believe, however, that it would be most helpful to clear the air
once and for all in this regard.*

Goldwater promptly produced the correct answer:

*I was urging in effect that we understand and view the great
problems of the day in their essence and not be diverted by glib political
catchwords. . . . If I were to paraphrase the two sentences in question
in the context in which I uttered them I would do it by saying that
wholehearted devotion to liberty is unassailable and that half-hearted
devotion to justice is indefensible.*

On August 12, Goldwater came to Hershey to meet with leading
Republicans—among them Eisenhower, Nixon, Rockefeller, and Scranton,
all of whom sat at a triangular table in a locked room and held a discussion that by most accounts was interminable. "Unity means, if a party is
going to be a national party . . . that there has to be room for disagreement, honest disagreement," Nixon said. Goldwater promised that before
he appointed anyone secretary of state or defense "or other critical national
security posts" he'd talk it over with Eisenhower and Nixon "and other experienced leaders." He also defended his record on civil rights, despite his
opposition to the public accommodations clause in the 1964 Civil Rights
Act that had passed the Senate on June 19. In what was probably the oddest remark of the day, Eisenhower said that Roy Wilkins, the head of the
NAACP, had scolded him for having spoken at the convention about crim-
inals "roaming the streets with a switchblade knife." Wilkins in a column
had written, "The phrase 'switchblade knife' means 'Negro' to the average
white American." Eisenhower said that he was amazed to hear that: "I
didn't associate switchblade knives with Negroes," he said. "So I am going
to have an aide write to this fellow and say, 'Well, for God's sake, that's
the last thing on my mind.' As a matter of fact, I thought switchblade
knives were always—and I hope there are no Italians here—identified with
Italians."

As they left town, Rockefeller wished the ticket well, although he would be too busy in New York to campaign outside the state. Scranton said that he'd be willing to leave Pennsylvania, but didn't sound eager, and Eisenhower said, "I'll be seventy-four in October." Nixon, though, planned to deliver more than a hundred speeches in thirty states in behalf of the ticket and for local candidates. He knew that Goldwater was going to lose—and lose badly. He had seen it coming after his own defeat four years earlier; during a post-election meeting with Eisenhower, he'd said that any "cold-blooded analyst" would know that a candidate with Goldwater's views would have lost to Kennedy by seven or eight million votes. Nixon also knew that he was going to be remembered as someone willing to go down the lonely road for Republicans in a difficult year and that Goldwater's loss could bring with it the defeat of other Republicans—people of the sort that Eisenhower was always trying to "bring up." Back then, when Ike looked at the roster of Republican talent and made one of his lists, Nixon was usually included. The result of a debacle in 1964 might well leave him standing pretty much alone.

3

As Americans cast 43 million votes for Johnson and 27 million for Goldwater, there was also a shift in voting patterns, particularly the defection of black voters in northern and industrial states, where as many as 90 percent chose the Democratic ticket, a shift that helped Robert Kennedy defeat Kenneth Keating in their New York Senate race. The numbers seemed to prove that the United States was indisputably centrist, and the centrist commentators sounded as if they were gloating. "The returns, which leave the Republican Party with virtually nothing more than a handful of states, won by racist votes, is a squalid and humiliating consequence of the San Francisco surrender," Walter Lippmann wrote, and one could imagine him scrubbing his hands to remove the dirt of Goldwaterism. Such assertions fit the comforting theory that Goldwater's strain of conservatism—far more benign and naive than its detractors realized—had been killed off. In the immediate aftermath, Nixon decided that the party unity he'd sought in Hershey was a thing of the past; he observed its expiration by calling Nelson Rockefeller "the principal divider" of the Republican Party, which Rockefeller called "a peevish post-election utterance." The loathing between them was like a peat fire that kept smoldering.

Eisenhower came to New York on December 9 as a guest of the Life Insurance Association of America, to whom he said, as if channeling Goldwater, "An all-powerful government can rob a whole people just as surely as a pickpocket can steal from an individual." Nixon had made plans to see him at the Waldorf Towers, and, as it turned out, Goldwater showed up, too; the three of them had a cordial and highly unpleasant meeting at which they discussed—in Nixon's words—"how to heal the rift" in the party and after which Goldwater said, "We want to see no blood dropped on the ground," although a purge of Goldwater people in the party's leadership had already begun. "It is remarkable," the columnist Murray Kempton observed, "how brilliantly the winning side is able to capture the General as soon as he has calculated what the winning side is."

CHAPTER 24

The Rehearsal

1

Eisenhower at the start of 1965 sent his usual birthday greeting to Nixon ("for a youngster like yourself I am certain it will be an occasion for a celebration") and admired a photograph of nineteen-year-old Tricia Nixon at the International Debutante Ball, where she was being courted by another young New Yorker, Edward Finch Cox, a student at Princeton. "I will have to admit," Nixon wrote in return, "that seeing Tricia in her debutante gown made me realize how the years have gone by since we first brought the girls in to meet Mrs. Eisenhower and you in the Brown Palace in Denver in 1952."

Even then, two months after Goldwater's defeat, it was reasonable to think that Nixon, although alert to the increasingly faint heartbeat of moderation in his party, was contemplating another run for president—that the columnist William S. White was right when he said that what defined Nixon was "the quality of an absolute tirelessness wrapped in a total determination." Yet although circumstances had changed since the move to Manhattan (which had promised an escape from all that), it was still not easy for him to overtly hint at his intentions, which would have undercut the goodwill at his law firm; and it would be even harder at home, where Pat viewed the prospect of another national campaign with anguish. He could, however, joke about it, and did so that January at the Alfalfa Club, a Washington institution that exists simply because it has existed—in its case since 1913, when its Confederate roots were more visible (its annual banquet honors the birthday of Robert E. Lee). The club's humor is at about the level of the Gridiron Club, but instead of skits and song parodies, it nominates an Alfalfa candidate for president. "We revel in failure," the club president said that year, which earned him roars of laughter. The nomination is not always a joke, though, since the club's prophetic choices have included Ronald Reagan (1974), George W. Bush (1998), and in 1965, Nixon, who, in the absence of the real president (Johnson), began by saying, "I thank you for the nomination on behalf of my wife, Pat Bird, my daughters, Julie Bird and Tricia Bird, and my car, Thunder Bird. I would also thank you on behalf of my dog, Checker Bird, but, as you know, unfortunately she died this year." (Checkers at age twelve had died in the late summer; newspaper accounts even took note of her burial at the Bide-a-Wee Home Association, a pet cemetery in Wantagh, Long Island.) After that grim beginning, Nixon made reference to something that had plagued him for five years:

I have some things going for me too. After all, look at my political background.

I can say without fear of contradiction that I have studied with the best.

After all, my political tutor was General Eisenhower.

General Eisenhower taught me many things about practical politics.

And, if you give me a week, I might think of one.

It was Nixon's funniest line, but he must have worried that Ike would not appreciate the jest because a day later he wrote to him to say, "As you will recall, the 'Alfalfa candidate' is expected to direct his needles to the top leaders of both major parties—thus the facetious reference to you. . . . It occurred to me that by using the phrase 'If you will give me a week' in a speech which everyone knows is completely in jest, I might point up the fact that your use of that term in 1960 was also intended to be facetious." For Nixon, too, the word "facetious" did not always mean what it was supposed to mean.

• • •

Nixon's colleagues at the law firm were always aware that, despite all disclaimers, the name partner was a major political figure—and a relatively young man in the small universe of major political figures. The artifacts of his office like those in his apartment bespoke both his passions and his past, particularly his ties to Eisenhower. A visitor might notice, along with the signed portraits of world figures, a golf scorecard that showed that he had made a hole-in-one (his party that day in Bel Air included the actor Randolph Scott), and a picture of Hannah Nixon, who not long before had suffered a stroke and had moved to a nursing home in La Habra. Rose Mary Woods, who had begun working for Nixon when he was a congressman, sat close by, and a part-timer who called herself "Miss Ryan"—a/k/a Pat Nixon—sometimes came in to help out with the mail and telephones and sometimes stayed late.

Nixon did not spend much time cultivating what he would call "buddy-buddy" relationships; yet his stiff formality and physical awkwardness, which sometimes made strangers uncomfortable, almost endeared him to colleagues. "Would anybody like a cigar?" he might ask, and the answer would usually be affirmative just so whoever was present could watch him fumbling around with the cigar, which sometimes bounced off his cheek and fell to the floor. Then he'd pick it up and routinely cut off the wrong end—an inadvertent comedy routine, although his audience tried to suppress its laughter. If he spent time away from the office for speeches or travel, that was perfectly acceptable; as the name partner he brought in a lot of business from clients like Donald Kendall (Pepsi-Cola) and Elmer Bobst (Warner-Lambert). Nothing could ever be compartmentalized in a life that was so immersed in politics.

His acquaintanceship with the Jewish, Brooklyn-born Leonard Garment, a senior litigator, was probably the closest that he came to a buddy-buddy relationship, one that was unlike any that Garment had ever experienced. Garment was enthralled; it was as if he were observing Nixon from a distance even as he drew closer to him. "To me it was like constantly being at the picture show—Nixon!" Garment said. "He's sitting there, talking on the telephone. . . . That was his basic business—learning more and more and feeding the machinery of his political intelligence so that it could operate twenty-four hours a day whether he was asleep or awake and not miss an opportunity." There were strange encounters, moments that Garment thought about only years later because they represented things about Nixon that he couldn't understand. Nixon would sometimes call Garment and ask him to come to his apartment, "And I'd get up there and ring on the buzzer and a long time would go by. I mean I knew he was there, because I'd just talked to him on the phone. He just took his sweet time coming to the door, whether getting dressed or coming from the bathroom, or gathering his thoughts together—not rushing." Nixon once advised Garment, "Never rush into a public place."

He always found time for his political life. In early August 1965, at Eisenhower's Gettysburg farm, Nixon took part in a party finance committee meeting, where the real subject seemed to be Lyndon Johnson's conduct of the rapidly escalating war in Vietnam. In March, Johnson had sent America's first ground combat troops, 3,500 Marines, to South Vietnam. By the time of the Gettysburg meeting, he had agreed to General William Westmoreland's request to send 200,000 additional American soldiers. Eisenhower wanted to be supportive, and he used the word "rot" to describe what people were saying about his purported differences with Johnson. "I've done everything I can to show I'm behind him," the general said. But it was difficult to hide the divisions that were already emerging among Republicans and others, or to forget that Eisenhower when he was president had never favored military involvement in South Vietnam. Now he found himself caught in the web of Johnson's war, and didn't much like it. A month earlier, he told Johnson "when you go into a place merely to hold sections or enclaves you are paying a price and not winning. When you once appeal to force in an international situation involving military help or a nation, you have to go all out! This is a war." It was a little different with Nixon. He endorsed what Ike had said in support of Johnson, but he had never really changed the views that had got him into trouble in 1954, when he was vice president and the French were about to be driven out of Indochina.

Soon after the Gettysburg meeting, Nixon visited Vietnam—it was described as a business trip in behalf of his law firm—and when he returned, he appeared on *Meet the Press* and said that the fight against the Communists had "turned the corner" and that he favored increasing military pressure; he specified a sea blockade of North Vietnam, increased bombing of the north, and a future commitment of American ground troops. The war had not yet become a nationally divisive issue, and Nixon was after all merely a corporate lawyer expressing a personal view. But as if in slow motion these questions as well as the politics of 1968 were approaching.

It was at about this time that Eisenhower published *Waging Peace,* the second volume of his White House memoirs, in which he discussed not only his most difficult moments as president—Suez, Little Rock, the 1958 Taiwan Strait crisis—but his health. A month later, in November, he suffered his second coronary. It had been ten years since his heart attack as president, and while this recent one was described as relatively mild, his condition was serious enough to keep him in an Army hospital near Augusta for two weeks, after which he went by train to Walter Reed, where he remained for nearly a month.

2

One day toward the end of 1965, Nixon in behalf of his firm went on a recruiting trip to Harvard; he spoke to the Graduate Students' Young Republican Club and even invited the group to visit him in New York. A month later, five of the students accepted the invitation, and Nixon at his apartment treated them well: they were served cocktails, filet of sole *bonne femme,* and baked Alaska, along with cigars and brandy after the meal. It was Nixon at his most expansive—he held forth on many subjects, mostly political, until about eleven-thirty, after which one person stayed behind—a twenty-seven-year-old business school student named Donald W. Riegle, who told Nixon that he'd been approached about running for Congress in Michigan, his home state. His wife, though, didn't want him to run, he told his host. It was a dilemma that Nixon addressed by saying, "If you don't run, you'll regret it for the rest of your life. And your wife will regret it. You'll wonder what might have happened if you'd run."

Nixon talked to Riegle about politics in personal terms. "He took me into his bedroom, where he had photographs in glassine sheets," Riegle said. "And one of the photographs was him as a young candidate with his young daughters, and he pointed that out to me, which I remember because he knew *I* had young daughters. And I think there were enough parallels." Riegle continued, "He encouraged me to run and said he would come out to campaign for me in Flint, and that he might also be able to introduce me to President Eisenhower." At about midnight, Nixon said, "Get your wife on the phone," and Riegle did as he was told, waking her with the words, "Honey, Richard Nixon would like to talk to you."

Nixon's encouragement of Riegle was probably not part of a political master plan, but by early 1966, his attention was ever more focused on the dozens of upcoming contests for state and local office—races that let him look over the next hill, toward 1968, and to once more view the presidency. Some of the offices at 20 Broad Street were becoming an informal clearinghouse for the furtherance of his political interests. One new employee was Dwight Chapin, a twenty-five-year-old who had worked with H. R. Haldeman at the California office of J. Walter Thompson; after he was transferred to the East Coast office, he spent some of his evenings at 20 Broad Street and helped out, sometimes when Pat Nixon was around. Chapin eventually became Nixon's full-time personal aide. Nixon also hired a speechwriter, the Washington-born, Jesuit-trained, full-bore conservative Patrick J. Buchanan, who had once caddied for him at Burning Tree. Buchanan was twenty-seven and before coming to work as a staffer for Nixon, he wrote editorials for the right-leaning *St. Louis Globe Democrat*. Then there was John Sears, a twenty-five-year-old Syracuse native who had clerked at the New York Court of Appeals, the state's highest court. When Sears came in for a job interview in 1965, he'd already had an offer to work at Dewey, Ballantine, Bushby, Palmer & Wood (Tom Dewey's firm), but Nixon, Mudge was willing to pay $500 more than Dewey, Ballantine and in addition give Sears some of the litigation work that he was eager to take on. Sears learned that new associates were expected to meet the name partner and, he said, "I was just ushered into his presence. I had the impression that he was more nervous than I was, ill at ease. But he saw on my résumé that I'd had some experience in public speaking and we did talk a bit about that." What soon became evident to Nixon was that Sears had rare political instincts—he was a sort of prodigy. "I used to get little memos that I first thought was somebody trying to play a joke on me, which was just asking for some suggestions on a speech or something," Sears said. "And I'd just write back."

By the summer, Evans and Novak were writing about what they called Nixon's "second presidential campaign." Nixon had set up an informal group called Congress '66, which had the obvious goal of electing Republicans in the midterms and the less obvious goal of helping Richard Nixon. The group included people like Peter Flanigan of Dillon, Read; Hobart Lewis, the top editor at *Reader's Digest*; Eisenhower's budget director, Maurice Stans, the publicist-speechwriter William Safire, whom Nixon had met during his 1959 Moscow visit, and people from the firm: John Sears, and the senior partners Thomas Evans and Len Garment. What Nixon didn't say, and didn't need to, was that anyone who won a seat in Congress in 1966 would be a delegate to the Republican National Convention in the summer of 1968.

3

Lyndon Johnson never sounded particularly pleased with decisions that got the country more deeply involved in Vietnam, perhaps because he had solemnly promised not to make them. But having told so many untruths and having committed so many Americans to the war, Johnson was eager for the support of General Eisenhower, who felt pulled in several directions: aversion to an Asian war, concern over the consequences of a victory by the Communist North, and what he felt was a duty to support his commander in chief. Johnson became a regular caller, and on the telephone he was by turns confiding and needy and flattering—almost frantic for Ike's approval. "There's nobody in this government that's been more valuable to me and been more comforting to me than you have," LBJ said during one conversation, and "I have told [people] in the meetings that at times I have asked your judgment and talked to you about various things and every time I have found it to be wise and good and. . . . If there ever was a patriot, you are it. And I'm awfully thankful the good Lord has spared you so you can help me. And I'm going to need all of it I can get."

Since leaving office, though, Ike had not been wholly predictable; there were times when he simply sounded cranky, as he had at the 1964 convention with remarks about switchblade knives and newspaper columnists. Yet he was still Ike, and still beloved; and when it came to questions of war and peace, no one spoke with more authority. So it was something of a surprise when the former president at a press conference in October 1966 said, "I'd take any action to win" in Vietnam, adding that he would not "automatically preclude anything," including nuclear weapons. That was enough to set off multiple alarms; Senator John O. Pastore, a Rhode Island Democrat, said, "If we do, all I can say is, God help us. God help us."

During the any-action-to-win controversy, it was Eisenhower's turn to call Johnson, who spoke as usual in bursts of ingratiation—"I saw you on color television the other day . . . and you just looked wonderful, just like you were coming back from the War." But Ike quickly changed the subject, he wanted to explain those stories that made him sound ready to use atomic weapons, and all at once he was at his wisest and best:

> I'll tell you, Mr. President, what bothers me is this: You see, in the Korean War, these people tried this thing, "Now, you said 'so and so' on the Korean War." I said, "My friends, no two military situations are the same. And no two political situations [are the same]." Here is a war that is the most nasty and unpredictable thing we've ever been in. And it's just as much political as it is military. Therefore, when I said, in Korea, I didn't say I'd use atomic bombs. I said that I would no more be inhibited or limited by the gentleman's agreement that [had] been prevailing at the time I got there.

Eisenhower knew that he needed to talk again to reporters, as he'd done when he was president and compared nuclear devices to bullets, and a few days later he said, "This is silly. How would you use nuclear weapons in Vietnam?" But at the core of Eisenhower's "clarification" was something more interesting than a rejection of nuclear weaponry. As he'd told Johnson, he viewed the Vietnam conflict as "the most nasty and unpredictable thing we've ever been in," which was not something that he'd said publicly. What he did say was that the United States needed to end the war quickly because otherwise "it will grow in costs, both in money and lives, and the nation's morale will be lowered." And he continued, "The morale of a nation is just as important a factor—probably a more important factor—in determining its capacity to lead as is its military or economic strength."

That idea seemed to elude Johnson and his advisers, who continued to widen the war without any coherent plan to end it. When Arthur Goldberg, the ambassador to the United Nations, announced that the United States was prepared to halt all bombing of North Vietnam "the moment we are assured privately or otherwise that this step will be answered promptly by a corresponding de-escalation from the other side," Nixon thought that he'd heard the sound of desperation, which he remarked upon in a note to Eisenhower: "This statement, it seems to me, runs directly contrary to the principle that you and Foster Dulles insisted upon in dealing with the communists—that we should never rely on communist promises—but should always insist on guaranteed deeds."

In fact, Eisenhower told Nixon, he'd also written to Goldberg—"I decided that the Ambassador meant to emphasize the word 'assured' as a condition for cessation of bombing"—and went on, with sarcasm and annoyance, to talk about the recent criticism that he'd been getting:

> The complaint is that I am "urging" the use of atomic bombs. I think even such great military experts as some of these senators would know that you could scarcely use this kind of weapon in South Vietnam where friends would be as badly exposed as one's enemies. Frankly, it seems that the Vietnam War is creating more whimperings and whinings from some frustrated partisans than it's inspiring a unification of all America in the solution of a national problem.

Nixon wrote back to say that he "could not agree more with your comments concerning the whimperings and whinings caused by the Vietnam War." It was as if the general and Nixon had the same view of the war, but in fact they were talking about different things. Eisenhower was once more looking for a semblance of national unity, to quiet passions, while Nixon seemed far more focused on how to fight the war. His occasional comments got under Johnson's skin. Johnson didn't trust him—didn't like the way Nixon would seem to suggest that there were better ways to prosecute the war. To Eisenhower, Johnson had said, "Nixon got out and said we ought to increase the ground forces twenty-five per cent. And then he said we're getting into a land war—we ought to get in more with bombers. . . . He changes each day or two. . . . And I don't get irritated any more. I just kind of, like you do . . ." Eisenhower, though, either didn't hear him, or pretended not to. Whatever his feelings about Nixon, he was not about to confide them to Lyndon Johnson.

October 14, 1966, was the general's seventy-sixth birthday. He appeared to have made a full recovery from the heart attack he'd suffered the previous November. The Nixons sent a greeting to which the former president replied with affection, saying that he was "always delighted to hear from my friends, particularly those who have been so close to me as you two," and adding that "seventy-six is a formidable number and I would like it to be my golf score rather than my age." Nixon by then was absorbed by the midterm elections; he was available to speak for anyone labeled "Republican" while also finding the soft spots in Lyndon Johnson's presidency and attacking them. A perfect opportunity came after the so-called Manila Conference—Johnson had flown to the Philippines to meet with the leaders of South Vietnam and other Pacific nations who had troops in Vietnam. The conference, which ended in late October with a "declaration of peace" and a call for mutual withdrawal of forces, was an empty exercise, and Nixon was ready to pounce. Thanks to luck and a skillful intercession by the publicist William Safire, his appraisal of the Manila communiqué was treated as front-page news by the *New York Times,* which also published a full page of text. His analysis—it appeared just before the midterm election—had a judicious tone, but was by any measure a merciless assessment: "While the mission . . . had a welcome effect on our friends it had no effect on our enemies and peace is no nearer," he wrote. Johnson's reaction bordered on fury. He called Nixon "a chronic campaigner" who likes to "find fault with his country and with his government during a period of October every two years," and he brought up—and misquoted—Ike's much quoted remark from 1960: "You remember what President Eisenhower said, that if you would give him a week or so he would figure out what he was doing." If that wasn't enough for Johnson, and it wasn't, he finished by saying, "Mr. Nixon doesn't serve his country well" in raising questions about the Manila meetings.

Because Johnson had used Eisenhower's words to attack Nixon, he more or less forced Ike to defend his former vice president, which he did, saying that "Dick Nixon, for whom I have always had the highest personal and official regard, was one of the best informed, most capable and most industrious Vice Presidents in the history of the United States." Nixon knew that being the center of President Johnson's attention was a rare opportunity—the columnist Mary McGrory called it "the best thing that has happened to Nixon since November, 1962"—and he replied in the prim language that made his critics shudder with helpless anger. He told reporters that Johnson had "broken the bipartisan front of support" for the war "with a personal assault against me." And yet despite his "shocking display of temper . . . my policy will continue to be to give him all-out support—which his own party has not done—for his goal of no reward for aggression in Vietnam." As for fighting the war, Nixon was sure that he had the better argument, especially when he could point out that General Eisenhower didn't believe in "gradualism" in a war. "I believe in putting in the kind of military strength we need to win and getting it over with as soon as possible," Nixon said, and added, "I know of no successful military effort that ever keyed its own intensity simply to match that of the aggressor." The conduct of the war and how to pay for it, Nixon said, were the issues—not "the President's temper or the fact that I was his target."

On the eve of the vote, Nixon spoke for the Republicans on national television (NBC gave half an hour of airtime to each party) and in his closing remarks, directed at Johnson, said, "I respect you for the great energies you devote to your office . . . and my respect has not changed because of the personal attack you made on me. You see," he added, now both patronizing and autobiographical, "I think I can understand how a man can be very tired and how temper can be very short." He rented a suite at the Drake Hotel in New York, and about forty people showed up, including his daughter Julie, a freshman at Smith College, and David Eisenhower, the general's grandson, a freshman at Amherst; they were both eighteen years old and had only recently become reacquainted. David didn't know Nixon very well, though he'd met him now and then when his grandfather was president, and had sometimes thought of him as a sort of uncle. As the returns came in, the celebration moved from the Drake to El Morocco, and Nixon was a little giddy, realizing that he could take at least partial credit for many of the local victories. By the end of the night, Republicans had picked up forty-seven House seats, including one that Don Riegle (who had met and been photographed with Eisenhower in Gettysburg) won. The party also gained three Senate seats, including one that Charles Percy took from Paul Douglas in Illinois; and eight governorships, among them California's, where the film and television actor Ronald Reagan defeated the incumbent Pat Brown by a large margin and Nixon's old friend Bob Finch won the race for lieutenant governor by an even wider margin.

On the Sunday before the vote, Nixon went on ABC's *Issues and Answers* and was asked yet again about running for president in 1968. "After this election, I am going to take a holiday from politics for at least six months," he said. He intended to travel and study and think, and as if to prove it, right after the Christmas holidays the family went to Key Biscayne. But despite this professed hiatus, he was not about to surrender his future—to content himself with life as a prosperous Wall Street lawyer. "Once you've hit the big leagues," he told the journalist Jules Witcover, "it's awfully hard to resign yourself to just puttering around." One afternoon in Florida, Pat, Tricia, and Julie sat on the beach, a day that Julie remembered as being bleak, with a wind so cold that they wore sweaters and wrapped towels around their legs; she recalled that her mother, in an almost toneless voice, had said that she couldn't face another run for the White House: "She spoke of the 'humiliation' of defeat. It was apparent to us that she simply no longer had the heart to fight the battle."

CHAPTER 25

"That Job Is So Big, the Forces Are So Great"

1

Richard Nixon, the constant sports fan, was like a crafty baseball manager, analyzing the lineups of opposing teams while assessing his own strengths and weaknesses. "They still call me 'Tricky Dick.' It's a brutal thing to fight," he said to James J. Kilpatrick for a *National Review* story. He didn't worry much about the designated front-runner, the Michigan governor George Romney—"he's a little bit thick, gonna stumble," he told Len Garment—nor did he think that Nelson Rockefeller had much of a chance in 1968. "If I can't establish in these miserable primaries that I *am* a winner, I'm out of it," he told Kilpatrick. "There won't be any 'brokered' or 'negotiated' nomination for me." He was pretty sure that in a brokered convention, the delegates would choose Ronald Reagan, to whom the party's conservatives had quickly turned after Goldwater's defeat. Although Reagan had been governor for only a few months, Nixon knew his party well enough to know that Reagan was already his most formidable rival. He knew that his party bore increasingly less resemblance to the party of Dewey and Eisenhower or, for that matter, Robert Taft. Yet if he no longer quite fit in, he was granted a sort of dispensation for his Red-hunting past, his pure strain of Cold War anticommunism, his work for Goldwater. He did not broadcast views that he shared privately, as when he remarked to an aide, John Whittaker, that "the far right kooks are just like the nuts on the left, they're door bell ringers and balloon blowers but they turn out to vote. There is only one thing as bad as a far left liberal and that's a damn right wing conservative."

Reagan in early 1967 wasn't announcing any presidential aspirations, but he made a pilgrimage to Palm Desert, to see his California neighbor General Eisenhower. After a lunch that lasted two and a half hours, the general held an impromptu press conference at the gate of the Eldorado Country Club (nonmembers are still not welcome on club grounds) and said, first, that Reagan would "make his own decision" about going after the nomination in 1968, followed by, "There are a number of men who would make fine Presidents in our party. Governor Reagan is one of the men I admire most in the world." And then, like some other words that Eisenhower had uttered over the years, he wished that there was a way to erase these, mostly because this time he probably hadn't said them. In a memorandum to himself, Ike said that he had been misquoted—that when he'd spoken about "one of the ablest men I knew and a man that I admired deeply and for whom I had a great affection" he was referring to Nixon, not Reagan. He telephoned Walter Cronkite, who had repeated the story on the air, and who, Eisenhower noted, was "chagrined to admit that his information came from a newspaper and he hoped sometime to change it." But there was no way to take it back; Eisenhower couldn't issue a "clarification." That would only insult Reagan, and Nixon, for the same reason, couldn't ask for one.

Eisenhower returned to Gettysburg in the spring, and in early April it was Nixon's turn to have lunch with the general. Eisenhower could see at once that this was a new iteration of Dick Nixon. His hair was thinning, even going a little gray, and he'd put on enough weight to look the part of a wealthy corporate lawyer. Eisenhower by contrast looked frail. At the end of 1966, he'd been hospitalized for gall bladder surgery, and by now his medical history was a chain of illnesses. Mamie worried about him. "He is thin and he doesn't seem to be able to put any weight on him— 159 lb is too light," she said in a note to Pat Nixon after Dick's visit. But the general was no less involved with the world when Nixon showed up accompanied by Dwight Chapin, who recalled, as others have, that Eisenhower had "these incredible blue eyes . . . they just go right through you." They covered a great many subjects. Eisenhower in particular had growing doubts about the way that Lyndon Johnson was handling the Asian war; he reminded Nixon that Robert E. Lee had had much greater success in Virginia than he'd had in Pennsylvania and Maryland, where the local population was not friendly to his cause. When they talked about 1968, Eisenhower told Nixon that he was the most qualified Republican—and furthermore, that was what he always told people. That was true enough, but not the whole truth. In fact, two weeks after the Gettysburg visit, Rose Mary Woods learned that the general had told Billy Graham that he "had some doubts about whether Nixon could win." Woods also informed Nixon that Graham had told Jack Paar's former producer Paul Keyes that "he thought you would get the nomination but that Ron Reagan was the one who would be a sure winner!!"

After seeing Nixon, Eisenhower summed up his real views about the next presidential race in a letter to his former treasury secretary, George Humphrey. Of Nixon, he said, "As you know I've always liked and respected him; he is now even more mature and well-informed than when he was Vice President." But he went on to express his doubts about Nixon in curiously critical language: "He himself openly recognizes that he has never projected well, and particularly on TV, and I'm certain that he is determined to overcome so far as possible, his weakness in this regard." In an interview with ABC's Bill Lawrence later that summer, the former president was his old evasive self. "I've often expressed my admiration for Dick Nixon, and I can certainly support him without any equivocation, without any reluctance whatsoever," he said. "But that doesn't mean that I'm going to try to substitute my own judgment for that of the party."

2

As General Eisenhower approached his seventy-seventh birthday, he talked more about slowing down without actually doing so. "I'm not so strong as I used to be," he told a reporter. "I'm going to get some lighter clubs. My game is terrible now and they may help." He said that he'd like to visit

Southeast Asia, "But my health is so tricky the doctors won't give me an okay." In a note to Nixon in late summer, he said, "When you come to see me please allow plenty of time. Although it is true that I have to take certain amounts of rest time, I think I can still perform that little chore and at the same time have plenty of time for a long talk with you." But it was not as though he had withdrawn from intellectual engagement. Along with the former Illinois senator Paul Douglas, a Democrat, and his wartime comrade General Omar Bradley, he announced that he was trying to "formulate a more sensible policy on Vietnam," although he didn't say that Lyndon Johnson was pursuing an *unsensible* policy. "Everybody is frustrated when things do not come out right," he said, adding, "All wars are nasty and this one is particularly bad. This is about as different as the one I had a part in as day and night." *The one I had a part in.* There were times when Ike could say a lot without actually saying it.

On the actual day of his birthday, October 14, he spoke to reporters on the campus of Gettysburg College. He was accompanied by Mamie and sounded almost melancholy when he talked about the growing protests on campuses and elsewhere against the expanding war. "Those speaking against Administration practices are exercising their right of dissent, but we need to be moderate in tone and emphasis," he said. "No one can be all-seeing." As for presidential politics, he mentioned, as he had before, a number of governors—not only Rockefeller, Reagan, and Romney, but James Rhodes of Ohio and Daniel Evans of Washington. It was at that point that Mrs. Eisenhower whispered something in his ear and the general hastened to add the name of his former vice president. That Nixon had been defeated, he said, shouldn't be held against him; after all, Lincoln had been defeated, too.

Nixon had set the end of the year as the date to make his final decision on running—the go or no-go moment—as if to put drama or suspense into an occasion that lacked both. Yet he liked to mull over his choices and then think over what he'd mulled and consider all the pros and then the cons; and there were still those times when he said that he was going to abandon public life altogether, just as he'd said it during his most painful moments as vice president. None of this, though, was real; it was, rather, a slightly narcissistic workout, a version of a thought experiment in which he would imagine himself in pursuit of the office he desired and then imagine his life after giving up the quest. When he gave an interview, as he did with Hugh Sidey for *Life* magazine, one could hear him trying to sound ever more presidential, as when he said "A President's energies, his creative energies, must be reserved for the great decisions which only he can make and which mean war or peace" (Ike had used almost exactly those words when he spoke to Nixon after his stroke) and when promising a strong, independent cabinet. "You only develop big men by giving them big jobs," he said, and added, "That job is so big, the forces are so great, I'm not sure any man can—by himself—be an adequate President of the United States at this time." Sidey was carried away enough to write that after years of absence from Washington, "He savors those memories as he stares down the shadowed financial canyon." Nixon was pleased enough with the article to send a tear sheet to Eisenhower, who wrote back and reminded Nixon of the importance of establishing order in the White House:

> I quite agree with your statement, ". . . I'm not sure any man can—*by himself*—be an adequate President." The secret is adequate and skillful organization. You have described the necessity for surrounding the President with individuals of strong convictions, properly organized, so that necessary information and opinion come to him in usable form. Without such personnel and such organization, errors of great magnitude are bound to occur in times of crisis.

Eisenhower added a P.S.—"I shall make an attempt to reach you for a telephone conversation before Mamie and I start for California on November 28. I should like to relate to you some of the gossip I have picked up here and there"—by which he meant the growing ties between his grandson and Nixon's younger daughter.

A couple of weeks after this exchange, Eisenhower, accompanied by General Bradley, appeared on CBS and talked about the war. The general said that he favored "hot pursuit"—that he was all for letting American troops invade the demilitarized zone and follow Communist forces into Cambodia and Laos. "This respecting of boundary lines," he said. "I think you can overdo it." Then, in a way that would not have been imaginable eight years earlier, Nixon disagreed, as if to show that he was no longer anyone's vice president but, rather, a mature politician with a long and complex history, a man approaching his fifty-fourth birthday and made of strong enough stuff to question the wisdom of the man who led the Allied Expeditionary Force. "I do not question General Eisenhower's military judgment," he said, not surprisingly, and then continued, "But the United States should be very cautious about taking any action that could be interpreted as widening the war. From a political standpoint, I would be very reluctant to take action that would be regarded as an invasion of North Vietnam, Cambodia, or Laos." It was in retrospect an odd moment—not only for Ike, who not long before had described the war as "the most nasty and unpredictable thing we've ever been in," but for Nixon, who, were he able to view the future, would have seen himself doing precisely what he had warned against.

CHAPTER 26

David and Julie

1

When Julie Nixon and David Eisenhower traveled to New York for the 1966 Republican victory celebration it was technically their second date, but they'd been seeing a lot of each other since someone at the Hadley Republican Women's Club realized that an Eisenhower and a Nixon were first-year college students and were living close by. The two famously named eighteen-year-olds turned down an invitation to speak to club-women, but David wondered what had become of Julie, whom he hadn't seen since they were children, and he hitchhiked the seven miles from the Amherst campus to the Smith campus to say hello. They went out for ice cream and realized right away that they not only enjoyed each other's company but had something in common that no one else could possibly have understood.

They had never been playmates—in fact had only met a few times, including an Opening Day game in 1959, at Griffith Stadium, when the vice president threw out the first ball, and David, some of his classmates, and the four Nixons sat together on the third base side. And once, when they were eight years old and watching the second inaugural, someone took a great picture: the president was standing behind the children and suggested that Julie, who had been in a sledding accident, turn her head to hide a prominent black eye. As a result, David appears to be staring directly and intently at Julie. But that encounter was an exception. David's family lived in Alexandria, Virginia, until 1959 (he attended St. Stephen's School there), and then in a house on the grounds of the Gettysburg farm, although they still made lengthy visits to the White House. Julie's schools and friends were several miles away, in upper Northwest Washington. David had never been anonymous (he was after all named Dwight D. Eisenhower II), but he had grown up away from the intense scrutiny that had rarely brought the Nixon family much joy.

Two days after the ice cream excursion, David came by again and, as they sometimes like to tell the story (almost a "meet-cute" variation), a girl who announced callers to Baldwin House residents said that "some guy named Eisenhower" was calling for "Miss Nixon." Almost from then on, they were together constantly—for study dates at the Amherst library or in David's room; they'd go to movies and fraternity parties (David belonged to Alpha Delta Phi), or to popular college hangouts in Hadley or Holyoke. Fred Grandy, who had been David's roommate when they attended Exeter, recalled a phone call during which David informed him, "Hey, I'm actually going out with Julie Nixon." They were crazy about each other and were recognized by their classmates as a couple, although at that point in the American 1960s, a somewhat out-of-time couple.

A few days before Christmas 1966, the fashion writer and columnist Eugenia Sheppard spent time with Julie Nixon, who was home for the holidays and was about to be escorted by David Eisenhower to the International Debutante Ball. Julie liked to see herself as anti-society, although not antisocial. "Of course the whole debutante thing is a little ridiculous," she said to Sheppard, who had been the fashion editor of the *Herald Tribune* (the *Trib* had folded the previous August). "I think most of us feel the same way about debutante parties." She also told Sheppard that she liked simple clothes and didn't mind being told that she looked like her father (although the blond Tricia's resemblance to her father is considerably more striking), because she shared many of his tastes, such as studying history and campaigning.

Some parts of the ball were televised by a local TV station, so New Yorkers of every class and circumstance could watch as the young women made their bows to about a thousand guests, including the Nixons as well as Mr. and Mrs. Jack Paar, whose daughter, Randy, also made her debut. A few days later, General Eisenhower took formal and sentimental note of the moment in his somewhat repetitive annual birthday greeting to Nixon: "Seeing your lovely Julie and David grown up enough to be at a formal Ball makes me, at least, realize how much time has passed since 1952 and our first convention," he said.

2

David Eisenhower knew that his grandfather wasn't particularly happy that he was seeing so much of Julie Nixon. The general worried in particular that an early marriage might derail his grandson's career, a subject that he discussed with the couple when they came to see him in Gettysburg. He quizzed his grandson on how he was using his time and on whether he was neglecting his health. He didn't tell them to slow things down, but there was little doubt that it was his wish. It was a discouraging, upsetting conversation for the two teenagers, but particularly for David; he hated to displease his formidable grandfather, who was used to being obeyed even if he didn't actually issue a direct order. He also disapproved of David's habit of hitchhiking the short distance between Amherst and Smith; when Nixon visited the general in April 1967, Eisenhower had mentioned in passing that David and Julie had ridden in a vehicle filled with beer cans. "They are unspoiled," Nixon said, and added, as if to reassure the general, "They don't drink."

David at least was getting support from his grandmother—"Mimi," as the family called her—who had encouraged him to see Julie in Massachusetts and who wrote to Pat Nixon to say "The friendship of Julie and David is heartwarming. They are both full of fun but still so sensible." Two months later, in June, Julie visited Gettysburg again, and this time Mamie wrote to tell Pat Nixon "how much we enjoyed Julie's short visit. . . . She is an adorable girl." In the summer of 1967 when school was out, David took a job in Chicago as a trainee for Sears Roebuck but the distance didn't keep them apart; Julie went out to see him, and found him working for the complaint department "being hounded," as she put it, "by ladies whose refrigerator doors fell off." On Julie's nineteenth birthday, July 5, David flew to Key Biscayne to spend time with all the Nixons.

Julie told reporters that summer that "I just enjoy being with him because we have a lot of fun" and that it was just a "lighthearted friendship" ("Well, you know how kids are," her father said), a fib that got them a few months of relative privacy. They—and Tricia Nixon—tried to laugh at the attention being paid to them and they gave themselves initials to fit their brand-new public images. Tricia, diminutive and blond, was "F. P." (Fairy Princess); Julie was "N.C.P.D." (No Cream Puff Deb), and David was "T.C.C." (Teen Carbon Copy). Julie and David knew that this was a lot more than a lighthearted friendship; in fact, although it was a secret, they had already decided to get married, definitely before they graduated.

Julie, though, knew that there was no way to separate what they were planning for themselves from what Julie's father might have in store for himself—unless and until he forswore any interest in pursuing the presidency. She had been reared in a far more political environment than David, having witnessed and suffered through her father's two losing campaigns and the strain of his never-ending tours during each election cycle. She once observed that she could have written that part of Alice Roosevelt Longworth's autobiography in which she said, "I find it hard to remember a time when I was not aware of the existence of politics and politicians." If her father were to run for president in 1968, as she had every reason to suspect, David's grandfather would inevitably be drawn into it.

"Of course I am pleased to hear you speak of your fondness of Julie," the general wrote to his grandson in September 1967. "She is a great favorite of Mimi's and mine, not only because of her natural charm but because she seems to have both feet solidly on the ground." But then Ike set down some of the reservations to which he had alluded in earlier conversations:

> As I see it you will have some 6–10 years of education still ahead of you, depending upon your choice of profession. If you go in for law, or a business career, probably the shorter term; if medicine, the longer. . . . By no means would I want you to abandon a social life, but at this stage it

should not interfere with health and education. I merely remind you that you are building a sturdy foundation for a future life of usefulness. That means a vigorous mind in a strong body and these together do much to make a happy life.

David wasn't particularly interested in a career in medicine or law, although he later went to law school and spoke of one day becoming a Supreme Court justice; and he'd gone to Amherst despite feeling some pressure to attend West Point, as his grandfather and father had. "I didn't realize until I was eighteen years old that I was disappointing anybody," David told the Eisenhower family biographer Steve Neal, "and it turned out I disappointed everybody." He wasn't being fair to himself. David's father, too, was more inclined to writing and teaching than to soldiering; David's deep interests included not only military and political history but baseball. (Forty years after the fact, he could still excitedly discuss the disastrous trade that the old Washington Senators made to acquire the pitcher Denny McLain from Detroit.)

As the 1967 holidays approached, Julie and David knew that they needed to tell their families that their relationship had reached this serious point, although the secret was getting out and it would not surprise Julie's mother and sister or some of the Eisenhowers.

Julie thought that her father's first reaction was something close to silence, but it was more like another instance of his sometimes unnerving stiffness; later that night, he slipped a note under her door which said in part, "I suppose no father believes any boy is good enough for his daughter. But I believe both David and you are lucky to have found each other." David was leery and even a little afraid of his grandfather's reaction and decided to give the news to the Eisenhowers en masse—his parents, his grandparents, his siblings—when they showed up in Gettysburg for Thanksgiving. Mamie Eisenhower was enthusiastic—after all, she'd been only nineteen when she'd married Lieutenant Eisenhower—and she went to fetch her mother's engagement ring for David to present to Julie. It was different with the general; he was uncommunicative after the announcement. "For two days, I awkwardly evaded mentioning the engagement in Granddad's presence," David recalled. He thought that they'd finally get around to discussing it just before he left Gettysburg to return to school, and at the end of this long Thanksgiving weekend, after lunch, he went to see his grandfather, who was in his bedroom getting ready for a nap. He looked tired, David thought, and they didn't have a real conversation although the general did ask about Amherst and told his grandson about his plans to spend the winter in the desert. After about half an hour, he asked what time it was and told David to have his valet wake him up in an hour; and then he fell asleep.

After David returned to Amherst, he got a letter from his grandfather that cheered him. "I am more than delighted that the two of you feel such a deep mutual affection," the general wrote. "You are both the kind of people who will, throughout your lives, enrich America. Moreover, a love, shared by two young and intelligent people, is one of heaven's greatest gifts to humanity."

David replied at once—he was sorry, he said, for being afraid of the general's reaction. But this time, his grandfather replied in a somewhat less affectionate tone:

> In your reply to my letter of a couple of weeks ago you seemed to conclude that I was disappointed by your failure, earlier, to tell Mimi and me of the then imminent "engagement." I was quite astonished that you made such an interpretation of my letter, because my only purpose was to comment a bit on the natural shyness that seems almost invariably to develop in the personal relationship between any two Nordic males, who are bound together by a mutual affection.

As if to soften that mild reproach—and those quotation marks around the word "engagement"—the general also offered some grandfatherly advice about healthy eating:

> All my life I've "bolted" my food—and, according to [the doctors], all the troubles I've had stem from that terrible habit. They say that if I had always eaten slowly, masticating my food until every mouthful is a liquid before swallowing, I would not only have avoided all my illnesses, but would still have a life expectancy of something like ninety.... If you

have formed any bad habits of this kind please ask Julie to help you break them.

Ike hadn't taken back what he'd said about "two young and intelligent people," but neither did he sound overjoyed; and he wasn't. One family friend ran into David during the first weeks of the engagement and found him deeply upset by the response from his family. "He loved Julie and he had—he was very loyal to his father and his grandfather—and he found it a very difficult position to be in," the friend said. David's father was no more pleased than his grandfather; at one point, John S. D. Eisenhower, some of whose friends believed that he disliked Nixon, perhaps because he thought that Nixon was usurping his paternal role, muttered to an acquaintance that the match was "social-climbing" by the Nixons.

The newspapers feasted on news of a Nixon-Eisenhower engagement. On December 1, right after the Thanksgiving holiday, it was a front-page story in the *New York Times* (EISENHOWER'S GRANDSON TO WED A NIXON DAUGHTER). "We won't get married for a while," Julie told a reporter. "I didn't expect all this publicity. I felt I just wasn't that important." Her father made an awkward, cringe-inducing joke: "They are both remarkable young people. And I'd say that even if they weren't both Republicans." General Eisenhower was on his way to Palm Desert, and when he arrived, he said of his grandson, "We're proud of him. We think he made a wonderful pick."

3

David and Julie sometimes felt estranged from their classmates and from their times and the more that they became public figures, the more likely they were to be ridiculed for being so determinedly out of step with the antiwar movement and the counterculture. "By their own admission," one newspaper story began, they'd never read the poetry of Allen Ginsberg. "They were a TV show from the Eisenhower era looked in on after ten years," Garry Wills wrote. "Mr. and Mrs. Howdy Doody about to set up housekeeping," and Wills went on to express scornful amazement that they could actually like the music of Dave Brubeck. On the Amherst campus,

David had come to represent the contented Establishment. "After all, he asked to be a symbol," the Student Council president said. He hadn't asked for that role, and he had many friends at Amherst, but he knew that his position was inescapable; and he knew that he stood out on a campus where he had counted only fourteen Republicans, including himself, among the twelve hundred students. It was harder being Richard Nixon's daughter. "I hate being a celebrity—and I use that word hesitantly," Julie wrote in her diary. "I am a 'celebrity' only in that I am stared at when I walk on campus, eyes and heads turn. Sometimes, when I am speaking I feel as if people were taking mental notes. And sometimes I feel so disgusted later when I *have* to put on a show."

Nixon, meanwhile, was still acting as if he wasn't going to make up his mind about a presidential run until the end of the year, much like a restless racehorse that, having trained for sixteen years and having reached the starting gate, was not sure whether to get back onto the track. What made this last-minute indecision so strange was that he insisted on having the people closest to him share in the false tension of his fictional narrative. By the end of the year, everyone was increasingly aware of the personal issues that his candidacy would raise; Nixon himself was willing to address the problem. After a dinner at the Nixons' apartment, David and Julie discussed a wedding date, and brought up the idea of having it sooner than anyone had expected—perhaps in June 1968. In a diary entry, Julie wrote:

> Daddy mentioned that a June wedding would cause people to say it was an attempt to bind DDE-Nixon families closer together and to attract publicity. Somehow, however, David and I questioned D's [Daddy's] nervousness. . . . I just wanted him to speak frankly—I wanted to know what he really felt. I am still not sure but I think his main objection was the reaction of David's grandfather. D finally said he was concerned, frankly, that if we married in June, DDE would blame Daddy. When we became engaged, DDE asked David to wait until graduation before we were married. D is afraid that DDE will think he pushed it and then make things difficult for RN. I can see D's point; it is likely that this would happen.

They needn't have worried. Despite a looming familial tie, the general was not about to break precedent when it came to endorsing a Republican candidate or when it came to expressing doubts about Richard Nixon. His views this time were filtered through Felix Belair Jr., the *New York Times* reporter who still managed to show up whenever the post-presidential Ike had something interesting to say. Belair thought that the former president looked a little paler than the last time he'd seen him, but he kept his old habits—he couldn't sit still for more than a few minutes, gesturing and pacing; that eternal restiveness overtook his frailty. His views on Nixon were attributed to a "golfing crony" to whom Ike had purportedly said, "Even if I had the power to name the next Republican Presidential nominee, I would not necessarily select the man I thought best qualified to be President." The "crony" continued, "My reason for that is that no matter how well qualified I may think a man might be, he still has to get elected. And I would like to see the convention pick a man who can win over Johnson next November." In Eisenhower's favored indirect fashion, this meant he believed Nixon still could not overcome the stigma of "they-say-he-can't-win," and of simply being Richard Nixon.

Julie Nixon encountered another sort of pervasive anti-Nixon sentiment when she showed up at the Smith government department's mock Republican convention, an episode that she recorded in her diary:

> It was hell on earth for me. My friend Marsha Cohen was asked to give R.N.'s speech, because there were no volunteers. As she spoke the word "selflessly," it came out "selfishly worked for his party." The audience loved it. And then another laugh when she praised Daddy. I just couldn't bear it. I was sitting in the back of the room, and walked out.

Julie Nixon, who was born with a surplus of cheery optimism and daughterly devotion, thought that she knew why she'd gone: "It wasn't for self-torture," the diarist wrote. "It was because I had a secret hope that perhaps there would be genuine response for my father."

CHAPTER 27

Family Ties

1

The holidays of 1967 were unusually busy for Richard Nixon, and one day, December 22, was especially crowded, for it included a lunch with his partners, a meeting with political advisers, and a Christmas party at his apartment—an annual event since the family had moved to New York. At some point, Nixon could be counted upon to play carols on the piano, sometimes thumpingly and still in the key of G. The party was an impressive display of New York wealth and power, and among the hundred or so invited guests was the firm's new partner, John Mitchell, a stocky man with a slight tremor, who was considered the nation's leading expert in municipal bonds, someone who had become wealthy and well connected simply by doing business with so many municipal leaders. At the end of the year, his firm, Caldwell, Trimble & Mitchell, merged with Nixon, Mudge, and the new entity—Nixon Mudge Rose Guthrie Alexander and Mitchell—employed 120 lawyers and occupied most of five floors at 20 Broad Street.

The evening at the Nixons' was fascinating for people like a Pennsylvania high school English teacher named William Gavin, who earlier that year had sent Nixon a rambling note that quoted Ortega y Gasset and urged him to run "boldly" for president, a letter that so appealed to Len Garment that he invited Gavin to lunch and asked him to send along ideas, some of which—often a single phrase—made their way into the speeches that Nixon was giving. That is why when Gavin and his wife showed up at the Nixons', someone, probably Dwight Chapin, made the introduction, and Nixon turned around and said, "The one-liner man," a gratifying moment of recognition. The party was not much fun for John Mitchell. He had brought his wife, Martha, who had been under psychiatric care and was being treated for alcoholism; she was hyperactive all night, much the way that she'd been at the firm's Christmas dinner, where she had sat next to Nixon and commanded his attention for the entire evening.

Nixon, meanwhile, refused to give up his own drama. After the guests left, he went into his office, picked up a yellow legal pad, and wrote, "I have decided personally against becoming a candidate." In this exercise Nixon also asked himself whether he still had the heart for another run. Julie in her diary wrote: "Daddy called Tricia and me in separately and told us that he had decided—almost definitely—not to run. He was very depressed. I had never known him to be depressed before—not even after 1962." Then, on Christmas Day, Nixon talked to his family and seemed to hear them out. Pat was still reluctant, but said that she'd help if he decided to go ahead. Julie and Tricia urged him to run, with Tricia saying, bluntly, "If you don't run, Daddy, you really have nothing to live for."

It is impossible, though, to imagine that Nixon's wife and daughters (or David Eisenhower) ever doubted his intentions—after all, he'd been plotting with his law partners, hiring and firing a campaign professional (a man named Gaylord Parkinson, who had helped elect Ronald Reagan), adding staff (most notably Ray Price, the former editorial page editor of the *Herald Tribune,* whose streak of naive honesty endeared him to journalists as well as to the Nixon family), and submitting to interviews in which he spoke about what kind of president he'd be. His personality, though, was compelling enough to lure his family into the game. In any case, three days after Christmas Nixon went alone to Key Biscayne to deal with "the most important decision of my life," a stay that included a walk on the beach with Billy Graham, who unhesitatingly urged him to run. He could not quite let go of this artificial play, and its last act took place when he returned to New York for a family dinner that included Rose Mary Woods and the Nixons' servants, Fina and Manolo Sanchez, and during which, as Julie recorded in her diary, Fina said "that in the world there are few men that are born to do something and that D was one of them," adding that those words "brought tears to his eyes and to Mother's too." Now that his future was settled, a June wedding was out of the question—"Since Daddy has decided to run, we can't," Julie wrote. "It would look politically contrived"—and the awkwardness that Nixon's candidacy might create for David and the Eisenhowers still needed to be addressed.

Nixon waited until January 31—three hours before the filing deadline—to enter his name in the March 12 New Hampshire primary. It was not the best time to announce his plans. Just as riots in Detroit, Newark, and elsewhere had made it seem as if America was facing an indefinite period of racial violence, the war in Vietnam took a bad turn. On the eve of Tet—the Lunar New Year—Vietcong raiders made surprise attacks on several South Vietnamese cities, and although the raids were not a military victory for the North, their impact required another sort of measurement. How could you defeat an enemy that was able to launch such surprises and was prepared to fight battles of attrition on its home territory? So not a lot of attention was paid to Richard Nixon when he appeared at a Manchester Holiday Inn on a near-freezing, foggy February day to tell the world what the world already thought it knew.

The nasty weather affected the family's plans. New England airports were fogged in, which forced Tricia and Pat to drive up from New York. Nixon's aide Dwight Chapin telephoned Julie at Smith and asked if David or perhaps another friend could drive her to Manchester, a distance of about 125 miles. The presence of General Eisenhower's grandson at Nixon's first campaign event would not go unnoticed—just the sort of thing that Julie had fretted over. Would it imply that Ike was already in the Nixon camp? Or would it put pressure on the general that he might resent? On the other hand, if David hurried back to Amherst, would that mean that he *wasn't* supporting his future father-in-law? David knew that his grandfather had doubts about Nixon's candidacy (he had only to read the newspapers) and that his father was skeptical, too. When John S. D. Eisenhower talked to friends at about this time, he would say things like, "Dick's about to make a fool of himself again."

As it turned out, David remained in New Hampshire where Nixon, in his first formal speech of the 1968 campaign, said that America faced a "crisis of the spirit" and that new leadership would give the nation "the lift of a driving dream"—a Ray Price phrase that did not quite match the candidate's earthbound demeanor. Later, the Nixon entourage held an open house at St. Anselm's College, where two thousand people showed up and waited in line to meet these political celebrities—the four Nixons and David Eisenhower, who was asked his opinion of miniskirts and replied that he liked them but didn't want Julie to wear one. Journalists described David and Julie as types. Julie was "bubbly" or "vivacious" or "talkative and uninhibited . . . with a heart-shaped face, brown eyes"; David was "a gangly boy with saucer ears and his grandfather's winning grin," not to mention "tousled" hair. Garry Wills was not the first, or the last, to invoke Howdy Doody.

General Eisenhower despite his doubts was perfectly willing to be supportive. To his former personal secretary, Ann Whitman, he wrote that "One of the stranger factors in all of the free political prognostication that comes my way is the confidence that Dick Nixon is a well prepared man for the Presidency, to which is added the further assertion that he is about the only one that could *not* possibly be elected." But the former president still wasn't ready to endorse Nixon. When he talked to reporters, he said only that Nixon is "a very good man," and "much better than a lot [of people] think," adding that because Nixon "didn't have a warm personal magnetism . . . people may tend to discount his experience, logical brain and courage."

Nelson Rockefeller in early February insisted that he was "absolutely not" a candidate "and never will be," after which Eisenhower told Nixon "I believe that he is completely honest when he says he does *not want* to get into the race." But Rockefeller was never completely honest when it came to this subject, and who knew what Ronald Reagan was thinking? Nixon at any rate was waging another, more personal campaign: to win Eisenhower's open support. Even though it should not have mattered, and even though the seventy-seven-year-old former president had very little influence in the post-Goldwater Republican Party, Nixon was no less eager for his backing than he had been eight years earlier, when Eisenhower had made him wait and fret. Nixon sensed that he could not press, so he used emissaries and indirect appeals, techniques of the sort that Ike liked to employ. David Eisenhower had a role in this, although not a very assertive one. "What's understood is what a lion Dwight D. Eisenhower was," he said, recalling himself at age twenty. "He wasn't somebody that you pressured. He wasn't someone that you even hinted around." In mid-February, Nixon sent Bob Ellsworth, a former Kansas congressman who had taken over Nixon-for-president duties, to see Eisenhower at his office at the Jackie Cochran–Floyd Odlum ranch, in Indio, to get some idea of how things stood. Ellsworth spent an hour with the general and brought Nixon no closer to his goal. Some of the talk was personal, even gossipy—the family business, so to speak; Ike for instance had heard that Tricia Nixon, a senior at Finch College, was jealous of all the attention being paid to her younger sister. He told Ellsworth that people shouldn't "comment in too much detail" about the war—"the important thing is we have to win—we have to succeed." And he worried about Johnson's attempts to micromanage the fighting. "He thinks that is Johnson's big trouble," Ellsworth informed Nixon. "He is doing too many things others should be doing for him." As for Nixon's political rivals, Eisenhower had come to think less of Governor Romney—he "has a genius for talking about things he is not informed of"—and seemed to have grown doubtful about Governor Reagan.

Then, at the end of February, Romney dropped out—simply quit the race two weeks before the New Hampshire primary. Nixon had reckoned all along that Romney would do himself in, either from ineptitude or inexperience, but this premature surrender was a surprise; people compared Romney to a fighter who wouldn't even climb into the ring. Nixon became suspicious—he had become increasingly suspicious of people's motives over the years—and wondered if there was a plot afoot, something that involved Rockefeller.

After Romney's withdrawal, the outcome looked inevitable, and for those who couldn't bear the prospect of having to choose between Richard Nixon and Lyndon Johnson, the approaching election was like an advancing toxic cloud. Walter Lippmann had become so disheartened by the war and by Johnson's governance that he had uprooted himself from his Washington home on Woodley Road, opposite the Cathedral, and settled in New York. Johnson, he wrote, "has driven a whole generation of

Americans into open or implicit revolt against their government and their own society." He had come to see Nixon as someone with a "long and rich experience in national government and in national politics" (Lippmann's detestation of Johnson was so limitless that Nixon's stature had ballooned) but found him lacking knowledge of local and regional politics—"where the action is"—and concluded that Rockefeller was the person to deal with the range of problems facing America: the war, the cities, the economy, race. Nixon's margin of victory in New Hampshire was a nearly meaningless 80 percent; the more interesting result was the Democratic one, where the antiwar candidate, Senator Eugene McCarthy, won 42 percent and Johnson, who was not on the ballot, did not surpass 50 percent. Four days later, Senator Robert Kennedy entered the race.

On March 31, before he was fated to lose a primary in Wisconsin, President Johnson abdicated. At the same time he ordered a halt to the bombing of North Vietnam. He has "the whole country puzzled," Eisenhower said, but privately he saw Johnson as a little craven, someone willing to abandon not only his office but his commitment to the war he had joined and expanded. He was not yet confident about Nixon's chances, though, if only because the networks were giving endless publicity to, as he put it, "such characters as Kennedy, McCarthy and [Vice President Hubert H.] Humphrey" while "Nixon scarcely exists."

Then came the much chronicled double nightmare: four days after Johnson's withdrawal, Martin Luther King Jr. was killed by a sniper in Memphis, a murder that set off riots in dozens of cities, including Chicago, Detroit, Boston, Newark, and Washington. The killing was "nothing less than a disaster" for the nation, Eisenhower wrote to his friend Admiral Lewis Strauss. "These are truly troubled times." Nixon suspended his campaign; he sent a telegram to Coretta Scott King, calling her husband's death "a great personal tragedy for everyone who knew him and a great tragedy for the nation." A public funeral was set for April 9, in Atlanta, but, oddly, Nixon at first acted as if he wasn't sure that he should go and at one point said, "In the long run, politicians who try to capitalize on this could be hurt. There can't be any grandstanding." Bill Safire reminded Nixon that "grandstanding" was the word he had used in 1960 when he was urged to make a telephone call in behalf of Dr. King. Nixon acted as if he were deliberating, although, as was often the case, he had already made up his mind. Two days before the funeral, he flew to Atlanta, where he saw members of the King family and spoke with them almost as if he were an old friend, which, in a distant and awkward way, he was. "He first went to the home of my sister-in-law, Coretta," Christine King Farris, Dr. King's sister, said. "I happened to be with her at that point. Then he said that he'd go to my parents' home"—a ranch house in Collier Heights, a prosperous Atlanta neighborhood. "He was amazed. He said, 'I think you call it a *split level.*'" Dr. Farris recalled Nixon's surprise at how well the King family lived and continued, "He was by himself. He didn't stay that long—I guess about thirty or forty minutes. He seemed to have been very moved and very sympathetic." There was no press coverage of Nixon's visit, and he left town as quietly as he'd come.

He returned to Atlanta two days later for the funeral, and found himself in the company of, among others, Gene McCarthy, Robert Kennedy, and Nelson Rockefeller. Teddy Kennedy was there, and Jacqueline Kennedy Onassis. And in the crowd were many well-known faces—Bill Cosby, Jackie Robinson, Hubert Humphrey, Wilt Chamberlain, Marlon Brando, Harry Belafonte, and the George Romneys. Dwight Chapin, who accompanied the former vice president, remembered getting out of a car and being surrounded. "I remember he said, 'We're just going to take this very easy' as we started into this crowd, this immense crowd." After the service at Ebenezer Baptist Church, Nixon didn't stay to march in the three-and-a-half-mile procession from the church to Morehouse College, King's alma mater. That would have been grandstanding.

Nelson Rockefeller in April declared that he was "available" after all and began hiring a campaign staff that once more included Emmet Hughes—a move that so displeased Eisenhower that he wrote to Ann Whitman, who had gone to work for Rockefeller, and said, "I can scarcely think of anything that could be less helpful to the Governor." Rockefeller still believed that no one was more qualified than himself—and that that was reason enough for him to win. He was out of shape, though; he appeared before the American Society of Newspaper Editors and delivered what was judged to be an overweight speech on the problems of the cities. Nixon—"smiling, confident, and clearly at ease," as the *New York Times* described him—spoke without a text and answered questions for forty-five minutes, getting (as a reporter tallied them up) ten rounds of applause and twelve bursts of laughter. He asked people to stop criticizing Johnson's war policies as long as there was a chance for successful negotiations (which also allowed Nixon to keep his silence) and disagreed with Gene McCarthy's suggestion that Dean Rusk, the secretary of state, should resign. When he was a congressman, Nixon said, he had demanded the resignation of Dean Acheson—and, in a moment of rare repentance, added, "I was wrong then." Eisenhower wrote to compliment Nixon, adding, "At first, all the self-appointed experts were still saying 'Dick is well prepared for the Presidency, but he cannot be elected.' Now by and large . . . the refrain has changed to 'Of course, Nixon is well prepared for the Presidency, now we must see if we can elect him.'" Eisenhower signed this note "Devotedly, Ike E."

A week later, Eisenhower suffered his fourth heart attack; he had been limiting his golf to "pitch and putt" exercises near Palm Springs, but on the morning of April 29 he couldn't resist an invitation from his friend Freeman Gosden to play a round. Mamie asked him to take it easy—temperatures were in the 90s—and by the time the golfers had reached the ninth hole, every shot had become an effort; by then it was too late. The coronary again was described as mild, but the general was expected to stay in the hospital for several weeks and was soon transferred to Walter Reed.

Nixon thought it likely that he'd be facing Senator Robert Kennedy in the general election. The Kennedy campaign had been passionate and in certain moments it took on an almost malarial heat. When shortly after midnight on June 5, Kennedy was mortally wounded by a man with a gun, this second Kennedy assassination awakened something not quite fathomable, even among people who could never have imagined voting for him. You did not have to care very much about American politics to feel trapped by malicious circumstance.

2

Although David Eisenhower by late spring was actively campaigning for his prospective father-in-law, speaking to small crowds and passing out a button that said NIXON BUTTON (Mamie Eisenhower, too, wore a large NIXON button and handed them out to visitors at Walter Reed), something was missing without a word from the general. There was that hesitant history between them—or a painful absence of history—and no one was more aware of it, or more sensitive about it, than Nixon.

He sent several emissaries to Walter Reed to see Eisenhower, and by far the most important one was Bryce Harlow, the former Eisenhower aide who was now a lobbyist for Procter & Gamble. On June 12, Harlow urged Eisenhower to speak out for Nixon. But, the general replied, if Nixon was bound to get the nomination wouldn't it make more sense to stay neutral until the convention was over? Then if there were party divisions, he'd be in a good position to help patch them up. Harlow did not think much of that reasoning, but he saved his argument for a letter in which he said that Ike's concern about party unity was fine, but that was Nixon's strength, too. On the other hand, without an immediate statement that Ike, as Harlow phrased it, was "hot for Dick," voters might "be open to the snide argument that as a good Republican you are only doing what you have to do." That letter, though, did not reach Eisenhower because the general had suffered his fifth heart attack, this one more serious than any of those that had gone before.

The endorsement campaign waited until Eisenhower began to regain strength, and then went into its most intense phase; at times, it was as if the general was as encircled by political operatives as he was by family and friends. On July 14, three weeks before the Republican convention opened in Miami Beach, Harlow let Rose Mary Woods know that Eisenhower had been "fussing" with an endorsement but wanted to see Nixon in person. Nixon needed to be more aggressive, Harlow believed, and he even composed some dialogue for Nixon to use when he saw the general: *I am not going to lose this nomination—I am not thinking about that—I am thinking of your own peace of mind, I know you are for me and I don't want anyone to be able to say that you were not for me until after the convention. Of course I would prize it tremendously myself.* The next day, Nixon went to see Eisenhower. He did not stay long, and when he wrote to him afterward, his impossible ultra-formality took hold and he sounded like someone writing a business letter to a stranger: "I greatly enjoyed our visit this morning and I want you to know how deeply grateful I am for your words of encouragement for the months ahead." Nixon added that if a "bandwagon psychology" set in, "the sophisticated press and TV observers would reach the conclusion that it was all over but the shouting"; and then he made Harlow's point—that they faced "the distinct possibility that in the public mind the decision would have been made before your endorsement was announced." He continued:

> I hesitate to bring these additional facts up for consideration because I shall indeed be most grateful for your announcement of support whenever it comes. In view of our discussion, however, I felt that you should know of these possibilities since they bear on the critical question of the timing of your announcement and the relationship of that timing to the effect your announcement will have on the voters in November.
>
> I was delighted to see that you were looking so fit after the rugged experiences you have gone through over the past few weeks.

Eisenhower finally did it. On July 18, three days after Nixon's bedside visit, he saw reporters at Walter Reed and, sitting up, read a statement that said, "I do this not only for my appreciation of his great service to the country during the years of my administration but rather and far more because of his personal qualities. He's a man of great reading, a man of great intelligence, and a man of great decisiveness. He's had a great experience over the years and he's still quite a young man." When he was asked about those persistent stories that he didn't truly value Nixon's talents and that they were not personally close, he said that was a "complete misapprehension" and added, "I have admired and respected this man and have liked him since I first met him in 1952."

CHAPTER 28

A Soldier's Serenade

1

The gossips of Washington liked to talk about the Eisenhower-Nixon relationship, and only rarely in a charitable spirit. "Now that the Eisenhowers are has-beens and Nixon is the one who keeps them in the news, the Eisenhowers are much more friendly to Nixon," Lorraine Cooper, the wife of a Republican senator, remarked to the journalist Henry Brandon at a Georgetown dinner party. Mrs. Cooper seemed amused by this change of fortune and grudgingly gave Nixon credit as a creature of ambition. "He is a success story," she said. "He has had nothing, he has had all these setbacks and still is about to succeed." On August 5, the first night of the 1968 Republican National Convention—almost certain to be Nixon's convention—General Eisenhower, looking alarmingly skeletal, addressed the delegates on closed-circuit television. He had taped the speech earlier that day in the living room of Ward 8, the VIP section at Walter Reed, and he'd worked hard on it; he'd gotten a haircut, and Sergeant John Moaney, who had been the general's valet since the war, helped to dress him for television. But Eisenhower had never been good at delivering prepared remarks, and even discounting his midwestern monotone, this wasn't a strong speech; his first attempt had been interrupted by a coughing fit. He stumbled over words, and his sentences were clotted with phrases like "the lawless acts of some minorities that so crowd the TV screen" and suggestions that Communists "covertly labor to deepen citizen discontent to incite violence, and to rend the fabric of our society." He didn't mention Nixon's name, but referred instead to an unnamed eventual nominee—the delegates after all had not yet made their decision. Watching the convention from the hospital, Ike and Mamie could see how their family was being drawn into the Nixon universe. Whenever Ike's grandson was photographed, he was close to the Nixons' younger daughter; their son, John, was in Miami Beach and so was a granddaughter, eighteen-year-old Barbara Anne.

Less than twelve hours after the speech was broadcast, Eisenhower suffered his third myocardial infarction in less than four months, and although his doctors did not blame it on the strain of giving the speech, the connection was obvious. This time, Ike's prognosis was "guarded." John Eisenhower and Barbara Anne immediately left for Washington.

The general wasn't strong enough to watch more of the proceedings, but he was informed that Nixon on Wednesday had won the nomination on the first ballot. (Governors Rockefeller and Reagan, both of whom were nominated and hoped to win enough delegates to stop Nixon, fell far short.) The delegates were not unhappy with the outcome, but neither were they thrilled. Reagan would have thrilled them—Reagan and John Wayne got the biggest cheers of the week—but they liked Nixon well enough, and he was as familiar to them as someone like plump Len Hall, the former Republican National Committee chairman, who was also in Miami Beach, and other party old-timers. The constant worry about Nixon was that he was fated to lose yet again.

Before arriving in Miami Beach on a Monday, Nixon spent a few days in Montauk Point, Long Island, a favorite spot, to work on his acceptance speech. Ray Price and Pat Buchanan were there, but Nixon, always in search of solitude, stayed mostly in his own cabin. Price and Buchanan would send along ideas and research material, and one idea came from someone who wasn't there—Bill Gavin, the "one-liner man," who thought that Nixon needed to show another side, something personal, even at the risk of sounding mawkish and awakening memories of the Checkers speech. And on Thursday night, Nixon addressed the hall and the nation, the embodiment of a will to succeed. His voice was, as always, perfect for radio—a "buttery baritone," a *Time* writer once said—but his gestures were exaggerated and he blinked nervously; he looked as always like an imperfect politician. When he invoked Eisenhower's name, as if marking a political continuum, there was something not quite believable in what he said, as if he was trying to play Pat O'Brien's Knute Rockne while the actor who played the Gipper was in town: "General Eisenhower, as you know, lies critically ill in the Walter Reed Hospital tonight. I have talked, however, with Mrs. Eisenhower on the telephone. She tells me that his heart is with us. She says that there is nothing that he lives more for, and there is nothing that would lift him more than for us to win in November. And I say, let's win this one for Ike!"

Bill Gavin's suggestion was the line "Tonight, I see the face of a child." Nixon liked the idea—and the "I-see-a" cadence—and in its final version the line had mutated into "That child . . . is America. . . . He is everything we ever hoped to be and everything we dare to dream to be," and from there to a memory of himself as a child in East Whittier, who "hears the trains go by at night and he dreams of faraway places where he'd like to go." The next day, when he met with his campaign staff, he took Gavin aside, put an arm around his shoulder, and invited him to come along on the campaign. "It was as if some kid from Podunk went to the Los Angeles Lakers, made three lucky shots, and they put him in as the No. 6 man," Gavin said.

As for picking a vice president, Nixon had asked for suggestions, a futile exercise, because everyone knew that he would choose without prompting from anyone and, furthermore, he knew that he needed to satisfy Strom Thurmond, the South Carolina senator, who had helped him to win the support of southern convention delegates. The selection of the Maryland governor, Spiro Agnew, a dull-witted, provincial politician, was an astonishingly bad choice ("Promise me, Dick, that if you're elected, you'll *always* make Governor Agnew travel with you on your plane," Alice Roosevelt Longworth said to him), but he was acceptable to Thurmond; and Nixon, as in 1960, was not going to risk losing southern white votes in pursuit of northern black ones. This time, his far more overt Southern Strategy, as it came to be known, angered black leaders, among them his onetime ally Jackie Robinson, who had been upset by the hidden messages of the 1964 Goldwater campaign and now called Nixon a "double-talker, a two-time loser, an adjustable man with a convertible conscience."

On August 16, General Eisenhower suffered yet another heart attack. John Eisenhower stayed by his side and David Eisenhower flew in from California, where he had been staying with the Nixons. Even the most advanced procedures, such as the insertion of a temporary electrical pacer, didn't appear to be helping. Nixon, too, hurried to Walter Reed, where he saw Mamie Eisenhower, although not the general, and afterward praised Ike's "magnificent spirit." That was language that one employs when death is near (Nixon had spoken of Dulles's "jaunty spirit" at the end of *his* life). Lyndon Johnson at about that time was explaining to the Soviet ambassador Anatoly Dobrynin (they were conferring after the Soviet attempt to crush democratic impulses in Czechoslovakia) what would happen when Ike died. "It's a six-day affair," Johnson said, adding that on the fifth day, Eisenhower would be buried in Kansas. "He still has a strong heart because *so* many heart attacks, and he still survives," Dobrynin remarked. "It's unbelievable."

Eisenhower did survive this time—he even took a turn for the better—and by the end of August was off the critical list. He was not yet permitted to sit up in bed, but Leonard Heaton, Eisenhower's surgeon and now the Army surgeon general, said, "It is scarcely an exaggeration to state that he 'died' quote-unquote, fourteen times." By mid-September, Heaton said that the former president had achieved "really a miraculous turnabout," although he was not out of danger and was not being allowed to read the newspapers. "They keep him from anything that would worry him," Mamie Eisenhower explained.

The general might have worried if he'd been reading newspapers and watching television, which only heightened the volume of the presidential contest. The Nixon campaign drew on some of the era's language and emotion in its commercials. On one—accompanied by piercing music, the rat-a-tat of drums, bloodied faces, and urban fires—Nixon, in a voice-over, said, "Dissent is a necessary ingredient of change, but in a system of government that provides for peaceful change there is no cause that justifies resort to violence." Another ad, almost a reverse image, showed happy faces, black and white, and crowds peaceably assembled, with Nixon saying, "The next president must unite America. He must calm its anger, ease its terrible frictions, bring its people together." The crazed Democratic convention in Chicago, where Hubert Humphrey was nominated, had provided much material. "How can a party that can't unite itself unite the nation?" another campaign spot asked.

One of Nixon's coaches was Paul Keyes, by then a writer for the popular NBC program *Rowan & Martin's Laugh-In*, and something of an outlier in that world. "Paul tended to be far right in attitude, if not in proclamation" was Hugh Downs's recollection; and Keyes was determined, as he put it, to help Nixon "appear much less mechanical and more human," even suggesting that he needed to "pause as if 'to think' before making a statement." Nixon was probably the first major presidential candidate to appear on a comedy show, and thanks to Keyes, and after several takes, he delivered the program's signature line, "Sock it to me." With his recognizable nose in profile, Nixon slowly turned to the camera and converted the phrase into a question: "Sock it to *me?*" Everything helped.

John Mitchell, the law firm's municipal bond expert, was named campaign manager, and while Mitchell did not know a lot about electoral politics, people like John Sears (traveling with Agnew) understood the rules and so by now did Bob Haldeman, who was actually trying to run the operation. Mitchell, though, knew a lot of people and how to analyze polling data; and he knew Nixon, to whom he sometimes referred disrespectfully as "Milhous," the middle name that Nixon had excised from his press releases. One of Mitchell's tasks was to give constant reassurance; if something upset Nixon, Mitchell would say to him, "Dick that's taken care of, don't worry about it."

When the family and David Eisenhower traveled together, Nixon gave Haldeman detailed instructions on the choreography, including seating arrangements. Nixon would usually sit with Haldeman in the forward cabin of the plane, while Pat would stay in the staff section, sitting next to Rose Woods or her old friend Helene Drown. David, Julie, and Tricia were in the next cabin back, and at every stop the two Nixon daughters and David would walk forward, fetch Pat, and when they all got to the front, Nixon would meet them. When the door of the airplane opened, David and the four Nixons would emerge, smiling, ready to greet each new crowd on the tarmac.

John Whittaker, who scheduled Nixon's appearances, says that Julie Nixon was particularly good at alerting the campaign to possible snafus—"When something would go wrong, Julie would call me directly and we'd get it fixed." They had fun. David got into the spirit of uttering nonsensical political rhetoric; at a Herald Square rally in late October, referring to a Hubert Humphrey promise to "wage a Truman-type campaign," he said things like "It's one thing to give 'em hell and another thing to give 'em Humphrey." Pat Nixon was having less fun than her daughters and future son-in-law, though her unhappiness was rarely visible. Gloria Steinem, on assignment for *New York* magazine, traveled briefly with Mrs. Nixon and ran into what all reporters fear: a subject who refuses to be drawn out. It was only when Steinem asked what woman she most admired that Mrs. Nixon opened up, almost: "I never had time to dream about being anyone else," she told Steinem, speaking softly. "I had to work. My parents died when I was a teenager, and I had to work my way through college. . . . I worked in a bank while Dick was in the service. Oh, I could have sat for those months doing nothing like everybody else, but I worked in the bank and talked with people and learned about their funny little customs. . . . I don't have time to worry about who I admire or who I identify with. I've never had it easy. I'm not like all you . . . all those people who had it easy."

By early October, the polls gave Nixon a comfortable lead. The influence of newspaper columnists was no longer what it had been a decade earlier, but Walter Lippmann still counted, and Lippmann in his biweekly *Newsweek* column (a version of which appeared in many newspapers) endorsed Nixon for president. He "is a very much better man today than he was ten years ago," he wrote, "and I have lived too long myself to think that men are what they are forever and ever." Lippmann, who was then seventy-nine, referred to the "Johnson disaster" and called Hubert Humphrey "Lyndon Johnson's creature," and suggested that in the absence of domestic tranquility "necessity may dictate the repression of uncontrollable violence." He concluded that "Nixon is the only one who may be able to produce a government that can govern."

2

Doctors in the late fall lifted the restrictions on what Eisenhower could see and read. He was sitting up and walking the few steps from his bed to a chair in his room, and not only was he plowing through western novels but even a door-stopping memoir by the journalist Arthur Krock. On his seventy-eighth birthday, October 14, the Army band stood below his third-floor window and for fifteen minutes played some of his favorite tunes, including "The Yellow Rose of Texas" and "The Caissons Go Rolling Along." When they got to "The Beer Barrel Polka," Ike came to the window and kept time with a tiny flag that had five white stars on a dark background; it was the first time in six months that the public could see the general, who now weighed 148 pounds, and, as it turned out, it was the last time. All of this—the music and the sight and sound of people cheering—was enough to make him dab his eyes with a handkerchief.

Eisenhower said that he'd like to do some television spots in Nixon's behalf. That wasn't possible, but he sounded ready for a fight. Humphrey, he wrote to Nixon, was trying to "belittle you with what he thinks to be clever insinuations," and he added, "I would pay no attention to him whatsoever, but I do wish, at times, that someone would really describe the little fellow as he really is." (He signed that letter "Ike"—a name by which Nixon had never addressed him and never would.) Two weeks before the election, he sent Nixon a letter that was meant for publication and concluded with "one final, heartfelt comment" regarding Vietnam:

> . . . perhaps because of my own background I have watched with particular interest what you have done and said in the heat of campaigning about so delicate a matter concerning our country as the Vietnam war. You have stood steady and talked straight, despite what must have been heavy pressures and temptations to reach for popular support through irresponsibility, I commend you especially for this; it befits you and befits our country.

Ike had also said that he wasn't worried about "any real danger of the misfortunes of 1948"—the Truman upset—but Nixon certainly was. In the campaign's final days, his lead began steadily to shrink, in fact alarmingly so. The pre-election Gallup Poll put him ahead by a margin of 42–40, with the third-party candidate, the segregationist governor George Wallace, at 14 percent, and it showed what Gallup called "dramatic gains" for Humphrey. Part of the shift came from Democrats returning to their party, but Humphrey was also helped by President Johnson's announcement on October 31—just days before the election—that he was ordering a new halt to the bombing of North Vietnam as an incentive to reach a settlement in Paris, where peace talks had been in progress for some time.

That was not good news for Nixon, who in any case was unable to stop thinking about what had happened in 1960 and 1962 and was becoming obsessed with the possibility of losing yet again. When he was feeling dispirited and couldn't sleep, a not infrequent occurrence, he would ask whoever was around to "Get Len on the phone," and soon enough the aide would locate Leonard Garment, who was usually in New York. "He'd call me at night from the road," Garment said. "That was his way of going to sleep"—simply hearing Garment's reassuring, faraway voice. "And he'd have a drink and he'd have his pill"—a Seconal—"and he would talk to me. It was so strange. And he was out on the road and the time differential resulted in my getting calls at strange hours, when he would just talk and then finally go to sleep."

Lyndon Johnson had given Nixon, Humphrey, and George Wallace advance word of the bombing halt, and he quickly came to suspect that the Nixon campaign was trying to sabotage the peace talks in order to increase his odds of winning. Nixon was certainly saying the right thing—at a rally in Madison Square Garden he said that he supported Johnson "if the bombings can be ended in a way that will speed an honorable peace" and on *Meet the Press* he said that "the key point, of course, is to get the South Vietnamese to the conference table"—but he definitely wasn't pleased by the timing. There were reasons to suspect that he was behaving badly—that there was something to the stories that Anna Chennault (the widow of General Claire Chennault of the Flying Tigers, who was close to the Republican Party and the Nixon campaign) had gotten word to South Vietnam's president Nguyen Van Thieu that he would get a better deal from

Nixon than from Johnson and ought to boycott the peace talks. These intrigues even involved the Harvard professor and Rockefeller adviser and loyalist, Henry Kissinger, who had been following events closely; he was passing the latest intelligence from Paris to the Nixon campaign and at the same time telling Humphrey's foreign affairs adviser, Zbigniew Brzezinski, "Look, I've hated Nixon for years."

Johnson and Nixon spoke by telephone a few days before the election, and Johnson came very close to accusing him of betraying American interests while Nixon tried to assure Johnson that he was playing it straight—that "Any rumblings around about somebody trying to sabotage the Saigon government's attitude absolutely have no credibility as far as I'm concerned." When Johnson mentioned that just that sort of thing was being said, Nixon replied, "My God I would never encourage Saigon not to come to the table because that's what you got out of your bombing pause. . . . I'm not trying to interfere with your conduct of it. . . . I'll only do what you and [Secretary of State Dean] Rusk want me to do. I'll do anything. I just want to get this God damn war off the plate." Johnson said he was glad to hear that, but did not sound convinced. "The important thing is for your people—if they'll tell them just what you tell me it'll be the best for all concerned," he said.

Johnson's suspicions about Nixon were being fed by the reports he was getting from the FBI, which, on his orders, had agents shadowing Chennault as she went around Washington in a maroon Lincoln Continental and stopped at the Vietnamese embassy as well as offices belonging to the Nixon campaign. As if that wasn't enough, the third-ranking State Department official, Eugene V. Rostow, a strong supporter of the war, reported that a "man of experience" in New York had told him that Nixon "was trying to frustrate the President, by inciting Saigon to step up its demands"—that he was creating difficulties that would make it easier to settle "on terms that [Johnson] would not accept."

No doubt at the urging of the Nixon campaign, Eisenhower's aide, General Schulz, released an election-eve statement purportedly written by the general in which he did the very un-Ike thing of questioning President Johnson's motives—suggesting that they were political. The statement, some of which was read on the air by his grandson during a telethon, was almost certainly drafted by Bryce Harlow; it said that Nixon's conduct warranted national commendation, and added that it would "be supreme irony if these statesmanlike positions of Richard Nixon . . . should now be turned into instruments of political injury to him," and furthermore that "Nixon deserves the plaudits of the American people for his extraordinarily responsible conduct of his campaign respecting Vietnam."

That was being far too generous. Nixon was not being particularly responsible and Lyndon Johnson, who had more or less held his temper when they spoke, never stopped believing that Nixon—or people working in his behalf—were directly interfering with the peace talks. Johnson used his strongest language—"He oughtn't be doin' this—this is treason"—in a call to Senator Everett Dirksen, in which he added, "Nixon ought to play it just like he has all along, 'that I want to see peace come the first day we can, that it's not going to affect the election one way or the other.' . . . Tell them that their people are messing around with this thing and if they don't want it on the front pages they'd better quit it." Whether or not Nixon was actively "messing around" with the peace talks, he was not, to put it charitably, eager for a pre-election breakthrough in Paris. He was deeply worried by how the bombing halt would affect the vote and there is every reason to believe that his wishes were clear to President Thieu even if he never expressed them directly.

3

On election night, the Nixon entourage and guests filled many of the rooms on the thirty-fifth floor of the Waldorf, where one could wander past television sets and unappetizing refreshments and all those telephones. It was a party with an uncertain ending and an odd mixture of guests; Nixon's law partner Tom Evans shared a couch with Strom Thurmond, the liberal New York senator Jacob Javits, and a former Miss South Carolina, the dark-haired twenty-two-year-old Nancy Moore, who was about to marry the sixty-six-year-old Thurmond. Nixon stayed mostly by himself, watching television, making his own calculations, occasionally talking to his family, but even Pat and their daughters tried to leave him alone as the returns came in. Nixon at first was ahead, and then, at about midnight, one could sense a slight momentum toward Humphrey. Ray Price recalled that "for the first time my own characteristic optimism turned to a queasy pessimism." The networks waited until nearly eight A.M. Wednesday to call the election for Nixon, whose victory was almost as narrow as his loss to Kennedy. When Nixon spoke to the cameras early that morning, he said that he intended to "bring the American people together."

Lyndon Johnson sent a plane to New York to ferry the victorious party to Key Biscayne. The plane was a converted jet tanker, the only one in the fleet of Air Force jets that was windowless; its passengers dubbed it "Air Force Five." On their way south, they stopped at Andrews Air Force Base so that the Nixons and David Eisenhower could pay a call on General Eisenhower. The atmosphere in Ward 8 was festive; a nurse's note said, "Monitor stable throughout—observed by Doctors . . . enjoyed visit tremendously—cheerful during and after." The moment remained vivid for Dwight Chapin, the outsider and observer, who watched as the president-elect leaned over the bed of the former president, and began holding the old man's hand.

CHAPTER 29

Victory Laps

1

The nation's mood, insofar as a nation's mood is measurable, did not brighten after the election; nor did Nixon dispel the doubts of those who were inclined to doubt him. The prospect of a Nixon presidency was so unnerving to James Reston that in an Election Day story headlined WITH-OUT A WINNER, he suggested that Nixon should parcel out his executive duties—that with the popular vote so close, "the case for the formation of a nonpartisan Administration or national government of the leaders of both major parties seemed to be indicated." That was never going to happen, although Nixon's early talk about unity had a practical basis; it was the first presidential election since Zachary Taylor's in 1848 that left the opposition in control of the House and the Senate. Nixon's own mood ought to have been very good. His achievement—one that had eluded such accomplished serial losers as Tom Dewey, Adlai Stevenson, and William Jennings Bryan—made political writers search for synonyms for "Lazarus." Lee Huebner, who was about to join Nixon's staff as a speechwriter, remembers making his way into the Waldorf and congratulating the president-elect. "And he shook his head and said, 'No, no, we lost both houses of the Congress. The press is really going to be upset.' He was depressed," Huebner recalled. "It was like whenever he was up, he had to pull himself down." On

Wednesday morning, before the family left New York, Nixon had allowed himself a moment that was like an exultant victory dance: he returned to his apartment, went to his powerful stereo rig, put on a recording of Richard Rodgers's *Victory at Sea*, and blasted the music through an open window to the press corps on the street below. After sixteen years of sometimes painful association with Dwight D. Eisenhower, Richard Nixon could feel as if they had become equals, a shift in status that was enhanced three weeks later by the announcement that Julie Nixon and Dwight David Eisenhower II would be married on December 22. The ceremony was to be performed at the Marble Collegiate Church by Norman Vincent Peale.

So they were family now, the Nixons and the Eisenhowers, and for the first time they celebrated Thanksgiving together, in Ward 8 at Walter Reed, where they had a traditional meal with turkey, stuffing, and a pumpkin pie baked by Delores Moaney, Sergeant Moaney's wife. The general was confined to his bed—"The blueness of his eyes was startling in his dead-white face," Julie Nixon thought—and members of both families took turns with him: Tricia Nixon and Susan Eisenhower, one of Ike's three granddaughters, joined him for juice, and Pat Nixon and John Eisenhower's wife, Barbara, for pumpkin pie. The three men—John, David, and the president-elect—spent about fifteen minutes with the general and then Nixon saw him alone for forty-five minutes. Afterward, in his most solemn voice, Nixon said that they'd discussed staffing decisions: "He made some recommendations and I discussed some of the problems I am confronting and got some advice and counsel from him." It sounded very much like the sort of thing that President Eisenhower might have said in 1952, after chatting with his young vice president.

A few days later, Eisenhower wrote to Nixon to review some of what they'd talked about and what he'd left out—namely "two rather personal matters that I wanted to mention but with so many people present I thought it better to write you personally, making sure you got the letter yourself." That sounded dramatic, but all that Eisenhower wanted were small favors for two friends, one of them Robert Woodruff, the longtime president of Coca-Cola, who had made a "significant contribution" to Nixon's campaign and deserved "a note of appreciation." The other concerned retaining Leonard Heaton as Army surgeon general—"an extremely able man." The general finished by saying "I cannot tell you how much I enjoyed the visit you and your family made to Mamie and me on Thanksgiving Day. That occasion has been the highlight of seven long months in a hospital room."

Nixon remembered the mild scolding that he'd gotten from Eisenhower after the 1960 election and asked Rose Mary Woods to "have Haldeman ride herd to see if there are any others of this type who should have letters from me. I don't want things to fall between the stools as they did in 1960." He was willing to write a letter for Heaton if need be, but the surgeon general was sixty-six and already two years past the mandatory retirement age, and he left his post in 1969.

2

Nixon had chosen Bob Haldeman, the campaign's chief of staff, as the White House chief of staff; and John D. Ehrlichman, a Seattle lawyer who had been the "tour director" of the campaign, became counsel to the president. He tried to move quickly to fill other top jobs, but getting people to serve was not always easy, not even when it came to secretary of state. That went to Nixon's old friend William Rogers, but he'd not been the first choice; rather, soon after the election Nixon had tried to recruit William Scranton, the former Pennsylvania governor and an Eisenhower favorite. Scranton knew that interesting times lay ahead; Nixon had talked to him about fresh initiatives, including a diplomatic opening to mainland China at which he'd hinted a year earlier in the quarterly *Foreign Affairs*, an essay ghostwritten by Ray Price in which he'd said "Taking the long view, we simply cannot afford to leave China forever outside the family of nations, there to nurture its fantasies, cherish its hates and threaten its neighbors." Scranton, though, had little interest—not least because he would have found it difficult to work for Nixon. "Although I admired his mind—Dick was a very bright guy—I could not deal with a guy that was, that every time I met with him I didn't know what he was trying to get at," Scranton said. "It wasn't that you don't *like* him, it's that working with him was difficult. . . . He always had the idea that people were trying to get him somehow, and you didn't know whether you were one of them or not."

Nixon offered Henry Kissinger the job of assistant for national security affairs, willing to overlook his close ties to Rockefeller as well as his previously dismissive attitude toward himself. Kissinger in his White House memoir said that he'd met Nixon just once, at a Christmas party the year before, and that Nixon had told him that he'd read Kissinger's *Nuclear Weapons and Foreign Policy* and written an admiring note—"which to my embarrassment I had forgotten." Kissinger also managed to forget that ten years earlier, in 1958, he'd invited Nixon to participate in the International Seminar at Harvard. Nixon in the end did not attend, but he had replied with enthusiasm, writing, "I not only would enjoy visiting Harvard and attending the seminar, but I would also welcome the opportunity to discuss some of our current international problems with you." Was Kissinger in 1958 perhaps advertising himself to a man he thought might win the presidency two years hence? Dr. Kissinger, as he liked to be addressed, was a master of office politics and a jealous servant when it came to influencing policy, so his appointment set up an inevitable clash over turf and responsibility with Bill Rogers at State.

There did not seem to be much of a role for Spiro Agnew, who wasn't included in what was emerging as an inner circle—Haldeman, Ehrlichman, Kissinger, Nixon's old friend Bob Finch, and the Oklahoman Bryce Harlow, who was quickly named as congressional liaison. Nixon knew what it felt like to be a vice president serving at the whim of a president, but Agnew had not impressed him during the campaign and was rarely if ever mentioned; he seemed suddenly to have realized that he'd given his old job to a subpar politician, and long before Agnew resigned amid allegations of bribery, Nixon was ready to replace him. He did recruit one prominent Democrat: Daniel Patrick Moynihan, the director of the Harvard-MIT Joint Center for Urban Studies, who was to run the new Council on Urban Affairs, which was seen as a domestic counterpart to the National Security Council.

Nixon presented his cabinet to the nation in a thirty-minute television program on December 11, and it turned out to consist of twelve Republican white men. Some appointees were distinguished, among them George Shultz, the dean of the University of Chicago's Graduate School of Business, who was named labor secretary; and some were problematic. Just before the election, Nixon had promised that the next attorney general would be a man "experienced in law enforcement at the highest levels whose national reputation will command immediate respect." His choice was John Mitchell, who had no relevant experience and furthermore didn't really want the job.

Eisenhower generally approved—"I think you have named a fine cabinet, one that ought to attain rather a very fine standing in public esteem," he wrote to Nixon, although he had some reservations about Nixon's defense secretary, Congressman Melvin Laird. He said that he was "quite anxious to meet the ones I do not know," and Nixon dutifully sent most of them to Walter Reed to pay a call on the general, who also had "some personal ideas" about the Supreme Court. Chief Justice Warren had already announced his intention to retire; after President Johnson's choice to succeed him—Associate Justice Abe Fortas—was blocked by a Senate filibuster, Ike suggested giving the job to Herbert Brownell. The general had even entertained the idea of seeking a job for himself, of asking to become a "senior counsel ex-officio" to the incoming administration. His health would never have allowed it, but it would have been fascinating to watch it unfold.

3

The press never lost its appetite for stories about Julie Nixon and David Eisenhower, even reporting on the premarital counseling that they got from Norman Vincent Peale. At seventy, Peale had abandoned the politics of 1960; he was an amiable, reassuring presence, and when he handed out copies of his famous "How Cards" (No. 3 was titled "How to Have a Happy Marriage" and said "Marriage is for the mature, not the infantile") he seemed to be gently conversing rather than preaching. For all his good-humored salesmanship, though, darkness sometimes pierced his positive thinking. "This is an awful world, just simply frightful, and we're stuck with it," Peale told an interviewer at about that time.

For the Nixons, the wedding was a happy interlude in a time that didn't promise a lot of them. Many of the five hundred or so guests were neither famous nor rich. They included family friends like the Drown family, and Johnnie Musante, who had delivered vegetables when they'd lived in California, and Manolo and Fina Sanchez, the family's servants. The Nixon side of the family was represented by the two surviving Nixon brothers, Donald and Edward, and the Ryan side by Pat Nixon's two brothers and a half brother. There were not many Eisenhowers apart from David's parents and three sisters, but there were friends, including Ike's Palm Desert golfing companion, Freeman Gosden, and Gosden's son, Craig, a classmate of David's. The Agnews sat next to the Nixons in a front pew, and members of the new cabinet were there, along with their wives; there were others, like Tom Dewey and Clare Boothe Luce, whose history with both families had been long and somewhat complicated; and the Norman Chandlers, whose *Los Angeles Times* had meant so much to young Dick Nixon; and the Cuban-born banker Charles (Bebe) Rebozo and Elmer Bobst, who had helped to recruit Nixon to his law firm and whose shadowy side—tales of incest and anti-Semitism—was kept hidden until well after his death in 1978.

The ceremony was ecumenical; David was Episcopalian and Julie, who regarded herself as a Quaker, had asked Peale to use the Quaker thee and thou and ye. When the guests filed in, they heard not only seasonal music—Christmas carols and Handel—but popular tunes, such as "The Impossible Dream" and the theme from *Friendly Persuasion,* the film about a Quaker family during the Civil War; the movie was adapted from the novel by the Nixon cousin Jessamyn West. The entrance of ten ushers was accompanied by Jeremiah Clarke's "The Trumpet Voluntary"; Tricia Nixon was maid of honor and David's best man was Fred Grandy, his roommate at Exeter, who later won a seat in Congress and, as an actor, became known as "Gopher" on *The Love Boat.* The ceremony took just fifteen minutes, and the sensation-starved press reported the single surprise, which the president-elect, with unusual woodenness, provided at the photo session. "Julie, wait a minute," he said, as his daughter and David were trying to leave the room. "I'd like to say one thing. At the ceremony everything went as rehearsed except when I put her hand in David's. She turned around and kissed me. That wasn't part of the ceremony. That was her idea." The Eisenhowers had hoped to watch the wedding on a closed-circuit hookup that NBC was going to provide, and it was reported that they had enjoyed the service. But they actually hadn't seen any of it; the video connection hadn't worked and they'd had to rely on audio alone.

At a reception in the Grand Ballroom of the Plaza, Nixon gave a toast in which he mentioned the Apollo 8 astronauts, whose mission—the first to carry humans to the moon, and then around the moon—was half completed. The president-elect's every gesture and comment was noted. He was overheard greeting the speechwriter Bill Safire and his wife, saying with a quick smile, "Let's get the suggestions for the Inaugural in by January fifth." Even then, the job seeking had begun. Soon after the wedding, Hobart Lewis (of *Reader's Digest*) called Rose Mary Woods to say that the Reverend Peale would like to be appointed ambassador to Switzerland, a suggestion that Nixon did not dismiss out of hand, although he believed that the job had already been promised; and, besides, they had a rule of not appointing ambassadors over the age of seventy. Peale stayed with his ministerial calling.

4

After the wedding, Nixon returned to Florida, taking some of his staff along. He was once more in an odd mood, at least to judge from the memoranda that he sent flying out, mostly to Haldeman and Ehrlichman, covering any number of subjects—issuing orders as if he were just learning how to flex his presidential muscles. He told Ehrlichman that he wanted an update on the status of *Six Crises,* in particular how the book, which had been reissued before the convention, had sold, suggesting that this might be an opportune moment to sell more copies. He was determined to avoid the traps of protocol: he would talk to any head of government and give a dinner for a head of state, but "under *no* circumstances, regardless of the character of the visit, will I go to a return dinner or luncheon or reception of any kind which is put on by the foreign visitor. I realize that this will break some china in State, but it is time to make this shift of policy now and to carry it out in the future. This decision, incidentally, is not subject to further discussion."

The memoranda kept jetting out, some of them suggesting hyperactivity and others coming close to moments of self-glorification. Who could blame him? He asked Ehrlichman to propose that someone write a "book or major article entitled 'The Great Come-backs in American

Political History.' " If something of "broader scope" was wanted, then simply "The Great Political Come-backs," which Nixon believed would make "a very exciting book or article if we could get somebody of real stature to undertake it." Old hostilities, a nagging feeling of having been wronged, bubbled up in these memoranda, as in a note to Ehrlichman on the subject of "Attacks on RN." Referring to himself in the third person, Nixon said that he wanted someone to "go back through the last twenty years and pick up all of the unfair attacks that have been made on RN, inadvertently and otherwise." That would be a "rich harvest," he thought, and just saying this gave him an idea for another article or a short book with a title like "RN, The Most Maligned Political Figure of the Twentieth Century." This note was sent just two weeks before Nixon was to be sworn in as the thirty-seventh president; it was as if he'd suddenly undergone a mysterious change of outlook, as if those generous impulses of November had been replaced by the resentful whims of a petty, slightly batty tyrant. Nixon even sent formal memoranda to Pat (with headings like *"TO: Mrs. Nixon FROM: The President"* and *"TO: Mrs. RN FROM: The President"*) in which he gave detailed instructions on how to work with a decorator on fixing up a hideaway office in the Old Executive Office Building or arranging for an end table in his bedroom "like the one on the right side of the bed which will accommodate *two* dictaphones as well as a telephone."

For much of the time that he spent in Florida, Nixon stayed in his house on the west side of the island, and his staff stayed in a hotel on the east side. He still thrived on solitude, communing with his yellow legal pads, blotting out the world, taking out the pipe that he sometimes smoked when he was by himself. He appeared confident, but anyone who had watched his career unfold—from the House and Senate to the vice presidency to Wall Street to this—might have remembered Eisenhower's advice in 1956: that Nixon needed the experience of actually running something. "You know, I know Dick knows what to do," the general said to the former staffer William Ewald when Ewald came to see him at Walter Reed on November 19. "I just question whether he knows how to organize the government to get it done."

• • •

Nixon spoke regularly with Eisenhower, who, although he was bedridden and exhausted, remained agitatedly engaged, and even sent a birthday greeting: "Imagine you have been so busy that you forgot about your birthday, therefore, I wanted to be sure that I conveyed warm thoughts and best wishes to you on this special occasion." This note—the last that he'd ever write to Nixon—was again signed "Ike." Nixon spent this birthday, his fifty-sixth, in Northampton, where his extended family got together at the young Eisenhowers' apartment and Julie cooked a chicken casserole; about two hundred Smith students conducted a vigil out of eyesight of the president-elect. Then he returned to New York, and to Florida, and once more began sending out memoranda and thinking about what he'd say on January 20.

When he was vice president, Nixon was no fan of what had seemed to him an endless series of meetings (Ike's weekly sessions with the cabinet, the National Security Council, and legislative leaders); to John Sears he once said, "Meetings are a bunch of shit, you can't decide anything in a meeting, and the only reason to have a meeting is so the people there feel as though they're important." Now he had to think about how he was going to do it, and he wanted his inaugural speech to boldly declare his ambitions. "It's a time when great decisions are going to be made," he told Ray Price, "and when we can all be a part of history." He received memoranda from many acquaintances, including Moynihan and Billy Graham and Paul Keyes, the comedy writer and itinerant political adviser, but he was mostly alone with his own thoughts, the drafts that he got from Price that he reworked and the revisions that came back typed from Rose Mary Woods. He returned to New York on the weekend before the inaugural—January 20 fell on a Monday—and on that Sunday, Eisenhower telephoned. It was, he told Nixon, his last chance to say, "Hi, Dick!" After that, it was going to be "Mr. President."

CHAPTER 30

Eulogies

1

Nixon was sworn in by Chief Justice Warren, and the seventeen-minute speech that followed was gentle and conciliatory, almost as if yet another Richard Nixon had emerged from the shell of the former candidate and the person who fretted and sent out goofy memos from his lair in Florida. To blacks who worried about the advent of his administration, he said, "No man can be fully free while his neighbor is not. To go forward at all is to go forward together." And if there was an overarching theme, it was the unity that he'd talked about on the morning after the election: "We will strive to listen in new ways—to the voices of quiet anguish, the voices that speak without words, the voices of the heart—to the injured voices, the anxious voices, the voices that have been left out, we will try to bring in." The speech could not have been less like the one delivered by Jack Kennedy, with its rhetorical inversions and Cold War language. After the lunch at the Capitol with legislators and the members of the new cabinet, the president and his entourage ran into the angry rhetoric that he had just been talking about. Nothing like it had ever been seen at an inaugural. Some demonstrators threw rocks and bottles and smoke bombs and eggs at the passing limousines, and chanted "Ho, Ho, Ho Chi Minh, the N.L.F. is going to win." Some of the chants and shouts were hard to interpret, but no one missed the meaning of "Four more years of death!" and "Nixon's the One—the No. 1 War Criminal," a premature insult for someone who'd only been president for an hour or so. So much for the honeymoon; Tricky Dick was at the helm and the nation was going to hell.

Andrew Goodpaster, Ike's former staff secretary and now a general and the deputy commander of the American forces in Vietnam, had returned to Washington to help with the transition, and three days after the inauguration, when he paid a call on General Eisenhower, he took Kissinger along. Kissinger had never met Eisenhower, and his first impression was of an emaciated old man confined to bed; he'd expected, as he put it, to meet the "genial but inarticulate war hero" of popular prejudice. He quickly realized that Eisenhower was still a formidable presence. His syntax, he wrote, "became much more graphic when enlivened by his cold, deep blue, extraordinarily penetrating eyes and when given emphasis by his still commanding voice."

Ten days later, Nixon went to see Eisenhower—his first visit as president—and Kissinger accompanied him. The general this time was sitting up in a gold-colored wing chair; Nixon sat in a smaller chair to his left. "Mr. President, I'm glad to see you," Eisenhower said, and Nixon, mildly embarrassed, referred to him several times as "General," although he now and then slipped into "Mr. President," too. Eisenhower was deeply interested in the subject of the moment—pressure on the United States to play a larger diplomatic role in the Middle East after years in which the Johnson administration had been relatively inactive. He was still averse to American involvement in the region; he thought that would inevitably lead to the United States becoming the guarantor of any final agreement, which would commit the nation to a long-term role. (Kissinger thought, but did not say, that Eisenhower's Suez policy had been in his words "deplorable.") What particularly annoyed Eisenhower—he mentioned it several times to Nixon and Kissinger—were leaks from the National Security Council.

The next day, Eisenhower telephoned Kissinger. He had seen a *New York Times* story based on a National Security Council leak that said America now intended to follow a more active policy in the Middle East. With what Kissinger called a "graphic vocabulary," the former president scolded him for letting Nixon down by not restricting the number of participants at the NSC meeting. It was, Eisenhower said, Kissinger's duty to "prevent attempts by the bureaucracy to stampede the President with news leaks," and what had happened only proved his other point: the United States should keep its hands off the Middle East. Kissinger himself was a notorious leaker, but if Eisenhower knew that, he pretended not to.

In late February, as Nixon was preparing to leave Washington for his first trip abroad as president, to Europe, Eisenhower developed signs of a serious intestinal obstruction; doctors at first tried to relieve the symptoms with a method that involved using a suction tube that went through the nose, down the throat, and into the stomach. When that didn't help, a Walter Reed surgical team led by General Heaton performed a three-hour operation; they had been reluctant to perform major surgery on someone who had suffered seven heart attacks, but they told reporters that the obstruction would have been fatal if they hadn't gone ahead. Haldeman in his diary recorded a conversation with Nixon, who had already decided to cancel the trip "if and when anything happens." On the day of the procedure, Mamie Eisenhower wrote to Pat Nixon ("Dearest 'Pat' ") and said, "There is nothing I can do but sit here and pray and hope."

About a week after undergoing abdominal surgery, Eisenhower developed pneumonia in his right lung, which put more strain on his heart. No one said that he was dying, but no one needed to. In the fall and early winter, old friends like George Allen and General Alfred Gruenther and Admiral Lewis Strauss could just drop by Walter Reed and spend as much as an hour with Ike. So would people like Jock Whitney and Bill Robinson, who would come (although no one said it) to say goodbye; even more casual acquaintances like the Bob Hopes, with whom the Eisenhowers had sometimes socialized in Palm Desert, visited Ward 8. The visits slowed as Ike grew weaker, and in early March, when he began to see people again, the stays were a lot shorter than they had been; the careful handwritten logbook kept by his steadfast military aide, General Robert Schulz, showed a steady procession of people closest to the general. David and Julie Eisenhower came on March 2 and stayed for five minutes, and a day later, John Eisenhower and Sergeant Moaney had equally brief visits. His last days were spent mostly with his family. Pat Nixon looked in and so did Tricia and Julie together. David and Julie saw him almost as often as John and Barbara Eisenhower.

President Nixon saw him again on March 19—it had been a month since his last visit. He had just returned from his European trip and as so often happened when he traveled abroad, he had seemed almost carefree, even transformed, loving his new job. Kissinger believed that he'd witnessed rare moments of "nearly spontaneous joy"—Nixon in Europe "was exuberant. . . . To land with Air Force One on foreign soil, to be greeted by a King and then a Prime Minister, to review honor guards . . . all this was the culmination of his youthful dreams." That could just as well have been Kissinger describing his own youthful dreams—the immigrant German Jew who adored vestigial ceremonies at least as much as a politician who rarely showed signs of pure happiness. But Nixon *had* found pleasure in the trip, perhaps above all in seeing Charles de Gaulle, who had welcomed Nixon when he was out of office and who, as Nixon has said, had also gone "into the wilderness" and returned to power. He admired de Gaulle's cultivation of mystery, his comfort with solitude and silence, which Nixon understood but could never quite carry off, although even without a mystique Nixon could seem mysterious to his countrymen.

Nixon was startled by Eisenhower's appearance. He looked like a corpse, he thought; his face was waxen, although he showed more life when Nixon raised his hand and said, "Hi!" They spent about a quarter of an hour together, during which the president recounted a little of the European trip and passed along greetings. They discussed the administration's plan to develop an antiballistic missile system that was meant to stop or deflect a Chinese rocket. Nixon knew that the general was opposed to spending large sums on a technology that was, and would continue to be, unproven, just as he was opposed to the lunar program, but he wasn't about to change Nixon's mind. "You've done great," the general told him. "No big mistakes." Nixon afterward said that the former president was "in good spirits," and General Schulz in his logbook wrote "DDE really enjoyed + tolerated well." The general's overall condition, though, was rapidly getting worse; two days later, doctors revealed that he had suffered an episode of congestive heart failure. "Doctors say DDE failing fast, probably go today or tomorrow," Haldeman wrote in his diary. Haldeman was a little premature, although not by much. On Monday, March 24, at noon, the general's kidneys briefly stopped functioning; then at six P.M., when doctors told him that he seemed to be getting better, he started to curse—he was ready to die.

On March 25, the hospital issued a particularly pessimistic bulletin, which prompted Nixon the next day to pay another call—his final one, as it turned out, and a visit that General Schulz recorded as lasting seventeen minutes. Nixon later recalled a moment that is not entirely believable, but is certainly the way that he would have *liked* their last conversation to have gone:

> I turned impulsively and tried to keep the emotion out of my voice as I said, "General, I just want you to know how all the free people of Europe and millions of others in the world will forever be in your debt for the leadership you provided in war and peace. You can always take great pride in the fact that no man in our history has done more to make America and the world a better and safer place in which to live." His eyes were closed as I spoke, but after a brief moment he opened them and lifted his head from the pillow. With an unusual formality he said, "Mr. President, you do me great honor in what you have just said." Then he slowly raised his hand to his forehead in a final salute.

In this fantastical exchange, Nixon had found a closeness with Ike, a glimmer of solidarity and friendship.

The medical bulletins persuaded David and Julie Eisenhower, who had been on a spring semester vacation in Key Biscayne, to hurry back to Washington on the night of March 27; they were able to spend three minutes with the general, whose only other visitors that day had been his brother Milton and General Goodpaster. John Eisenhower has described how his father the next day, a Friday, suddenly issued an order—"Lower the shades!"—and how, when the room was barely illuminated by streaks of sunlight, the general issued another order: "Pull me up." When they reached a point that they thought was high enough, the general muttered, "Two big men. Higher." And they pulled him higher. Then, his son wrote, "Dad looked up at me and said softly, 'I want to go; God take me.' " John, and the general's grandson, David, were at his bedside when he died, on March 28, 1969, at 12:35 P.M. David Brinkley reported the death of the former president at about one P.M., breaking into regular programming on NBC; his announcement was short and unusually apt: "General Eisenhower died today. His death was peaceful and natural. He was seventy-eight and it was the end of a life so filled with achievement and honors that even though it was a long life it could hardly have held any more."

When Nixon heard the news, just before a meeting that was to include Kissinger, Haldeman, and Defense Secretary Laird, he turned away and looked out the window; then he began to cry. "He was such a strong man," he said, before going into a small adjoining office. When he returned to the Oval room, his eyes were red.

Nixon called Pat and then Tricia; and he told Dwight Chapin to reach Bill Rogers and Bryce Harlow. He left almost immediately for Walter Reed, accompanied by Pat as well as Laird, Rogers, Kissinger, Haldeman, and Harlow. At the hospital, the president spent twenty-five minutes with the family—Mamie, as well as John, David, and Julie. Even before other visitors began arriving—among them Milton Eisenhower and General Omar Bradley—Nixon was starting to feel under the weather, as if some minor flu bug had just gotten him. On the drive back to the White House, he decided that he'd go to Camp David to work on a eulogy. Pat Nixon thought that was a bad idea, but Nixon asked Haldeman to make the case for him, which Haldeman swiftly did, squelching the domestic disagreement; and soon enough Nixon was off by helicopter to the Catoctin Mountains.

Kissinger called Ann Whitman to let her know that she was going to be invited to the funeral, a somewhat sensitive issue because Mamie Eisenhower had never stopped being a little jealous of Whitman, who was Ike's constant, protective attendant during his presidency. "President Nixon was marvelous, and he is flying all the members of the family by plane," Kissinger told Mrs. Whitman, adding, "He couldn't be more broken up." She told Kissinger that Eisenhower had often talked to her about death, but then, because Rose Woods was calling on another line, she had to break off the conversation.

As Lyndon Johnson had explained to the Russian ambassador, the funeral plans had long been ready, and included a small private service on Sunday morning, at the Washington Cathedral; then Eisenhower's body would lie in state in the Capitol Rotunda, where Nixon on Sunday afternoon would deliver a eulogy. On Monday, after a state funeral at the

Cathedral, the coffin would be taken to Union Station and then carried by train to Abilene. Ike was to be buried there on Wednesday, April 2.

Nixon telephoned Mamie Eisenhower shortly after he arrived at Camp David, and they spoke for about five minutes. He had given some thought to seeing General Goodpaster and Ellsworth Bunker, the U.S. ambassador to Vietnam, but changed his mind; that could wait. "He wants to start work on his eulogy," Haldeman told Kissinger. "He wants some time to collect himself; he was shook—but he's in good shape."

He had asked Ray Price to join him in the mountains, and talking about the eulogy put Nixon in a curious mood. Everybody loved Eisenhower, Price suggested, and Nixon then began creating for himself a portrait of an idealized and unreal Ike who didn't hate his enemies ("He was puzzled by McCarthy"), a semi-naive soul who needed to learn what Dick Nixon already knew about the intentions of the Soviet Union. "I remember talking with Foster Dulles, about how he even loved Khrushchev and the Russians," Nixon told Price in a brief excursion into myths about himself and Eisenhower, who had no love at all for Khrushchev. "When Khrushchev was here at Camp David," Nixon continued, "Ike got the message, and he toughened up." Nixon kept jotting notes on one of his yellow pads, often repeating himself as he descended into banality: *Commanded respect. No one treated him familiarly . . . The grin—the warm personality—but the inner dignity . . . —a smile that warmed up a room . . . a mind cutting through non essentials to heart of problem. But an inner dignity, strength. . . . Why was he great? . . . Mysteries—of greatness.* But Nixon's mind was elsewhere, too—even on Senator Edward Kennedy: "R.N. attacks. Who is going to take Teddy on" a note says; and in a corner of the page he wrote, "Haldeman: Handling Agnew (not)." Through all this he was still feeling unwell, and he stayed most of the time in bed, with a croup kettle steaming up the room.

Nixon returned to Washington on Sunday morning, a cold, cloudy day, and in his speech that afternoon in the Rotunda, witnessed by just about every person in Washington with an official job, he said, "Many leaders are known and respected outside their own countries. Very few are loved . . . Dwight Eisenhower was one of the few." He said that Ike's greatness "derived not from his office but from his character, from a unique moral force that transcended national boundaries. . . . This man who led the most powerful armies that the world has ever seen, this man who led the most powerful nation in the world; this essentially good and gentle and kind man—that moral force was his greatness." Nixon's military aide, Don Hughes—he was now Colonel Hughes and would soon become a brigadier general—was sitting close to the president and saw that as he left the Rotunda he broke down again. It is hard, though, to imagine that those were tears of grief. They are better explained by Nixon's continuing sadness at never having been admitted to the general's small, rarely expanded circle, the one that he reserved for friends. Nixon was outside that circle even when his daughter became an Eisenhower and now it was closed to him forever.

Haldeman and Kissinger discussed the protocol for Monday: there would be a reception in the evening, but what about serving drinks? (They agreed that serving drinks might be misunderstood by many Americans.) Nixon met visiting foreign leaders before and after the state funeral, starting with General de Gaulle, with whom he spent nearly an hour. De Gaulle and Nixon had discussed Vietnam when Nixon was in Paris, and de Gaulle returned to the subject in Washington; he believed that the United States needed to leave Indochina as quickly as possible—although not precipitously, not, as he put it to Nixon, *"en catastrophe"*—and predicted that American power and prestige would be enhanced if and when he managed to carry it off. Nixon agreed, but his timetable had no resemblance to the hasty one that de Gaulle was proposing. Before the evening reception for congressional leaders and foreign leaders, Nixon continued discussions about Vietnam with Ambassador Bunker, General Goodpaster, Kissinger, and Henry Cabot Lodge, the chief American negotiator in Paris.

On Tuesday, he met for nearly half an hour with Vietnam's vice president, Nguyen Cao Ky, and then with the Shah of Iran, the West German chancellor, and quite a few others. As vice president, he had often met with foreign leaders, and sometimes, as he had with de Gaulle and with West Germany's Konrad Adenauer, established personal ties. But he had never before had to talk to any of them or face any of these problems without the counsel, or at least the potential counsel, of Eisenhower, something that he could count on even when their relationship was at its most difficult and delicate. It was a new sensation that would strike him more often in the months ahead, when he would think—and almost say to himself—"I need to tell the President something."

2

A flag and black crepe identified baggage car No. 314 on the funeral train as the one that carried the general's body. Among the passengers were Mamie Eisenhower; Ike's brother Edgar; his son, John, and John's wife, Barbara; his four grandchildren and Julie Eisenhower; and Master Sergeant and Mrs. John Moaney Jr. Milton Eisenhower had become dizzy during the funeral service at the Cathedral and was taken to Walter Reed where, doctors believed, he had suffered a "transient episode of coronary insufficiency," and where he stayed when the train arrived in Abilene before dawn, after a thirty-hour journey across mid-America. People stood along the tracks to watch as the train rolled through West Virginia, Ohio, Indiana, Missouri; in Seymour, Indiana, a town of about thirteen thousand, nearly six thousand turned out. Some of the onlookers were the no-longer-young veterans of the war. In St. Louis, where the train stopped for maintenance, Mamie Eisenhower came out to the platform of the same Santa Fe observation car in which the Eisenhowers often traveled, much as she'd done during the 1952 campaign. Her grandson stood with her and held her hand as she said, "I am most grateful for all these expressions of respect and love. I am very proud."

One of the general's granddaughters, Susan Eisenhower, remembers waking up on the train—"the moon shadows playing tricks on my eyes"— and looking out to see a solitary figure standing straight on a small slope. In the "clear moonlit sky, he raised his hand in salute as the train passed by. He remained at attention until we had gone." The train brought the general's body through Lawrence and Topeka, the tall prairie grass around Manhattan and Junction City, and arrived a little before seven A.M., at the Union Pacific depot in Abilene. Nearly two hours later, the Nixon party—a contingent of about twenty, including wire service reporters— arrived on Air Force One, which landed in Salina, a town with a larger airport, about twenty miles away, and this group traveled from there to

Abilene by helicopter and automobile. Another member of the official party was unannounced: Lyndon Johnson, whose private JetStar landed at the Salina airport just before the Nixon group arrived. Johnson had come and gone almost invisibly at the funeral and had apparently decided at the last minute to travel to Abilene where he'd been once before, in May 1962, for the dedication of the Eisenhower Library building. It was Nixon's first visit to Ike's hometown.

Abilene had not changed much since Dwight had left in 1911 to attend West Point; although he often returned to visit, and to be celebrated, he had never lived there again. An honor guard and pallbearers stood in lines at the train station as the Nixon and Eisenhower families met. The Fifth Army Band began playing "Ruffles and Flourishes," "Hail to the Chief," and then the hymn "God of Our Fathers," during which the coffin was taken from the funeral car and moved to a waiting hearse in preparation for the slow walk to the grounds of the Eisenhower Center, where the general would be buried. The procession moved south along Buckeye Avenue, the main thoroughfare of Abilene, and then east on South Fourth Street, toward the buildings that made up the center—a library, a museum, Ike's boyhood home, and the Chapel of Meditation, where he would be buried and where Doud Dwight—Icky—the Eisenhowers' firstborn, had been reinterred some years earlier. More than four hundred soldiers in dress uniform stood along the procession route; the honorary pallbearers included some of the military men who had been closest to Ike—Generals Omar Bradley and Alfred Gruenther and Master Sergeant Moaney, the only black man in sight. The crowd in Abilene numbered somewhere between seventy and a hundred thousand; traffic was backed up for three miles on I-70, and people were standing six or seven deep along the downtown processional route, just to get a glimpse or to say that they were there.

The service was held outdoors between the Eisenhower library and the museum. Mamie Eisenhower wore a black broadtail fur coat and a pill-box hat with a heavy veil; she sat with her son, resting a hand on his arm. Behind them were John's wife, David and Julie Eisenhower, and David's three sisters. Behind them were President and Mrs. Nixon, Tricia, and former President Johnson. It was a cloudless April day, but they all sat in shadow and everyone felt the chill of a north wind; and everyone could see that Mamie Eisenhower, who had been so stoic until then, had begun to weep.

Two and a half hours after the service, after Nixon and his entourage left for Washington and the crowds had dispersed, Mrs. Eisenhower, accompanied by her son, the Moaneys, and David and Julie returned to the chapel. There she put gladiolus on the general's crypt and chrysanthemums on Icky's grave. At that moment in the late afternoon, and after nearly nineteen years of association, the Eisenhowers and the Nixons had become like any grieving family; there in that chapel in Kansas, they were bound together not only by history but by blood.

CHAPTER 31

What Happened Next

1

President Nixon at the end of 1970 sent a memorandum to Haldeman in which he discussed among other topics his capacity for "warmth" and his regret that so few were aware of it. He wrote about "the way we have gone far beyond any previous President in this century in breaking our backs to be nicey-nice" and he mentioned "such little things such as the treatment of household staff, the elevator operators, the office staff, the calls that I make to people when they are sick." Rose Mary Woods, he said, could remember when "I took dolls out to a couple of children at a hospital, when I was presiding over the Senate, who were dying with leukemia," and he wanted Haldeman to know that "a very important point to underline is that we do not try to broker such items. We allow them to be discovered. For example, I would be horrified at the idea of putting out the fact that I called some mothers and wives of men that had been killed in Vietnam shortly after I met with the POW wives."

One can sympathize with Nixon even while cringing at his language and worrying about his state of mind. He really did want people to see him as a warm man, someone who did good deeds with anonymous benevolence; and in fact all through his life he *was* responsible for many unpublicized acts of kindness. There were little things, such as trying to make sure that his fifth-grade teacher and "the daughter of the doctor who took care of me when I fell out of the buggy as a child" got answers to their letters; and heartfelt sympathy notes, such as one he sent to the columnist Murray Kempton on the death of a son. He spent too much time thinking about the prospect of having to someday face Senator Edward Kennedy (within weeks of taking office, he suggested inviting Gene McCarthy to the White House only because "it would be well to worry Teddy a bit") and yet in November 1973, when the Watergate scandal was nearing its most virulent stage, he telephoned Ted Kennedy's son when he was about to have a cancerous leg amputated. Eunice Kennedy Shriver, who was in the hospital room when her nephew got the call, wrote to Nixon to say "This is a gesture of unselfishness and nobility." None of these gestures—there were many of them—were "brokered," although they were appreciated; but even so, there was something about Nixon that made people question his motives, and as he worked his way through this exercise in image and artifice, he glimpsed as he often did the large shadow of Eisenhower—"a bigger figure than life when he went into the Presidency," and someone who never had a warmth problem.

Nixon knew better, though. "He justifiably, in the Presidency, was known as a warm, kindly, fair man," he told Haldeman, but then added, "If you talked to members of his staff this is really mythology in a sense, because while this was his *public* impression, he was distant and all business—military in a sense—with the members of his staff, except possibly for very close intimates." Or, as he wrote later, "Beneath that sunny, warm Eisenhower exterior was a cold and when necessary even ruthless executive who often used others to carry out unpleasant assignments." He was, he told Monica Crowley, an assistant in the 1990s, "a hard-ass . . . a tough son of a bitch. . . . [He] used me, but he used me well."

Nixon envied Eisenhower's ability not only to project warmth but to inspire warm feelings in others, and he could acknowledge—and resent—the importance of personality. To Walter Judd, a veteran Minnesota congressman, he recalled how Ike had once said to him, "Dick, you don't seem to take people into your confidence. You don't tell them about your boyhood. You don't tell them about your hardships. . . . You don't talk about your family. You don't talk about your religion. You don't say anything about what you believe most deeply." After recounting this, Nixon said, ruefully, "Ike does this so naturally, you know. He's an extrovert. He likes people obviously. It's the easiest thing in the world for him to talk about what he did when they were boys [in Abilene]. . . . He tells all these stories, and people identify with him immediately—'Well, that's how it was in my home town too.' They sense a kinship."

Nixon did not inspire feelings of kinship—often the opposite. The British journalist Henry Brandon after interviewing him in 1971 jotted down his impressions and wrote, "He prefers to look in front of himself, but occasionally he turned around and seemed to look not into my eyes, but somewhere on my lapel. His eyes seemed to me ugly and cruel"; and the observant White House watcher John Osborne took note of "his restless hands, those usually unmanaged and seemingly unmanageable hands, and his mouth, that mean and twitching mouth and the frozen smile that could appear in an instant and vanish in the next instant." Nixon told some of his aides that Eisenhower did not have enough "heart" and was all too willing to drop loyal people if they might endanger his reputation. But Nixon also shed old loyalists, such as the journalist Ralph de Toledano, who in 1970 wrote to William F. Buckley Jr., to say, "My years of faithful service to what Whittaker [Chambers] used to call The Man have been rewarded by calculated standoffishness," and who told Murray Chotiner (another loyalist dropped), "He's lost the best friend he had in the press." De Toledano had a point; he had willingly bent journalistic standards in behalf of Nixon. In early 1960, for instance, he let Nixon see an early version of a *Newsweek* story which mentioned the vice president's doubts about administration policy during the 1956 Suez crisis; Nixon asked de Toledano to "delete any idea that I did not support the Administration's position in fact as well as in words," and he got his wish. Bryce Harlow believed that "Since he did not really trust people, people did not really trust him," and he could become so tightly wound and suspicious that even the most commonplace moments could be misconstrued. Don Hughes, recalled a time when Nixon was giving a speech and, as he headed to the stage and a band started to play—General Hughes hummed a few bars of "For He's a Jolly Good Fellow"—Nixon heard something else: "He grabs me and says, 'Don, why are they playing "The Bear Went over the Mountain"?'"

2

Dwight D. Eisenhower and Richard M. Nixon understood that their association was unusual, in part because it lasted so long and went through so many stages, but also because they were so unalike. They were certainly not close and their personal contacts were stilted. "Eisenhower was always telling Nixon to straighten his tie or pull back his shoulders, or speak up or shut up," Dr. Albert Hutschnecker told the author Anthony Summers. "He *made* himself like Nixon," John S. D. Eisenhower told the biographer Evan Thomas, and Bryce Harlow once said simply that Eisenhower was "not fond" of him. But it's hard to believe that the former British prime minister Harold Macmillan had it right when he told a biographer that "Ike always hated him . . . always regarded him as a sharp lawyer."

Politically, Nixon found it easier than Eisenhower to connect to the conservative Republican base, and yet on most domestic issues he was considerably more progressive than Ike, at least as that term is understood in modern times. As the Eisenhower adviser Gabriel Hauge said, Nixon "took a less-than-evangelical view of the dangers of budget deficits and went well beyond Eisenhower and his Cabinet in urging federal intervention into social programs." He advocated educational opportunity for lower-income Americans, student exchanges, and more open immigration policies. From the time that he was elected to the House in 1946, he sought a larger federal role in health care, especially for those who faced the cost of catastrophic illness, which the Nixon family had faced in Whittier. Eisenhower, the West Point graduate and career military officer, never had to worry about educational opportunity or medical care, and while he might express concern for the needs of pensioners, one rarely sensed much passion for the issue. The *Brown* decision, which Nixon publicly supported, made Eisenhower uneasy. "As a matter of fact, I personally think the decision was wrong," Ike told a surprised aide, Arthur Larson; even while the case was being decided, he spoke to Chief Justice Warren at a White House dinner and, referring to the southern states, said, "These are not bad people. All they are concerned about is to see that their sweet little girls are not required to sit in school alongside some big, overgrown Negroes."

Eisenhower shrugged off Sputnik in 1957 and in the mid-1960s was scornful of the proposed manned mission to the moon. Nixon from the moment that the first artificial satellite was launched understood what the space program meant for the nation's idea of its destiny; when he was president, he even urged support of the fiscally irrational but emotionally appealing supersonic transport, the SST, once remarking, "I understand why some oppose it . . . but let's not let this be a pattern of turning away from exploring the unknown, turning inward, not meeting our responsibilities in the world, and so forth." As president, he wondered whether it was feasible to invite a Russian astronaut "to go along on our next space trip," and he had every right to take some credit when he welcomed the Apollo 11 astronauts back from the moon.

For all this, a *New York Times* editorial writer considered "The First Hundred Days" of Nixon's presidency and tried to characterize them as "Eisenhower-ism without Eisenhower," finding both relief and satisfaction in the presence of such familiar faces as Bryce Harlow, William Rogers, and the economic adviser Arthur Burns. In fact the first months of Nixon's presidency were less like a resuscitated Eisenhower era and more like a policy making laboratory with beakers bubbling in every corner. Here was Daniel Patrick Moynihan, composing rambling memoranda that rivaled anything that C. D. Jackson ever sent to Ike, worried about racial issues and urging experiments with welfare, in particular the Family Security System, a passionate cause that Nixon encouraged for a time. And there was the conservative economist Martin Anderson, who had helped persuade Nixon to end the military draft; and Senator J. William Fulbright, a strong critic of the war, invited to come by for what Henry Kissinger called "an informal, unpublished chat," with a promise that "there will not be any name-calling"; and there of all people was Dean Acheson, who was about to turn seventy-six and whom Nixon made it a point to invite to a dinner for NATO foreign ministers. In his memoirs, Nixon described Acheson, once a favored campaign target, as a "friend."

The administration was open to domestic originality. It created a department—the Environmental Protection Agency—to police and try to eliminate the pollution of America's air and water; it supported the doomed Equal Rights Amendment (an extra push for that came from Julie Nixon Eisenhower); it supported national health insurance and increased spending for the arts, and it effectively moved to desegregate southern schools. While the Family Security Plan was never passed by Congress and Nixon himself backed away from it, Vincent and Vee Burke, in their book, *Nixon's Good Deed,* have pointed out that "it put income guarantees on the national political agenda . . . led directly to our first national cash-income guarantee, Supplemental Security Income [and] dramatized the antiwork, antifather, antifamily pressures of welfare policy." In foreign policy, the administration in its first four years repaired relations with Western Europe, which had deteriorated under Johnson, negotiated an arms reduction treaty with the Soviet Union, and established ties to mainland China after twenty years of Chinese isolation. But because of Vietnam—the war that Eisenhower in 1954 was determined to avoid—none of this counted for very much at the time, and Nixon steadily lost support, even from people like Donald Riegle, whom he had urged to run for Congress when he was still a graduate student and who, after meeting with Nixon in 1967, had come away encouraged that he intended to end the fighting within months of taking office. Riegle's opposition to administration policies finally got him to switch parties. Nixon could not see a quick or easy way out—certainly not the way that the former war correspondent David Halberstam recommended when he wrote, just as Nixon took office, that the new president "must know by now that the war is unwinnable" and that his chance to get out

> . . . will come perhaps in the first four months, and if he fails, then his speeches will have to justify the war, and the failure to end the war, and soon it will no longer be Johnson's war, it will be Nixon's. He will find himself justifying it more and more, and slowly but surely, without even realizing it, he will be pulled by the powerful currents around him into the same course as Johnson.

Nixon all along had believed that the United States had to be militarily credible in order to reach his geopolitical goals with Russia and China, the two major Communist countries. "The U.S. can't fold," he told the *New York Times*'s C. L. Sulzberger. "We would destroy ourselves if we pulled out in a way that really wasn't honorable." Yet he told his onetime speechwriter Richard Whalen that "there's no way to win the war . . . we can't say that, of course. In fact, we have to seem to say the opposite, just to keep some degree of bargaining leverage." Soon enough, the Vietnam conflict did become his conflict; the domestic violence that it provoked came to obsess him and to shape the contours of his presidency. Some 58,000 Americans were killed in the fighting, along with uncounted Vietnamese; of that number, 18,000 died during Nixon's first term with the majority of those deaths occurring in 1969. He withdrew Americans from combat and promised to reduce the U.S. role, but what was most remembered in the first term was the speech that he delivered on April 30, 1970, when he appeared to be expanding the war, when he said that American forces were being sent to "clean out major enemy sanctuaries on the Cambodian-Vietnam border" and that if "the world's most powerful nation . . . acts like a pitiful, helpless giant, the forces of totalitarianism and anarchy will threaten free nations and free institutions throughout the world." The speech, written by Pat Buchanan, was considered a disaster even by Buchanan's White House colleagues; protests flared up on campuses all over the country and on May 4, four students were killed and nine wounded by National Guardsmen who shot protesters at Kent State in Ohio. "I was paranoiac, or almost a basket case with regard to secrecy," Nixon admitted to Frank Gannon in one of his post-presidential interviews. Vietnam, to use the language of Watergate, became the cancer on his presidency.

Even without being asked, those who knew and admired Nixon often talk about how his presidency might have avoided its basipetal course. For a man of his experience and political intelligence, how could it have gone so wrong? His duties as vice president had included performing Eisenhower's most onerous tasks (taking on Joe McCarthy, helping to get rid of Sherman Adams, going on the political offense, sometimes excessively so). But what he learned then wasn't useful when he had to deal with problems of his own making, which were compounded by his own fears and suspicions. Almost from the start, a fretful atmosphere developed in the Nixon White House. Bob Haldeman was no Sherman Adams and seemed actually to enjoy creating stress—"[I] have, I think, shook them to the core," he said after delivering a scolding to an agency head over a minor matter. Staff people would arrive at their desks to find distressing messages, usually delivered by a Haldeman lieutenant, touching on matters as small as the competence of the projectionist at Camp David or the tides in the Potomac when the USS *Sequoia,* the presidential yacht, was out or the absence of ketchup at a table—each message hinting at the distant displeasure of a president who had a curious obsession with the minutiae of White House life. "We had titles, we had perks, but I got to the point where I was getting nasty notes about the steak being too well done," Don Hughes said. The contagion became increasingly mean-spirited and malevolent—even Edward Nixon found it hard to get through to his older brother.

It is often said that Nixon was changed—and permanently embittered—by his loss to Kennedy in 1960 (less so by losing to Pat Brown in 1962); he undoubtedly suffered the stresses of desperate uncertainty during his vice presidential years. But beyond that, nothing made President Nixon as agitated as Vietnam. On June 17, 1971, and four days after the *New York Times* began printing the confidential history of the war known as the Pentagon Papers, he demanded to know what had become of the so-called bombing halt file—the possible record of who had done and said what just before the 1968 election. He had an almost frantic interest in its whereabouts, perhaps fearing that it might contain something about the campaign's pre-election contacts with the Thieu government. As he talked with Kissinger, Haldeman, and Ehrlichman, Nixon ordered *someone* to get that file, if need be "on a thievery basis. Goddamn it, get in and get those files. Blow the safe and get it."

No one blew the safe—the file was believed to be at the Brookings Institution—but a year later, a break-in at Democratic headquarters in the Watergate complex touched off a scandal that extended far beyond that curious burglary. Nixon didn't know how to respond to questions about it and he had no one to help him respond. He had liked to see himself as someone who remained cool in a crisis, like Eisenhower, about whom he'd said, "I was impressed by the fact that the hotter the discussion became, the cooler he became." Nixon though simply froze; he lashed out; he lied and covered up and then he got caught doing both. The onetime Eisenhower aide William Ewald remembers Ike's brother Milton telling him "I'm glad that the President did not live to see the things that man did." It is natural to wonder whether Watergate and all of its tributaries would ever have materialized if the patriarch had lived beyond the first two months of the Nixon presidency.

3

David and Julie Eisenhower left Massachusetts in May 1970; classes were canceled after the Kent State killings. But even before that, Julie had asked John Ehrlichman to dissuade her father from attending her graduation. "The temper up here is ugly," she wrote to Ehrlichman. "At a rally . . . one of the Chicago Seven led the audience of 10,000 in a chant of 'fuck Julie and David Eisenhower.'" The journalist I. F. Stone, known for his strong anti-administration views, spoke at the Amherst graduation, which came about a month after the Kent State killings. Like his wife, David Eisenhower wasn't present (his diploma and honors thesis were mailed), but his name, when it was called, was greeted by boos and hisses as well as applause.

After Nixon resigned, in August 1974, the young Eisenhowers first lived in Capistrano Beach, California, close to Julie's parents, and then in a suburb of Philadelphia. Julie worked for *The Saturday Evening Post,* editing and writing; her work included a children's story called "Pasha Passes By" and a profile of Alice Roosevelt Longworth. A year after her father left office, she published *Julie Eisenhower's Cookbook for Children,* which included recipes from family ("Mamie Eisenhower's Turkey") and famous friends ("Barbara Walters's Brownies"), and which omitted the "Nixon" from her name. David in 1976 intended to work at a Wall Street law firm (after Navy service, he'd studied law at the George Washington University), but didn't much care for that life and, like Julie—and his father—became a writer. Julie in 1976 published *Special People,* portraits of people like Ruth Bell Graham, Golda Meir, Anne Morrow Lindbergh, and Charles, Prince of Wales (and restored the "Nixon" to her name). David in the fall of 1986 published a widely praised book about his grandfather, *Eisenhower at War, 1943–1945;* Julie a month later published an intimate biography of her mother, *Pat Nixon: The Untold Story.* She continued as a consulting editor for *The Saturday Evening Post* and David began an academic career at the University of Pennsylvania. In 2010 they collaborated on an engaging book about the post-presidential General Eisenhower (*Going Home to Glory*). The Eisenhowers aren't very public figures, though in 2008 Julie, as well as David's sister Susan, worked in behalf of the presidential candidacy of Senator Barack Obama.

Mamie Eisenhower after her husband's death had no plans to return to Gettysburg; she postponed the decision by living in Brussels with her son, whom Nixon in 1969 had named ambassador to Belgium. But life in Brussels was a weary existence and she returned to the farm, the closest place to a home that she'd known. Her life there could be isolated, but she had regular visits from her grandchildren; and from the John S. D. Eisenhowers—he resigned his ambassadorship in July 1971—who lived in Valley Forge. Mamie would take breaks from the farm by visiting the new Eisenhower College (it closed in 1982) in Seneca Falls, New York; or staying at "Mamie's Cabin" at Augusta National; or traveling to Abilene to visit the Chapel of Meditation. In the year after Ike died, Abilene experienced a boom in tourism, which, although it didn't last long, brought more motels and chain restaurants; the town even got a tame strip joint, the Red Pussycat. The year before Mamie's death, in November 1979, David and Julie Eisenhower had their first child, a daughter they named Jennie—Pat and Dick's first grandchild and Mamie's first great-grandchild.

Pat and Dick always welcomed Mamie to the White House and frequently included her in social and ceremonial occasions; she called him "Dick." Mamie was grateful for their constant attention and thoughtfulness, and as the Watergate scandal began to unfold, she worried about them. In May of 1973, a month after Nixon fired Haldeman and Ehrlichman and the new attorney general, Elliot Richardson, appointed a special prosecutor, she wrote:

Dearest "Pat"

Just a line to let you know how much I love you and the President. My heart has been heavy for you both but do assure the President that the whole country is really behind him and that folks know what it means when your friends that you trust let you down—We all live in glass houses. Naturally he must shoulder the blame but it hurts. So glad you have Julie with you. Devotedly your friend,

Mamie Eisenhower

By March of 1974, when Nixon's presidency appeared to be fatally wounded by the scandal, Mamie wrote to her granddaughter Susan, "Nixon is our heartbreaking worry here. Feel so sorry for the family." On August 6, 1974, just before Richard Nixon announced his resignation, she wrote again:

Dearest "Pat"

I only want to say I am thinking of you today—always you will have my warm affection as will your husband President Nixon.

Your friend
Mamie Eisenhower

Nixon died in April 1994—he outlived Eisenhower by a quarter century—and in the nearly twenty years after his presidency, he traveled frequently; his stops included Russia and China, the loci of the old Cold War that he'd helped to end. He also produced a number of books, the best of which is probably *Leaders*, a collaboration with Ray Price that was published in 1982 and included portraits of de Gaulle, Churchill, Adenauer, and others. There was no separate chapter on Eisenhower, one in which Nixon might have examined what the general had done to shape the postwar world—a place and time that were filled with great danger, skillful diplomacy, and ideological reversals; and which, when Eisenhower died and the Nixon administration was new, bore little resemblance to the place once inhabited by the intense Orange County congressman and the war hero from Kansas. In that window of time—the first months of 1969—it was still possible to look past the hideous war and glimpse the shape of a post-Eisenhower presidency that could have been defined by domestic innovation and creative foreign policy, and that might at the very least have given the illusion of an enduring, peaceful center.

ACKNOWLEDGMENTS

Priscilla Painton, Simon & Schuster's executive editor, saw me through this project with energy, creative intelligence, and a sympathetic appreciation of what I was up to. I was wildly lucky to work with her and also fortunate to have the wholehearted backing of our publisher, the ingenious Jonathan Karp. It's my fourth book with Simon & Schuster, and I'm always mightily impressed. Publicity manager Anne Tate and marketing manager Nina Pajak gave me terrific advice. The production manager John Wahler (then) and Lisa Erwin (now); senior production editor Lisa Healy; designer Akasha Archer; associate editor Michael Szczerban; proofreader Bill Molesky, indexer Charles Newman, and copy editor extraordinaire Fred Chase were among those who made every page better.

It's sometimes hard to say how a book gets started, but in this case it came out of conversations with the talented Sarah Hochman and the publisher David Rosenthal, with whom I'd talked about growing up in Washington when Eisenhower was president and Nixon could be spotted in the lower grandstand at Griffith Stadium. It was followed by an essential, enthusiastic push from Tina Bennett, a wise counselor, a brilliant critic, and a friend as well as my literary agent for more than a decade.

None of this would have gotten very far without the men and women at the National Archives and Records Administration (NARA), which oversees the presidential libraries. At the Dwight D. Eisenhower Presidential Library and Museum in Abilene, Kansas, I'm particularly grateful to Valoise Armstrong—for her knowledge and all-around niceness, who was always able to help me solve riddles, even by long-distance. The library's director, Karl Weissenbach; deputy director Tim Rives; audiovisual archivist Kathy Struss; and archives technicians Chalsea Millner and Catherine Cain all helped; retired archivist David Haight saved me at least once from embarrassment.

I was just as privileged at the Nixon Presidential Library and Museum in Yorba Linda, California, where my expert guide was Supervisory Archivist Gregory Cumming, who understood my absorption with the subject, and where more help came from archives technicians Craig Ellefson, Carla Braswell, Dorissa Martinez, and audio-video archives technician Pamla Eisenberg. The library's former director, Timothy Naftali, brought the commitment of a serious historian; he was unfailingly supportive, as was Paul Wormser, who became acting director in 2011. Paul Musgrave, now a doctoral candidate at Georgetown University and formerly a special assistant to the director, gave me sound advice.

Relations between the Nixon Library, which is under the auspices of NARA, and the privately supported Richard Nixon Foundation have not been easy; in fact, that's understating years of mutual bad feelings between the Library, with its recent focus on Watergate, and the Foundation. But that had little or no effect on my project. I appreciated the openness and assistance I got from Richard (Sandy) Quinn, president of the Foundation; from his predecessor Ronald H. Walker, now chairman of the Foundation; and Cheryl Saremi, secretary to the Foundation. They had every reason to suspect my intentions—not least because I'd worked for a dozen years at *The Washington Post*—but they trusted me to be fair. I hope they conclude that I was.

At the Hoover Institution at Stanford University, I owe an enormous debt to Mandy MacCalla, the executive assistant to the deputy director. Much appreciation goes to the librarian Paul Thomas, assistant archivist for reference, Carol A. Leadenham, and especially the audio specialist Jim Sam. The staff at the Manuscript Division of the Library of Congress was always accommodating, and particularly so were Mary Rich in the Law Library and Lewis Wyman. At Columbia University's Butler Library many thanks to Charis Emily Shafter; at the J. Willard Marriott Library at the University of Utah I'm indebted to librarian Paul A. Mogren and especially to the moving image and sound archivist Molly R. Creel. Researcher Virginia Martin assisted with the Harold Stassen Papers at the Minnesota Historical Society; Kathy Petersen, at the Bowdoin College Library, led me through the papers of James Bassett. More thanks to Christian C. Goos, at the Gerald R. Ford Presidential Library; Eric R. Cuellar at the

Lyndon B. Johnson Library; Sam Rushay, at the Harry S. Truman Library; the librarians at Olin Library, Cornell University and at the Multnomah County Library in Portland, Oregon; the documentarians George Colburn and Deborah Blum; Christine A. Lutz, at the Seeley G. Mudd Manuscript Library, at Princeton; the New York Society Library, and the indispensable New York Public Library.

I'm especially obliged to those who read some early parts of the manuscript: the historian David Greenberg, who years ago warned me of the danger of Nixon obsession, made valuable and important suggestions; more good advice came from Jodie Allen, my smart former boss at *The Washington Post*, as well as two masters of nonfiction narrative, Philip Gourevitch and David Grann, friends and former *New Yorker* colleagues. Mary Norris, one of the magazine's peerless O.K.ers, gave the book a painstaking read. Thanks also to Robert K. Nedelkoff; Skye Gurney, and those who were kind enough to come to my aid, among them: Chris Donovan, a producer with *Meet the Press*; Katherine Connell, research director at *National Review;* Kenneth Adelman; Cynthia Bassett; Christopher Buckley; Mark Feldstein; Laurie Heineman; Michael Isikoff; David L. Robb; Adele Ruxton, who's in charge of the underfunded Indian Wells Historical Society and showed me around the Coachella Valley, where Eisenhower spent post-presidential winters; Yvette Siegert; my former assistant at *The New Yorker,* who volunteered valuable pro bono research, and Robbyn Swan, who went far out of her way to help. I have gratitude left over for the nearly seventy men and women who agreed to be interviewed and whose recollections and shrewd interpretations I appreciated and appropriated whenever I could. Above all, I relied on my amazing wife, Diana, for her acumen, support, and encouragement throughout this multiyear venture.

NOTES

Frequently Used Abbreviations
Collections

ACW: Ann C. Whitman Diary Series, at the Eisenhower Library

COHP: Columbia University Oral History Project

DDE: Dwight D. Eisenhower Diary Series, at the Eisenhower Library

DDEL: Dwight D. Eisenhower Presidential Library and Museum

ELOH: Eisenhower Library Oral History

EP: *The Papers of Dwight David Eisenhower*, Johns Hopkins University Press

FRUS: *Foreign Relations of the United States*

HI: Hoover Institution Library and Archives, Stanford University, Palo Alto, California

HSTL: Harry S. Truman Library and Museum, Independence, Missouri

LOC: Library of Congress Manuscript Division

LWH: The posthumous political memoirs of Leonard Wood Hall, at the Eisenhower Library

RNL: Nixon Presidential Library and Museum, Yorba Linda, California

"UYLM": "Ugly Year, Lonely Man," James Bassett's unpublished journal, at the Bowdoin College Library

WHSF: White House Special Files, Nixon Presidential Returned Materials Collection, at the Nixon Library

Newspapers and Magazines

BG: *Boston Globe*

CT: *Chicago Tribune*

LAT: *Los Angeles Times*

NYHT: *New York Herald Tribune*

NYT: *New York Times*
NYTM: *New York Times Magazine*
SEP: *The Saturday Evening Post*
TNR: *The New Republic*
TNY: *The New Yorker*
USN&WR: *U.S. News & World Report*
WP: *Washington Post* (also: *WP&TH,* the *Washington Post & Times Herald,* the newspaper's masthead from 1954 until 1973)
WSJ: *The Wall Street Journal*

Prologue

PAGE
1   *A million citizens watched:* WP, 6/19/45, p. 2.
2   *With music provided by the Army band:* NYT, 6/15/45, p. 5; NYT, 6/20/45, pp. 6, 7; "Home to Abilene," *Time,* 7/2/45.
2   *"Maybe I just think it was that way":* Robert Coughlan, "Success Story of a Vice President," *Life,* 12/14/53, p. 146; NYT, 9/25/52, p. 21; Richard Nixon, *RN,* p. 80.
3   *"like a junior officer":* Richard Nixon, *Six Crises,* p. 76.
3   *"There were times when I would find Nixon":* Ralph de Toledano, *Notes from the Underground,* p. 232.
4   *"a painfully lonesome man":* Russell Baker, *The Good Times,* pp. 313–14.
4   *"I'm not exactly amused to see myself":* Bela Kornitzer, *The Real Nixon,* p. 223.
4   *"spatulate nose":* Garry Wills, *Nixon Agonistes,* p. 169.
5   *Ike's appearance sometimes seemed to change:* "Eisenhower and His Task," *TNR,* 6/5/51, p. 11.
5   *"those cold blue laserlike eyes":* Douglas Price, interview by author, January 26, 2011.
5   *"those blue eyes of his turned crystal cold":* Kenneth Thompson, ed., *The Eisenhower Presidency,* pp. 148, 151.
5   *"We are very close":* Press conference, 3/14/56; transcript: http://www.presidency.ucsb.edu/ws/index.php?pid=10752#axzz1nyFRqlfb.
5   *"a far more complex and devious man":* Nixon, *Six Crises,* p. 160.
6   *"tight-lipped, over-tense, and slightly perspiring":* William S. White, "Nixon: What Kind of President?," *Harper's,* 1/58, p. 26.
6   *"I was constantly aware of an inner man":* DDEL, George B. Bookman Papers, unpublished Gabriel Hauge autobiography.
6   *Nixon kept count:* USN&WR, 5/16/60, p. 98+; NYT, 3/29/59, p. 1+.
7   *"The same slanted, almost Slavic eyes":* Jessamyn West, "The Real Pat Nixon," *Good Housekeeping,* 2/71, p. 68.
7   *"a very studious individual":* LOC, Joseph and Stewart Alsop Papers, Box 47.
8   *"Somebody related a secondhand story":* RNL, Series 320, Box 324, Harvey, 9/1/60.
8   *"Lt. Nixon comes from good Quaker stock":* Roy O. Day, ELOH.
8   *"a natural-born leader":* LAT, 11/29/45, p. 10.
8   *"He has terrifically large feet":* Day, ELOH.
9   *had prepared himself, as if for a chess match:* Edward Nixon, interview by author, February 19, 2009; Day, ELOH.
9   *People who had known him:* Henry D. Spalding, *The Nixon Nobody Knows,* p. 168.

9 *Nixon was tutored by Murray Chotiner:* See Chotiner's "Fundamentals of Campaign Organization," his "course" on campaign tactics. RNL, RNC "campaign school," 9/55–10/55. Also: *NYT,* 5/13/56, p. 65. More on the early Chotiner: *LAT,* 9/11/48, p. 4; *The Nation,* 7/2/55, pp. 4–7.

10 *"The cheering in the streets will die down":* WP, 6/9/45, p. 7.

10 *When he was asked about politics:* WP, 6/23/45, p. 2; NYT, 6/23/45, p. 1+; *Abilene Reflector-Chronicle,* Eisenhower Memorial Edition.

10 *"suddenly turned toward me":* Dwight D. Eisenhower, *Crusade in Europe,* p. 444.

11 *"complete chimera":* Alsops, *LAT,* 5/10/46, p. A4.

11 *In fact, on the morning after:* Peter Lyon, *Eisenhower,* pp. 390–91.

12 *drawn to the twists and mysteries:* Stacy A. Cordery, *Alice: Alice Roosevelt Longworth, from White House Princess to Washington Power Broker,* p. 440.

12 *"Hamburg, Berlin and the other German cities":* LOC, Alsop Papers, Box 47.

12 *Congressman Nixon in 1947:* HI, Ralph de Toledano column draft, King features syndicate, 10/10/68.

12 *"a dapper little man":* Carey McWilliams, "Bungling in California," *The Nation,* 11/4/50, p. 411.

13 *his first memories of "the war":* Dwight D. Eisenhower, *At Ease,* p. 41.

13 *"the mobility of the new technical society":* Arthur Schlesinger Jr., "A Skeptical Democrat Looks at President Nixon," *NYTM,* 11/17/68, p. 45+.

13 *made many journalists wary of him:* Helen Thomas, interview by author, May 3, 2011.

13 *always liked to have people around:* David Eisenhower, *Going Home to Glory,* p. 66.

13 *"His temper could blaze":* Dwight D. Eisenhower, *At Ease,* p. 304.

14 *"It was his temper that impressed me":* Nixon, *RN,* p. 6. David Eisenhower, in an interview by author, September 29, 2010, pointed out the similarities between Hannah Nixon and Ida Eisenhower.

14 *"My father was very firm in that idea":* RNL, interview by Jonathan Aitken, Aitken Collection, Boxes 9, 10.

14 *Everyone adored Harold:* Edward Nixon, interview by author, February 19, 2009.

14 *a "brighter, more handsome fellow":* People, 8/11/75, pp. 27–28.

14 *His parents were members of the River Brethren:* DDEL, Jehovah's Witnesses Abilene Congregation; Jerry Bergman, abstract from the *JW Research Journal,* vol. 6, no. 2, July-December 1999; Dwight D. Eisenhower, *At Ease,* p. 305.

14 *"I have never known such a blow":* Dwight D. Eisenhower, *At Ease,* p. 181.

15 *"goddamned old fool":* DDEL, Henry W. Hoagland Papers, the posthumous, unpublished autobiography of Leonard Wood Hall, edited by William J. Casey, p. 158 (hereafter: LWH).

15 *"a senile old bastard.":* William Bragg Ewald Jr., *Eisenhower the President,* p. 14.

15 *"After Nixon got elected":* John Sears, interviews by author, August 27, 2010, August 10, 2011.

1. The Men's Club

PAGE

17 *Bohemian Club:* William Domhoff, *The Bohemian Grove and Other Retreats: A Study in Ruling Class Cohesiveness,* p. 33. Domhoff's subtitle suggests his point of view; his history of the club is entertaining and useful.

18 *These private ceremonies have become less secret:* For example: http://video.google.com/video play?docid=5617720002953136903#.

18 *"My dear Mr. Congressman":* This and subsequent Hoover letters to Nixon are in RNL, Series 320, Hoover, Boxes 351, 352, letters 1/22/50, 3/31/51, 4/3/51, 4/19/51.

18 *Fred Gurley, the railroad man: EP,* Volume 11, Part 4, Chapter 9, p. 1188, 6/29/50.

19 *"was deferential":* Nixon, *RN,* p. 81.

19 *in the funeral cortege for General John J. Pershing:* William Arnold, *Back When It All Began,* p. 8.

19 *"It was not a polished speech": RN,* pp. 80–81.

20 *when they came to a room with a piano:* Greg Mitchell, *Tricky Dick and the Pink Lady,* p. 242; a later clip of Nixon at the piano can be seen at http://www.stream.efootage. com/clips/DV-130/38588.mov.

20 *"Watch that boy!": Covina Argus-Citizen,* 4/18/52, p. 1.

20 *"Your victory was the greatest good":* RNL, Series 320, Box 351, Hoover, 11/8/50, 12/11/50.

20 *"Governor, if you are not going to run": Meet the Press,* transcript, 10/15/50.

21 *"He fascinates them":* Gênet (Janet Flanner), "Letter from S.H.A.P.E.," *TNY,* 10/27/51, pp. 120–24.

21 *without carrying his service revolver:* Arthur Larson, *Eisenhower,* p. 88.

21 *a group of relatively new friends:* Fletcher Knebel, "Ike's Cronies," *Look,* 6/1/54, p. 57+; "Our Om-nescient President," *TNR,* 6/1/59, p. 11+; Clifford Roberts, COHP.

21 *was probably most comfortable:* David Eisenhower, interview by author, 5/21/12.

22 *Douglas pointed out that the two parties: WP,* 6/3/51, p. B1.

22 *"You don't suppose a man":* Ronald Steele, *Walter Lippmann and the American Century,* p. 481.

22 *"a round, bald little man":* Peter Edson, in a column for the Newspaper Enterprise Association, 8/31/51.

22 *"General Eisenhower feels a need":* RNL, Series 320, Kohlberg, Box 423, 5/1/51.

22 *they were holding open May 18:* DDEL, Pre-Presidential Papers, 1916–52, Principal File, Box 87.

22 *Nixon later told Kohlberg:* RNL, Series 320, Kohlberg, Box 423, 5/30/51.

23 *"was erect and vital":* Nixon, *RN,* p. 81.

23 *the general invited Nixon:* Richard Nixon, *In the Arena,* p. 144; HSTL, Summaries of Meetings Between Milton Katz and President Eisenhower, Milton Katz papers, memo of conversation, 4/27/57.

23 *"I was impressed, let me say parenthetically": Congressional Record,* 6/5/51, p. 6138.

23 *"the importance of non-military strength":* Nixon, *RN,* pp. 81–82.

23 *"I felt that I was in the presence":* Ibid.

24 *"Harry fell in love with Eisenhower":* Ralph G. Martin, *Henry and Clare,* p. 291.

24 *Cecil Beaton supposedly described her:* Martin, *Henry and Clare,* p. 104.

24 *"the future of the country": EP,* Volume 10, Part 3, Chapter 7, 9/27/49, p. 755.

24 *knew everyone in the business:* Lyon, *Eisenhower,* p. 427.

24 *embarrassed by an unusual number of scandals:* Andrew J. Dunar, *The Truman Scandals and the Politics of Morality,* pp. 65, 97; Fletcher Knebel and Jack Wilson, "The Scandalous Years," *Look,* 5/22/51.

25 *The initial reaction:* Richard H. Rovere and Arthur Schlesinger, *The General and the President,* 12.

25 *"At rare intervals in the life of a free people": NYHT,* 10/25/51, p. 1.

25 *A Citizens for Eisenhower group:* DDEL, George Lodge account, Eisenhower Administrative Series, Box 23; Stanley Rumbough, interview by author, February 8, 2011. This history in some form also appears in most standard biographies.

25 *"There is one question"*: NYT, 1/7/52, p. 9.
26 *The declaration was enough for Truman*: WP, 1/11/52, p. 1+.
26 *"I do not feel that I have any duty"*: EP, Volume 13, 1/1/52, pp. 830–31.
26 *"As a Californian, I am ashamed"*: RNL, Special Files, PPS 324 (1), 1/17/52.
26 *"I suppose that defamatory attacks"*: Ibid., 1/28/52.
26 *"The political pot is really boiling"*: RNL, Jack and Helene Drown Collection, 2/2/52.
27 *"burst into tears"*: Jacqueline Cochran, ELOH.
27 *"a real emotional experience"*: EP, Volume 13, Part 4, Chapter 7, pp. 971–72.
27 *Jackie Cochran, a self-made cosmetics entrepreneur*: See Doris Rich, *Jackie Cochran*, which recounts her surprising life.

2. The Ticket

28 *he could summon a fiery, even evangelical rhythm*: One can hear the Nixon of 1952 in a speech to California's Commonwealth Club, 2/14/52.
28 *"Too many people don't like us both"*: Stewart Alsop, *Nixon and Rockefeller*, p. 55.
28 *"on the whole"*: Wolcott Gibbs, *More in Sorrow*, pp. 143–44.
29 *"should offer . . . a program"*: NYT, 5/9/52, p. 1+.
29 *"That was a terrific speech"*: RNL, Series 320, Box 214, Dewey, letter to Dewey, 1/15/61.
29 *"He had a very fine voting record"*: Dewey, COHP.
29 *"only a polite gesture"*: RNL, Series 320, Dewey, 1/15/61.
30 *what struck viewers*: "Homecoming," *Time*, 6/15/52; Marquis Childs, *Eisenhower*, p. 139; Lyon, *Eisenhower*, p. 440.
30 *"a parvenu, an amateur"*: Richard Rovere, "Letter from Chicago," TNY, 7/19/52, p. 74.
30 *Seven large cameras*: "The Eye of the Nation, *Time*, 7/14/52.
31 *The TV critic . . . was annoyed*: NYT, 7/13/52, p. X9.
31 *"Nixon is a dyed-in-the-wool Ikeman"*: Bowdoin College Library, George J. Mitchell Department of Special Collections and Archives, James E. Bassett Jr. Papers, 1929–1977, Box 1, Correspondence, 7/9/52 (hereafter: Bassett correspondence).
31 *"Mr. Nixon through backdoor tactics"*: LAT, 5/13/62, p. B1.
31 *"deep sense of fear"*: NYT, 7/10/52, p. 21; NYT, 7/8/52, pp. 1, 18; CT, 7/8/52, p. 1+; Time, 7/14/52.
31 *"We were in fear"*: Bassett correspondence, 7/9/52.
31 *Eisenhower could be stopped*: General Albert Wedemeyer, HI, Oral History Collection.
32 *since he'd played football at UCLA*: Dean J. Kotlowski, *Nixon's Civil Rights*, p. 163.
32 *knew something was going on*: Dorothy Cox Donnelly, interview by author, May 2, 2011.
32 *he was one of seven people in contention*: NYT, 7/9/52, p. 1.
32 *he had already met at least once with Herbert Brownell*: RNL, Series 320, Box 20, Sherman Adams, Nixon letter to Adams, 12/31/58.
32 *Nixon kept dodging*: LAT, 7/10/52, p. A; NYT, 7/10/52, p. 1.
32 *"As you know"*: EP, Volume 12, Part 5, Chapter 10, p. 1308, 8/2/63.
33 *"reminded me of a ward committee"*: Sherman Adams, *Firsthand Report*, p. 35.
33 *"primarily because he is young"*: C. L. Sulzberger, *A Long Row of Candles*, p. 773.
33 *"he is dynamic, direct and square"*: EP, Volume 13, Part 5, Chapter 10, p. 1307, 8/2/52.
33 *"Could you recall for us, sir"*: Press conference, 5/31/55; transcript: http://www.presidency.ucsb.edu/ws/index.php?pid=10246#axzz1nyFRqlfb. See also: DDEL, Herbert Brownell Papers, Box 108, letter to Dewey, 4/1/70; Jack Bell, COHP; Sherman Adams, COHP; Clifford Roberts, COHP.

34 *"the worst part"*: Nixon, *RN*, p. 85.
34 *"There comes a point"*: Nixon, *RN*, p. 86.
34 *"The room was not air-conditioned"*: Ibid.
35 the Carrier Corporation: *CT*, 7/9/52, p. 13.
35 the hotel's Saddle and Sirloin Coffee Shop: *LAT*, 7/14/52, B1.
35 *"This is Herb Brownell"*: Pat Hillings, *The Irrepressible Irishman*, p. 56.
35 *"with the damndest wet tropical wind"*: Bassett correspondence, 7/21/52.
35 *"I felt hot, sleepy, and grubby"*: Nixon, *RN*, p. 87.
36 *"a little coolness developing*: RNL, Series 320, Box 20, Nixon to Stewart Alsop, 12/31/58; Nixon/Gannon interviews, Day 1, Tape 2; Day 3, Tape 3.
36 *"That bite of sandwich popped right out of my mouth"*: Patricia Ryan Nixon, "I Say He's a Wonderful Guy," *SEP*, 9/6/52, p. 94.
36 *"I could hear the stuff coming in on the radio"*: Stephen Hess, interview by author, September 18, 2008.
37 *"I sensed when I held the general's arm up"*: Nixon/Gannon interviews, Day 3, Tape 2; you can see this moment at http://www.youtube.com/watch?v=GFSOocR2ddo.
37 *"You're the prettiest thing!"*: Julie Nixon Eisenhower, *Pat Nixon*, p. 116.

3. The Silent Treatment

38 *"I'm sure that Sherman Adams"*: Stephen Benedict, interview by author, January 31, 2009.
38 *The general was an expert*: Merriman Smith, *Meet Mister Eisenhower*, p. 148.
38 the tutoring was not a success: Nixon talked about that moment with Frank Gannon: Day 3, Tape 2; there is some newsreel footage at http://www.britishpathe.com/record.php?id=62145.
38 *"above-the-battle position"*: Nixon, *RN*, p. 88.
39 *"When we are through"*: *WSJ*, 10/20/52, p. 1+.
39 *"mouse-like dependence on Harry Truman"*: *NYT*, 10/2/52 p. 22; *The Reporter*, 10/19/56, p. 16.
39 *"traitors to the high principles"*: *LAT*, 10/28/52, p. 2+; Robert H. Ferrell, ed., *Off the Record*, p. 341.
39 *"Secret Nixon Fund!"*: *New York Post*, 9/18/52, pp. 1, 6.
39 *"[T]here was considerable doubt"*: RNL, Series 320, Box 236, Edson, 7/27/52.
40 *"to give America what everybody wants"*: *NYHT*, 9/19/52, p. 1+.
40 *"I believe Dick Nixon to be an honest man"*: Dwight D. Eisenhower, *Mandate for Change*, pp. 1, 65; "The Remarkable Tornado," *Time*, 9/29/52.
40 *"If Ike can't make up his mind on this"*: *WSJ*, 9/25/52, p. 1+.
40 *"the purpose of those smears"*: *WP*, 9/20/52, p. 1; *LAT*, 9/20/52, p. 2.
41 a resident of Pasadena: *NYT*, 9/22/53, p. 9.
41 *"I do not see how we can win"*: Thompson ed., *The Eisenhower Presidency*, p. 183.
41 *"Honesty is the best policy"*: *NYT*, 9/21/52, p. 1+.
41 made him uncomfortable: *NYT*, 9/25/52, p. 20.
41 *"God—I tell you, in five minutes"*: Milton Eisenhower, COHP.
42 *"The proper course for Senator Nixon"*: *NYHT*, 9/20/52, p. 13.
42 *"it occurred to me"*: Nixon, *Six Crises*, p. 86.
42 *"no one can afford to act on a hair-trigger"*: *EP*, Volume 13, Part 5, Chapter 10, p. 1360, 9/20/52.

42 *"The thing just kind of snowballed"*: Marjorie Acker, interviews by author, 11/10/2010, 11/18/2010, 12/15/2010, 1/26/2011.

42 *"No mink coats for Pat Nixon"*: *LAT*, 9/20/52, p. 2; *LAT*, 9/21/52, p. 1+.

43 *"a great fold of muscle and flesh"*: Harry A. McPherson, *A Political Education*, p. 74.

43 *to play the role of a relief pitcher*: Adams, *Firsthand Report*, p. 4; Earl Mazo, *Richard Nixon*, pp. 115–16.

43 *"There was all kinds of stuff going on"*: Acker, interviews by author, 11/10/2010, 11/18/2010, 12/15/2010, 1/26/2011.

43 *the candidate was being pulled in different directions*: See various accounts in, for example, Dwight D. Eisenhower, *Mandate for Change*, p. 65; *Time*, 9/29/52; *WSJ*, 9/20/52, p. 1+; Milton Eisenhower, COHP.

43 *an extra burden for Nixon's office*: Dorothy Cox Donnelly, interview by author, May 2, 2011; Rose Mary Woods, as told to Don Murray, "Nixon's My Boss," *SEP*, 12/28/57, p. 77; Mazo, *Richard Nixon*, pp. 115–16.

43 *"That's a question I'm not going to answer"*: *WP*, 9/22/52, p. 1.

44 *"In the long run it will also strengthen you"*: Mazo, *Richard Nixon*, p. 120; Nixon, *Six Crises*, p. 98.

44 *"was ready"*: Mazo, *Richard Nixon*, p. 120.

44 *in a survey of a hundred newspapers*: *NYT*, 9/21/52, p. 1+.

44 *When he was handed a telegram from his mother*: Hillings, *The Irrepressible Irishman*, p. 66; Mazo, *Richard Nixon*, p. 121.

44 *At Temple Beth Israel*: *Oregonian*, 9/22/52, pp. 1, 15.

45 *"was not sympathetic to Nixon's predicament"*: Herbert Brownell, *Advising Ike*, pp. 124–26.

45 *"I will not crawl"*: Mazo, *Richard Nixon*, p. 121.

45 *"What do you plan to do?"*: Harold Lavine, ed., *Smoke-Filled Rooms*, pp. 83–84.

46 *Adams said that he was willing to give it a try*: Ewald, *Eisenhower the President*, p. 53.

46 *"You've been taking a lot of heat"*: I rely in these paragraphs on many sources, including notes that Nixon took as he was speaking to Eisenhower: RNL, Campaign 1952, Box 174, Correspondence, September 20–23, notes, 9/20/52; Nixon, *Six Crises*, pp. 99–100; Nixon, *RN*, pp. 97–98; Mazo, *Richard Nixon*, p. 121.

47 *contracted for a national hookup*: Mazo, *Richard Nixon*, p. 121.

47 *Nixon walked the nearby streets*: John C. Lungren and John C. Lungren Jr., *Healing Richard Nixon*, p. 48.

47 *took note of Senator Knowland's presence*: *WSJ*, 9/22/52, p. 1+.

47 *"A high ethical level in government requires"*: *NYHT*, 9/22/52, p. 15.

47 *"has been thrown to the wolves"*: *WSJ*, 9/23/53, p. 2; *NYT*, 9/23/52, p. 1+; Herbert G. Klein, *Making It Perfectly Clear*, p. 372.

48 *to pray for him*: Maureen Drown Nunn, interview by author, October 28, 2010.

48 *"Just before the broadcast I had my worst moment"*: Stewart Alsop, "The Mystery of Richard Nixon," *SEP*, 7/12/58, p. 29+; Nixon/Gannon interviews, Day 3, Tape 2; Nixon, *RN*, pp. 102–3.

48 *Dewey knew that Ike wanted Nixon to resign*: *NYT*, 3/15/62, p. 51; Richard Norton Smith, *Thomas E. Dewey and His Times*, p. 601.

49 *"Well, what shall I tell them"*: RNL, Campaign 1952, Box 174, September 20–23, 9/23/52.

49 *"Dick looked like someone had smashed him"*: Mazo, *Richard Nixon*, p. 127.

4. "The Greatest Moment of My Life"

50 *Nixon's speech:* The entire Checkers speech may be watched at http://www.american rhetoric.com/speeches/richardnixoncheckers.html.

52 *A claim by the columnist Drew Pearson:* Tyler Abell, ed., *Drew Pearson Diaries,* pp. 227–28.

55 *the telephone lines were jammed:* Acker, interviews by author, 11/10/2010, 11/18/2010, 12/15/2010, 1/26/2011.

55 *he was cheered by people:* LAT, 9/24/52, p. 2.

55 *about four thousand an hour:* NYT, 9/25/52, p. 1+.

55 *after the speech, she stayed put:* Loie Gaunt, interview by author, March 13, 2009.

55 *"will emerge from this ordeal":* NYHT, 9/25/52, p. 13.

56 *"this mawkish ooze":* Robert Coughlan, "Success Story of a Vice President," *Life,* 12/14/53, p. 165.

56 *"He talked well and to the point":* Anthony Trollope, *Orley Farm.*

56 *"enthusiastic Nixon supporter":* Lavine, ed., *Smoke-Filled Rooms,* pp. 91–92; "Nixon Fights, Wins and Weeps," *Life,* 10/6/52, p. 26+; Robert Cutler, *No Time for Rest,* p. 285.

56 *"I have seen many brave men":* NYT, 9/24/52, p. 24.

57 *"I could insist on stay":* RNL, 1952 campaign, Nixon's handwritten notes.

57 *revealing how a special tax decision:* Stewart Alsop, *Nixon and Rockefeller,* p. 65; Tom Wicker, *One of Us,* p. 101.

57 *"Your presentation":* Nixon, *RN,* p. 105.

57 *he'd expected a decisive answer:* Ibid., p. 105.

58 *"Tell the sisters":* RNL, Drown Collection, 9/24/52.

58 *"It was like before starting in a football game":* Robert Coughlan, "Success Story of a Vice-President," *Life,* 12/14/53, p. 158.

58 *"tell him to intercept Dick":* DDEL, Robert Humphreys Papers, Box 6, RN (2).

59 *"not a GI in this war":* WSJ, 9/25/52, p. 1+.

59 *"Your presentation was magnificent":* Nixon, *RN,* p. 105; NYT, 9/24/52, p. 1+.

59 *Eisenhower had waited for about forty-five minutes:* Lavine, *Smoke-Filled Rooms,* pp. 94–96; "Nixon Fights, Wins and Weeps," *Life,* 10/6/52, p. 26.

60 *"We weren't sure who was going to meet us":* Acker, interviews by author, 11/10/2010, 11/18/2010, 12/15/2010, 1/26/2011.

60 *"You run interference":* CT, 9/25/52, p. 1+.

60 *Every detail was scrutinized by reporters: Wheeling Intelligencer,* 9/24/52, p. 1.

60 *"You've had a hard time, young fellow":* Thompson, ed., *The Eisenhower Presidency,* p. 182; Adams, *Firsthand Report,* pp. 41–42.

60 *"But you just don't realize":* Julie Nixon Eisenhower, *Pat Nixon,* p. 125.

60 *"Mom trusted Eisenhower":* Edward Nixon, interviews by author, February 19, 2009, April 25, 2010.

61 *two occasions:* NYT, 9/25/52, p. 21.

61 *"the greatest moment of my life":* Ibid.

61 *"Good old Bill":* Mazo, *Richard Nixon,* p. 134.

61 *fresh rumors concerning his finances:* Nixon, *RN,* p. 107.

62 *"left a deep scar":* Nixon, *Six Crises,* p. 128.

62 *"Do we have to talk about this?":* Julie Nixon Eisenhower, *Pat Nixon,* p. 126.

5. President Eisenhower

PAGE

63 *had predicted that Governor Stevenson: NYT,* 9/25/52, p. 23.

63 *"I just remember him looking very serene":* Benedict, interview by author, January 31, 2009.

63 *"forgo the diversions":* "I Shall Go to Korea," *Time,* 11/3/52.

63 *a young, dandyish* Life *editor:* Benjamin Bradlee, interview by author, April 27, 2010; Martin, *Henry and Clare,* p. 287.

64 *"That's the speech that will beat us":* Porter McKeever, *Adlai Stevenson,* p. 44.

64 *"I have long felt that the Founding Fathers": LAT,* 11/9/52, p. 9; LAT, 11/12/52, p. 6.

64 *"pounding the gavel":* "Nixon's Own Story of 7 Years in the Vice Presidency," *USN&WR,* 5/16/60, p. 98+; Nixon, *RN,* p. 88.

64 *other professional politicians had joined the administration: NYT,* 2/17/53, p. 16; *WP,* 2/17/53, p. 4; DDEL, C. D. Jackson Papers, Box 50, 1953.

65 *"I believe him to be": EP,* Volume 14, Part 2, Chapter 3, p. 226, 5/14/53.

66 *Ann Cook Whitman: NYHT,* 12/10/57, p. 9; Robert J. Donovan, *Confidential Secretary,* pp. 2, 14; Roberts, COHP.

66 *"I'll do whatever General Eisenhower wants": NYT,* 11/25/52, p. 1+.

66 *"We could not stand forever":* Dwight D. Eisenhower, *Mandate for Change,* p. 95.

66 *"My first day at President's Desk": EP,* Volume 14, Part One, Chapter 1, p. 5, 1/23/53.

67 *Eisenhower and Nixon stayed in the reviewing stand: LAT,* 1/20/52, p. 2.

67 *impressed at meeting Eisenhower:* Edward Nixon, interviews by author, February 9, 2009, April 25, 2010.

67 *"an incredible appointment": NYT,* 12/9/52, p. 26.

68 *"technical matter":* Ibid.

68 *"general field of personality": EP,* Volume 14, Part 2, Chapter 3, pp. 224–30, 5/14/53; Emmet John Hughes, *The Ordeal of Power,* p. 51.

68 *which Eisenhower tried to hold every Friday:* Bradley Patterson, interview by author, September 20, 2008. From the start, Eisenhower tried hard to organize the policy planning process. See, for example, Fred I. Greenstein and Richard H. Immerman, "Effective National Security Advising: Recovering the Eisenhower Legacy," *Political Science Quarterly,* Vol. 115, No. 3 (2000).

68 *"not particularly persuasive in presentation": EP,* Volume 14, Part 2, Chapter 3, pp. 224–30, 5/14/53.

69 *"He was always there":* Henry Roemer McPhee, interview by author, October 4, 2010.

69 *"steered a canny course": NYT,* 6/28/53, p. E6.

69 *had three offices:* Bowdoin College Library, George J. Mitchell Department of Special Collections and Archives, James E. Bassett Jr. Papers, 1929–1977, unpublished journal, "Ugly Year, Lonely Man," Boxes 3, 4 (hereafter: Bassett, "UYLM"), 3/6/54.

69 *"able and serious": WP,* 5/18/53, p. 8.

69 *"I am riskfully enclosing":* RNL, Series 320, Box 226, Drummond, 7/2/53.

70 *"He participates in more activities":* RNL, PPS 325, V.P. Work Files, Box 3, Folder 3, 6/1/53.

70 *"Well, anything you like":* Richard Nixon oral history, recorded 3/5/65, John Foster Dulles Oral History Collection, Seeley G. Mudd Manuscript Library, Princeton University.

70 *"is not only bright, quick and energetic": EP,* Diary, Volume 14, Part 2, Chapter 4, p. 266, 6/1/53.

70 *"probably the only place in the world"*: Bassett, correspondence, 2/28/54. A day earlier, Jim Bassett told his wife about a mildly uncomfortable visit to Burning Tree: the president sat at a communal table next to theirs—"grinning, laughing and joking, with his foursome"—followed by a moment on the links as "Ike and his party were breathing on our group's necks . . . [and] after some slight Alphonsing & Gastoning, the Presidential group went through."

70 *"quite a while"*: NYT, 8/10/53, p. 24.

70 *"It was just like a professional golf tournament"*: Lawrence Radak, interview by author, November 23, 2009.

71 *one of Ike's favorite courses*: Merriman Smith, *Meet Mister Eisenhower*, p. 75.

71 *"Just get up there and hit"*: NYT, 9/12/53, p. 1+.

6. Diplomatic Vistas

72 *"I think it would be a very fine"*: EP, Volume 14, Part 2, Chapter 5, pp. 378–79, 7/10/53.

72 *employment ads for "men"*: Chicago Defender National Edition, 5/8/54, p. 11. When the Capital Transit Co. in Washington announced on January 13, 1955, that it would hire Negro bus and streetcar drivers, Nixon, speaking in behalf of Eisenhower, said it was "a testament to the ideal of human dignity and liberty cherished by us all" (WP&TH, 1/14/55, p. 25).

73 *"not good"*: LOC, Roy Wilkins Papers, 8/26/52. WSJ, 11/27/57, p. 1+.

73 *also a short drive*: Merriman Smith, *Meet Mister Eisenhower*, p. 75.

73 *"The war is over"*: NYT, 7/27/53, p. 1+.

73 *"serious hip ailment"*: NYT, 7/30/53, p. 1.

74 *"I found him extraordinarily 'leftish'"*: EP, Volume 15, Part 4, Chapter 8, p. 827, 1/18/54; see also James Patterson's thorough biography, *Mr. Republican*.

74 *"He was a . . . prospector"*: Richard Rovere, *Senator Joe McCarthy*, p. 72.

74 *"nothing will be so effective"*: EP, Volume 14, Part 1, Chapter 2, p. 136, 4/1/53.

74 *"conspiracy so immense"*: NYT, 6/15/51, p. 3.

74 *"This was, of course, completely untrue"*: Dwight D. Eisenhower, *Mandate for Change*, pp. 318–19.

75 *"George will not tell you"*: Childs, *Eisenhower*, p. 68.

75 *"Always understate"*: Mazo, *Richard Nixon*, p. 140.

75 *"It was a sort of game for us"*: Edwin R. Bayley, *Joe McCarthy and the Press*, p. 68.

75 *the fight at the Sulgrave Club*: Ralph de Toledano, *Nixon*, 167–68; Bayley, *Joe McCarthy and the Press*, pp. 166–67.

75 *"I don't believe we can live in fear"*: Press conference, 11/18/53; transcript: http://www.presidency.ucsb.edu/ws/index.php?pid=9766#axzz1nKIgtLav.

75 *"The raw, harsh, unpleasant fact"*: NYT, 11/25/53, p. 1+.

76 *"I believe I can safely say"*: RNL, PPS 325, V.P. Work Files, Box 3, Folder 3, 6/16/53.

76 *"This is war"*: WP, 3/23/53, p. 9.

76 *would come east*: Julie Nixon Eisenhower, "Introducing Read Aloud," SEP, 1/2/74, p. 74.

76 *"Ho Chi Minh is finished"*: RNL, PPS 325, V.P. Work Files, Box 2, Folder 1, handwritten Indochina notes.

76 *"It is impossible to lay down arms"*: NYT, 11/5/53, p. 8.

76 *"extremely successful"*: FRUS, vol. 13, 1952–54, Part 1, 11/26/53, pp. 857–58.

77 *"he has a knack"*: NYT, 12/14/53, p. 1+.

77 *"a mover and shaper"*: Robert Coughlan, "Success Story of a Vice President," Life, 12/14/53, p. 146+.

77 *"mollifier to prevent an open breach"*: NYT, 12/20/53, p. E7.

77 *held out his hand*: WP, 12/15/53, p. 1+.

77 *"missed your wise counsel"*: EP, Volume 15, Part 4, Chapter 8, p. 761, 12/14/53.

78 *a memorandum for the National Security Council*: FRUS, 1952–54, 12/23/53, pp. 929–30; RNL, PPS 325, V.P. Work Files, Box 2, Briefing Notes, Folders 21, 22.

7. The Troublesome Senator

PAGE

79 *a Steuben glass cup*: WP&TH, 1/21/54, p. 23.

79 *he gave a dinner with music*: WP&TH, 1/20/54, p. 23; CT, p. 3.

79 *"At eight promptly"*: Ellis Slater, *The Ike I Knew*, pp. 66–67.

80 *he had mastered the art*: James Keogh, *This Is Nixon*, pp. 66–67.

80 *"Damon to Nixon's Pythias"*: WP&TH, 12/12/56, p. A15.

80 *"he's in one of his lonesome-lost"*: Bassett correspondence, 6/3/54.

80 *"Darned if I know"*: Ibid., 2/28/54, 3/6/54.

80 *Among the guests*: WP, 1/20/54, p. 23; CT, p. 3.

80 *spent time with McCarthy in Key Biscayne*: NYT, 1/10/54, p. E4; Herbert Parmet, *Richard Nixon and His America*, p. 339.

81 *"There may be a time"*: RNL, PPS 325, Box 3, Folder 3, handwritten notes, 6/16/53; Ralph de Toledano, *One Man Alone*, p. 183.

81 *"coddle and promote communists"*: NYT, 2/22/54, p. 2.

81 *an embarrassment for everyone*: DDEL, Legislative Meeting Series, 1954, Supplementary Notes, 3/1/54, p. 2.

81 *That was the topic*: RNL, Vice Presidential Work Files, PPS 325, "A Chronology of Joe McCarthy."

81 *"the atmosphere suggests"*: WP&TH, 2/28/54, p. B5.

81 *"It's probably time"*: Bassett, "UYLM," 2/24/54.

82 *"disagreeable labor camps"*: NYT, 3/2/54, p. 1+.

82 *"Where one party says"*: NYT, 3/7/54, p. 62.

82 *"one must conclude"*: NYT, 3/10/54, p. 1+.

82 *"pimple on the path"*: DDEL, Hagerty Diary, 3/8/54.

82 *"alleged Communist infiltration"*: NYT, 3/9/54, p. 1.

83 *"There was a meeting"*: Press conference, 3/10/54; transcript: http://www.presidency.ucsb.edu/ws/index.php?pid=10177#axzz1nKIgtLav.

83 *"in agony"*: Bassett, "UYLM," 3/8/54.

83 *"This is one I can't win"*: de Toledano, *One Man Alone*, p. 186.

83 *"As in any battle"*: DDEL, Robert Ferrell, ed., *The Diary of James C. Hagerty*, p. 10.

83 *"He said that first"*: Nixon, RN, p. 145.

83 *rarely seen Nixon so angry*: David Halberstam, *The Fifties*, p. 328.

84 *"He pointed out"*: Nixon, RN, p. 145.

84 *to show a kinescope*: Bassett, "UYLM," 3/10/54.

85 *"Now, I can imagine"*: NYT, 3/14/54, p. 44.

86 *"It was just right, Dick"*: Bassett, "UYLM," 3/13/54; Nixon, RN, p. 147.

86 *"the very delicate circumstances"*: HI, George Sokolsky Papers, Box 92, 3/13/54.

86 *in a curious mood*: Bassett, "UYLM," 3/13/54; WP&TH, 2/27/54, p. 7, 3/1/54, p. 10.

86 *"That prick Nixon"*: Thomas C. Reeves, *The Life and Times of Joe McCarthy*, p. 578.

86 *"Did you by any chance"*: RNL, Series 320, Box 291, Godfrey, 3/15/54, 12/15/57.

8. "Mr. Nixon's War"

PAGE

87 *alarm at the advance of Communism:* See *FRUS,* 1952–54, Vol. 13, 9/9/53, pp. 780–89.

87 *"the sudden day":* Sidney Hyman, "Between Throttlebottom and Jefferson," *NYTM,* 3/28/54, p. 64.

87 *"We must see to it":* NYT, 11/5/53, p. 8.

88 *"Who lost Indochina?":* Townsend Hoopes, *The Devil and John Foster Dulles,* p. 211.

88 *"gregarious and outgoing":* Nixon oral history, 3/5/65, John Foster Dulles Oral History Collection, Seeley G. Mudd Manuscript Library, Princeton University.

88 *"a palpably physical intensity":* Hoopes, *The Devil and John Foster Dulles,* p. 36.

88 *"long pauses between"; "candle wax":* Roderic O'Connor, COHP; Hoopes, *The Devil and John Foster Dulles,* pp. 36, 144.

88 *drop by the Nixons' home:* Julie Nixon Eisenhower, interview by author, September 29, 2010.

89 *"I cherished my relationship":* Nixon oral history, 3/5/65, John Foster Dulles Oral History Collection, Seeley G. Mudd Manuscript Library, Princeton University.

89 *"No one could be more bitterly opposed":* Press conference 2/10/54; transcript: http://www.presidency.ucsb.edu/ws/index.php?pid=10130#axzz1nKIgtLav.

89 *was stealthily doing:* See Melanie Billings-Yun, *Decision Against War: Eisenhower and Dien Bien Phu, 1954.*

89 *"Dulles presented":* Nixon, *RN,* p. 151.

90 *he'd go around a long octagonal table:* Cutler, *No Time for Rest,* p. 303; DDEL, doodles; Bassett, "UYLM," 3/5/54; Cabell Phillips, "The Super-Cabinet for Our Security," *NYTM,* 4/4/1954, p. 14+.

90 *"You have a row of dominoes":* Press conference, 4/7/54; transcript: http://www.presidency.ucsb.edu/ws/index.php?pid=10202#axzz1nyFRqlfb.

91 *The United States is the leader:* Many news accounts; see also Keogh, *This Is Nixon,* p. 141.

91 *"would be a grave threat":* NYT, 4/18/54, p. 1+.

91 *"It was mine":* Nixon oral history, 3/5/65, John Foster Dulles Oral History Collection, Seeley G. Mudd Manuscript Library, Princeton University.

91 *"brief interpretive statement":* FRUS, 1952–54, Volume 13, pp. 1346–48, 4/17/54.

91 *"whooping it up for war":* WP&TH, 4/20/54, p. 6.

92 *"is not in the position":* RNL, PPS 325, Box 3, Folder 3, "Memorandum on the Duties of a V.P.," 6/16/53.

92 *a conversation with James Reston:* NYT, 4/20/54, p. 1+.

92 *"immediately stepped in":* Nixon, *RN,* p. 153.

92 *"They are very volatile":* Ferrell, ed., *The Diary of James C. Hagerty,* p. 48.

93 *"an assortment of ideas":* WP&TH, 4/20/54, p. 13.

93 *The National Security Council met again on April 29:* FRUS, 1952–54, Volume 13, pp. 1270–1.

93 *"If the French indeed collapsed":* This debate went on for some time. See FRUS, 1952–54, Volume 13, pp. 1437–43, 4/29/54.

95 *"The only language the Communists understand":* NYT, 6/27/54, p. 37; NYT, 6/28/54, p. 2; WP&TH, 6/27/54, p. M1.

95 *"since his remarkably successful":* NYT, 6/28/54, p. 2.

95 *"The hatchet boys (and girls)":* Bassett, "UYLM," 6/29/54.

96 *"Will you drop in to see me":* EP, Volume 15, Part 5, Chapter 11, p. 1155, 6/28/54.

96 "*the impulse . . . to lash out*": Ibid.
96 *Nixon protested:* ACW, Box 2, June, 6/29/54.
97 *planting a question:* Bassett, "UYLM," 6/29/54.
97 "*First of all, let's recognize*": Press conference, 6/30/54; transcript: http://www
.presidency.ucsb.edu/ws/index.php?pid=9938#axzz1nKIgtLav.
97 "*policy of weakness*": WP&TH, 7/4/54, p. 2.

9. The Pounding

PAGE
98 "*the people like a fighter*": RNL, Chotiner's "Fundamentals of Campaign Organization,"
9/7–10/55.
98 "*so delicate and tenuous*": Julie Nixon Eisenhower, *Pat Nixon*, p. 151.
98 "*After a few hours*": Nixon, *RN*, p. 161.
98 "*Sure, I know*": Bassett "UYLM," 7/23/54.
98 "*No man on earth*": DDE, Box 2, 11/24/54.
99 "*give our great President*": Cabell Phillips, "One Man Task Force," *NYTM*, 10/24/54,
pp. 17–21.
99 "*balloon blowers*": *NYT*, 9/2/54, p. 1.
99 "*There is no reason*": RNL, Speech File, Campaign 1954, Appearances; *NYT*, 10/1/54.
100 "*The more I saw of you*": RNL, Series 320, Box 420, Kihss, 10/4/54.
100 "*millions of loyal Democrats*": *NYT*, 10/23/54, p. 7; *The Reporter*, 10/19/56, p. 16.
100 "*It wasn't I who swore*": WP&TH, 10/15/54, p. 2.
100 "*Throw him out*": DDEL, William Rogers Papers, Box 50, Nixon-VP correspondence,
10/29/54; *NYT*, 10/30/54.
100 "*on a number of occasions*": Nixon, *RN*, p. 161.
101 *that "no matter how difficult*": Richard Rovere, "Letter from Washington," *TNY*,
11/13/54, p. 116.
101 "*Chamber of Smears*": *NYT*, 10/23/54, p. 1+; *NYT*, 1/13/55, p. 1+.
101 "*I have listened lately*": Press conference, 10/27/54; transcript: http://www.presidency
.ucsb.edu/ws/index.php?pid=10110#axzz1nKIgtLav.
101 "*I was out front*": Nixon, *RN*, p. 163.
102 "*I don't think I have ever seen*": DDEL, C. D. Jackson Papers, Box 70, 12/18/54.
102 "*the mood and tenor*": Ibid., 12/21/54.
102 "*the greater likelihood*": *EP*, Volume 15, Part 6, Chapter 13, p. 1404, 11/20/54.
102 "*We must present the able*": DDEL, C. D. Jackson Papers, Box 70, 12/21/54.
103 "*Take Bob Anderson*": Ibid.
103 *the only real job:* "What Goes On at Ike's Dinners: President Puts Old-Time Cracker-
Barrel Idea to Work," *USN&WR*, 2/4/55, p. 34+.
103 "*attributes for a man of destiny*": RNL, Series 320, Box 364, Arnold A. Hutschnecker,
4/12/55.
103 "*were much more virulent*": *EP*, Volume 16, Part 7, Chapter 15, pp. 1617–18, 3/14/55.
104 "*completely reckless*": ACW, Box 4, 3/26/55.
104 "*new and powerful weapons*": DDEL, John Foster Dulles Papers, White House memoranda, Box 3, March 7, 1955 (7); *NYT*, 3/16/55, p. 1+; WP&TH, 3/16/55, p. 1+.
104 "*We have been*": Press conference, 3/16/55; transcript: http://www.presidency.ucsb.edu/
ws/index.php?pid=10434#axzz1nKIgtLav.
105 "*by a sudden sneak attack*": DDE, Box 8, 10/4/54.
105 "*The failure to have this showdown*": Henry Cabot Lodge, *As It Was*, p. 73.

105 *"Tactical atomic explosives":* CT, 3/18/55, p. 1+; NYT, 3/18/55, p. 16.
105 *"when you get into actual war":* Press conference, 3/23/55; transcript: http://www
.presidency.ucsb.edu/ws/index.php?pid=10437#axzz1nKIgtLav.
106 *"only thing you* know*":* RNL, PPS 325, Box 6, handwritten note, undated.

10. Mortal Man

PAGE
107 *"For six weeks now":* Richard Rovere, *Affairs of State,* p. 313.
108 *made no effort:* Mazo, *Richard Nixon,* p. 196.
108 *"I never saw the President look better":* NYT, 9/6/55, p. 1+; WP&TH, 9/6/55, p. 1+.
108 *"Personally, I have felt better":* DDEL, Milton Eisenhower Papers, Correspondence Series, Box 14, 9/17/55.
108 *"Humans are frail":* "Ike Outlines His Political Creed: Government Should Only Do What Individual Can't Do for Himself," USN&WR, 9/23/55, p. 116.
108 *slight indigestion:* Adams, *Firsthand Report,* p. 183.
109 *"With a full head":* Leonard Heaton, ELOH.
109 *"is really not capable":* EP, Volume 15, Part 6, Chapter 13, p. 14, 11/20/54.
109 *the only man in the world:* Donovan, *Confidential Secretary,* p. 92.
109 *meeting informally with wire service reporters:* Alvin Spivak, interview by author, May 19, 2011.
110 *"How's his tummy?":* Nixon, *Six Crises,* pp. 131–32.
110 *"Let me know":* The Diary of James C. Hagerty, p. 234.
110 *Nixon just sat:* RNL, PPS 325, Box 5, Folder 21, Executive Branch Files, 9/24/55; Mazo, *Richard Nixon,* p. 189.
110 *"This is really going to be":* RNL, PPS 325, Box 5, Folder 21, Executive Branch Files, 9/26/55.
110 *Hagerty was on the phone: Diary of James C. Hagerty,* p. 237.
110 *"We had just arrived":* Brownell, *Advising Ike,* p. 274.
111 *"I realized that":* Kornitzer, *The Real Nixon,* p. 332.
111 *"We had to employ a strategy":* Ibid., p. 322; Robert J. Donovan, *Eisenhower,* p. 369.
111 *"I don't have the vaguest idea":* Jonathan Aitken, *Nixon,* p. 236.
111 *He didn't go to bed:* RNL, V.P. Work Files, PPS 325, Folder 26, 9/25/55.
111 *"an all-night ham radio contest":* Anthony Rogers, interview by author, March 12, 2009.
111 *"During the three years":* Nixon, *Six Crises,* p. 142.
112 *"It was a very tense night":* Rogers, interview by author, March 12, 2009.
112 *Nixon returned home:* Julie Nixon Eisenhower, *Pat Nixon,* p. 154.
112 *planning to resign:* CT, 9/27/55, p. 1+.
112 *"was not particularly apt":* James (Don) Hughes, interview by author, October 10, 2010.
112 *"a madhouse around here":* RNL, Helene and Jack Drown Collection, undated letter.
112 *Foster Dulles and Nixon conferred:* DDEL, John Foster Dulles Papers, Telephone Conversation Series, 9/25/55.
113 *"is pretty much out of it":* RNL, PPS 325, Folder 6, 9/25/55.
113 *"He never mentioned Ike's situation":* LWH, p. 99.
113 *"needed to keep business of government going":* RNL, PPS 325, Box 5, Folder 27, handwritten notes for cabinet meeting, 9/30/55.
114 *Dulles spoke up, praising:* RNL, PPS 325, Box 5, Folder 27, 9/30/55; DDEL, John Foster Dulles Telephone Series, 9/30/55; Ezra Taft Benson, *Cross Fire,* pp. 271–72; Donovan, *Inside Story,* p. 371; Nixon, *Six Crises,* pp. 143–44, 148–49.

114 *"Dulles was my major adviser":* Nixon oral history, 3/5/65, John Foster Dulles Oral History Collection, Seeley G. Mudd Manuscript Library, Princeton University.

114 *"cold, gray chaotic nightmare":* NYT, 9/26/55, p. 15.

114 *Journalistic reinforcements rushed out:* Spivak, interview by author, May 19, 2011.

114 *a story of good luck:* See Clarence G. Lasby's fascinating *Eisenhower's Heart Attack,* University Press of Kansas, Lawrence, KS, 1997, particularly pages 73–112.

115 *"I hope you will continue":* NYT, 10/4/55, p. 1+.

115 *"looked startlingly thin and pale":* Nixon, *Six Crises,* p. 151.

115 *"a crippled old man":* RNL PPS 325, Box 5, Folder 24, handwritten notes, October 8–9, 1955.

115 *but hadn't realized:* RNL, PPS 325, Box 5, Folder 24, handwritten notes, October 8–9, 1955.

115 *Nixon met with reporters:* CT, WP&TH, NYT, all 10/9/55, p. 1+.

115 *"appearing to assume":* Adams, *Firsthand Report,* p. 182.

115 *Dulles didn't trust Harold Stassen:* RNL, PPS 325, Box 5, Folder 24, handwritten notes, 10/8–9/55.

116 *"Everyone was so conscious":* Milton Eisenhower, COHP.

116 *"council of state":* WP&TH, 9/27/55, p. 15.

116 *"What happens under the Constitution":* Brownell, *Advising Ike,* pp. 274, 278.

116 *"it was generally agreed":* NYT, 9/25/55, p. 1+.

116 *"about 100-to-1 against":* Eric Sevareid, "The Longest Campaign in History," *The Reporter,* 11/5/55, p. 18.

117 *"Like half the world":* RNL, Series 320, Box 464, Henry and Clare Luce, 10/8/55.

118 *"my brilliant future":* Nixon, *Six Crises,* p. 150.

118 *"As you know, my attitude":* RNL, PPS 325, Box 6, Folder 1, transcribed by Rose Mary Woods, 10/10/55.

118 *the farm in Gettysburg:* NYT, 3/29/69, p. 20.

118 *"there was no personal thank you":* Nixon, *Six Crises,* p. 152.

118 *the president played bridge:* Presidential Papers of DDE, Chronology, November 1955: http://www.eisenhowermemorial.org/presidential-papers/first-term/chronology/index.htm.

119 *"a maturity of intellect":* DDE Personal Diary, Box 9, 11/10/55.

119 *But Nixon was Nixon:* Kornitzer, *The Real Nixon,* p. 330.

119 *"heir to one of the greatest":* NYT, 9/26/55, p. 1+.

11. Survivor

PAGE

120 *"He is just about the ablest man":* Everett E. Hazlett, *Ike's Letters to a Friend,* p. 138.

121 *"delve into the deepest of subjects":* Robert Keith Gray, *Eighteen Acres Under Glass,* pp. 116–18.

121 *ability as a briefer:* William Bragg Ewald Jr., interviews by author, September 11, 2008, October 16, 2008, December 9, 2008.

121 *a political basis:* Gerald Anderson, interview by author, March 9, 2008.

121 *"a bald and bouncy":* "The Mahout from Oyster Bay," *Time,* 3/12/56.

121 *"really a wonderful fellow":* EP, Volume 16, Part 9, Chapter 19, p. 2063, 3/12/56.

122 *"He could also be evasive":* LWH, p. 97; other accounts of this visit: Allen Drury, "The Enigma of Gettysburg," *The Reporter,* 12/29/55, p. 21; *NYT,* 11/29/55, p. 1+; "If He Feels Able," *Time,* 12/12/55; *WP&TH,* 11/29/55, p. 1.

122 *"most disappointing":* Nixon, *Six Crises,* p. 159; WP&TH, 11/18/55, p. 37.

123 *taking a cabinet job:* Nixon, *Six Crises,* p. 158.

123 *conflict with . . . Nelson Rockefeller:* DDEL, C. D. Jackson Papers, Box 70, 10/26/55.
123 *"I have no secrets from you":* ACW, Box 8, 1/11/56.
123 *Ike had been brooding:* Nixon, *RN,* p. 168.
124 *"I want each one of you fellows":* LWH, p. 100.
124 *The group then talked for hours:* DDEL, John Foster Dulles Papers, White House Memoranda Series, Box 8, 1/13/56; LWH, 99–100; Wilton Persons, COHP.
124 *Nixon spoke in Chicago:* CT, 1/21/56, p. 11.
124 *"I would devoutly wish":* WP&TH, 1/21/56, p. 1+.
124 *"fatigue is a central problem":* DDEL, C. D. Jackson Papers, Box 71, 1/23/56.
124 *He told Jackson:* Ibid.
125 *"You might want to make him Secretary of State":* DDEL, John Foster Dulles Papers, White House Memoranda Series, Box 8, 2/27/56.
125 *"all these paid off":* RNL, PPS 325, Box 6, undated.
125 *"General Clay is a mysterious figure":* RNL, PPS 325, Box 7, 1/13/55.
126 *began to brainstorm:* ACW, Box 8, 2/9/56.
126 *"The one that would be the shocker would be Lausche":* Ibid.
127 *"be very, very gentle":* Ibid.
127 *"hit in the solar plexus":* LWH, p. 107.
127 *"Len Hall called":* DDE Diary Series, Box 13, February, 1956, Misc. (4).
127 *ordered General Omar Bradley:* John S. D. Eisenhower, *General Ike,* p. 66.
128 *"I consented to four years only":* DDE Diary Series, Box 9, 2/7/56.
128 *no vice president since Martin Van Buren:* Nixon, *RN,* p. 167.
128 *"However, if you calculate":* ACW, Box 8, 2/9/56.
128 *"absolutely indescribable anguish":* John Osborne, "Gabbing with Harlow," *TNR,* 5/15/78, pp. 12–14; Nixon, *Six Crises,* p. 160.
128 *"No man elected President at 65":* TNR, 3/5/56, p. 3.
129 *"As a matter of fact":* Press conference, 2/29/56; transcript: http://www.presidency.ucsb.edu/ws/index.php?pid=10742#axzz1nKIgtLav.
129 *"President Eisenhower's":* WP&TH, 2/14/56, p. 1+.
129 *"ruthless partisan":* WP&TH, 2/18/56, p. 15.
129 *"Once a man has passed":* Press conference, 2/29/56.
130 *"What kind of man is he?":* LWH, p. 156.
130 *"The field is wide open":* RNL, PPS 325, Box 6, handwritten notes, 3/1/56.
130 *"so aggressive and gangster-like":* WP&TH, 3/1/56, p. 15.
130 *"Nixon is in some way connected":* ACW, Box 8, 3/19/56.
131 *"chart out his own course":* Press conference, 3/7/56; transcript: http://www.presidency.ucsb.edu/ws/index.php?pid=10749#axzz1nKIgtLav.
131 *"As long as I am potential candidate":* RNL, PPS 325, Box 6, handwritten notes, 3/1/56.
131 *The plan was for Ike to say:* ACW, Box 8, 3/13/56.
132 *"Anyone who attempts to drive a wedge":* Press conference, 3/14/56; transcript: http://www.presidency.ucsb.edu/ws/index.php?pid=10752#axzz1nKIgtLav.
132 *"I suggested to our friend":* EP, Volume 16, Part 9, Chapter 19, p. 2130, 4/24/56.
132 *"Well, he hasn't reported back":* Press conference, 4/25/56; transcript: http://www.presidency.ucsb.edu/ws/index.php?pid=10787#axzz1nKIgtLav.
133 *"The only reason I waited":* Mazo, *Richard Nixon,* p. 167; Nixon, *RN,* pp. 171–72.
133 *"If they want me":* DDE Diary Series, Box 13, 4/26/56.
133 *"it was a mutual thing":* DDEL, Administrative Series, Box 28, Nixon, 4/26/56.
133 *"Dick always says":* DDEL, John Foster Dulles Papers, Telephone Call Series, 4/27/56.
134 *He joked with Bob Hope:* WP&TH, 6/9/56, p. 1+.

134 *"Cut it down to one pack"*: Quentin Reynolds, "Mr. President Eisenhower," *Life*, 4/15/50, p. 144+.

134 *Hagerty called Nixon:* Nixon, RN, p. 173.

134 *"an attack of ileitis"*: WP&TH, 6/9/56, p. 1+; NYT, 6/9/56, p. 1+.

135 *they had no choice:* ACW, Box 8, 6/8/56, 6/9–11/56.

135 *an ileotransverse colostomy:* NYT, 6/9/56, p. 1+; NYT, 6/10/56, p. 60.

135 *might resume playing golf:* NYT, 6/10/56, p. 60.

135 *"an amiable but aging"*: WP&TH, 7/15/56, p. E5.

135 *"Who is in fact likely"*: WP&TH, 7/12/56, p. 15.

135 *"The man who should speak"*: WP&TH, 6/19/56, p. 1+.

136 *"if his health permits"*: NYT, 7/10/56, p. 18.

136 *Len Hall and Jim Hagerty to Gettysburg:* WP&TH, 7/13/56, p.1+; LWH, p. 111.

136 *"it wasn't a gasp"*: LWH, p. 111.

136 *what he'd told Herter:* WP&TH, 7/24/56, p. 1+.

137 *"so long as he did not purport"*: Hughes, *The Ordeal of Power*, p. 173.

137 *set off for Panama:* NYT, 7/21/56, p. 1+.

137 *"join in supporting Chris Herter"*: RNL, Series 320, Stassen, Boxes 724–25, 7/23/56.

137 *replacing Herbert Hoover Jr.:* "Childe Harold's Pilgrimage," *Time*, 8/6/56.

137 *"We have been close friends"*: Christian Herter Papers, Houghton Library, pp. 1073–75, 7/25/56.

137 *"So I walked into the President's office"*: LWH, p. 112.

138 *Russell Baker pointed out:* NYT, 8/5/56, p. E4.

138 *Milton quickly wrote Nixon:* RNL, Milton Eisenhower Series, Series 320, Box 238, 8/6/56, 8/16/56.

138 *"a man can be drafted at any time"*: NYT, 8/18/56, p. 10.

138 *Herbert Brownell suggested:* Brownell, *Advising Ike*, p. 299.

138 *"and join wholeheartedly and cheerfully"*: RNL, Series 320, Box 724, Stassen, 8/22/56; WP&TH, 8/23/56, p. 8.

138 *"Any comment"*: NYT, 8/23/56, p. 1+.

139 *"Richard Nixon has a moral blank"*: Glen Harold Stassen, interview by author, July 31, 2009.

139 *his father was mortally ill:* NYT, 8/23/56, p. 1+.

139 *"I'd really like to talk to Fulton Lewis Jr."*: Edward Nixon, interviews by author, February 19, 2009, April 25, 2010.

139 *"Hell, I offered him anything"*: Dwight D. Eisenhower, *Waging Peace*, pp. 6–9; Ewald, *Eisenhower the President*, p. 200.

139 *he told his brother Milton:* George S. Wills, interview by author, January 28, 2011.

140 *"at least had the President's acquiescence"*: NYT, 7/24/56, p. 1+.

140 *"Oh, certainly"*: Stassen, COHP.

12. The Liberation of Richard Nixon

PAGE

141 *"I think today you ought to take notice"*: RNL, DDE Special File, PPS 324, 9/12/56, memo to file from Nixon; DDE, Box 18, telephone calls, 9/12/56.

142 *"the peace and prosperity"*: DDE, Box 18, telephone calls, 9/12/56.

142 *"Everyone shares in sympathy"*: WP&TH, 9/14/56, p. 1+.

142 *"we should point out that he is wrong"*: RNL, Eisenhower Special File, PPS 324, 9/12/56, memo to file from RN.

142 *"There is no man"*: NYT, 9/13/56, p. 22.

142 *he took Nixon and Len Hall: NYT,* 9/13/56, p. 1+.

142 *"Do you know":* Theodore White, *The Making of the President, 1960,* p. 72.

142 *Mort Sahl's routine:* Quoted by Richard Rovere, "Letter from Washington," *TNY,* 9/29/56, p. 140.

143 *Stevenson who "quailed": NYT,* 9/27/56, p. 26.

143 *"a man who ranks":* Richard Rovere, "A Reporter at Large: The Campaign: Nixon," *TNY,* 10/13/56, pp. 168–77.

143 *"The free world suffered": NYT,* 10/28/56, p. 72.

143 *"has no standard of truth":* Ibid.

143 *"sly," "slippery," and "ruthless":* McKeever, *Adlai Stevenson,* pp. 418–19.

144 *"a country in which": NYT,* 9/27/56, p. 26.

144 *"And distasteful as this matter is": NYT,* 11/6/56, p. 18.

144 *took along a board:* HI, George Humphrey oral history.

145 *"I do not see how the economy": EP,* Volume 17, Part 10, Chapter 21, p. 2264, 9/2/56.

145 *"I did not participate":* Nixon oral history, John Foster Dulles Papers, Seeley G. Mudd Manuscript Library, Princeton University, 2/21/66.

146 *to the British MP Julian Amery:* RNL, Aitken Collection, Box 10, 12/21/83.

146 *to his biographer:* Aitken, *Nixon: A Life,* p. 244.

146 *and in casual conversations:* RNL, Aitken Collection, Box 10; also: Nixon tapes, 11/29/71, 8:38–10:42 A.M.

146 *"a positive orgy": WP&TH,* 11/14/56, p. A15.

146 *"the most crowded":* Dwight D. Eisenhower, *Waging Peace,* p. 58.

146 *"rightness of the liberation position": WP&TH,* 11/19/56, p. 4.

146 *"verge of a nervous breakdown":* ACW, Box 8, 11/19/56.

146 *"quite certain that the implications": EP,* Volume 17, Part 11, Chapter 22, pp. 2398–99, 11/19/56.

146 *"I cannot sleep at night":* LOC, Clare Boothe Luce Papers, Box 631, Memoranda, 11/19/56.

147 *a Christmas night television program: NYT,* 12/25/56, p. 39; *NYT,* 12/26/56, p. 1+.

147 *"to get needed flexibility":* ACW, Box 8, 12/26/58.

147 *"high quality of these refugees":* DDEL, Eisenhower Papers as President, Legislative Meeting Series, Box 2, 1/1/57.

147 *"In these past four years":* RNL, DDS Special File, PPS 324 (1), 12/28/56.

13. "Once an Oppressed People Rise"

PAGE

148 *"the greatest cross":* E. Frederic Morrow, *Black Man in the White House,* pp. 8, 9, 215.

148 *"sly, morally sinuous":* Joseph Alsop, *I've Seen the Best of It,* p. 357.

148 *"He felt that I must":* Morrow, *Black Man in the White House,* p. 174.

149 *saw him as an ally:* Andrew Young, interview by author, October 15, 2010; Morrow, *Black Man in the White House,* p. 83.

149 *"the coming continent":* DDEL, John Foster Dulles Papers, Telephone Call Series, 1/8/57.

149 *"Fred, how would you":* DDEL, E. Frederic Morrow Papers, 2/14/57.

149 *"Mrs. Nixon patted babies":* Morrow, *Black Man in the White House,* p. 92.

149 *"lacked warmth, soul, sincerity":* Pittsburgh Courier, 5/25/57, p. B1.

150 *"American Show Boy":* Chicago Defender, 3/4/57, p. 3.

150 *"two great Americans met":* Atlanta Daily World, 3/13/57, p. 6.

150 *urged Nixon to speak out:* Amsterdam News, 3/9/57, p. 1+.

150 *"He has a genius"*: Martin Luther King Jr. Papers, Volume 4, 9/9/58, letter to Mazo, pp. 481–83.

150 *"It will be a pleasure"*: RNL, Series 320, Box 411, 5/23/57.

150 *"I am looking forward"*: RNL, Series 320, Box 411, 5/28/57.

150 *"Ann, you would feel differently"*: Ann Whitman, ELOH.

151 *"I think that no other"*: Hazlett, *Ike's Letters to a Friend*, 7/22/57, p. 186.

151 *the Court should have started*: ACW, Box 8, 8/14/56.

151 *"shamefacedly admitted"*: Ibid., 1/3/57.

151 *"Once an oppressed people rise"*: RNL, Series 320, Box 411, Martin Luther King, handwritten notes on meeting.

151 *"a step in that direction"*: Chicago Defender, 6/18/57, p. 6.

152 *"the most dangerous man in America"*: Martin Luther King Jr. Papers, Volume 4, 9/9/58, letter to Mazo, pp. 481–83.

152 *"a vote against the right to vote"*: NYT, 8/6/57, p. 1+.

152 *conservative Republicans complained*: WP&TH, 8/2/57, p. A12.

153 *"the most distinguished member"*: WP&TH, 8/31/57, p. 1+.

153 *complex and ever-shifting*: For a larger picture, see Robert Caro's excellent *Master of the Senate*, pp. 853–935.

153 *"much better than no bill"*: RNL, Series 320, Box 411, King, 9/17/57.

153 *"I and many others"*: RNL, Series 320, Box 649, Robinson, 8/2/57.

153 *"I will long remember"*: RNL, Series 320, Box 411, King, 8/30/57.

154 *"I am sure you know"*: RNL, Series 320, Box 411, King, 9/17/57.

154 *About a year later*: Rocco Siciliano, *Walking on Sand*, 162–64.

154 *"an empty still life"*: Taylor Branch, *Parting the Waters*, p. 236.

154 *"epochal nature"*: Rocco Siciliano, interview by author, January 10, 2009; Siciliano, *Walking on Sand*, p. 168.

155 *political liquidation of Harold Stassen*: DDEL, John Foster Dulles Papers, Subject Files, 5/15/57.

155 *considering his unique job*: DDEL, John Foster Dulles Papers, Box 6, Nixon-2; 8/24/57.

155 *"My basic thought is"*: Ibid., 9/2/57.

155 *near the Naval War College*: John W. Kennedy, interview by author, July 25, 2010.

155 *"the customs and fears"*: Hazlett, *Ike's Letters to a Friend*, pp. 183, 186–187.

156 *"Every instance of prejudice"*: DDEL, Administration Series, Box No. 28, Report to the President, 4/5/57.

156 *"In my career I learned"*: Brownell, *Advising Ike*, p. 211.

156 *rumors that he was unhappy*: WP&TH, 8/5/57, p. A2.

156 *"Nixon had a full realization"*: Siciliano, interview by author, January 10, 2009.

14. Worn Down

PAGE

157 *"another military development"*: WP&TH, 11/3/54, p. 15.

157 *"It is a grim business"*: WP&TH, 10/10/57, p. A15.

157 *"Any of you fellows"*: Ewald, *Eisenhower the President*, pp. 285, 287–88.

158 *"the serving of science"*: NYT, 10/20/57, p. E1.

158 *"it does definitely prove"*: Press conference; 10/9/57, transcript: http://www.presidency.ucsb.edu/ws/index.php?pid=10924#axzz1nKIgtLav.

158 *"ceases to be great"*: Nixon, *RN*, p. 429; see also: Robert H. Ferrell, ed., *Inside the Nixon Administration*, p. 38.

158 *"We could make no greater mistake"*: NYT, 10/17/57, p. 32.

158 *"there was practically nothing done"*: DDEL, John Foster Dulles Papers, Subject Series, Nixon, Box 6, 10/9/57.

159 *"two so-called intelligence people"*: FRUS, 1955–57, Volume 11, 10/10/57, p. 760.

160 *"we should answer inquiries"*: Ibid., p. 761; *NYT,* 10/1/57, p. E3.

160 *"I have a feeling"*: LOC, Alsop Papers, Box 21, 10/15/57.

160 *"was frankly facing"*: *NYT,* 10/30/57, p. 9.

160 *"what is or will be"*: *NYT,* 10/17/57, p. 32.

160 *"Control of space"*: Robert Divine, *The Sputnik Challenge,* p. 79.

160 phrases like *"nuclear blackmail"*: DDEL, Vincent Ford Papers, unpublished manuscript, "Twenty-Four Minutes to Checkmate," 1953–1957.

160 *"Thank God Mr. Nixon"*: Ibid.; see also Neil Sheehan's excellent, carefully researched *A Fiery Peace in a Cold War.*

161 *Jupiter, Thor, and Atlas*: FRUS, 1955–57, Volume 19, pp. 401–3, 1/11/57.

161 *"Well, I will tell you"*: Press conference, 10/30/57; transcript: http://www.presidency .ucsb.edu/ws/index.php?pid=10943#axzz1nKIgtLav.

162 *"screaming about it too"*: DDEL, John Foster Dulles Papers, Telephone Call Series, Box 7, 12/6/57.

162 *"great Department of Space"*: DDEL, Legislative Leadership Meeting, Supplementary Notes, 2/4/58.

162 *"I'd rather have a good Redstone"*: Ibid.

163 *"I tell you one thing"*: LOC, Joseph and Stewart Alsop Papers, Box 47, undated 1958.

164 *"When I wake up in the morning"*: DDE, Box 28, Correspondence, 11/8/57.

15. Should He Resign?

PAGE

165 *pulled out a handkerchief*: *WP&TH,* 11/26/57, p. 1+.

165 *"seemed literally to run off"*: Dwight D. Eisenhower, *Waging Peace,* p. 227.

166 *"These . . . darned . . . glasses"*: Gray, interview by author, July 23, 2010; Gray, *Eighteen Acres Under Glass,* pp. 197–200.

166 *"The President has gone back"*: Adams, *Firsthand Report,* p. 195.

166 *"get you to bed"*: Dwight D. Eisenhower, *Waging Peace,* pp. 227–28.

167 *"What are you doing up, Ike?"*: John S. D. Eisenhower, *Strictly Personal,* p. 196.

167 *"I am perfectly all right!"*: Adams, *Firsthand Report,* p. 196.

167 *"If I cannot attend"*: John S. D. Eisenhower, *Strictly Personal,* p. 197; Adams, *Firsthand Report,* p. 196.

167 *"This is a terribly, terribly"*: Nixon, *Six Crises,* pp. 170–71.

168 *"This really is too much"*: Ibid., pp. 172–73.

168 *Ike had suffered a stroke*: *NYT,* 11/27/57, p. 1+.

168 *"beating the bedclothes with his fists"*: John S. D. Eisenhower, *Strictly Personal,* p. 196.

168 *"This third sickness"*: *The Reporter,* 12/12/57, p. 2.

168 *"we were all just holding fire, waiting"*: Siciliano, interview by author, January 10, 2009.

168 *"What is in the offing"*: BG, 12/4/57, p. 22.

169 *"The issue"*: *NYT,* 11/29/57, p. 29.

169 *"We are in a race"*: *NYT,* 12/8/57, p. E10.

169 *"who has been maturing successfully"*: *WP&TH,* 11/28, p. A21. Similarly, Richard Rovere, in *The New Yorker,* wrote, "power vacuums are always filled in ways that are strange to tradition . . . [Nixon] will fill part of it, as he already has, and there is every reason to believe that he will do it with éclat and intelligence and a sense of responsibility." "Letter from Washington," *TNY,* 12/7/57, p. 152+.

169 *"No President since Washington"*: NYHT, 11/27/57, p. 15.

169 *On the Wednesday before Thanksgiving*: ACW, Box 9, President's Illness, 11/27/57; Second-term Chronology, searchable by date: http://www.eisenhowermemorial.org/presidential-papers/second-term/chronology/index.htm.

169 *"Slight difficulty on long words"*: NYT, 11/28/57, p. 34.

170 The New Republic *thought*: "Responsible Rule and the President," TNR, 12/16/57, p. 5.

170 *"There is actually, I would say"*: ACW, Box 9, President's Illness, 11/27/55; NYT, 11/28/57, p. 35.

171 *He had heard the president say "window"*: Nixon/Gannon interviews, Day 5, Tape 1.

171 *"he could not go to NATO"*: DDEL, John Foster Dulles Papers, Telephone Call Series, 11/30/57.

171 *"'55—had to prove self with Cabinet"*: RNL, PPS 325, Box 8, Folder 1, undated 1957, journal notes.

171 *"even looks different"*: NYT, 11/28/57, p. 1+.

172 *"a complete phony"*: Ann Whitman, ELOH.

172 *make it a little more "punchy"*: DDEL, John Foster Dulles Papers, Telephone Call Series, 11/29/57.

172 *"his big problem was whether to resign or not"*: Roberts, COHP.

173 *"would be able to exercise judgment or control"*: DDEL, John Foster Dulles Papers, White House Memoranda Series, Box 6, 12/1/57.

173 *"but this was a concern that I had"*: Lucius Clay, COHP.

173 *"reproduction of the Wilson problem"*: DDEL, John Foster Dulles Papers, White House Memoranda Series, Box 6, 12/1/57.

173 *The upsetting commentary*: NYT, 12/1/57, p. 229, p. 236.

174 *Dulles had asked Stevenson*: DDEL, John Foster Dulles Papers, Telephone Call Series, 10/28/57.

174 *"expressed enthusiasm"*: DDEL, John Foster Dulles Papers, Subject Files, Box 6, Nixon (2), 10/30/57.

174 *over-fondness for "phrase-making"*: HSTL, Summaries of Meetings Between Milton Katz and President Eisenhower, Milton Katz Papers, memo of conversation, 1/21/60.

174 *role of "consultant"*: NYT, 11/13/57, p. 1+; NYT, 11/19/57, p. 1+.

174 *the vice president would probably attend*: DDEL, John Foster Dulles Papers, Telephone Call Series, 11/26/57; John Foster Dulles Papers, Conversations and Memoranda, 12/1/57; NYT, 11/27/57, p. 1+.

174 *"I don't know whether"*: NYT, 12/4/57, p. 1+.

174 *"unless there were compelling"*: DDEL, Name Series, Box 32, Adlai Stevenson, 12/3/57.

175 *"What the hell does that mean?"*: DDE, Box 29, Telephone Calls; RNL, PPS 325, Box 8, Folder 1, 12/3/57.

175 *"precise clinical data alone"*: RNL, Series 320, Albert Hutschnecker, Box 364, 11/28/57.

175 *continue in office or "abdicate"*: DDEL, John Foster Dulles Papers, Box 6, White House Memoranda, 12/2/57.

175 *"very hard and tough thinking"*: RNL, PPS 325, Box 8, Folder 1, Nixon memo, 12/3/57.

175 *"This was the only point in the conversation"*: Ibid.

176 *the president would not let him go*: ACW, Box 9, President's Illness, 12/3/57.

176 *Rogers . . . also sensed*: DDEL, William P. Rogers Papers, Box 50, memo after stroke, 12/3/57.

176 *"The earliest symptoms"*: DDE, Diary Series, Dictation, Box 29, 12/4/57.

176 *if not, he would resign*: Dwight D. Eisenhower, Waging Peace, p. 230.

176 *onlookers called out "Good luck":* NYT, 12/14/57, p. 1+.
176 *panic in the press corps:* Spivak, interview by author, May 19, 2011.
177 *Mrs. Eisenhower never took her eyes off her husband:* NYT, 1/10/58, p. 8.
177 *"When it is remembered":* State of the Union speech, 1/9/58; transcript: http://www
.presidency.ucsb.edu/ws/index.php?pid=11162#axzz1nKIgtLav.
177 *"May I say once again how grateful":* RNL, PPS 324, 1/7/58.
177 *"I feel very well indeed":* Press conference, 1/15/58; transcript: http://www.presidency
.ucsb.edu/ws/index.php?pid=11063#axzz1nKIgtLav.
177 *"for a period of some weeks and months":* Bryce Harlow, COHP.
177 *"After that stroke":* Robert D. Novak, interview by author, October 17, 2008.

16. Dirty Work

179 *"The existence of this agreement":* EP, "Disability of President Memo," Volume 19, Part
4, Chapter 8, p. 711+, 2/5/58.
179 *"No, this isn't a pact":* Press conference, 3/5/58; transcript: http://www.presidency.ucsb
.edu/ws/index.php?pid=11315#axzz1nKIgtLav.
179 *the case of Governor Henry Horner:* DDEL, William P. Rogers Papers, Box 51, undated
memoranda, early 1958.
180 *"realization by the Framers":* LOC, Felix Frankfurter Papers, Box 97, 2/19/58.
180 *"uncertainty as to whether the office":* Ibid., 2/21/58.
180 *"Once you convert the court":* DDEL, William P. Rogers Papers, Box 51, undated Malcolm Wilkey memo, early 1958.
181 *a design that would have worked:* On October 12, 1961, in a conversation with CBS's
Walter Cronkite, Eisenhower said, "Now, I made up my mind the thing to do was to
make [Nixon] the judge. I trusted him and I knew that the people around him would
be also of a like mind. . . . There was no quarrel between him and me. So I just told
him he would be the man to determine when I was unable to do the job, and I'd be the
man to say when I was able to take it back."
182 *"I think there is a lot of darn good men":* Press conference, 4/30/58, transcript: http://
www.presidency.ucsb.edu/ws/index.php?pid=11365#axzz1nKIgtLav.
182 *"proper and only position":* NYT, 5/4/58, p. 30.
182 *"Those who seek the Presidency":* NYT, 5/6/58, p. 1+.
182 *a trip that ended abruptly in Caracas:* Hughes, interview by author, October 5, 2010;
Nixon, RN, pp. 234, 241; Mazo, Richard Nixon, p. 213; Nixon/Gannon interviews,
Day 9, Tape 3.
183 *"a roaring conflagration":* DDEL, Humphreys Papers, Box 7, Richard Nixon, 5/16/58.
183 *"You cannot allow it to appear":* DDE, Box 35, Staff Notes, 7/15/58; ACW, Box 10,
7/15/58; Bernard Shanley, COHP; Nixon, RN, p. 195; NYT, 7/16/58, p. 1+.
183 *the Communist bloc wouldn't drop atomic bombs:* DDE, Box 35, Staff Notes (2), 8/14/58.
184 *"plush Boston hotel":* WP&TH, 6/11/58, p. A1.
184 *unreported cash payments:* Arthur Schlesinger Jr., Robert Kennedy and His Times, p. 878.
184 *"I need him":* Press conference, 6/18/58; transcript: http://www.presidency.ucsb.edu/ws/
index.php?pid=11098#axzz1nKIgtLav.
185 *"I would be less than candid":* ACW, Dictated Memo, Box 10, 7/15/58.
185 *he called Foster Dulles:* DDEL, John Foster Dulles Papers, Telephone Call Series,
7/15/58.
186 *"Every vacation we had planned":* Nixon, RN, p. 195.
186 *"He hasn't told me to tell you this":* Ibid., p. 196.

186 *"I don't want to imply"*: Henry D. Spalding, *The Nixon Nobody Knows*, p. 338.
186 *"I'm going to play some golf this afternoon"*: Nixon, *RN*, p. 196.
187 *that he did not know who could replace him*: DDEL, Administration, Box 28, RMN, 1958–61, Ann Whitman's diary, written 9/1/58.
187 *"Eisenhower's face flushed"*: Ibid.
187 *"My mother would remember"*: Julie Nixon Eisenhower, *Pat Nixon*, p. 179.
187 *ADAMS STILL IN JOB*: *WP&TH*, 8/30/58, p. A2.
187 *"how this is striking people"*: Meade Alcorn, COHP.
188 *jeopardizing those with a political future*: ACW, Box 10, 9/4/58.
188 *" 'What's the President think?' "*: Alcorn, COHP.
188 *say that Adams was treated too harshly*: WH Tapes, 3/13/72, 3:48 P.M.–6:03 P.M.
188 *who told Ehrlichman*: H. R. Haldeman, *The Haldeman Diaries*, pp. 665–66.
188 *" 'I was just Ike's prat-boy' "*: Nixon/Gannon interviews, Day 3, Tape 4; Nixon, *RN*, p. 198.

17. Unstoppable

189 *"that ugly man"*: Mazo, *Richard Nixon*, p. 8.
190 *"make him a leader of men"*: RNL, "Cushman Files," PPS 325, Box 10, 1958–July 1959.
190 *"Don't take anyone"*: DDEL, John Foster Dulles Papers, Telephone Call Series, 5/19/55.
190 *"He loved you"*: RNL, John Foster Dulles Papers, Series 320, Box 229, handwritten note, 6/2/59.
190 *"telling of his great admiration etc"*: DDEL, John Foster Dulles Papers, Box 6 (Nixon), memorandum of telephone call from Herbert Hoover Jr., 4/29/59.
190 *"I don't know anybody"*: Mazo, *Richard Nixon*, p. 258.
190 *"after looking everybody over"*: DDEL, John Foster Dulles Papers, Box 6 (Nixon), memorandum of telephone call from Hoover, 5/4/59.
190 *"We should be careful to understand"*: Press conference, 7/22/59; transcript: http://www.presidency.ucsb.edu/ws/index.php?pid=11453#axzz1nKIgtLav.
191 *"we will make some yardage"*: *NYT*, 7/24/59, p. 1.
191 *"got so ridiculous"*: RNL, Pre-Presidential Papers, "Cushman Files," 8/19/59.
191 *"I felt like a fighter"*: *The Observer* (London), 11/24/68, p. 21.
191 *"came back terribly upset"*: Michael Beschloss, *Mayday*, p. 183.
192 *it was "a dangerous thing"*: RNL, Woods to Nixon, PPS 325, Box 12, 8/15/59.
192 *"it just didn't sound like Nelson at all"*: ACW, Box 11, 8/14/59.
192 *"My concern about the matter"*: RNL, Eisenhower Special Files, 324 (2), 8/15/59.
193 *"It is terrible"*: ACW, Box 10, 6/11/59.
193 *Khrushchev's designated escort*: Henry Cabot Lodge, *The Storm Has Many Eyes*, p. 178.
193 *"Delicate question"*: ACW, Box 11, 9/16/59.
193 *"he was irritated at the way people raised this question"*: RNL, PPS 325, Box 12, note to Rose Mary Woods, 3/26/59.
193 *"I wouldn't have him on the place"*: Bradlee, *Conversations With Kennedy*, 225.
194 *"fabulous and fantastic"*: *NYT*, 12/24/59, p. 1+.
194 *"the certain nominee"*: *NYT*, 12/27/59, p. E3.
194 *Nixon had lunch*: DDEL, C. D. Jackson Papers, Box 69, Log, 1/11/60.
195 *I would just say*: Press conference, 1/13/60; transcript: http://www.presidency.ucsb.edu/ws/index.php?pid=12131#axzz1nyFR qlfb.
195 *"we're all human"*: Press conference, 2/3/60, transcript: http://www.presidency.ucsb.edu/ws/index.php?pid=11884#axzz1nKIgtLav.

195 *"Would it get some Republican interest":* EP, Volume 20, Part 9, Chapter 22, p. 1942, 5/9/60.

196 *"Was there any doubt":* Press conference, 3/16/60; transcript: http://www.presidency .ucsb.edu/ws/index.php?pid=12157#axzz1nKIgtLav.

196 *"Inherent in his comments":* Dwight D. Eisenhower, *Waging Peace,* p. 592.

196 *"fine hand of Emmet":* "A Fine Hand," *Time,* 6/20/60.

196 *"The path of a great leadership":* WP&TH, 6/9/60, p. A1+; NYT, 6/9/60, p. 16.

196 *saw Eisenhower turn bright red:* Frank van der Linden, letter to author, August 10, 2010.

196 *"dangerously vulnerable to Soviet attack":* CT, 6/9/60, p. 1+.

197 *When Kissinger expressed:* NYT, 8/1/57, p. 1+; Mike Wallace interview, 7/13/58, http:// www.hrc.utexas.edu/multimedia/video/2008/wallace/kissinger_henry.html; NYT, 2/1/59, p. 2.

197 *"The other one is not easy":* DDE, Box 50, 6/11/60.

197 *complained about him to the president:* DDEL, John Foster Dulles Papers, Subject Files, Box 7, 7/13/55, 7/30/55, 8/5/55.

197 *"was too used to borrowing brains":* DDE, Box 9, 10/10/55.

197 *"off again, on again":* ACW, Box 11, 6/9/60; DDE, Box 50, Telephone Calls, 6/11/60.

197 *"howled like a stuck pig":* Bassett correspondence, 5/16/54.

198 *"haunting doubts":* WP&TH, p. A15.

198 *"There is a new Nixon":* Meg Greenfield, "The Prose of Richard M. Nixon," *The Reporter,* 9/29/60, p. 15.

198 *"Do you wish you could call back":* HI, *Open End,* sound recording of television program, 5/15/60.

198 *"When people say there is a new Nixon":* CBS, Cronkite interview, 9/13/60.

199 *"I would say that these strikes":* Open End audio, 5/15/60.

199 *"The Governor has suggested":* NYT, 6/10/60, p. 14.

200 *"We all thought it was excellent":* RNL, Eisenhower Special Files, PPS 324 (2), 6/12/60.

200 *a surprise party:* Bassett correspondence, 6/24/60.

200 *Nixon had known John F. Kennedy:* RNL, PPS 325, Box 3, Folder 3, 6/16/53.

200 *he had sponsored:* RNL, PPS 320, JFK to RN, 2/4/54; Jacqueline Bouvier Kennedy to RN, 12/5/54.

200 *"I don't think there is anyone":* RNL, Series 320, Box 405, John F. Kennedy, 12/5/54.

200 *would exchange greetings:* Hughes, interview by author, October 5, 2010; Dorothy Cox Donnelly, interview by author, May 2, 2011; Christopher Matthews, *Kennedy and Nixon,* 17; Cabell Phillips, "How to Be a Presidential Candidate," NYTM, 7/13/58, p. 11.

200 *"the sort of person I like":* John P. Mallan, "Massachusetts, Liberal and Corrupt," TNR, 10/14/52, p. 10.

200 *"might make a pretty good President":* HSTL, Summaries of Meetings Between Milton Katz and President Eisenhower, Milton Katz Papers, memo of conversation, 1/21/60.

201 *"a sort of an idiot":* Ibid.

201 *civil rights planks:* For a detailed look at these maneuverings, see Robert Caro's *The Passage of Power,* the fourth book in his biography of Lyndon Johnson, especially pages 75–143.

201 *turned down a request:* WP&TH, 7/18/60, p. A2; NYT, 7/19/60, p. 1+.

201 *the illusion of party unity:* NYT, 7/24/60, p. 1.

201 *When Nixon telephoned:* DDE, Box 51, Telephone Calls, 7/23/60,

201 *"This is a disaster!":* Melvin Laird, interview by author, October 4, 2009.

202 *He stood in an open limousine:* NYT, 7/27/60, p. 1+, p. 59.
202 *many thought he'd done it maliciously:* LWH, p. 144.
202 *"the look of a playboy":* "GOP on TV," *The Nation,* 8/6/60, p. 67.
202 *"I have never had a manager":* LWH, p. 144.
202 *"Pat and I were happier":* Nixon, *RN,* p. 40.
203 *"King was greatly impressed":* RNL, Series 320, Box 298, Graham, 8/23/60.

18. "If You Give Me a Week, I Might Think of One"

204 *"I've got a lot of other responsibilities":* Press conference, 8/10/60; transcript: http://www
     .presidency.ucsb.edu/ws/index.php?pid=11902#axzz1nKIgtLav.
204 *"The first reaction":* Ewald, interviews by author, October 8, 2008, December 9, 2008.
204 *more severe than a mere bump:* Hughes, interview by author, October 5, 2010.
205 *"If you give me a week":* Press conference, 8/24/60; transcript: http://www.presidency
     .ucsb.edu/ws/index.php?pid=11915#axzz1nKIgtLav.
205 *"I get a picture":* USN&WR, 5/16/60, p. 98+; NYT, 8/25/60, p. 22.
206 *"immediately knew":* Nixon, *RN,* 219.
206 *"I wish to hell I'd never said it":* Benedict, interview by author, January 31, 2009.
206 *"to avoid a Hagerty":* David Eisenhower, interview by author, September 29, 2010.
206 *"provoked a riot":* WP&TH, 8/25/60, p. 1+.
206 *may have been "facetious":* Richard Whalen, *Catch the Falling Flag,* p. 13.
206 *"had struck a nerve":* Ewald, interviews by author, September 11, 2008, October 8,
     2008, December 9, 2008; also: Ewald, *Eisenhower the President.*
207 *"actually the President stated the case exactly":* NYT, 8/26/60, p. 1+; NYT, 8/26/60, p. 6;
     LAT, 8/26/60, p. 2.
208 *"the majordomo":* Hugh Downs, E-mail to author, August 17, 2011.
208 *"Just who gains from all this":* LAT, 8/28/60, p. B1.
208 *"cheered up":* Bassett, correspondence, 9/4/60.
208 *"Later, the President":* ACW, Box 11, 8/30/60.
209 *"the finest team":* NYT, 9/13/60, p. 1+.
209 *"so damned human looking":* Bassett correspondence, 9/18/60.
209 *"Dick Nixon has the broadest":* NYT, 9/30/60, p. 10.
209 *"Well, I would suggest Mr. Vanocur":* See debate transcript, 9/26/60, http://www
     .debates.org/index.php?page=september-26-1960-debate-transcript.
209 *"Your chap's beat":* Alistair Horne, *Harold Macmillan, Volume II: 1957–1986,* p. 280.
210 *"drive the small percentage of Catholic voters":* RNL, Series 320, Henry & Clare Boothe
     Luce, undated letter to Clare during Nixon's stay at Walter Reed Hospital, Box 464.
210 *"throughout Protestantism":* RNL, Series 320, Billy Graham, Box 298, 8/22/60.
210 *"when the chips are down":* RNL, Series 320, Box 298, Graham, see for example letters
     sent 10/21/55, 6/4/56, 12/2/57.
210 *"solidifying the Protestant vote":* RNL, Series 320, Box 298, Graham, 6/21/60.
210 *"to align American foreign policy with the Vatican's":* NYT, 9/8/60, p. 1+; WP&TH,
     9/8/60, p.1+.
210 *"Mr. Nixon and I agreed":* Press conference, 9/7/60; transcript: http://www.presidency
     .ucsb.edu/ws/index.php?pid=11933#axzz1nKIgtLav.
211 *"taken the job I wanted him to":* ACW, Box 11, 10/4/60.
211 *"That goddamned old fool":* LWH, p. 158.

211 *"What the hell's the matter with that guy?":* LWH, p. 159; Ewald, *Eisenhower the President,* pp. 311–12; WH chronology, 10/31/60.

211 *"Well I carried out exactly":* Today, interview with Eisenhower, October 27, 1965.

212 *"almost in tears":* Nixon, *RN,* p. 222.

212 *Eisenhower himself seemed to acknowledge:* Richard L. Tobin, "Dwight D. Eisenhower: What I Have Learned," *Saturday Review,* 9/10/66, pp. 29–33; Nixon/Gannon interviews, Tape 3, Day 4; Ted Lewis column, *New York Daily News,* 9/9/66.

212 *"a road paved with glittery promises":* NYT, 9/20/60, p. 30; WP&TH, 11/2/60, p. 1+.

212 *"I believe completely":* RNL, Series 320, Box 311, Haldeman, 5/22/56, undated, probably May or June 1956.

213 *"We were in Iowa I think":* McPhee, interview by author, October 4, 2010.

213 *"Nixon began to kick the back of Hughes's seat":* Haldeman, *The Haldeman Diaries,* pp. 74–75.

213 *"We were all tired":* Hughes, interview by author, October 4, 2010.

213 *"Well, I don't know how":* LWH, p. 151.

213 *a Negro in the cabinet:* DDEL, Fred Seaton Papers, Box 9, 3/12/64 memorandum.

214 *"some hang-up occurred someplace":* Robert Finch, COHP.

214 *their first big social event:* "The Maturing Richard Nixon," *Look,* 9/3/57, p. 70.

214 *Frederic Morrow had joined the Nixon campaign:* E. Frederic Morrow, *Forty Years a Guinea Pig,* p. 206.

214 *"frequently counseled with Dr. King":* Michael G. Long ed., *First Class Citizenship,* Nixon letter to Robinson, pp. 114–15, 11/4/60.

215 *"I am not making myself a party":* DDE, Box 54, 11/5/60.

215 *"a heavy heart":* RNL, Series 320, Hutschnecker, Box 364, 2/10/61.

215 *"suffered a debilitating, painful and depressing rejection":* Arnold A. Hutschnecker, *The Drive for Power,* p. 54.

215 *"was astonished":* DDE, Diary Series, Box 53, 11/8/60; *NYT,* 11/7/60, p. 1+, p. 31; Ewald, *Eisenhower the President,* p. 312.

215 *"I was really mad":* The details of this episode went unreported until 1968, when Drew Pearson wrote about it: http://www.aladin0.wrlc.org/gsdl/cgi-bin/library?e=d-01000 -00—off-0pearson—00-1—0-10-0—0—0prompt-10—4——0-11—11-en-50—20 -home—00-3-1-00-0-0-11-0-0utfZz-8-00&a=d&cl=CL2.37&d=HASH016316f03c0 7bb5924afae82 The Pearson column prompted Hart to call Rose Mary Woods, who took notes: RNL, Donated Nixon Documents, campaign activities, 10/7/68.

216 *"C'mon, I'm going to show you guys":* Hughes, interview by author, October 4, 2010.

216 *"the next few hours":* The account of Nixon's trek was based on: Hughes, interview by author, October 4, 2010; also: Klein, *Making It Perfectly Clear,* pp. 51–52; RNL, Aitken Papers, Rose Mary Woods interview; *LAT,* 11/8/60, p. D1; *LAT,* 11/9/60, p. A1.

217 *"if the present trend continues":* WP&TH, 11/9/60, p. 1+.

217 *an emaciated look:* Bassett correspondence, 9/25/60.

217 *"if by some miracle":* DDE, Box 54, Telephone Calls, 11/9/60.

218 *he didn't want to create a "constitutional crisis":* CT, 11/16/60, p. 14; David Greenberg, *Slate,* 10/16/2000, www.slate.com/id/91350.

218 *"Well, this is the biggest defeat":* Slater, *The Ike I Knew,* p. 235.

218 *"more tired and discouraged":* RNL, Series 320, J. S. D. Eisenhower, Box 238, 6/14/62.

219 *"On the personal side":* RNL, Eisenhower Special Files, PPS 324 (2), 11/9/60.

219 *"just killed us in the South":* DDE, Staff Notes, December 1960, 12/28/60.

220 *"It seems to me fundamentally unjust":* NYT, 12/14/60, p. 24; *NYT,* 12/15/60, p. 30.

220 *"I always felt that Nixon lost a real opportunity"*: John F. Kennedy Presidential Library and Museum, Martin Luther King Jr., Oral History Interview, 3/9/64.

220 *"completely irrational"*: ACW, Box 11, 12/6/60.

221 *"such a hassle arose"*: RNL, PPS 320, Vice Presidential General Correspondence, Box 238, 1/11/61.

221 *"We won, but they stole it from us"*: Ewald, interviews by author, September 11, 2008, October 8, 2008, December 9, 2008.

19. The Good Life

PAGE

222 *Jacqueline Cochran and her husband:* Rich, *Jackie Cochran*, p. 21.

222 *his rank as a five-star general:* David Eisenhower, *Going Home to Glory*, p. 15.

223 *where he now socialized:* Jack Muse, interview by author, November 4, 2011.

223 *"I am sorry that"*: RNL, Eisenhower Special Files, PPS 324 (2), 1/6/61.

223 *"every public man should write a book"*: Nixon, *Six Crises*, p. xi.

224 *"Honest to Pete, I'm no gourmet"*: "The Private Life of Pat Nixon," *Look*, 7/27/54, p. 23.

224 *"Come show me how you work this goddamned thing!"*: Stephen Ambrose, *Eisenhower: The President*, p. 617.

224 *"At the end of the last Cabinet meeting Friday"*: RNL, Eisenhower Special Files, PPS 324 (2), 1/15/61.

225 *"the sun will always shine on your life"*: RNL, Eisenhower Special Files, PPS 324 (1), 1/15/61.

225 *"putting a period to our long"*: Ibid., 1/19/61.

225 *"If you come out this way"*: Ibid., 2/21/61.

226 *on the eleventh fairway:* CT, 3/5/61, p. 33.

226 *"must be pretty hectic"*: RNL, PPS 324 (2), 3/17/61.

226 *the Nixons looked at Hancock Park:* LAT, 3/3/61, p. B1.

226 *he was met by flashbulbs:* LAT, 3/15/61, p. B1.

226 *a movie called* PT-109: LAT, 3/9/61, p. B11.

226 *"I preferred to be alone"*: Nixon, *RN*, pp. 231–32.

226 *"My God, what do you do out here?"*: Robert D. Novak, *The Agony of the G.O.P.*, p. 50.

226 *with neighbors like Alfred Hitchcock:* WP&TH, 11/7/61, p. A1+.

226 *"He is bored out of his mind"*: Hess, interview by author, September 18, 2008.

227 *"There is one thing"*: RNL, Eisenhower Special Files, PPS 324 (1), 4/25/61.

227 *"Every time I see something"*: Hess, interview by author, September 18, 2008.

228 *"Let's say he got ten thousand dollars"*: Ibid.

228 *"no fair-minded person"*: RNL, Series 320, Box 320, Bryce Harlow, 4/11/61.

228 *"very dreary account"*: DDEL, Augusta–Walter Reed Series, Box 1, Cuba (2) April–June 1962, 6/5/61.

228 *"It is essential that you act"*: BG, 6/27/61, p. 1+.

229 *"I guess it's a hard one to miss"*: WSJ, 5/10/61, p. 14.

229 *"likeliest immediate turn of fate"*: LAT, 5/25/61, p. B4.

229 *"It is a very difficult decision"*: RNL, Eisenhower Special Files, PPS 324 (1), 7/13/61.

229 *"I would be virtually finished"*: Ibid., 7/25/61; Nixon, *RN*, p. 238; Julie Nixon Eisenhower, *Pat Nixon*, p. 207.

230 *"Over the years I have wrestled"*: RNL, Eisenhower Special Files, PPS 324 (1), 8/8/61.

230 *"I can find no alternative"*: Ibid., 9/11/61.

231 *"If you ever run for office again"*: Fawn Brodie, *Richard Nixon*, p. 451 (source: Adela Rogers St. Johns letter to Brodie).

20. The Obituary Writers

PAGE

232 *carrying framed photographs to his car:* Richard (Sandy) Quinn, interview by author, October 26, 2010.

232 *"are now nothing but rubble":* RNL, Series 320, letter to Fr. J. F. Cronin, Box 192, 11/11/61; Stephen Hess and David Broder, *The Republican Establishment,* p. 141; *CT,* 11/7/61, p. 1+; *WP&TH,* 11/7/61, p. 1+; *LAT* 11/7/61, p. 1+.

233 *Knight accused Nixon: LAT,* 9/30/61, p. 1.

233 *"I know this is a difficult blow": NYT,* 1/17/62, p. 1+.

233 *the "kingmakers" had made sure:* Marquis Childs, *WP&TH,* 4/2/62, p. 20.

233 *"the repetition of things":* Mark Harris, *Mark the Glove Boy,* p. 81.

233 *his heart was never in it:* Quinn, interview by author, October 26, 2010.

234 *whose supporters included: WP&TH,* 11/7/61, p. A4.

234 *"hear them crackling there in the head":* Nixon/Gannon interviews, Day 9, Tape 1.

234 *"I think it would be a great tragedy":* Richard Nixon at the Commonwealth Club ("An Evening with Richard Nixon"), 6/11/59; audio at the Hoover Institution Library.

234 *"the kitchen is an electronic marvel":* RNL, Eisenhower Special Files, PPS 324 (2), 1/4/62.

234 *This one, at 410 Martin Lane:* Parmet, *Richard Nixon and His America,* p. 421; visit by author.

235 *"I had no sooner entered":* Harris, *Mark the Glove Boy,* p. 37.

235 *"so much the better":* RNL, Eisenhower Special Files, PPS 324, 2/5/62.

235 *he told Nixon how impressed he was:* Ibid., 2/14/62.

235 *"do call or drop me a line":* RNL, Eisenhower Special Files, PPS 324 (2), 2/20/62.

235 *"This was my first effort in the literary field":* DDEL, Post-Presidential Principal File, 1961–62, 2/20/62.

236 *"I thought it was time to take on the lunatic fringe":* RNL, Eisenhower Special Files, PPS 324, 3/5/62.

236 *"in large measure":* Ibid., 3/6/62.

236 *to get out of it "forthwith": LAT,* 3/4/62, p. F1.

236 *"I interviewed him on all the five crises":* Alvin Moscow, interview by author, September 30, 2009.

236 *working in the desert town of Apple Valley:* Hughes, interview by author, October 4, 2010.

236 *"We would go line by line":* Moscow, interview by author, September 30, 2009.

237 *"had a quality of reserve":* Nixon, *Six Crises,* p. 76.

237 *"Tell me about Eisenhower":* Moscow, interview by author, September 30, 2009; Nixon, *Six Crises,* pp. 160–61.

237 *The book sold more than:* Daniel Frick, *Reinventing Richard Nixon,* p. 18.

237 *"I do wish you and Pat":* DDEL, Post-Presidential Principal File, 1961–62, 5/2/62.

238 *Eisenhower campaigned alongside his former vice president: LAT,* 10/9/62, p. 1+; *CT,* 10/9/62, p. A2.

238 *"I read, with some surprise":* RNL, Series 320, Box 313, Leonard Hall, 11/20/61.

238 *"If I have any greater interest than politics":* Harris, *Mark the Glove Boy,* p. 84.

238 *"Dear Dick—I pray you'll win!":* RNL, Series 320, Paar, Box 575, undated note.

239 *"rambling elocution of a Bowery wino":* John Ehrlichman, *Witness to Power,* p. 37.

239 *"I got a copy of the book":* Moscow, interview by author, September 30, 2009.

239 *met outside by two old friends: LAT,* 5/3/63, p. 23.
239 *There were rumors:* Anthony Summers, *The Arrogance of Power,* p. 234.
239 *susceptible to rages:* Sears, interviews by author, August 27, 2010, August 11, 2011; Raymond K. Price, interviews by author, December 12, 2007, July 1, 2008, January 21, 2009, January 10, 2010, July 28, 2010.
239 *"There was a sadness":* Julie Nixon Eisenhower, *Pat Nixon,* p. 216.
239 *"He's too able a man":* DDEL, Post-Presidential Principal File, 1961–62, 11/62 undated; *BG,* 11/19/62, p. 5; David Eisenhower, *Going Home to Glory,* p. 100; RNL, Series 320, Box 320, Harlow, note from Rose Mary Woods, 1/2/63; *NYT,* 11/15/62, p. 34; *CT,* 11/14/62, p. 1+.
240 *turned on him: WP&TH,* 11/12/62, p. A23.
240 *"The fact is, of course":* Hughes, *The Ordeal of Power,* 173; *NYT,* 11/20/62, p. 25.
240 *he might have said Nixon wasn't ready: NYT,* 12/2/62, p. 4; *LAT,* 12/2/62, p. 1.

21. Easterners

241 *their "eyrie-like" home: LAT,* 11/15/62, p. L1.
241 *"recover his equilibrium":* RNL, Series 320, Box 320, Bryce Harlow letter to Rose Woods, 1/2/63.
242 *"Dick, are you really going to practice law?":* Thomas Evans, interviews by author, February 17, 2008, August 31, 2010; Elmer Holmes Bobst, *The Autobiography of a Pharmaceutical Pioneer,* pp. 269, 327.
242 *"Whether or not it was wise":* Dwight D. Eisenhower, "Danger from Within," *SEP,* 1/26/63, p. 15.
242 *he wrote to his new friend, Paul Keyes:* RNL, Series 320, Paar, Box 575, 3/11/63, and Keyes, Box 409, 2/25/63.
243 *he played the piano:* Some of this may be watched on YouTube: http://www.youtube .com/watch?v=x-ihI5_Vg6A.
243 *"If Jack and Lyndon could get together": NYT,* 4/21/62, p. 1+.
244 *"emerging as the clearest and most constructive voice": WP&TH,* 4/24/63, p. A17.
244 *"That is categorical": WP&TH,* 5/13/62, p. A16.
245 *"I say categorically":* Ibid.
245 *"It took her half a second": WP&TH,* 5/15/63, p. A19.
245 *Thomas Evans . . . has observed:* Evans, interviews by author, 2/17/08 and 8/31/10.
245 *"wish you every success":* RNL, Special Files, PPS 324 (2), 5/15/63.
245 *wanted him to run for president: LAT,* 5/22/63, p. 12.
245 *"We like the life there": WP&TH,* 5/15/63, p. A19.
245 *the children of John Birchers:* Nixon/Gannon interviews, Day 9, Tape 1.
246 *He said his formal goodbyes: LAT,* 6/8/63, p. A10; *NYT,* 6/8/63, p. 23.
246 *a chance to behave like a former vice president:* Maureen Drown Nunn, interview by author, October 28, 2010.
246 *"One of those frank and firm personalities":* Brian Crozier, *De Gaulle,* p. 560.
246 *"I am not a Johnny-come-lately in this field": LAT,* 6/24/63, p. 2.
247 *"He's told me he positively": LAT,* 8/16/63, p. 3.
247 *"Your visit . . . must have brought back":* RNL, Eisenhower Special Files, PPS 324 (2), 8/16/63.
247 *"The only difference I have found":* Ibid., 8/19/63.
248 *"It appears that the newspaper people":* Ibid., 9/25/63.
248 *"I don't think he wants it": CT,* 10/9/63, p. 1+.

248 *"Strangely enough that impression"*: WP&TH, 11/11/63, p. 1; NYT, 11/11/63, p. 12; NYT, 11/15/63, p. 50.

249 *"deadlocks are a thing of the past"*: NYT, 11/12/63, p. 28.

249 *"This whole thing stinks with murder"*: LOC, Clare Boothe Luce Papers, Box 218, 11/4/63.

249 *"I hesitate to bring a discordant note"*: Ibid., 12/12/63.

249 *"JFK has bungled it"*: Ibid., 11/12/63, 11/15/63.

249 *"I rather suspect the Diem affair"*: RNL, Eisenhower Special Files, PPS 324 (2), 11/11/63.

22. The "Moratorium"

PAGE

251 *"I'm not going to predict anything like that"*: NYT, 11/23/63, p. 12.

252 *"I'm the first person he's seen"*: Hess, interview by author, September 18, 2008; Nixon-Gannon interviews, Day 8, Tape 1.

252 *it was never rescheduled:* Novak, *The Agony of the G.O.P.,* p. 258.

253 *"While the hand of fate"*: RNL, PPS 320, Box 21, John Fitzgerald Kennedy, 1960–67.

253 *"Dear Mr. Vice President"*: Ibid.

254 *"the political consequences of what happened"*: Hess, interview by author, September 18, 2008.

254 *a Goldwater candidacy was a lot less appealing:* See Warren Weaver's analysis, NYT, 12/1/63, p. 247.

255 *"General Eisenhower continues to regard"*: NYT, 12/8/63, p. 1+.

255 *"He's an old friend"*: NYT, 12/9/63, p. 1+.

256 *"It was not a deep discussion"*: NYT, 12/10/63, p. 46; "Republicans: I Do," *Time,* 12/27/63.

256 *"radiant smile"*: Evans, interviews by author, February 17, 2008, August 31, 2010.

256 *he was already a candidate:* Stewart Alsop, "The Logical Candidate," SEP, 1/18/64, p. 15.

256 *Nixon didn't want to comment:* NYT, 12/12/63, p. 32.

257 *"Richard M. Nixon is a happy New Yorker"*: NYT, 12/29/63, p. 1+.

257 *"You have to bone up to keep alive"*: Robert J. Donovan, "Over-Nominated Under-Elected, Still a Promising Candidate," NYTM, 4/25/64, p. 14+.

257 *"The disease of the cities is a great tragedy"*: NYT, 12/29/63, p. 1+.

257 *He tried to blend in:* Various snapshots of the Nixon family's life in Manhattan appear in Jules Witcover, *The Resurrection of Richard Nixon,* p. 50; NYT, 12/29/63, p. 1+; Robert J. Donovan, "Over-Nominated Under-Elected, Still a Promising Candidate," NYTM, 4/25/64, p. 14+; WP&TH, 12/15/68, p. G1.

258 *invited Tricia and Julie:* NYT, 6/5/12, p. B10.

258 *Harry Truman and Dick Nixon shook hands:* NYT, 12/25/63, p. 23.

23. Private Agendas

PAGE

259 *the first choice of Republican voters:* LAT, 1/5/64, p. N2.

259 *"He's got everything but brains"*: Larson, *Eisenhower,* p. 6.

260 *neither Goldwater nor Rockefeller could win the nomination:* Novak, interview by author, October 17, 2008; WP&TH, 3/10/63, p. A17.

260 *When Nixon talked over the results:* DDEL, Fred Seaton Papers, Nixon–1964 Campaign–Memos of Conversations, Box 9, 3/12/64.

260 *"another gold star"*: Ibid.; *NYT*, 3/17/64, p. 11.

261 *"I know it would mean a great deal"*: RNL, Eisenhower Special Files, PPS 324 (2), 3/13/64.

261 *" 'If you're going out for a canter' "*: *CT*, 5/16/64, p. S3.

261 *ghostwrote the article:* Raymond K. Price, interviews by author, December 12, 2007, July 1, 2008, January 21, 2009, January 10, 2010, July 28, 2010.

261 *"the responsible, forward-looking"*: *NYHT*, 5/25/64, pp. 1, 4.

262 *"If former President Eisenhower can have his way"*: Ibid.

262 *"Let him try to fit that shoe"*: *NYHT*, 5/26/64, p. 1+.

262 *"You might kill a lot of monkeys"*: *NYT*, 5/27/64, p. 22.

262 *how the great press lords:* Novak, interview by author, October 17, 2008.

262 *"It's between you and Nixon"*: Stewart Alsop, "The Logical Candidate," *SEP*, 1/18/64, p. 15.

263 *"And that was a hard one to handle"*: William W. Scranton, interview by author, May 26, 2010.

263 *could barely reply:* Robert Novak, *The Agony of the G.O.P. 1964*, pp. 429–30; see also Rick Perlstein's splendid history of that period, *Before the Storm*, p. 277.

263 *a phantom write-in candidate:* DDE, Fred Seaton Papers, Box 9, Nixon–1964 campaign–Memos of conversations, 4/22/64.

263 *"I still feel Nixon"*: *CT*, 6/10/64, p. 2.

263 *"a political ghost"*: Rowland Evans and Robert Novak, "The Unmaking of a President," *Esquire*, 9/64, p. 91+.

263 *"My role will be one of neutrality"*: *NYT*, 6/13/64, p. 9; *CT*, 6/10/64, p. 1+.

263 *"things didn't develop"*: *WP&TH*, 6/12/64, p. A2; UPI dispatch, 7/13/64; *CT*, 7/16/64, p. 1+; Rick Perlstein, *Before the Storm*, p. 381.

263 *"Because Dick Nixon has never been really accepted"*: DDEL, Post-Presidential Principal File, Box 51, 6/30/64.

264 *"I felt almost physically sick"*: Nixon, *RN*, p. 260.

264 *"I have received several inquiries"*: *CT*, 8/8/64, p. A6; *NYT*, 8/10/64, p. 1+.

265 *"I was urging in effect that we understand"*: Ibid.

265 *"Unity means"*: Lyndon Baines Johnson Library and Museum, White House Central Files, Box 117, Folder PL6-3, Republican Party.

265 *"I didn't associate switchblade knives with Negroes"*: Ibid.

266 *As they left town:* WSJ, 8/13/64, p. 2; *NYT*, 8/13/54, p. 1+; *CT*, 8/13/64, p. 1+.

266 *more than a hundred speeches:* *WP&TH*, 9/21/64, p. A15.

266 *"cold-blooded analyst"*: DDE, Staff Notes, December 1960 (Harlow), 12/28/60.

266 *"a squalid and humiliating consequence"*: *WP&TH*, 11/5/64, p. A25.

267 *"a peevish post-election utterance"*: *CT*, 11/6/64, p. 1+; *NYT*, 11/6/64, p. 1+.

267 *Eisenhower came to New York:* *CT*, 12/10/64, p. 1+; *LAT*, 12/10/64, p. 1+; *NYT*, 12/10/64, p. 1+; *NYT*, 12/11/64, p. 1+.

267 *"It is remarkable"*: Murray Kempton, "The General Had to Dress for Dinner," *TNR*, 12/19/65, p. 6.

24. The Rehearsal

PAGE

268 *usual birthday greeting to Nixon:* RNL, Eisenhower Special Files, PPS 324 (2), 1/13/65.

268 *"the quality of an absolute tirelessness"*: *WP&TH*, 10/8/65, p. A20.

269 *"We revel in failure"*: *WP&TH*, 1/24/65, p. A2.

269 *"she died this year"*: DDEL, Fred Seaton Papers, Box 10 (Nixon–Political 1965), 1/23/65.

269 *Checkers at age twelve had died:* LAT, 9/9/64, p. 2; NYT, 12/31/64, p. 13.

269 *"I have some things going for me too":* DDEL, Fred Seaton Papers, Box 10, (Nixon–Political 1965), 1/23/65.

269 *"As you will recall":* RNL, Eisenhower Special Files, PPS 324 (2), 1/25/65.

270 *A visitor might notice:* Dwight Chapin, interview by author, April 3, 2008; Evans, interviews by author, February 17, 2008, August 31, 2010; Robert J. Donovan, "Over-Nominated Under-Elected, Still a Promising Candidate," NYTM, 4/25/65, p. 14; Jules Witcover, *The Resurrection of Richard Nixon,* p. 50.

270 *"Would anybody like a cigar?":* Evans, interviews by author, February 17, 2008, August 31, 2010.

270 *"To me it was like constantly":* Leonard Garment, interview by author, January 30, 2008.

271 *"when you go into a place":* DDEL, Augusta–Walter Reed Series, Box 3, memorandum of telephone conversation with LBJ, 3, 7/2/65.

271 *"I've done everything I can":* NYT, 8/20/65, p. 1+.

271 *"turned the corner":* CT, 9/13/65, p. 3.

272 *"You'll wonder what might have happened":* Donald Riegle, interview by author, October 14, 2010; Evans, interviews by author, February 17, 2008, August 31, 2010.

272 *"He took me into his bedroom":* Riegle, interview by author, October 14, 2010.

273 *"And I'd just write back":* Sears, interviews by author, August 27, 2010, August 10, 2011.

274 *Congress '66:* Evans, interviews by author, February 17, 2008, August 31, 2010; William Safire, *Before the Fall,* p. 22; WP&TH, 8/25/66, p. 1+; 9/18/66, p. 1+; NYT, 9/4/66, p. 139.

274 *"There's nobody in this government":* LBJ, WH Tapes, 10/3/66.

275 *"automatically preclude anything":* WP&TH, 10/5/66, p. A16.

275 *"I'll tell you, Mr. President":* LBJ, WH Tapes, 10/3/66.

275 *"This is silly":* WP&TH, 10/5/66, p. A16; LAT, 10/11/66, p. 1.

275 *"The morale of a nation":* LAT, 10/11/66, p. 1+.

276 *"the moment we are assured":* NYT, 9/29/66, p. 13.

276 *Nixon thought that he'd heard:* DDEL, Post-Presidential Principal File, 1961–62, 10/4/66.

276 *"The complaint is":* DDEL, Post-Presidential Principal File, 10/7/66.

276 *"could not agree more":* RNL, Eisenhower Special Files, PPS 324 (2), 10/13/66.

276 *"Nixon got out and said":* LBJ, WH Tapes, 10/3/66.

277 *The Nixons sent a greeting:* DDEL, Post-Presidential Principal File, 10/13/66, 10/19/66.

277 *"and peace is no nearer":* NYT, 11/4/66, p. 18.

277 *"a chronic campaigner":* Press conference, 11/4/66, transcript: http://www.presidency.ucsb.edu/ws/index.php?pid=27990#axzz1nKIgtLav.

278 *"one of the best informed, most capable":* NYT, 11/6/66, p. 68.

278 *"the best thing that has happened to Nixon":* BG, 11/8/66, p. 20.

278 *"broken the bipartisan front":* NYT, 11/5/66, p. 1+; 11/6/66, p. 68; CT, 11/5/66, p. 1+.

278 *Eisenhower didn't believe in "gradualism":* CT, 11/5/66, p. 1+.

278 *"I think I can understand how a man can be very tired":* NYT, 11/7/66, p. 33; WP&TH, 11/7/66. p. A1+.

278 *as a sort of uncle:* BG, 7/14/68, p. 26.

279 *"Once you've hit the big leagues":* Jules Witcover, "Nixon for President in '68?," SEP, 2/25/67, pp. 94, 97.

279 *"she simply no longer had the heart":* Julie Nixon Eisenhower, *Pat Nixon,* p. 230.

25. "That Job Is So Big, the Forces Are So Great"

PAGE

280 *"It's a brutal thing to fight"*: James Jackson Kilpatrick, "Crisis Seven," *National Review,* 11/14/67, pp. 1263–74.

280 *"he's a little bit thick"*: Garment, interview by author, January 30, 2008.

280 *his most formidable rival:* Stewart Alsop, "Richard Nixon and the Locked Door," *SEP,* 12/2/67, p. 18.

281 *"There is only one thing as bad"*: John C. Whitaker, "Nixon's Domestic Policy: Both Liberal and Bold in Retrospect," *Presidential Studies Quarterly,* vol. 26, no. 1 (winter 1996), p. 131.

281 *"make his own decision"*: *NYT,* 3/14/67, p. 26.

281 *Ike said that he had been misquoted:* DDEL, Augusta–Walter Reed Series, Box 2, Politics, 1967–68, 3/14/67.

281 *Eisenhower by contrast looked frail:* Chapin, interview by author, April 3, 2008.

281 *"He is thin and he doesn't seem"*: RNL, PPS 324 (3), Mamie Eisenhower letter to Pat Nixon, 4/5/67.

282 *"these incredible blue eyes"*: Chapin, interview by author, April 3, 2008.

282 *They covered a great many subjects:* RNL, Eisenhower Special Files, PPS 324 (3), 4/2/67.

282 *"Ron Reagan was the one"*: Ibid., 4/18/67.

282 *"As you know I've always liked and respected him"*: DDEL, Augusta–Walter Reed Series, Box 2, Politics, 1967–68, 7/21/67.

282 *"I've often expressed my admiration for Dick Nixon"*: Who in 1968?, 8/17/67, ABC News Presentation with Bill Lawrence.

282 *"I'm not so strong as I used to be"*: WP&TH, 10/8/67, p. E1.

283 *"When you come to see me"*: RNL, Eisenhower Special Files, PPS 324 (3), 8/24/67.

283 *"All wars are nasty"*: CT, 10/8/67, p. A1+.

283 *Mrs. Eisenhower whispered something in his ear:* LAT, 10/14/67, p. 1+.

284 *"He savors those memories"*: Hugh Sidey, "Philosophy of Office and the Ache of Ambition," *Life,* 11/3/67, p. 30+.

284 *"I quite agree with your statement"*: RNL, Eisenhower Special Files, PPS 324 (3), 11/15/67.

284 *"I think you can overdo it"*: NYT, 11/30/67, p. 21.

285 *"I do not question General Eisenhower's military judgment"*: CT, 11/30/67, p. 7.

26. David and Julie

PAGE

286 *They went out for ice cream:* Julie Nixon Eisenhower, *Pat Nixon,* p. 229.

286 *Opening Day game in 1959:* NYT, 4/10/59, p. 33, photo; WP&TH, 4/10/59, p. D5; WP&TH, 12/22/68, p. H3.

287 *they were together constantly:* Julie and David Eisenhower, interview by author, September 29, 2010; Julie Nixon Eisenhower, *Pat Nixon,* pp. 229–30; David Eisenhower, *Going Home to Glory,* pp. 213–14; WP&TH, 12/17/67, p. G1; 12/22/68, pp. H1, 3.

287 *"Hey, I'm actually going out"*: Fred Grandy, interview by author, December 9, 2011.

287 *"Of course the whole debutante thing"*: WP&TH, 12/23/66, p. D3.

288 *"Seeing your lovely Julie and David"*: RNL, Eisenhower Special Files PPS 324 (3), 1/3/67.

288 *"They don't drink"*: RNL, Eisenhower Special Files, PPS 324 (3), 4/2/67.

288 *"The friendship of Julie and David is heartwarming"*: RNL, PPS 324 (3), Mamie Eisenhower letter to Pat Nixon, 4/5/67.

288 *"She is an adorable girl"*: RNL, Patricia Ryan Nixon Collection, Eisenhower Correspondence, 1959–1979, PPS 268, 6/2/67.

288 *"by ladies whose refrigerator doors fell off"*: BG, 12/3/67, p. 9.

289 *David flew to Key Biscayne*: David Eisenhower, *Going Home to Glory*, pp. 214–15.

289 *"I just enjoy being with him"*: Vera Glaser, "Julie and Tricia Nixon: When Father Is a Politician," *Parade*, 8/13/67, p. 14.

289 *"I find it hard to remember a time"*: Julie Nixon Eisenhower, "Teddy Roosevelt's Daughter at 90," *SEP*, 3/74, p. 42.

289 *"Of course I am pleased"*: DDEL, DDE, Augusta–Walter Reed Series, Box 5, drafts, undated.

290 *"I didn't realize until I was eighteen"*: Steve Neal, *The Eisenhowers*, p. 452.

290 *to acquire the pitcher Denny McLain*: Author conversation with David Eisenhower, May 2, 2011.

290 *give the news to the Eisenhowers en masse*: Julie Nixon Eisenhower, *Pat Nixon*, pp. 232–33.

291 *and then he fell asleep*: David Eisenhower, *Going Home to Glory*, p. 226.

291 *"You are both the kind of people"*: Ibid.

291 *"I was quite astonished that you made such an interpretation"*: DDEL, Augusta–Walter Reed Series, Box 5, undated; David Eisenhower, *Going Home to Glory*, pp. 228–29.

292 *"he found it a very difficult position to be in"*: Off-the-record interview by author.

292 *believed that he disliked Nixon*: James Humes, interview by author, June 7, 2011.

292 *"social-climbing"*: Off-the-record interview by author.

292 *The newspapers feasted*: NYT, 12/1/67, p. 1+; NYT, 12/3/67, p. 38; WP&TH, 12/17/67, p. G13.

292 *"By their own admission"*: WP&TH, 9/3/68, p. C1.

292 *"They were a TV show"*: Wills, *Nixon Agonistes*, p. 35.

293 *"After all, he asked to be a symbol"*: WP&TH, 10/25/68, p. C1.

293 *"I hate being a celebrity"*: Lynda Rosen Obst, *The Sixties*, p. 270.

293 *"Daddy mentioned that a June wedding"*: David Eisenhower, *Going Home to Glory*, p. 237.

294 *"Even if I had the power to name"*: NYT, 12/25/67, p. 1+.

294 *"It was hell on earth for me"*: Obst, *The Sixties*, p. 268.

27. Family Ties

296 *"The one-liner man"*: William Gavin, interview by author, October 4, 2010.

296 *she was hyperactive all night*: Thomas W. Evans, *Mudge Rose Guthrie Alexander & Ferdon*. (Unpublished history of the firm). Julie Nixon Eisenhower, *Pat Nixon*, p. 233.

296 *"I have decided"*: Julie Nixon Eisenhower, *Pat Nixon*, pp. 233–34.

296 *Julie in her diary*: Ibid.

296 *"you really have nothing to live for"*: Ibid., p. 233.

296 *"the most important"*: Ibid., pp. 233–34.

297 *"It would look politically contrived"*: Ibid.; Nixon/Gannon interviews, Day 9, Tape 2.

297 *"Dick's about to make a fool of himself again"*: Off-the-record interview by author.

297 *an enthusiastic supporter*: David Eisenhower, interview by author, 5/16/12.

298 *an open house at St. Anselm's College*: NYT, 2/4/68, p. 31; NYT, 2/27/68, p. 27;

WP&TH, 2/4/68, p. 1+; BG, 2/18/66, p. 66; Witcover, *The Resurrection of Richard Nixon*, pp. 239–40.

298 *"One of the stranger factors"*: DDEL, Post-Presidential Principal File, 1968, 5/17/68.

298 *"didn't have a warm personal magnetism"*: WP&TH, 4/3/68, p A4; LAT, 4/3/68, p. 3.

298 *"absolutely not"*: CT, 2/2/68, p. D9.

298 *"I believe that he is completely honest"*: DDEL, Post-Presidential Principal File, 1961–62, 3/13/68.

299 *"What's understood"*: David Eisenhower, interview by author, 5/16/12.

299 *Ellsworth spent an hour with the general:* RNL, Eisenhower Special Files, PPS 324 (3), 2/13/68.

299 *Nixon became suspicious:* Sears, interviews by author, August 27, 2010, August 10, 2011; NYT, 3/3/68, p. E2.

299 *"has driven a whole generation of Americans"*: WP&TH, 3/3/68, p. L1.

300 *"the whole country puzzled"*: LAT, 4/3/68, p. 3.

300 *"such characters as Kennedy"*: DDEL, Augusta–Walter Reed Series, Box 5, undated draft letter to Lewis Strauss, April 1968.

300 *"These are truly troubled times"*: Ibid.

300 *"a great personal tragedy"*: CT, 4/5/69, p. 23.

300 *Bill Safire reminded Nixon:* Safire, *Before the Fall*, 49; Novak, *The Agony of the G.O.P.*, p. 136.

301 *"He seemed to have been very moved"*: Christine King Farris, interview by author, October 20, 2010.

301 *Nixon didn't stay to march:* Chapin, interview by author, April 3, 2008.

301 *"I can scarcely think of anything"*: DDEL, Post-Presidential Principal File, 4/17/68. Mrs. Whitman wrote back to say, "You are, as you always have been, so right": 4/25/68.

301 *"smiling, confident, and clearly at ease"*: NYT, 4/20/68, p. 17; WP&TH, 4/20/68, p. W1.

302 *"now we must see if we can elect him"*: RNL, Eisenhower Special Files, PPS 324 (3), 4/23/68.

302 *Mamie asked him to take it easy:* David Eisenhower, *Going Home to Glory*, p. 251.

303 *"be open to the snide argument"*: RNL, Eisenhower Special Files, PPS 324 (3), Harlow letter, 6/17/68.

303 *suffered his fifth heart attack:* NYT, 6/17/68, p. 1; CT, 6/17/68, p. 1; NYT, 6/18/68, p. 20; BG, 4/27/68, p. 4.

303 *he even composed some dialogue for Nixon:* RNL, Eisenhower Special Files, PPS 324 (3), Harlow note, 7/14/68.

303 *"I greatly enjoyed our visit"*: RNL, Eisenhower Special Files, PPS 324 (3), 7/16/68.

304 *"I have admired and respected this man"*: CT, 7/19/68, p. 1+; WP&TH, 7/19/68, p. 1+.

28. A Soldier's Serenade

PAGE

305 *"He is a success story"*: LOC, Henry Brandon Papers, Box 60, Notebooks, 9/16/68.

305 *he'd gotten a haircut:* DDEL, General Robert Schulz Logbook, 8/5/68.

305 *interrupted by a coughing fit:* DDEL, CBS videotape.

306 *"the lawless acts of some minorities"*: NYT, 8/6/68, p. 22.

306 *Ike's prognosis was "guarded"*: WP&TH, 8/7/68, p. 1+; CT, 8/7/68, p. 1+.

306 *stayed mostly in his own cabin:* Price, interviews with author, December 12, 2007, July 1, 2008, January 21, 2009; January 10, 2010, July 28, 2010; Gavin, interview by author, October 4, 2010.

307 *"let's win this one for Ike!"*: Nixon, *Nixon Speaks Out*, pp. 290–91.

307 *"Tonight, I see the face of a child"*: Gavin, interview by author, October 4, 2010; Nixon, *Nixon Speaks Out*, pp. 290–91.

307 *"It was as if some kid from Podunk"*: Gavin, interview by author, October 4, 2010; Evans, interviews by author, February 17, 2008, August 31, 2010.

307 *"Promise me, Dick"*: Aitken, *Richard Nixon*, 357.

308 *"a double-talker"*: Chicago Daily Defender, 8/17/68, p. 10; *NYT*, 8/12/68, p. 1+.

308 *"magnificent spirit"*: *NYT*, 8/17/68; *NYT*, 8/18/68; *NYT*, 8/19/68, p. 1+; *CT*, 8/18/68, p. 1+; *CT*, 8/21/68, p. 3.

308 *"jaunty spirit"*: *NYT*, 4/13/59, p. 1+.

308 *"It's a six-day affair"*: FRUS, 1964–68, Volume 17, 8/20/68, 8:15 P.M., pp. 236–37.

308 *"It is scarcely an exaggeration"*: Heaton, ELOH; *NYT*, 9/20/68, p. 11; *LAT*, 10/3/68, p. G3.

309 *"How can a party that can't unite itself"*: Many of these political advertisements can be seen at http://www.livingroomcandidate.org/commercials/1968.

309 *"Paul tended to be far right in attitude"*: Hugh Downs, e-mail to author, August 17, 2011.

309 *"appear much less mechanical"*: Paul Keyes Papers, privately held.

309 *"Sock it to me?"*: See Nixon's appearance at http://www.youtube.com/watch?v=KFEh mF-cSi8.

309 *referred disrespectfully as "Milhous"*: James Rosen, *The Strong Man*, p. 35.

309 *One of Mitchell's tasks*: Evans, interviews by author, February 17, 2008, August 31, 2010.

310 *ready to greet each new crowd on the tarmac*: Ehrlichman, *Witness to Power*, pp. 55–56.

310 *"Julie would call me directly"*: John Whittaker, interview by author, May 27, 2011.

310 *"It's one thing to give 'em hell"*: *NYT*, 10/27/68, p. 72.

310 *"I've never had it easy"*: Gloria Steinem, *Outrageous Acts and Everyday Rebellions*, pp. 264–65.

310 *"is a very much better man today"*: WP&TH, 10/6/68, p. B2.

311 *Ike came to the window*: *NYT*, 10/15/68, p. 1+.

311 *"I would pay no attention to him"*: DDEL, Post-Presidential Principal File, 1968, 10/16/68.

311 *"one final, heartfelt comment"*: Ibid., 10/24/68.

312 *what Gallup called "dramatic gains"*: *NYT*, 11/4/68, p. 1+.

312 *"he would just talk and then finally go to sleep"*: Garment, interview by author, January 30, 2008.

312 *"in a way that will speed an honorable peace"*: *LAT*, 11/1/68, p. 9; *NYT*, 11/1/68, p. 1+; *NYT*, 11/2/68, p. 1+.

312 *"the key point"*: Meet the Press transcript, 11/3/68.

313 *"Look, I've hated Nixon for years"*: Walter Isaacson, *Kissinger*, p. 133.

313 *"The important thing is for your people"*: LBJ, WH Tape WH6811.02, 11/3/68.

313 *shadowing Chennault*: See the so-called "X" file at the LBJ Presidential Library (in the folder "South Vietnam and U.S. Policies"). The once top-secret file, which concerns Chennault's role around the time of the bombing halt, was first opened to researchers in the mid-1990s.

313 *was almost certainly drafted*: David Eisenhower, interview by author, 5/16/12.

314 *"Nixon deserves the plaudits"*: *NYT*, 11/5/68, p. 29; WP&TH, 11/5/68, p. A4.

314 *"Tell them that their people are messing around"*: LBJ, WH Tape 6811.01, 11/2/68.

314 *tried to leave him alone*: Evans, interviews by author, February 17, 2008, August 31, 2010; Klein, *Making It Perfectly Clear*, p. 36.

315 *"turned to a queasy pessimism"*: Raymond Price, *With Nixon*, p. 36.
315 *"Air Force Five"*: Acker, interviews by author, 11/10/2010, 11/18/2010, 12/15/2010, 1/26/2011; Klein, *Making It Perfectly Clear*, p. 38.
315 *"cheerful during and after"*: DDEL, General Robert Schulz Logbook, 11/6/68.
315 *the president-elect leaned over the bed:* Chapin, interview by author, April 3, 2008.

29. Victory Laps

PAGE
316 *"the case for the formation"*: *NYT,* 11/6/68, p. 1+.
316 *"He was depressed"*: Lee Huebner, interview by author, 5/2/12.
317 *put on a recording of Richard Rodgers's* Victory at Sea: Julie and David Eisenhower, interview by author, September 29, 2010; Nixon/Gannon interviews, Day 9, Tape 3.
317 *The ceremony was to be performed:* *NYT,* 11/23/68, p. 1+.
317 *"The blueness of his eyes was startling"*: Julie Nixon Eisenhower, *Special People*, p. 193.
317 *"He made some recommendations"*: *NYT,* 11/29/68, p. 1+; *LAT,* 11/29/68, p. 5; Julie Nixon Eisenhower, *Special People*, p. 193.
318 *"I cannot tell you how much I enjoyed the visit"*: RNL, Eisenhower Special Files, PPS 324 (3); 12/4/68.
318 *"have Haldeman ride herd"*: RNL, White House Special Files, Box 1, 1/8/69.
318 *"Taking the long view"*: Richard Nixon, "Asia After Vietnam," *Foreign Affairs,* 9/67, p. 111+.
318 *"He always had the idea that people were trying to get him"*: Scranton, interview by author, May 16, 2010.
319 *"which to my embarrassment I had forgotten"*: Henry Kissinger, *White House Years,* p. 9.
319 *"I not only would enjoy visiting Harvard"*: RNL, Series 320, Kissinger, Box 414, letter to Kissinger, July 7, 1958.
319 *Bryce Harlow, who was quickly named as congressional liaison:* *NYT,* 11/8/68, p. 1+.
319 *Nixon was ready to replace him:* A Nixon conversation on this subject, from 7/1/72, may be heard at http://nixon.archives.gov/virtuallibrary/tapeexcerpts/541-2-connally.mp3.
319 *He did recruit one prominent Democrat:* James A. Reichley, *Conservatives in an Age of Change,* p. 69.
320 *"experienced in law enforcement at the highest levels"*: *LAT,* 11/3/68, p. 1.
320 *"I think you have named a fine cabinet"*: RNL, Eisenhower Special Files, PPS 324 (3), 12/12/68; Nixon, *RN,* p. 289.
320 *Ike suggested giving the job to Herbert Brownell:* RNL, Eisenhower Special Files, PPS 324 (3), 12/13/68.
320 *"senior counsel ex-officio"*: David Eisenhower, *Going Home to Glory,* p. 265.
320 *The press never lost its appetite:* See, for example, *WP&TH,* 12/1/68, p. K1, and *NYT,* 1/16/69, p. 26.
320 *"How Cards"*: *BG,* 12/19/68, p. 21.
320 *"This is an awful world"*: *NYT,* 12/23/68, p. 53; *LAT,* 12/15/68, p. J5.
320 *Many of the five hundred or so guests:* *NYT,* 12/23/68, p. 53.
321 *The ceremony took just fifteen minutes:* Various newspaper accounts of the wedding: *NYT,* 12/23/68, p. 1+; *WP&TH,* 12/23/68, p. 1+, E2; *CT,* 12/23/68, p. 3; *LAT,* 12/23/68, p. 1+.
321 *"That wasn't part of the ceremony"*: *BG,* 10/23/68, p. 20.
321 *they'd had to rely on audio alone:* *CT,* 12/20/68, p. B14; David Eisenhower, *Going Home to Glory,* p. 267.

322 *Peale would like to be appointed ambassador:* RNL, WHSF, Box 1, 1/17/69.

322 *he wanted an update on the status of Six Crises:* Ibid., 1/4/69.

322 *"This decision, incidentally, is not subject to further discussion":* Ibid., 1/3/69.

322 *" 'The Great Come-backs' ":* Ibid., 1/15/69.

323 *"rich harvest:"* Ibid., 1/4/69.

323 *instructions on how to work with a decorator:* RNL, WHSF, Box 50, 2/5/69.

323 *"like the one":* RNL, President's Personal File, Memoranda from the President, 1969–74, 1/25/69.

323 *Nixon stayed in his house:* Kenneth W. Thompson, ed., *The Nixon Presidency*, p. 122.

323 *"I just question whether he knows how to organize the government":* Ewald, interviews by author, October 8, 2008, December 9, 2008.

324 *"Imagine you have been so busy":* RNL, Eisenhower Special Files, PPS 324 (3), 1/9/69.

324 *Smith students conducted a vigil:* BG, 1/10/69, p. 1+.

324 *"you can't decide anything in a meeting":* Sears, interviews by author, August 27, 2010, August 10, 2011.

324 *"It's a time when great decisions":* Price, *With Nixon*, pp. 42–43.

324 *his last chance to say "Hi, Dick!":* Price, interviews by author, December 12, 2007, July 1, 2008, January 21, 2009, January 10, 2010, July 28, 2010.

30. Eulogies

PAGE

326 *So much for the honeymoon:* NYT, 1/21/69, p. 24; NYT, 1/21/69, p. 1+; WP&TH, 1/21/69, p. D1; NYT, 1/21/69, p. 24; LAT, 1/21/69, p. 1+; NYT, 1/21/69, p. 23; NYT, 1/21/69, p. 22; CT, 1/21/69, p. 5; NYT, 1/21/69, p. 22; Price, interviews by author, December 12, 2007, July 1, 2008, January 21, 2009, January 10, 2010, July 28, 2010.

326 *Eisenhower was still a formidable presence:* Kissinger, *White House Years*, p. 45.

326 *"Mr. President, I'm glad to see you":* Ibid., p. 349.

326 *"graphic vocabulary":* Ibid., p. 351; Hartford Courant, 2/3/69, p. 23.

327 *a serious intestinal obstruction:* NYT, 4/23/69, p. 1+; NYT, 4/24/69, p. 1+; NYT, 4/25/69, p. 1+.

327 *"if and when anything happens":* Haldeman, *The Haldeman Diaries*, p. 31.

327 *"There is nothing I can do":* DDEL, Eisenhower Special Files, PPS 324 (3), 2/22/69.

327 *The visits slowed as Ike grew weaker:* General Schulz in his logbook recorded the time and duration of each visit.

328 *he had seemed almost carefree:* Robert Semple, interview by author, May 11, 2011; Thompson, ed., *The Nixon Presidency*, pp. 306–7.

328 *"the culmination of his youthful dreams":* Kissinger, *White House Years*, p. 93.

328 *"You've done great":* RNL, President's Personal File, Box 47, handwritten notes, 3/19/69.

328 *"in good spirits":* NYT, 3/20/69, p. 19.

328 *"DDE really enjoyed":* DDEL, General Robert Schulz Logbook, 3/19/69.

328 *"Doctors say DDE failing fast":* Haldeman, *The Haldeman Diaries*, pp. 39, 42; NYT, 3/22/69, p. 16; WP&TH, 3/25/69, p. 1+.

328 *he was ready to die:* RNL, HAK, telcon (Henry A. Kissinger telephone conversations), 3/28/69, 3:45 P.M.

329 *"I turned impulsively and tried":* Nixon, *RN*, p. 37.

329 *" 'I want to go; God take me' ":* General Robert Schulz Logbook; John S. D. Eisenhower, *Strictly Personal*, p. 336.

329 *"General Eisenhower died today":* David Brinkley's announcement: http://www.youtube.com/watch?v=ao7Balh1WoU.

330 *"He was such a strong man"*: RNL, White House Daily Diary, 3/28/69; Haldeman, *The Haldeman Diaries*, p. 44; Nixon/Gannon interviews, Day 3, Tape 1.

330 *other visitors began arriving:* Wills, interview by author, January 28, 2011.

330 *Pat Nixon thought that was a bad idea:* Haldeman, *The Haldeman Diaries*, p. 44.

330 *a little jealous of Whitman:* Susan Eisenhower, *Mrs. Ike*, p. 277.

330 *"He couldn't be more broken up"*: RNL, HAK, telcons, 3/28/69.

331 *they spoke for about five minutes:* White House Daily Diary, 3/28/69.

331 *"He wants to start work"*: RNL, HAK-Haldeman, telecon, 3/28/69, 6:05 P.M.

331 *"Ike got the message, and he toughened up"*: Price, *With Nixon*, p. 61.

331 *But Nixon's mind was elsewhere, too:* RNL, President's Personal File, handwritten notes, Box 47, 3/29/69.

331 *with a croup kettle steaming up the room:* Price, interviews by author, December 12, 2007, July 1, 2008, January 21, 2009, January 10, 2010, July 28, 2010.

331 *"Many leaders"*: http://www.presidency.ucsb.edu/ws/index.php?pid=19878st1=#axzzlvt AKOWKB.

332 *he broke down again:* Hughes, interview by author, October 5, 2010.

332 *Haldeman and Kissinger discussed the protocol:* RNL, HAK, telcon, 3/28/69, 6:05 P.M.

332 *Nixon met visiting foreign leaders:* Haldeman, *The Haldeman Diaries*, p. 46; White House Daily Diary, 3/31/69.

332 *predicted that American power and prestige would be enhanced:* Richard Nixon, *Leaders*, pp. 77–78.

333 *"I need to tell the President something"*: Edward F. Cox, interview by author, June 22, 2010.

333 *"transient episode of coronary insufficiency"*: CT, 4/5/69, p. 7.

333 *"I am very proud"*: LAT, 4/2/69, p. 6; CT, 3/30/69, p. 7; Hartford Courant, 4/2/69, p. 1+.

333 *"he raised his hand in salute"*: Susan Eisenhower, interviews by author, September 18, 2008, February 18, 2010; Susan Eisenhower, *Mrs. Ike*, p. 316.

335 *At that moment in the late afternoon:* Accounts of the train ride and burial from: Interviews by author with David, Julie (9/29/10), and Susan Eisenhower (9/18/8 and 2/18/10); WP&TH, 4/1/69, p. A+; WP&TH, 4/1/69, p. A14; Abilene Reflector-Chronicle, Eisenhower Memorial Edition; NYT, 4/3/69, p. 1+; WP&TH, 4/3/69, p. A1+; CT, 4/3/69, p. 1+; BG, 4/3/69, p. 1+.

31. What Happened Next

PAGE

336 *"For example, I would be horrified"*: RNL, RN to HRH, WHSF, Box 51, 12/4/70.

337 *"the daughter of the doctor"*: RNL, PPF, Memoranda from the President, Nixon to Rose Mary Woods, 2/17/69.

337 *such as the one he sent to the columnist Murray Kempton:* RNL, President's Personal File, Box 10, 11/28/71.

337 *"it would be well to worry Teddy a bit"*: RNL, President's Personal File, Box 1, 2/5/69.

337 *"This is a gesture of unselfishness and nobility"*: RNL, President's Personal File, Box 10, 11/16/73.

337 *"a bigger figure than life"*: RNL, RN to HRH, WHSF, Box 51, 12/4/70.

337 *"He justifiably"*: Ibid.

337 *"Beneath that sunny"*: Nixon, *In the Arena*, p. 274.

337 *"a hard-ass"*: Monica Crowley, *Nixon off the Record*, pp. 15–16.

338 *"They sense a kinship"*: Walter Judd, COHP.

338 *"His eyes seemed to me ugly and cruel"*: LOC, Henry Brandon Papers, Box 19, 2/26/71.

338 *"his restless hands"*: John Osborne, *The Last Nixon Watch*, p. 2.

338 *Ike was selfish*: Safire, *Before the Fall*, p. 623.

338 *"He's lost the best friend he had in the press"*: HI, Ralph de Toledano Papers, 5/23/70, 8/6/70.

338 *"delete any idea that I did not support"*: RNL, Series 320, Box 213, de Toledano, 2/28/60.

338 *"Very confidentially"*: RNL, Series 320, Ralph de Toledano, 3/4/59.

338 *"Since he did not really trust people"*: John Osborne, "White House Watch: Gabbing with Harlow," *TNR*, 5/13/78, pp. 12–14.

338 *"He grabs me and says"*: Hughes, interview by author, October 5, 2010.

339 *"Eisenhower was always telling Nixon"*: Summers, *The Arrogance of Power*, p. 147. Hutschnecker seemed to relish this association, and after Nixon's death, he began to talk about it, most volubly to Anthony Summers and his partner, Robbyn Swan, to whom he said, "He didn't have a serious psychiatric diagnosis. Nixon wasn't psychotic. He had no pathology. But he did have a good portion of neurotic symptoms."

339 *"He made himself" like Nixon*: Evan Thomas, *Ike's Bluff*, p. 176.

339 *"Ike always hated him"*: Horne, *Harold Macmillan*, pp. 131–32.

339 *"took a less-than-evangelical view"*: DDEL, Bookman Papers, Gabriel Hauge unpublished autobiography, Box 1.

339 *"I personally think the decision was wrong"*: Larson, *Eisenhower*, p. 12.

339 *"These are not bad people"*: Earl Warren, *Memoirs of Chief Justice Warren*, p. 291.

340 *"I understand why some oppose it"*: WH Tape, transcripts, Nixon to Kissinger, 4/8/71.

340 *"to go along on our next space trip"*: RNL, WHSF, Box 1, 1/8/69.

340 *"Eisenhower-ism without Eisenhower"*: *NYT*, 4/29/69, p. 44.

340 *"there will not be any name-calling"*: RNL, HAK, telcons, 3/25/69.

340 *as a "friend"*: Nixon, *RN*, p. 110.

341 *"it put income guarantees"*: Vincent J. and Vee Burke, *Nixon's Good Deed*, p. 219.

341 *Riegle's opposition to administration policies*: Riegle, interview by author, October 15, 2010; Paul (Pete) McCloskey, interview by author, October 15, 2010.

341 *"must know by now that the war is unwinnable"*: David Halberstam, "President Nixon and Vietnam," *Harper's*, 1/69, p. 22+.

341 *"The U.S. can't fold"*: C. L. Sulzberger, *The World and Richard Nixon*, p. 29.

341 *"there's no way"*: Richard Whalen, *Catch the Falling Flag*, p. 137.

342 *Some 58,000 Americans were killed*: See Melvin Small's *The Presidency of Richard Nixon*, p. 69.

342 *was considered a disaster*: Price, interviews by author, December 12, 2007, July 1, 2008, January 21, 2009, January 10, 2010, July 28, 2010.

342 *"I was paranoiac"*: Nixon/Gannon interviews, Day 3, Tape 1.

342 *"[I] have, I think, shook them to the core"*: HI, Lynn Nofziger Papers, Box 6, Folder 55, 11/69.

343 *even Edward Nixon*: Hughes, interview by author, October 5, 2010; Acker, interviews by author, 11/10/2010, 11/18/2010, 12/15/2010, 1/26/2011; Edward Nixon, interviews by author, February 19, 2009, April 25, 2010.

343 *"Blow the safe and get it"*: Hear this at www.whitehousetapes.net/transcript/nixon/525-001; 7/21/71.

343 *"the hotter the discussion became, the cooler he became"*: "Nixon's Own Story of 7 Years in the Vice Presidency," *USN&WR*, 5/17/60.

343 *"I'm glad that the President did not live to see"*: Ewald, interviews by author, September 11, 2008, October 8, 2008, December 9, 2008.

344 *"The temper up here is ugly"*: Ehrlichman, *Witness to Power*, p. 62.

344 *greeted by boos and hisses as well as applause*: NYT, 6/6/70, p. 17.

344 *"Pasha Passes By"*: Julie Nixon Eisenhower, *SEP*, 1/2/74, p. 74.

345 *Mamie would take breaks from the farm*: Susan Eisenhower, *Mrs. Ike*, pp. 317–18.

345 *the town even got a tame strip joint*: NYT, 4/20/70, p. 41.

345 *she called him "Dick"*: See for example, WH Tapes, 7/27/71, 11:53 A.M.–12:03 P.M.

345 *"Just a line to let you know"*: RNL, President's Personal File, 268, Patricia Ryan Nixon Collection, Eisenhower Correspondence, 1954–79, 5/4/73.

346 *"Nixon is our heartbreaking worry here"*: Susan Eisenhower, *Mrs. Ike*, p. 321.

346 *"I only want to say"*: RNL, President's Personal File, 268, Patricia Ryan Nixon Collection, Eisenhower Correspondence, 1973–74, 8/6/74.

SOURCES

For a couple of decades, books about Dwight D. Eisenhower's presidency have encouraged a wave of revisionism that is no longer revisionist—that is, few still believe, as many once did, that Eisenhower was an ineffectual, inarticulate, barely attentive leader. A more accurate view has been influenced by an expanding circle of historians, among them Princeton's Fred I. Greenstein, whose early, influential *The Hidden-Hand Presidency: Eisenhower as Leader* (1982), revealed a man skilled in the art of forceful indirection, and Stephen E. Ambrose, whose festive two-volume biography (1983, 1984), portrayed Eisenhower as a leader who had patience and purpose, particularly in foreign affairs. Some excellent recent books on his life and presidency include those by Jim Newton, David A. Nichols, Jean Edward Smith, and Evan Thomas.

Richard Nixon was a thirty-nine-year-old senator when he was picked to run for vice president, and even then was regarded by many contemporaries as slightly damaged goods, a view that despite his foreign policy successes and domestic innovation never changed much—especially in the aftermath of the scandal that ended his presidency. Yet for all the books that take a decidedly negative view of Nixon—for instance those by Roger Morris, Fawn Brodie, and William Costello—there are more balanced ones, such as those by David Greenberg, Herbert Parmet, Melvin Small, and Tom Wicker, as well as distinctly positive studies by, among others, Jonathan Aitken and Irwin F. Gellman. All the sources that I consulted contributed to my understanding of two complicated and, as I discovered, ever more elusive, unusual, and compelling figures.

Books

Abell, Tyler, ed., *Drew Pearson Diaries, 1949–1959*. New York: Holt, Rinehart & Winston, 1974.

Adams, Sherman. *Firsthand Report: The Story of the Eisenhower Administration*. New York: Harper & Brothers, 1961.

Aitken, Jonathan. *Nixon: A Life*. Washington, D.C.: Regnery, 1993.

Allen, George E. *Presidents Who Have Known Me*. New York: Simon & Schuster, 1960.

Alsop, Joseph W. (with Adam Platt). *I've Seen the Best of It*. New York: W. W. Norton, 1992.

Alsop, Joseph, and Stewart Alsop. *The Reporter's Trade*. New York: Reynal, 1958.

Alsop, Stewart. *The Center: People and Power in Political Washington*. New York: Harper & Row, 1968.

———. *Nixon and Rockefeller: A Double Portrait*. Garden City, New York: Doubleday, 1960.

Ambrose, Stephen E. *Eisenhower: Soldier, General of the Army, President-Elect, 1890–1952*. New York: Simon & Schuster, 1983.

———. *Eisenhower: The President*. New York: Simon & Schuster, 1984.

———. *Nixon: The Education of a Politician, 1913–1962*. New York: Simon & Schuster, 1987.

———. *Nixon: The Triumph of a Politician, 1962–1972*. New York: Simon & Schuster, 1989.

Anderson, Jack (with James Boyd). *Confessions of a Muckraker*. New York: Random House, 1979.

Anderson, Jack, and Ronald W. May. *McCarthy: The Man, the Senator, the "Ism."* London: Victor Gollancz, 1953.

Andrews, John A., III. *The Other Side of the Sixties: Young Americans for Freedom and the Rise of Conservative Politics*. New Brunswick, New Jersey: Rutgers University Press, 1997.

Arnold, William A. *Back When It All Began: The Early Nixon Years*. New York: Vantage, 1975.

Baker, Russell. *The Good Times*. New York: William Morrow, 1989.

Bayley, Edwin R. *Joe McCarthy and the Press*. Madison: University of Wisconsin Press, 1981.

Benson, Ezra Taft. *Cross Fire: The Eight Years with Eisenhower*. Garden City, New York: Doubleday, 1962.

Beschloss, Michael R. *The Crisis Years: Kennedy and Khrushchev, 1960–1963*. New York: HarperCollins, 1991.

———. *Eisenhower: A Centennial Life*. New York: Edward Burlingame/Harper-Collins, 1990.

———. *Mayday: Eisenhower, Khrushchev, and the U-2 Affair*. New York: Harper & Row, 1986.

Billings-Yun, Melanie. *Decision Against War: Eisenhower and Dien Bien Phu, 1954*. New York: Columbia University Press, 1988.

Black, Conrad. *Richard Nixon: A Life in Full*. New York: PublicAffairs, 2007.

Blumenson, Martin. *The Patton Papers, 1940–1945*. New York: Da Capo, 1996.

Bobst, Elmer Holmes. *Bobst: The Autobiography of a Pharmaceutical Pioneer*. New York: David McKay, 1973.

Branch, Taylor. *At Canaan's Edge: America in the King Years, 1965–68*. New York: Simon & Schuster, 2006.

———. *Parting the Waters: America in the King Years, 1954–63*. New York: Simon & Schuster, 1988.

———. *Pillar of Fire: America in the King Years, 1963–65*. New York: Simon & Schuster, 1998.

Brandon, Henry. *The Retreat of American Power: The Inside Story of How Nixon & Kissinger Changed American Foreign Policy for Years to Come*. Garden City, New York: Doubleday & Company, 1973.

Brands, H. W., Jr. *Cold Warriors: Eisenhower's Generation and American Foreign Policy*. New York: Columbia University Press, 1988.

Brinkley, Alan. *The Publisher: Henry Luce and His American Century*. New York: Alfred A. Knopf, 2010.

Brodie, Fawn. *Richard Nixon: The Shaping of His Character*. New York: W. W. Norton, 1981.

Brownell, Herbert (with John P. Burke). *Advising Ike: The Memoirs of Attorney General Herbert Brownell*. Lawrence: University Press of Kansas, 1993.

Burke, Bob, and Ralph G. Thompson. *Bryce Harlow: Mr. Integrity*. Oklahoma City: Oklahoma Heritage Association, 2000.

Burke, Vincent J., and Vee Burke. *Nixon's Good Deed: Welfare Reform.* New York: Columbia University Press, 1974.

Caro, Robert A. *The Years of Lyndon Johnson: Master of the Senate.* New York: Alfred A. Knopf, 2002.

Carson, Clayborne, Tenisha Armstrong, Susan Carson, Adrienne Clay, and Kieran Taylor, eds. *The Papers of Martin Luther King, Jr.* Berkeley: University of California Press, 2005 (also online: http://mlk-kpp01.stanford.edu/index .php/kingpapers).

Childs, Marquis. *Eisenhower: Captive Hero.* New York: Harcourt, Brace, 1958.

———. *Witness to Power.* New York: McGraw-Hill, 1975.

Cook, Blanche Wiesen. *The Declassified Eisenhower.* Garden City, New York: Doubleday, 1981.

Cordery, Stacy A. *Alice: Alice Roosevelt Longworth, from White House Princess to Washington Power Broker.* New York: Viking, 2007.

Costello, William. *The Facts About Nixon.* New York: Viking, 1960.

Crowley, Monica. *Nixon Off the Record.* New York: Random House, 1996.

Crozier, Brian. *De Gaulle.* New York: Charles Scribner's Sons, 1973.

Cutler, Robert. *No Time for Rest.* Boston: Little, Brown, 1966.

de Toledano, Ralph. *Nixon.* New York: Henry Holt, 1956.

———. *Notes from the Underground: The Whittaker Chambers–Ralph de Toledano Letters.* Washington, D.C.: Regnery, 1997.

———. *One Man Alone: Richard Nixon.* New York: Funk & Wagnalls, 1969.

Divine, Robert A. *The Sputnik Challenge: Eisenhower's Response to the Soviet Satellite.* New York: Oxford University Press, 1993.

Domhoff, William. *The Bohemian Grove and Other Retreats: A Study in Ruling Class Cohesiveness.* New York: Harper & Row, 1974.

Donovan, Robert J. *Confidential Secretary: Ann Whitman's 20 Years with Eisenhower and Rockefeller.* New York: E. P. Dutton, 1988.

———. *Eisenhower: The Inside Story.* New York: Harper & Brothers, 1956.

Drummond, Roscoe, and Gaston Coblentz. *Duel at the Brink: John Foster Dulles' Command of American Power.* Garden City, New York: Doubleday, 1960.

Dunar, Andrew J. *The Truman Scandals and the Politics of Morality.* Columbia: University of Missouri Press, 1984.

Ehrlichman, John D. *Witness to Power: The Nixon Years.* New York: Simon & Schuster, 1982.

Eisenhower, David (with Julie Nixon Eisenhower). *Going Home to Glory: A Memoir of Life with Dwight D. Eisenhower, 1961–1969*. New York: Simon & Schuster, 2010.

Eisenhower, Dwight D. *At Ease: Stories I Tell to Friends*. Garden City, New York: Doubleday, 1967.

———. *Crusade in Europe*. Baltimore: Johns Hopkins University Press, 1997.

———. *Mandate for Change: The White House Years, 1953–1956*. Garden City, New York: Doubleday, 1963.

———. *Waging Peace: The White House Years, 1956–1961*. Garden City, New York: Doubleday, 1965.

Eisenhower, John S. D. *General Ike: A Personal Reminiscence*. New York: Free Press, 2003.

———. *Strictly Personal*. Garden City, New York: Doubleday, 1974.

Eisenhower, Julie Nixon. *Pat Nixon: The Untold Story*. New York: Simon & Schuster, 1986.

———. *Special People*. New York: Simon & Schuster, 1977.

Eisenhower, Milton. *The President Is Calling*. New York: Atheneum, 1974.

Eisenhower, Susan. *Mrs. Ike: Memories and Reflections on the Life of Mamie Eisenhower*. New York: Farrar, Straus & Giroux, 1996.

Elson, Robert T. *The World of Time Inc.: The Intimate History of a Publishing Enterprise, 1941–1960*. Edited by Duncan Norton-Taylor. New York: Atheneum, 1973.

Evans, Thomas W. *Mudge Rose Guthrie Alexander & Ferdon*. New York. Unpublished history of the firm, 1994.

Ewald, William Bragg, Jr. *Eisenhower the President: Crucial Days, 1951–1960*. Englewood Cliffs, New Jersey: Prentice-Hall, 1981.

———. *Who Killed Joe McCarthy?* New York: Simon & Schuster, 1984.

Feldstein, Mark. *Poisoning the Press: Richard Nixon, Jack Anderson, and the Rise of Washington's Scandal Culture*. New York: Farrar, Straus & Giroux, 2010. Also: unpublished supplemental chapters provided by the author.

Ferrell, Robert H., ed. *The Eisenhower Diaries*. New York: W. W. Norton, 1981.

———, ed. *Inside the Nixon Administration: The Secret Diary of Arthur Burns, 1969–1974*. Lawrence: University Press of Kansas, 2010.

———, ed. *Off the Record: The Private Papers of Harry S. Truman*. New York: Harper & Row, 1980.

Frick, Daniel. *Reinventing Richard Nixon*. Lawrence: University Press of Kansas, 2008.

Garment, Leonard. *Crazy Rhythm: My Journey from Brooklyn, Jazz, and Wall Street to Nixon's White House, Watergate, and Beyond*. New York: Times Books, 1997.

Gellman, Irwin F. *The Contender: Richard Nixon: The Congress Years, 1946–1952*. New York: Free Press, 1999.

Gibbs, Wolcott. *More in Sorrow*. New York: Henry Holt, 1958.

Graham, Billy. *Just As I Am: The Autobiography of Billy Graham*. New York: HarperOne, 1997.

Gray, Robert Keith. *Eighteen Acres Under Glass*. Garden City, New York: Doubleday, 1962.

Greenberg, David. *Nixon's Shadow: The History of an Image*. New York: W. W. Norton, 2003.

Greenstein, Fred I. *The Hidden-Hand Presidency*. New York: Basic Books, 1982.

———. *The Presidential Difference*. New York: Free Press, 2000.

Hagerty, James. *The Diary of James C. Hagerty: Eisenhower in Mid-Course, 1954–1955*. Edited by Robert H. Ferrell. Bloomington: Indiana University Press, 1983.

Halberstam, David. *The Fifties*. New York: Villard, 1993.

———. *The Powers That Be*. New York: Alfred A. Knopf, 1979.

Haldeman, H. R. *The Haldeman Diaries: Inside the Nixon White House*. New York: G. P. Putnam's Sons, 1994.

Haldeman, H. R. (with Joseph DiMona). *The Ends of Power*. New York: Times Books, 1978.

Hall, Leonard Wood. Posthumous, unpublished autobiography, edited by William J. Casey, who was in Hall's law firm, Rogers and Wells, and later served as President Reagan's CIA director. (At the Dwight D. Eisenhower Presidential Library and Museum in the papers of Henry W. Hoagland, a staffer with the Republican Congressional Campaign Committee.)

Harris, Mark. *Mark the Glove Boy*. New York: Macmillan, 1964.

Hauge, Gabriel. Unpublished autobiography; manuscript in the George Bookman Papers at the Dwight D. Eisenhower Presidential Library and Museum.

Hazlett, Everett E. *Ike's Letters to a Friend, 1941–1958*. Edited by Robert W. Griffith. Lawrence: University Press of Kansas, 1984.

Hess, Stephen, and David S. Broder. *The Republican Establishment: The Present and Future of the G.O.P.* New York: Harper & Row, 1967.

Hill, Gladwin. *Dancing Bear: An Inside Look at California Politics.* Cleveland: World, 1968.

Hillings, Pat (with Howard Seelye). *The Irrepressible Irishman: A Republican Insider.* Howard D. Dean, 1994.

Hoff, Joan. *Nixon Reconsidered.* New York: Basic Books, 1997.

Hoopes, Townsend. *The Devil and John Foster Dulles.* Boston: Atlantic-Little, Brown, 1973.

Horne, Alistair. *Harold Macmillan: Volume II: 1957–1986.* New York: Viking, 1989.

Hughes, Emmet John. *The Ordeal of Power.* New York: Atheneum, 1963.

Humes, James C. *Confessions of a White House Ghostwriter: Five Presidents and Other Political Adventures.* Washington, D.C.: Regnery, 1997.

Hutschnecker, Arnold A. *The Drive for Power.* New York: M. Evans and Company, 1974.

———. *The Will to Live.* Thomas Y. Crowell Company, New York, 1951.

Isaacson, Walter. *Kissinger: A Biography.* New York: Simon & Schuster, 1992.

Jacobs, Travis Beal. *Eisenhower at Columbia.* New Brunswick, New Jersey: Transaction, 2001.

Jones, Charles O. *Passages to the Presidency: From Campaigning to Governing.* Washington, D.C.: Brookings Institution Press, 1998.

Kabaservice, Geoffrey. *Rule and Ruin: The Downfall of Moderation and the Destruction of the Republican Party from Eisenhower to the Tea Party.* New York: Oxford University Press, 2012.

Kempton, Murray. *Rebellions, Perversities and Main Events.* New York: Times Books, 1994.

Keogh, James. *This Is Nixon: The Man and His Work.* New York: G. P. Putnam's Sons, 1956.

Kissinger, Henry. *White House Years.* Boston: Little, Brown, 1979.

Klein, Herbert G. *Making It Perfectly Clear: An Inside Account of Nixon's Love-Hate Relationship with the Media.* Garden City, New York: Doubleday, 1980.

Kluger, Richard. *The Paper: The Life and Death of the New York Herald Tribune.* New York: Alfred A. Knopf, 1986.

Kotlowski, Dean J. *Nixon's Civil Rights: Politics, Principle, and Policy.* Cambridge: Harvard University Press, 2001.

Korda, Michael. *Ike: An American Hero.* New York: Harper, 2007.

Kornitzer, Bela. *The Real Nixon.* Chicago: Rand McNally, 1960.

Krock, Arthur. *Memoirs: Sixty Years on the Firing Line.* New York: Funk & Wagnalls, 1968.

Larson, Arthur. *Eisenhower: The President Nobody Knew.* New York: Charles Scribner's Sons, 1968.

Lasby, Clarence G. *Eisenhower's Heart Attack.* Lawrence: University Press of Kansas, 1997.

Lavine, Harold, ed. *Smoke-Filled Rooms: The Confidential Papers of Roberts Humphreys.* Englewood Cliffs, New Jersey: Prentice-Hall, 1970.

Lodge, Henry Cabot. *As It Was.* New York: W. W. Norton, 1976.

———. *The Storm Has Many Eyes.* New York: W. W. Norton, 1973.

Long, Michael G., ed. *First Class Citizenship.* New York: Times Books, 2007.

Lungren, John C., and John C. Lungren Jr. *Healing Richard Nixon: A Doctor's Memoir.* Lexington: University Press of Kentucky, 2003.

Lyon, Peter. *Eisenhower: Portrait of a Hero.* Boston: Little, Brown, 1974.

Mailer, Norman. *Some Honorable Men: Political Conventions, 1960–1972.* Boston: Little, Brown, 1976.

Martin, Ralph G. *Henry and Clare: An Intimate Portrait of the Luces.* New York: G. P. Putnam's Sons, 1991.

Matthews, Christopher. *Kennedy & Nixon: The Rivalry That Shaped Postwar America.* New York: Simon & Schuster, 1996.

Mazo, Earl. *Richard Nixon: A Political and Personal Portrait.* New York: Harper & Brothers, 1959.

Mazo, Earl, and Stephen Hess. *Richard Nixon: A Political Portrait.* New York: Harper & Row, 1967.

McCullough, David. *Truman.* New York: Simon & Schuster, 1992.

McKeever, Porter. *Adlai Stevenson: His Life and Legacy.* New York: William Morrow, 1989.

McPherson, Harry. *A Political Education: A Washington Memoir.* Boston: Houghton Mifflin, 1988.

Merson, Martin. *The Private Diary of a Public Servant.* New York: Macmillan, 1955.

Mitchell, Greg. *Tricky Dick and the Pink Lady*. New York: Random House, 1998.

Montgomery, Gayle B., and James W. Johnson. *One Step from the White House: The Rise and Fall of Senator William F. Knowland*. Berkeley: University of California Press, 1998.

Morris, Roger. *Richard Milhous Nixon: The Rise of an American Politician*. New York: Henry Holt, 1990.

Morrow, E. Frederic. *Black Man in the White House*. New York: Macfadden, 1963.

———. *Forty Years a Guinea Pig*. New York: Pilgrim Press, 1980.

Neal, Steve. *The Eisenhowers: Reluctant Dynasty*. Garden City, New York: Doubleday, 1978.

Neustadt, Richard E. *Presidential Power*. New York: Signet, 1964.

Newton, Jim. *Eisenhower: The White House Years*. New York: Riverhead, 2011.

Nichols, David A. *A Matter of Justice: Eisenhower and the Beginning of the Civil Rights Revolution*. New York: Simon & Schuster, 2007.

Nixon, Richard. *In the Arena: A Memoir of Victory, Defeat and Renewal*. New York: Simon & Schuster, 1990.

———. *Leaders*. New York: Warner Books, 1982.

———. *Nixon on the Issues*. New York: Nixon-Agnew Campaign Committee, 1968.

———. *Nixon Speaks Out: Major Speeches and Statements by Richard M. Nixon in the Presidential Campaign of 1968*. New York: Nixon-Agnew Campaign Committee, 1968.

———. *RN: The Memoirs of Richard Nixon*. New York: Grosset & Dunlap, 1978.

———. *Six Crises*. Garden City, New York: Doubleday, 1962.

Novak, Robert D. *The Agony of the G.O.P.* New York: Macmillan, 1965.

Novak, Robert, and Rowland Evans Jr. *Nixon in the White House*. New York: Random House, 1971.

Obst, Lynda Rosen. *The Sixties*. New York: Random House/Rolling Stone Press, 1977.

Osborne, John. *The Last Nixon Watch*. Washington, D.C.: New Republic Book Company, 1975.

———. *The Nixon Watch*. New York: Liveright, 1970.

Pach, Chester J., Jr., and Richardson, Elmo. *The Presidency of Dwight D. Eisenhower.* Lawrence: University Press of Kansas, 1991.

Parmet, Herbert S. *Eisenhower and the American Crusades.* New York: Macmillan, 1972.

———. *Richard Nixon and His America.* Boston: Little, Brown, 1990.

Patterson, Bradley. *The Ring of Power.* New York: Basic Books, 1988.

Patterson, James T. *Mr. Republican.* Boston: Houghton Mifflin, 1972.

Persico, Joseph E. *The Imperial Rockefeller.* New York: Simon & Schuster, 1982.

Perlstein, Rick. *Before the Storm.* New York: Nation Books, 2009.

———. *Nixonland: The Rise of a President and the Fracturing of America.* New York: Scribner, 2008.

Perret, Geoffrey. *Eisenhower.* New York: Random House, 1999.

Pipes, Kasey S. *Ike's Final Battle: The Road to Little Rock and the Challenge of Equality.* Los Angeles: World Ahead Publishing, 2007.

Price, Raymond. *With Nixon.* New York: Viking, 1977.

Reeves, Richard. *President Nixon: Alone in the White House.* New York: Simon & Schuster, 2001.

Reeves, Thomas C. *The Life and Times of Joe McCarthy.* New York: Stein & Day, 1982.

Reichley, James A. *Conservatives in an Age of Change.* Washington, D.C.: Brookings Institution, 1981.

Reston, James. *Deadline.* New York: Random House, 1991.

Rich, Doris L. *Jackie Cochran: Pilot in the Fastest Lane.* Gainesville: University Press of Florida, 2007.

Riegle, Donald W. (with Trevor Armbrister). *O Congress: A Young Congressman's Intimate Diary of Life on Capitol Hill.* New York: Doubleday, 1972.

Rosen, James. *The Strong Man: John Mitchell and the Secrets of Watergate.* New York: Doubleday, 2008.

Rovere, Richard H. *Affairs of State.* New York: Farrar, Straus and Cudahy, 1956.

———. *Arrivals and Departures: A Journalist's Memoirs.* New York: Macmillan, 1976.

———. *Senator Joe McCarthy.* Cleveland: Meridian, 1960.

Rovere, Richard H., and Arthur Schlesinger Jr. *The General and the President.* New York: Farrar, Straus and Young, 1951.

Safire, William. *Before the Fall: An Inside View of the Pre-Watergate White House.* Garden City, New York: Doubleday, 1978.

Schlesinger, Arthur M., Jr. *Journals, 1952–2000.* New York: Penguin, 2007.

———. *Robert Kennedy and His Times.* Boston: Mariner-Houghton Mifflin, 2002.

Sheed, Wilfrid. *Clare Boothe Luce.* New York: E. P. Dutton, 1982.

Sheehan, Neil. *A Bright Shining Lie: John Paul Vann and America in Vietnam.* New York: Random House, 1988.

———. *A Fiery Peace in a Cold War: Bernard Schriever and the Ultimate Weapon.* New York: Random House, 2009.

Siciliano, Rocco C. (with Drew M. Ross). *Walking on Sand.* Salt Lake City: University of Utah Press, 2004.

Slater, Ellis D. *The Ike I Knew.* Privately printed, 1980.

Small, Melvin, *The Presidency of Richard Nixon.* Lawrence: University Press of Kansas, 1999.

Smith, Jean Edward. *Eisenhower in War and Peace.* New York: Random House, 2012.

Smith, Merriman. *Meet Mister Eisenhower.* New York: Harper & Brothers, 1955.

Smith, Richard Norton. *Thomas E. Dewey and His Times.* New York: Simon & Schuster, 1982.

Spalding, Henry D. *The Nixon Nobody Knows.* Middle Village, New York: Jonathan David, 1972.

Steele, Ronald. *Walter Lippmann and the American Century.* Boston: Atlantic-Little, Brown, 1980.

Steinem, Gloria. *Outrageous Acts and Everyday Rebellions,* 2nd ed. New York: Henry Holt, 1995.

Strober, Gerald S., and Deborah Hart. *Nixon: An Oral History of His Presidency.* New York: HarperCollins, 1994.

Sulzberger, C. L. *The Last of the Giants.* New York: Macmillan, 1970.

———. *A Long Row of Candles: Memoirs and Diaries (1934–1954).* New York: Macmillan, 1969.

———. *The World and Richard Nixon.* New York: Prentice-Hall, 1987.

Summers, Anthony (with Robbyn Swan). *The Arrogance of Power: The Secret World of Richard Nixon*. New York: Viking, 2000.

Tanenhaus, Sam. *Whittaker Chambers*. New York: Random House/Modern Library, 1998.

Thomas, Evan. *Ike's Bluff: President Eisenhower's Secret Battle to Save the World*. New York: Little, Brown, 2012.

Thompson, Kenneth W., ed. *The Eisenhower Presidency: Eleven Intimate Perspectives of Dwight D. Eisenhower*. Lanham, Maryland: University Press of America, 1984.

———, ed. *The Nixon Presidency: Twenty-Two Intimate Perspectives of Richard M. Nixon*. Lanham, Maryland: University Press of America, 1987.

Truman, Harry S. *The Truman Memoirs, Volume II: Years of Trial and Hope*. New York: Doubleday, 1955.

Van Atta, Dale. *With Honor: Melvin Laird in War, Peace, and Politics*. Madison: University of Wisconsin Press, 2008.

Volkan, Vamik D., Norman Itzkowitz, and Andrew W. Dod. *Richard Nixon: A Psychobiography*. New York: Columbia University Press, 1997.

Warren, Earl. *Memoirs of Chief Justice Warren*. Garden City, New York: Doubleday & Company, Inc., 1977.

Whalen, Richard J. *Catch the Falling Flag*. Boston: Houghton Mifflin, 1972.

White, Theodore H. *The Making of the President, 1960*. New York: Atheneum, 1961.

———. *The Making of the President, 1964*. New York: Atheneum, 1965.

———. *The Making of the President, 1968*. New York: Atheneum, 1969.

Wicker, Tom. *One of Us: Richard Nixon and the American Dream*. New York: Random House, 1991.

Wills, Garry. *Nixon Agonistes: The Crisis of the Self-Made Man*. New York: Atheneum, 1969.

Witcover, Jules. *The Resurrection of Richard Nixon*. New York: G. P. Putnam's Sons, 1970.

Yoder, Edwin, Jr. *Joe Alsop's Cold War*. Chapel Hill: University of North Carolina Press, 1995.

Selected Magazine Articles

Alsop, Stewart. "The Mystery of Richard Nixon." *Saturday Evening Post*, 7/12/58, p. 29+.

———, (interviewer). "Nixon on Nixon." *Saturday Evening Post*, 7/12/58, p. 26+.

———. "The Logical Candidate." *Saturday Evening Post*, 1/18/64, p. 15.

———. "Richard Nixon and the Locked Door." *Saturday Evening Post*, 12/2/1967, p. 18+.

———. "If Nixon Stumbles." *Saturday Evening Post*, 2/10/68, p. 11.

Andrews, William G. "Rockefeller's Strategy." *The Nation*, 12/19/59, p. 464+.

Asbell, Bernard. "Does Robert Finch Have Soul?" *New York Times Magazine*, 4/6/69, p. 28+.

"Behind the Headlines: The Doctors and Mr. Eisenhower's Decision." *The New Republic*, 1/2/56, p. 11+.

Booker, Simeon. "What Republicans Must Do to Regain the Negro Vote." *Ebony*, 4/62, p. 47+.

Cater, Douglass. "The Unleashing of Richard M. Nixon." *The Reporter*, 9/1/60, p. 32+.

Coffin, Patrick. "The Private Life of Pat Nixon." *Look*, 7/27/54, p. 23+.

Collins, Frederic W. "Our Om-nescient President. Some Forces of His Not-Knowing." *The New Republic*, 6/1/58, p. 11+.

———. "How to Be a President's Brother." *New York Times Magazine*, 8/23/59, p. 10+.

Cort, David. "GOP on TV." *The Nation*, 8/6/60, p. 67.

Coughlan, Robert. "Success Story of a Vice President." *Life*, 12/14/53, p. 146+.

Davies, Gareth. "Richard Nixon and the Desegregation of Southern Schools." *The Journal of Policy History*, Vol. 19, No. 4 (2007).

Donovan, Robert J. "What Ike Will Do." *Saturday Evening Post*, 1/19/57, p. 31+.

———. "Over-Nominated Under-Elected, Still a Promising Candidate." *New York Times Magazine*, 4/25/65, p. SM13+.

Drury, Allen. "The Enigma of Gettysburg." *The Reporter*, 12/29/55, pp. 20–21.

Eisenhower, Dwight D. "My Views on Berlin." *Saturday Evening Post*, 12/9/61, pp. 15–18.

Eisenhower, Dwight D. "Danger from Within." *Saturday Evening Post*, 1/26/63, pp. 15–18.

Eisenhower, Julie Nixon. "Teddy Roosevelt's Daughter at 90." *Saturday Evening Post*, 3/74, pp. 42–45.

Evans, Rowland, and Robert Novak. "The Unmaking of a President." *Esquire*, 9/64, p. 91+.

———. "The Road to Miami Beach." *Harper's*, 1/68, p. 24+.

Flanner, Janet ("Genet"). "Letter from S.H.A.P.E." *The New Yorker*, 10/27/51, p. 120+.

———. "Letter from Paris." *The New Yorker*, 12/14/57, p. 132+.

Fleming, D. F. "Does Eisenhower Mean War?" *The Nation*, 5/25/52, p. 374+.

Gavin, William F. "His Heart's Abundance: Notes of a Nixon Speechwriter." *Presidential Studies Quarterly*, Vol. 31, No. 2 (June 2001), p. 358+.

Glaser, Vera. "Julie and Tricia Nixon: When Father Is a Politician." *Parade*, 8/13/67, p. 14+.

Greenberg, David. "Nixon in American Memory." Institutions of Public Memory, *Bulletin of the German Historical Institute*.

Greenfield, Meg. "The Prose of Richard M. Nixon." *The Reporter*, 12/29/60, p. 15+.

Greenstein, Fred I., and Richard H. Immerman. "Effective National Security Advising: Recovering the Eisenhower Legacy." *Political Science Quarterly*, Vol. 115, No. 3 (2000).

Halberstam, David. "President Nixon and Vietnam." *Harper's*, 1/69, p. 22+.

Harsch, Joseph C. "John Foster Dulles: A Very Complicated Man." *Harper's*, 9/56, p. 27+.

Honan, William H. "The Men Behind Nixon's Speeches." *New York Times Magazine*, 1/19/69, p. 21+.

Hoopes, Townsend. "The Legacy of the Cold War in Indochina." *Foreign Affairs*, 7/70, p. 601+.

Hughes, Emmet John. "The Politics of the Sixties—From the New Frontier to the New Revolution." *New York Times Magazine*, 4/4/71, p. 24+.

Hutschnecker, Arnold A. "The Mental Health of Our Leaders." *Look*, 7/15/69, pp. 51–54.

Hyman, Sidney. "Between Throttlebottom and Jefferson." *New York Times Magazine*, 3/28/54, p. 12+.

————. "Inner Circles of the White House." *New York Times Magazine*, 1/5/58, p. 10+.

————. "The Cabinet's Job as Eisenhower Sees It." *New York Times Magazine*, 7/30/58, p. 7+.

"Ike Outlines His Political Creed: Government Should Only Do What Individual Can't Do for Himself." *U.S. News & World Report*, 9/23/55, p. 115+.

Kempton, Murray. "The General Had to Dress for Dinner." *The New Republic*, 12/19/65, p. 6.

Knebel, Fletcher. "Ike's Cronies." *Look*, 6/1/54, p. 57+.

Knebel, Fletcher, and Jack Wilson. "The Scandalous Years." *Look*, 5/22/51.

Krock, Arthur. "Now the Political Tensions Mount." *New York Times Magazine*, 10/17/54, p. 9.

Lewis, Anthony. "Close-up of Our Lawyer in Chief." *New York Times Magazine*, 4/6/68, p. 22+.

Liddell Hart, B. H. "Eisenhower and His Task." *The New Republic*, 11/4/51, pp. 12–13.

Lukacs, John. "The Fifties: Another View: Revising the Eisenhower Era." *Harper's*, 1/2002, pp. 64–70.

Mallan, John P. "Massachusetts, Liberal and Corrupt." *The New Republic*, 10/14/52, pp. 10–11.

Mannes, Marya. "Rabbit Punches on TV: The Governor and the Lady." *The Reporter*, 11/25/52, p. 12.

Marine, Gene. "What's Wrong with Nixon?" *The Nation*, 8/18/56, p. 131+.

McKenzie, R. T. "Ike: Stuck with Dick." *The Nation*, 9/1/56, p. 170+.

McWillliams, Carey. "Bungling in California." *The Nation*, 11/4/50, p. 411+.

————. "Has Success Spoiled Dick Nixon?" *The Nation*, 6/2/62, p. 487+.

Miller, William Lee. "The Debating Career of Richard M. Nixon." *The Reporter*, 4/19/56, p. 11+.

Morrow, Hugh. "The Democrats' No. 1 Optimist." *Saturday Evening Post*, 7/28/56, p. 28+.

Nelson, Anna Kasten. "The 'Top of the Policy Hill': President Eisenhower and the National Security Council." *Diplomatic History*, Vol. 7 (Fall 1983), pp. 307–26.

Nixon, Patricia Ryan, as told to Joy Alex Morris. "I Say He's a Wonderful Guy." *Saturday Evening Post*, 9/6/52, p. 17+.

Nixon, Richard M. "Khrushchev's Hidden Weakness." *Saturday Evening Post,* 10/12/63, p. 23+.

———. "Asia After Vietnam." *Foreign Affairs,* 9/67, pp. 111–25.

"Nixon Fights, Wins and Weeps." *Life,* 10/6/52, p. 26+.

"Nixon's Own Story of 7 Years in the Vice Presidency: Exclusive Interview on How a Vice President for the First Time in History Serves as the President's 'Deputy,' " *U.S. News & World Report,* 5/16/60, p. 98+.

O'Donnell, Kenneth. "LBJ and the Kennedys." *Life,* 8/7/70, pp. 45–56.

Osborne, John. "What Are Nixon and Rockefeller Saying?" *The New Republic,* 6/29/68, pp. 15–17.

———. "Moynihan at Work in the White House." *The New Republic,* 3/22/69, p. 11+.

———. "The Nixon Watch: White House Who's Who." *The New Republic,* 10/18/69, p. 13+.

———. "The Nixon Watch: Where Is Pat?" *The New Republic,* 11/29/69, p. 15.

———. "White House Watch: Gabbing with Harlow." *The New Republic.* 5/13/78, p. 12+.

Phillips, Cabell. "Eisenhower's Harry Hopkins?" *New York Times Magazine,* 6/7/53, p. 13+.

———. "The Super-Cabinet for Our Security." *New York Times Magazine,* 4/4/54, p. 14+.

———. "One-Man Task Force of the G.O.P." *New York Times Magazine,* 10/24/54, p. 17+.

———. "How to Be a Presidential Candidate." *New York Times Magazine,* 7/13/58, p. 11+.

"The Presidency." *The New Republic,* 3/5/56, p. 3.

Reeves, Richard. "Nixon's Men Are Smart but No Swingers." *New York Times Magazine,* 9/29/68, p. 28+.

"The Reporter's Notes." *The Reporter,* 12/12/57, p. 3.

"Republican 'Pros' Size Up Rockefeller and Nixon. *U.S. News & World Report,* 1/30/59, p. 55+.

"Responsible Rule and the President." *The New Republic,* 12/16/57, p. 5.

Reynolds, Quentin. "Mr. President Eisenhower." *Life,* 4/17/50, p. 144.

Rovere, Richard H. "Letter from Washington." *The New Yorker,* 2/23/52, p. 87+.

———. "Letter from Washington." *The New Yorker,* 3/22/52, p. 116+.

————. "Letter from Chicago." *The New Yorker*, 7/19/52, p. 72+.

————. "Letter from Washington." *The New Yorker*, 11/15/52, p. 119+.

————. "Letter from Washington." *The New Yorker*, 1/23/53, p. 55+.

————. "Letter from Washington." *The New Yorker*, 4/17/54, p. 71+.

————. "Letter from Washington." *The New Yorker*, 11/13/54, p. 106+.

————. "Letter from Washington." *The New Yorker*, 12/18/54, p. 128+.

————. "Letter from Washington." *The New Yorker*, 3/26/55, p. 79+.

————. "Nixon: Most Likely to Succeed." *Harper's*, 9/55, p. 57+.

————. "Letter from Washington." *The New Yorker*, 10/8/55, p. 179+.

————. "Letter from Washington." *The New Yorker*, 3/10/56, p. 749+.

————. "Letter from Washington." *The New Yorker*, 5/19/56, p. 140+.

————. "Letter from Washington." *The New Yorker*, 6/23/56, p. 75+.

————. "Letter from Washington." *The New Yorker*, 9/29/56, p. 135+.

————. "A Reporter at Large: The Campaign: Nixon." *The New Yorker*, 10/13/56, p. 168+.

————. "A Reporter at Large: The Campaign: Stevenson & Co." *The New Yorker*, 10/27/56, p. 148+.

————. "Letter from Washington." *The New Yorker*, 10/5/57, p. 167+.

————. "Letter from Washington." *The New Yorker*, 12/7/57, p. 149+.

————. "Letter from Washington." *The New Yorker*, 1/25/64, p. 35+.

————. "Letter from Washington." *The New Yorker*, 6/13/64, p. 111+.

————. "Letter from Washington." *The New Yorker*, 7/25/64, p. 77+.

————. "Letter from Miami Beach." *The New Yorker*, 8/17/68, p. 93+.

————. "Letter from Chicago." *The New Yorker*, 9/7/68, p. 116+.

————. "Letter from Washington." *The New Yorker*, 10/12/68, p. 155+.

————. "Letter from Washington." *The New Yorker*, 12/21/68, p. 91+.

————. "Letter from Washington." *The New Yorker*, 2/1/69, p. 65+.

————. "Letter from Washington." *The New Yorker*, 4/19/69, p. 155+.

Schaap, Dick. "Pat Loves Everybody and Everybody Loves Pat." *Los Angeles Times*, 7/21/68, p. A12+.

Schlesinger, Arthur, Jr. "A Skeptical Democrat Looks at President Nixon." *New York Times Magazine*, 11/17/68, p. 45+.

Schoenbrun, David. "Five Weeks That Made a Politician." *The Reporter*, 8/5/52, p. 7+.

Schreiber, Flora Rheta. "I Didn't Want Dick to Run Again." *Good Housekeeping*, 7/68, p. 64+.

Semple, Robert B., Jr. "The Three Strategies of a Master Politician." *New York Times Magazine*, 11/1/70, p. 229+.

Sevareid, Eric. "The Longest Campaign in History." *The Reporter*, 11/5/55, p. 18.

Shearer, Lloyd. "Elder Statesman Eisenhower—At 77 He's Become an Artful Dodger." *Parade*, 5/12/68, p. 6.

Sidey, Hugh. "Philosophy of Office and the Ache of Ambition." *Life*, 11/3/67, p. 30+.

Smith, Beverly. "Campaigning with Kennedy." *Saturday Evening Post*, 10/1/60, p. 26+.

Smith, Merriman. "Ike Won't Run Again." *This Week*, 1/2/55, p. 7+.

Stokes, Thomas L. "The Cabinet Changes in Character, Too." *New York Times Magazine*, 4/12/53, p. 14+.

"The Team in Charge as President Rests." *Life*, 10/10/55, p. 38.

"They're Running Scared." *Newsweek*, 10/31/60, p. 19+.

Thimmesch, Nick. "Whatever Happened to Richard Nixon?" *Los Angeles Times*, 7/16/67, p. A10.

Tobin, Richard L. "Dwight D. Eisenhower: What I Have Learned." *Saturday Review*, 9/10/66, pp. 29–33.

"T.R.B. from Washington." *The New Republic*, 1/18/66, p. 6.

Viorst, Milton. "Nixon of the O.P.A." *New York Times Magazine*, 10/3/71, p. 70+.

West, Jessamyn. "The Real Pat Nixon." *Good Housekeeping*, 2/71, p. 67+.

"What Goes On at Ike's Dinners: President Puts Old-Time Cracker-Barrel Idea to Work," *U.S. News & World Report*, 2/4/55, p. 34+.

White, E. B. (unsigned). "Talk of the Town: Notes and Comment." *The New Yorker*, 10/4/52, p. 23.

White, Theodore H. "The Gentlemen from California." *Collier's*, 2/3/56, p. 40+.

White, William S. "Evolution of Eisenhower as Politician." *New York Times Magazine*, 10/23/56, p. 220+.

———. "Nixon: What Kind of President?" *Harper's*, 1/58, pp. 25–30.

Whittaker, John C. "Nixon's Domestic Policy: Both Liberal and Bold in Retrospect." *Presidential Studies Quarterly*, Volume 26, No. 1 (Winter, 1996), p. 131.

Wicker, Tom. "Anatomy of the Goldwater Boom." *New York Times Magazine,* 8/11/63, p. 171+.

Widick, B. J. "Romney: New Hope for the GOP?" *The Nation,* 2/3/62, p. 95+.

Wilson, Richard L. "The Big Change in Richard Nixon." *Look,* 9/3/57, pp. 66–69.

Wise, David. "The Twilight of a President." *New York Times Magazine,* 11/3/68, p. 278+.

Witcover, Jules. "Nixon for President in '68?" *Saturday Evening Post,* 2/25/67, pp. 93–97.

Woods, Rose Mary (as told to Don Murray). "Nixon's My Boss." *Saturday Evening Post,* 12/28/57, p. 21+.

Yagoda, Ben. "At Home with Julie and David." *Saturday Evening Post,* 1–2/87, p. 64+.

Yagoda, Ben. "At Home with Julie and David." *Saturday Evening Post,* 3/87, p. 68+.

Newspapers

(Abilene) *Reflector-Chronicle*
Amsterdam News
Atlanta Daily World
Boston Globe
Chicago Defender
Chicago Tribune
Covina Argus-Citizen
Hartford Courant
Los Angeles Times
New York Herald Tribune
New York Post
New York Times
Pittsburgh Courier
The (Portland) *Oregonian*
The Wall Street Journal
Washington Evening Star
Washington Post / Washington Post & Times Herald (masthead 1954–1973)

Selected Audio and Video

Open End (television program, sound recordings, 1960–1961). An audio of Nixon's three-plus-hour interview with David Susskind, at the Hoover Institution Library and Archives.

Dwight D. Eisenhower, speaking at the Commonwealth Club of California, 10/20/1960, at the Hoover Institution Library and Archives.

Richard Nixon at the Commonwealth Club ("The Issues for 1952"), 2/14/1952, at the Hoover Institution Library and Archives.

Richard Nixon at the Commonwealth Club ("An Evening with Richard Nixon"), 6/11/1959, at the Hoover Institution Library and Archives.

Nixon: American Experience (WGBH Educational Foundation, 1990).

Frost/Nixon: The Complete Interviews (Liberation). The 400 minutes inspired an entertaining if not quite accurate stage play and film.

The Making of the President: The 1960s (Athena, 2011).

Nixon: A Presidency Revealed and *Inside the Presidency: Eisenhower vs. Nixon* (History Channel, 2007).

Firing Line, Richard M. Nixon and William F. Buckley Jr., 9/14/67, Hoover Institution Video Library, Hoover Institution Library and Archives.

Biography: Richard Nixon (A&E).

Important Online Resources

The Complete Eisenhower Papers, from Johns Hopkins University Press (subscription required): http://eisenhower.press.jhu.edu/

The Eisenhower Papers: The Presidential Papers (free): http://www.eisenhower memorial.org/presidential-papers/index.htm

The Nixon Library "virtual library," a growing collection of documents, including the White House Special Files. Follow other links for oral histories, dictabelts, and some Watergate tapes: http://nixon.archives.gov/virtuallibrary/documents/index.php

Eisenhower Presidential Library: While not nearly as extensive as the Nixon Library's, many documents are online from Abilene: http://www.eisenhower.archives.gov/research/online_documents.html

Presidential News Conferences, year by year: http://www.presidency.ucsb.edu/news_conferences.php?year=1953&Submit=DISPLAY.

The "Papers of Martin Luther King, Jr.," edited by Professor Clairborne Carson et al., and searchable by date and name: http://mlk-kpp01.stanford.edu/index .php/kingpapers/article/king_paper_volumes1/

The Frank Gannon interviews with Richard Nixon. Gannon worked with Nixon on his memoir *RN*, and in 1983 conducted nine separate conversations with the former president. He was a sympathetic interlocutor, but his questions were direct and, thanks to his thorough knowledge of the subject, there is no better self-portrait of Nixon extant. A transcript of the Nixon/ Gannon Interviews: http://www.libs.uga.edu/media/collections/nixon/

Foreign Relations of the United States: the historical, declassified record of American foreign policy decisions and discussions: http://uwdc.library.wisc.edu/ collections/FRUS.

YouTube, that addictive site, where so much recorded history appears and, pursued by the Copyright Police, may disappear far too quickly.

Interviews by Author

Marjorie Acker (née Peterson)
Gerald Anderson
Stephen Benedict
Benjamin C. Bradlee
William F. Buckley Jr.
Dwight Chapin
Edward F. Cox
Dorothy Cox Donnelly
Hugh Downs (by e-mail)
David Eisenhower
Julie Nixon Eisenhower
Susan Eisenhower
Thomas W. Evans
William Bragg Ewald Jr.
Christine King Farris
Peter Flanigan
Frank Gannon
William Gavin
Leonard Garment
Loie Gaunt
Fred Grandy

Robert Keith Gray
Wendell Gubler
Stephen Hess
General James (Don) Hughes
Lee Huebner
James C. Humes
John W. Kennedy
Melvin Laird
Lois Lundberg
Paul (Pete) McCloskey
Henry Roemer McPhee
Alvin Moscow
Jack Muse
Edward Nixon
Robert D. Novak
Maureen Drown Nunn
Lee Page
Roger Parkinson
Bradley Patterson
Roswell Perkins
Douglas Price

Raymond K. Price

Richard (Sandy) Quinn

Lawrence Radak

Donald Riegle

Anthony Rogers

Susan Porter Rose

Stanley Rumbough

William Scranton

John Sears

Robert Semple

Rocco Siciliano

Hugh Sloan

Alvin Spivak

Glen Harold Stassen

Helen Thomas

Frank van der Linden (by mail)

Gerald Warren

John Whittaker

George S. Wills

Andrew Young

Oral Histories
Columbia University Oral History Project

Sherman Adams

Meade Alcorn

George E. Allen

Jack Bell

Herbert Brownell

Lucius Clay

Clifton Daniel

Thomas Dewey

Milton Eisenhower

Robert Finch

Edward T. Folliard

Barry Goldwater

Alfred Gruenther

Homer Gruenther

Leonard Hall

Bryce Harlow (Also, A. James

    Reichley's interview from the Gerald

    R. Ford Presidential Library)

Gabriel Hauge

Walter Judd

William Lawrence

Clare Boothe Luce

Earl Mazo

Kevin McCann

Roderic O'Connor

Wilton B. (Jerry) Persons

Clifford Roberts

Bernard Shanley

Harold Stassen

Thomas Stevens

Dwight D. Eisenhower Presidential Library and Museum

Herbert Brownell

Lucius Clay

Jacqueline Cochran

Roy Day

Milton Eisenhower

Leonard Heaton

Ann C. Whitman

Nixon Presidential Library and Museum

Dwight Chapin
Robert Ellsworth
Leonard Garment

Raymond K. Price
William Safire

Hoover Institution Library and Archives

George Humphrey
General Albert Wedemeyer

Sinclair Weeks

Other

Martin Luther King Jr. (Oral History Interview, March 9, 1964, Atlanta, Georgia, for the John F. Kennedy Presidential Library and Museum)
Joseph Rauh, Richard Strout, and Earl Warren (Harry S. Truman Library and Museum)

Archival Collections
Dwight D. Eisenhower Presidential Library and Museum, Abilene, Kansas

Ann C. Whitman Diary Series
Dwight D. Eisenhower Diary Series

Papers as President

1. Legislative Meeting Series
2. Augusta–Walter Reed Series
3. Administration Series (Box 28, Richard Nixon)
4. Cabinet Series
5. Post-Presidential Principal File
Sherman Adams (Name Files)
George B. Bookman Papers (includes the unpublished autobiography of Gabriel Hauge)
Herbert Brownell Papers
Jacqueline Cochran Papers
John Foster Dulles Papers
Milton Eisenhower Papers

Vincent Ford Papers (his unpublished manuscript, recalling ICBM
 development)
Alfred M. Gruenther Papers
Jamel Hagerty Papers
Christian Herter Papers
Henry W. Hoagland Papers (includes the posthumous political memoir of
 Leonard Wood Hall)
C. D. Jackson Papers
Arthur Larson Papers
E. Frederic Morrow Papers
William Robinson Papers
William B. Rogers Papers
Robert Schulz (Logbook)
Fred Seaton Papers
Bernard Shanley Diaries
Jehovah's Witnesses Abilene Congregation: Records and Related Materials,
 1912–1943

Nixon Presidential Library and Museum, Yorba Linda, California
General Correspondence, Series 320, 1946–1962

Sherman Adams
Meade Alcorn
Joseph and Stewart Alsop
Bert Andrews
James Bassett
Elmer Bobst
Norman Chandler
Otis Chandler
Fr. J. F. Cronin
Robert Cutler
Arthur Dean
Ralph de Toledano
Thomas E. Dewey
George Dixon
Roscoe Drummond
Peter Edson
John Ehrlichman
Milton Eisenhower

Bob Finch
Arthur Godfrey
Barry Goldwater
Billy Graham
H. R. Haldeman
Leonard Hall
Bryce Harlow
Paul Harvey
Gabriel Hauge
Herbert Hoover
Hedda Hopper
Hubert Humphrey
Arnold A. Hutschnecker
C. D. Jackson
Paul Keyes
Peter Kihss
Martin Luther King Jr.
Henry Kissinger

Goodwin Knight
Alfred Kohlberg
Victor Lasky
Walter Lippmann
Henry Cabot Lodge
Clare Boothe Luce and Henry Luce
Douglas MacArthur
Kevin McCann
Joe McCarthy
Jack Paar
Kyle Palmer
Norman Vincent Peale
Admiral Arthur Radford
Nelson Rockefeller
Jackie Robinson
William P. Rogers
Harold Stassen
Cyrus Sulzberger
Robert Taft
Colonel Vernon Walters
Rose Mary Woods
Dwight D. Eisenhower Special Files
(PPS 324 1, 2, 3)
Vice Presidential Work Files—
Executive Branch
(PPS 325)

Vice Presidential Papers, Special Files
(PPS 320)
President's Personal File, Boxes 1–4,
Memoranda from the President
Patricia Ryan Nixon Collection
(Eisenhower Correspondence,
1954–1979) (PPS 268)
Jonathan Aitken Collection
(Interviews)
Bob Abplanalp
H. R. Haldeman
Richard Nixon
Rose Mary Woods
Bryce Harlow Papers
Jack and Helene Drown Collection
1952 Campaign Material, Series I,
Series II
1952 Convention Material
1960 Campaign Material
Administration Series—Box 28 (Billy
Graham)
Nixon Presidential Returned
Materials Collection
White House Special Files
White House Special Files: Contested
Files

Library of Congress, Manuscript Division, Washington, D.C.

Joseph and Stewart Alsop Papers
Henry Brandon Papers
Felix Frankfurter Papers

Clare Boothe Luce Papers
John Osborne Papers
Roy W. Wilkins Papers

Hoover Institution Library and Archives, Stanford University, Palo Alto, California

William J. Casey Papers
Ralph de Toledano Papers
Allen Drury Papers

Alfred Kohlberg Papers
George Sokolsky Papers

Minnesota Historical Society, Manuscripts Collection, St. Paul, Minnesota

Harold Stassen Papers

J. Willard Marriott Library, University of Utah, Salt Lake City, Utah

Papers of Fawn Brodie, Special Collection. Her notes and/or recorded interviews with James Bassett, Robert Bergholz (*Los Angeles Times*), Colonel Robert Cushman, Ralph de Toledano, Robert Finch, Leonard Hall, Herbert G. Klein, Jessamyn West

Bowdoin College Library, Brunswick, Maine

George J. Mitchell Department of Special Collections and Archives
James E. Bassett Jr. Papers, 1929–1977
    Box 1: Correspondence
    Boxes 3, 4: Unpublished journal, "Ugly Year, Lonely Man"

Lyndon Baines Johnson Library and Museum, Austin, Texas

White House Central Files, Box 117, Folder PL6-3, Republican Party (report on the "Republican unity" meeting in Hershey, Pennsylvania, August 1964)
National Security File: Files of Walt W. Rostow. Nixon, Richard–Vietnam.
Chennault, Anna, from folder "South Vietnam and U.S. Policies (1 of 2)"

Harry S. Truman Library and Museum, Independence, Missouri

Summaries of meetings between Milton Katz and President Eisenhower, Milton Katz papers, memo of conversation

Houghton Library, Harvard University, Cambridge, Massachusetts

Christian Herter Papers

Seeley G. Mudd Manuscript Library, Princeton University, Princeton, New Jersey

John Foster Dulles Oral History Collection: Richard Nixon, interview, March 5, 1965

INDEX

Page numbers beginning with 352 refer to notes.

ABOUT THE AUTHOR

Jeffrey Frank was a senior editor at *The New Yorker* and the deputy editor of the *Washington Post*'s Outlook section. He is the author of four novels, including the Washington Trilogy—*The Columnist, Bad Publicity*, and *Trudy Hopedale*—and the co-translator, from the Danish, of *The Stories of Hans Christian Andersen*. He lives in Manhattan with his wife, Diana Crone Frank. They have one son.